Environmental Governance and Sustainability

THE IUCN ACADEMY OF ENVIRONMENTAL LAW SERIES

Series Editors: Kurt Deketelaere, *University of Leuven, Leuven, Belgium* and Zen Makuch, *Imperial College, London, UK*

As environmental law increases in importance as an area of legal research, this new series will bring together some of the most current research carried out by the IUCN Academy of Environmental Law, a global network of environmental law scholars. The important issues addressed in the papers in this series were first presented at the Academy's annual colloquia. The series will present original research analysis and assessment, along with a much-needed synthesis of the state of environmental law. Directions as to the positive role that environmental law can play at a global level are also emphasized. This series will prove essential reading for scholars throughout the world with an interest in cutting edge environment-related issues, and will no doubt play an important role in shaping future debate.

Titles in this series include:

Compliance and Enforcement in Environmental Law
Toward More Effective Implementation
Edited by LeRoy Paddock, Du Qun, Louis J. Kotzé, David L. Markell, Kenneth J. Markowitz and Durwood Zaelke

Environmental Law and Sustainability after Rio
Edited by Jamie Benidickson, Ben Boer, Antonio Herman Benjamin and Karen Morrow

Environmental Governance and Sustainability
Edited by Paul Martin, Li Zhiping, Qin Tianbao, Anel Du Plessis and Yves Le Bouthillier

Environmental Governance and Sustainability

Edited by

Paul Martin

Director, Australian Centre for Agriculture and Law, University of New England, Australia

Li Zhiping

Law School, Sun Yat-Sen University, China

Qin Tianbao

Professor of Environmental Law and International Law and Assistant Dean for International Affiliations, School of Law and Research Institute of Environmental Law (RIEL), Wuhan University, China

Anel Du Plessis

Faculty of Law, North-West University, South Africa

Yves Le Bouthillier

Faculty of Law, University of Ottawa, Canada

THE IUCN ACADEMY OF ENVIRONMENTAL LAW SERIES

Edward Elgar
Cheltenham, UK • Northampton, MA, USA

Published by
Edward Elgar Publishing Limited
The Lypiatts
15 Lansdown Road
Cheltenham
Glos GL50 2JA
UK

Edward Elgar Publishing, Inc.
William Pratt House
9 Dewey Court
Northampton
Massachusetts 01060
USA

A catalogue record for this book
is available from the British Library

Library of Congress Control Number: 2011936420

MIX
Paper from
responsible sources
FSC® C018575
FSC
www.fsc.org

ISBN 978 1 78100 047 2 (cased)

Typeset by Cambrian Typesetters, Camberley, Surrey
Printed and bound by MPG Books Group, UK

Contents

PART III THE INTERSECTION OF ECONOMICS AND SOCIAL JUSTICE AROUND WATER LAWS

PART IV LINKING LOCAL AND INTERNATIONAL LEGAL INNOVATIONS

Figures

Tables

Contributors

Ann Brower is a senior lecturer in public policy in the Faculty of Environment, Society and Design at Lincoln University, New Zealand.

Joseph W. Dellapenna is Professor of Law at the Villanova University School of Law, USA. He has an extensive background as a litigator and author on water and other policy matters.

Anel Du Plessis is Associate Professor, Faculty of Law, North-West University, South Africa.

Michael G. Faure is Professor of Comparative Private Law and Economics at the Erasmus University Rotterdam; and Professor of Comparative and International Environmental Law at Maastricht University, the Netherlands. He also holds other senior academic appointments.

Alex Gardner is an Associate Professor, The University of Western Australia, Faculty of Law; Adjunct Professor, The Australian National University, College of Law; and Chief Investigator of Program 5 of the National Centre for Groundwater Research and Training, Australia.

Nils Goeteyn is a PhD Candidate at Ghent University, Belgium.

Ke Jian is Associate Professor, Research Institute of Environmental Law, Wuhan University, China; and the General Secretary of the Academic Committee, Environmental and Natural Resources Law Department, China Law Society.

Amanda Kennedy is the Deputy Director of the Australian Centre for Agriculture and Law at the University of New England, Australia.

Kishan Khoday is the UNDP Deputy Resident Representative in Saudi Arabia. He was previously UNDP Assistant Resident Representative and Team Leader for Energy & Environment in China (2005–09) and UNDP Deputy Coordinator for Environment in Indonesia (1997–2005).

Robert Kibugi is a doctoral candidate in the Faculty of Law, University of Ottawa, Canada; and a tutorial fellow (on study leave), School of Law, University of Nairobi, Kenya.

Frank Maes is Professor in Public International Law at Ghent University, Belgium.

Paul Martin is the Director of the Australian Centre for Agriculture and Law at the University of New England, Australia.

Mei Hong is Associate Professor at the environmental law research institute at the Law and Politics School of Ocean University, China; and researcher at the postdoctoral center in Xiamen University, China.

Michèle Morel is a PhD candidate at the Law School, Ghent University, Belgium.

John Page is an Assistant Professor in Law in the Faculty of Law at Bond University, Australia. He was formerly at the School of Law, University of New England, Australia.

Qin Tianbao is Professor of Environmental Law and International Law and Assistant Dean for International Affiliations for School of Law and the Research Institute of Environmental Law (RIEL), Wuhan University, China.

Wang Huanhuan is a lecturer and post-doctoral researcher in the School of Law, Sun Yat-sen University in Guangzhou, China.

Jacqueline Williams is a Senior Researcher of the Australian Centre for Agriculture and Law at the University of New England, Australia.

Yin Yanjie is a lecturer at the School of Biological and Chemical Engineering, Qingdao Technical College, China.

Hao Zhang is a PhD candidate at the Centre for Resources, Energy and Environmental Law and the Asian Law Centre at Melbourne Law School of the University of Melbourne, Australia.

Zhou Chen is a PhD candidate in the International Public Law department, the Law School, Tilburg University, the Netherlands.

Table of cases

REGIONAL

European Court of Human Rights

NATIONAL

Australia

China

New Zealand

United States

Table of legislation

INTERNATIONAL

France

Germany

Kenya

New Zealand

United States

Introduction: the scholarship of environmental governance

This collection of scholarly works provides insights into emerging developments in the field of legal governance of the environment. Environmental governance is increasingly concerned with far more than legal doctrine, though environmental law stands at the heart of good environmental governance. It is concerned with the totality of arrangements through which power and resources are deployed to protect and restore natural resources, and how the costs and benefits of this are allocated. As such, how the community exercises its democratic rights; the ways in which government responds to the needs of current and future generations and balances the interests of the powerful with the powerless; the freedoms and responsibilities of commerce and the holders of property; and the ways in which laws and policies are informed by science and other perspectives are all important. The chapters in this book show the many ways in which legal scholarship is pivotal to good governance in all these respects, and the extent of innovation that is being generated by the ecological, economic and social challenges that are arising.

The content and scope of these chapters demonstrate clearly the increasing breadth and depth of environmental law scholarship. The chapters show the many ways in which community and political leadership towards sustainability is being translated into institutional arrangements in the international and national spheres. The book also demonstrates the many conflicts and potential conflicts inherent in a radical transformation of society and economy. Legal scholars are, as a result, being called to take a leadership role in some of the fundamental contests of ideas and of interests that are taking place across the planet, as societies try to find a way of living with the reality of our finite and declining resources.

The chapters in this book suggest that this requires significant legal and institutional innovations that are interlinked with scientific discovery and the march of community power (enabled in no small degree by technology). The chapters reflect a willingness on the part of legal scholars to question the received wisdom of economics, and to contest the entrenched power structures within societies in the interests of sustainability, social justice and future citizens.

Nowhere is this more evident than in China, which is struggling with the intersecting challenges of population and economic growth, burgeoning citizen rights-based environmental and social activism, and fundamental threats to ecological sustainability. The pivotal role of the law and lawyers in shaping the future of Chinese ecological sustainability and economic welfare is well illustrated within these pages. The contributions to this volume by a number of excellent Chinese legal scholars, including doctoral candidates, reflect the commitment of the International Union for the Conservation of Nature (IUCN) Academy of Environmental Law to advancing legal scholarship. This was particularly demonstrated by the holding of the 2009 IUCN Academy of Environmental Law Colloquium in Wuhan, China. It is from this event that the chapters in this book have evolved.

This book suggests the significance of the willingness of modern scholars to uphold the best traditions of jurisprudence: independence of thought, concern for the principled management of conflicts and conflicts of interests, and a willingness to stand up for the least privileged people or on unpopular political cause. This is evident in many ways. It is salutory to reflect that of the disciplines that are typically central to the development of sustainability in all jurisdictions, only the law brings to the table a culture and approach that places such values at the centre of how the craft is exercised. This suggests a unique opportunity and responsibility that may often be undervalued even by lawyers themselves.

Based on legal principles and the evidence of history, this book rationally contests the received wisdom in many policy and academic circles that markets are best able to solve natural resource management problems. A number of chapters provide reasons to believe that this paradigm, like all simple solutions to complex human problems, is intrinsically limited. In these chapters, it is suggested that more complete and nuanced solutions that reflect the great variations in social and ecological contexts are more likely to prove robust and reliable, and that when social justice and political economy concerns are added to the mix, the types of strategies and instruments that are used can vary markedly from what may seem to be as 'efficient' at first glance. Some authors provide specific directions for more robust governance arrangements, and for scholarship and policy practice that will be more inclusive and robust than current institutional and instrumental arrangements.

The chapters demonstrate the emergence of an increasingly transdisciplinary approach to the legal scholarship of environmental governance. Some of the chapters have been developed by teams that bring together high levels of legal capacity with ecology, economics, political science and management knowledge. The chapters that have been enriched in this way have put forward some challenging ideas about matters as fundamental as the nature of private property, and the architectural principles that ought to govern the design of environmental laws and resource governance arrangements. It is interesting to observe (as has been done at other times by other authors) that a distinguishng feature of environmental law is that it intrinsically requires an ability to ntegrate both ecological and social science insights, and to cope with the complexities that so often plague interdisciplinary thinking.

A number of chapters draw together the strands of social justice and ecological sustainability. Considering a variety of interlinked social and ecological issues in Africa, China, and other parts of the world, these authors suggest a number of practical interventions, supported by legal arrangements, that will best ensure social justice whilst pursuing ecological sustainability. The matters covered include the use of information technology to enable citizen-led governance; embedding stewardship capacity in natural resource governance arrangements; fairer and more effective management of ecological refugee issues; and more activist roles for existing legal institutions.

STRUCTURE AND CONTENT OF THIS BOOK

The structure of any book is limited by the fact that pages are put in sequence, even if the ideas contained within the chapters refuse such simple ordering. We have elected to sequence the book in the following manner, but in reality many important ideas that link different chapters are scattered in ways that would violate this structure. Therefore, some readers may find it more interesting to take a random walk through the book.

The Architectural Design of Environmental Governance

The chapters in the first part of the book consider the overall 'architecture' of environmental law and governance, following the lead provided by the keynote speech by Professor Michael Faure. His chapter ('Instruments for environmental governance: what works?') provides a solid context in which to consider the ways in which regulatory, market, taxation or other instruments might contribute to the advance of sustainability. From a survey of the empirical literature, he provides clear indications that whilst different types of instrument may be advocated as 'better' or 'best' for a wide variety of circumstances, the reality of their performance is much more nuanced. He demonstrates that it is not the instrument in isolation that is important, it is the instrument in context that ought be the matter of concern. He also points out that it is more likely that a suite of instruments of different types will be effective and less distorting than relying on any one type. This is an important strategic observation at a time when the trend in economic and natural resource management literature seems to be to seek a simple 'single instrument' solution to complex and multi-faceted problems; and to largely ignore the realities of implementation and implementation capacity. Professor Faure's chapter also places a great deal of emphasis on the political realities of 'public choice', and the market for political power, as frequently driving policies that entrench established interests and create perverse effects.

The second chapter provides a good indication of the innovative approaches that can come from thinking more broadly about environmental law scholarship. Informed by ecological system science and the pluralist school of interest group politics in political science, John Page and Ann Brower ('Does (property) diversity beget (landscape) sustainability?') develop the thesis that ecological sustainability is likely to be enhanced by a pluralistic ownership structure involving a mosaic of interests, rather than the traditional 'despotic dominion' view of ownership as intrinsically comprising use rights and exclusive domain. They suggest that the bundle of interests within property is best managed sustainably by fragmentation, with an emphasis upon the stewardship aspects of use rights. It should be noted that questions of ownership of use rights and sustainability are later considered in relation to water in chapters by John Dellapena and Alex Gardner, and that they too seem to suggest that issues of ownership and obligation need to be more effectively linked through the management of use rights. This chapter suggests that a rethinking of the legal and political conceptualization of the foundational concepts of property rights could in itself generate significant improvements in sustainable use of landscapes.

The following chapter ('Creating next generation rural landscape governance: the challenge for environmental law scholarship' by Paul Martin, Jacqueline Williams and Amanda Kennedy) supports and extends Professor Faure's observations, but also takes a somewhat radical look at the conceptualization of environmental law, in this case with a greater emphasis on the public law aspects. Also based upon empirical research, their work supports the conclusion that *ex-post* studies do not support the view that either market or regulatory instruments are intrinsically more effective or efficient, and that it is more likely that a suite of instruments, arrayed in a systematic manner, will work better and be less likely to introduce perverse effects. Their study goes on to provide a set of specific principles for governance innovation, with an emphasis upon the importance of creating integrated 'smart regulation' approaches which control the proliferation of instruments and agencies, at the same time as bringing greater sophistication to the behavioural design of legal instruments. Their chapter suggests a number of innovations that might improve the cost-effectiveness of environmental law. These include co-regulation, with industry supported by credible government oversight, greater use of the strength of consumer demands for sustainable production, far deeper engagement between legal experts and affected communities, a deeper role for systems thinking (with an emphasis on linking ecological, socio-economic and institutional systems), and a more sophisticated treatment of risk in legal and institutional arrangements.

Governance Innovation in China

A number of chapters are concerned with natural resource governance in China, and a few are assembled in this part. What many readers will be aware of is the spectacular economic growth that has occurred and continues to occur in China, and perhaps they will be aware of the many issues of pollution and resource degradation that have occurred along with this development. What fewer will be aware of is the quite fundamental shifts in the legal governance arrangements in China, with the high level commitment embodied in law of pursuing an 'ecological civilization' paradigm, as well as greatly enhanced human rights. The depth and variety of changes that this implies, and the governance innovations that have been introduced, are impressive, though, as most authors point out, the resistance and challenges at a local level are also significant.

The chapter by Kishan Khoday entitled 'Constitutionalism and the environment: the evolution of environmental governance in China's Socialist Market Economy' provides a clear description of the extent to which the government of China has come to grips with the 'existential threat' that is posed by ecological degradation, and how this has occurred at the same time as society has moved to greater political liberalism in its administrative arrangements and a deeper concern for the disadvantaged. This chapter details the rebalancing of the national paradigm away from a modernist view of the environment as a development resource towards a more harmonious development and conservation paradigm. The challenges that are embedded in making this adjustment are enormous. At a local provincial level, when faced with major regional economic and political challenges, the commitment to development and the interests of industry often proves stronger than any commitment to sustainability and social equity principles. However, a large number of governance innovations have been assembled to create pressure towards accepting the new priorities. These include strengthening citizen opportunities for access and participation, particularly with greater rights for environmental and social justice non-governmental organizations (NGOs), and new legal standing for citizens in civil and administrative suits. In terms of political rhetoric backed by institutional change, the commitment shown to sustainability is impressive compared with that which is ostensibly demonstrated by many other societies with less pressing economic challenges.

The depth of the doctrinal impediments to implementing this new order is well illustrated in the chapter 'Toward a more effective environmental criminal law in China' by Michael Faure and Hao Zhang. This chapter provides a detailed examination of the architecture of the relevant criminal and associated administrative laws in China. It demonstrates a complex interplay between national and regional, criminal and administrative, and statutory and judicial arrangements that together serve to make effective use of the criminal law to achieve national sustainability objectives difficult. The problem of messy architectures being an impediment to effective use of the law that is discussed in Chapter 3 is well illustrated in this detailed study. The chapter considers this doctrinal structure relative to an idealized arrangement of proportionate responses that are coordinated between administrative and criminal law, and finds the present arrangements fall well short of this ideal. We suspect that, in most countries, whilst the doctrinal details would differ, the conclusions would be similar. In China the legal instruments suggest a typology of crimes, potentially penalizing a variety of anti-environmental behaviours, actions with adverse consequences, and responsibility for circumstances that arise that are deemed to be wrongful at law. Issues of guilty intention, or preconditions for a breach of administrative requirements, materially reduce the ability for this suite of criminal sanctions to be deployed, and in some cases the penalties are weak sanctions compared to the potential economic gains from continued breaches of the law. As we see in a subsequent chapter concerned with water pollution, in some aspects of Chinese law these practical issues are being addressed, but systemically the issues of penalization and enforcement are of concern. Ultimately, the creation of high-level policy objectives for sustainability and harmony with nature will be of limited effectiveness unless criminal and administrative laws, and their implementation, are made more efficient and powerful.

The role of the civil law for damages and administrative appeals against environmentally harmful decisions emerges as a frontier of environmental law development in China, given the difficulties that are documented with the criminal law. At the intersection between public and private law is the role of the public prosecutor or people's procuratorate in China. In this arm of government, innovativeness and a desire to advance the national sustainability agenda is shown in the chapter 'A feasible approach to environmental public interest litigation: the people's procuratorate as plaintiff' by Mei Hong and Yin Yanjie. This chapter provides many instances where public agents have stepped in to fill the gap between private rights and the limits of criminal law, by supporting civil or administrative actions by citizens or acting as a representative citizen in taking such actions. The authors point to the long history of public prosecutorial authorities taking this role as an adjunct to their criminal law responsibilities, and point to the important consequences for public administration that have flowed from this initiative. The absence of a clear legal mandate and sufficient resources, however, limits this opportunity to advance public environmental policy and citizens' environmental rights in China. The chapter suggests a relatively simple and inexpensive way of furthering the public interest in the environment in China, which may also be relevant in many other jurisdictions.

Good environmental governance, wherever it is found in the world, requires transparency and public scrutiny. In China, as in many other parts of the world, increasingly this scrutiny is being driven by the use of the internet and other information technologies, which are breaking down the ability of administrators and others to control information flows. The chapter 'Environmental e-governance in China: insights from government-citizen interaction' by Qin Tianbao and Wang Huanhuan provides an illuminating view of the extent to which technology is now an important actor in environmental governance. The explosion of technology options and high rates of consumer adoption intersect with a more supportive national government view of the role of the citizen in advancing sustainability as both a legal and political interest, creating a dynamic and rapidly changing context for participation in and supervision of government environmental policy. The authors look at both official government portals and non-government uses of technology, and observe a complex and rapidly evolving governance dynamic. Other chapters in this book also illustrate the explosion of avenues for the citizen and the consumer to exercise power to force or support government in advancing sustainability, and this suggests some new directions for legal environmental scholarship. One wonders, for example, what an international standard of disclosure and participation in environmental governance might do to advance both sustainability and social justice, or how environmental legal aid might by reframed to be effective in a technology-enabled world. Administrative law and environmental law are likely to be materially altered by developments of the type highlighted by these authors.

The Intersection of Economics and Social Justice around Water Laws

Water and air are environmental assets that have an immediacy about them, as resource deprivation due to their contamination or lack is fatal. The links between fundamental human needs and fundamental human rights is clear in this aspect of natural resource governance. But water (and, in a different manner, air) is an industrial commodity as well as a human need, and how it is managed as an economic asset impacts economically, socially and environmentally. Water governance is rightly considered to be a particular focus for legal scholarship, but it also brings into focus other issues of natural resource governance and social justice more broadly.

In countries such as China, the issue of water quality and quantity is a topic of critical human concern for many millions of people, whereas in richer economies the focus tends to be upon its economic use. Joseph Dellapenna ('Global climate disruption and water law reform in the United States') explores the evolution and effectiveness of different legal arrangements for the allocation of water for economic purposes in the USA, and considers these in the light of climate change. He provides a critical review of the capacity of three water allocation regimes that exist in the USA, in the light of the anticipated increasing conflict over water allocation. This chapter provides insights into the inability of market instruments to effectively deal with water, but in the context of governance arrangements that fall short of 'full-blown' ownership of water allocation interests (which is considered in the following chapter). Professor Dellapena provides an insightful discussion of the realities of riparian interests, and their ineffectiveness in coping with conditions where supply falls chronically short of potential demand. In so doing he provides a timely critique of the view popularized by the Nobel prize winner, Eleanor Ostrom, that self-organized arrangements for common property are reliable mechanisms for dealing with resource scarcity. He points out that whilst such arrangements may be reliable in some settings, in a modern Western economy where interpersonal relationships are often temporary and therefore where realization of interdependency may be vague, such approaches are risky. He also provides a realistic critique of appropriative approaches (or 'prior appropriation'), and of regulated riparianism. Whilst he is most supportive of the concept of time-bound and administered allocation of water extraction licences, he points to the limits of such arrangements. Notably, and in common with Chapter 1 by Michael Faure, he points to the distortions that arise through the self-interested exercise of political power by those who control water and other resources, and highlights the fact that regulated riparianism in itself does not ensure the reallocation of water in ways that are more likely to ensure the ability of society to respond to climate change-induced shortages.

The Australian water management regime described by Alex Gardner in his chapter on 'The legal protection of Ramsar Wetlands: Australian reforms' goes a long way towards creating a fully private, property rights-based regime for managing water allocation. Whilst the focus of the chapter is upon the use of market allocations to ensure the sustainability of hydrological systems (and in particular, Ramsar listed wetlands within those systems), it of necessity describes in detail the operations of that market. Considering the criticisms of markets in John Dellapena's chapter, and the suggestion of more circumscribed rather than expanded property rights arrangements in the Page and Brower chapter, this does raise questions about the efficiency, effectiveness and equity of private rights in water. Alex Gardner's study highlights important developments in making sustainable extraction limits the touchstone of the cap on use, and the treatment of the environment (though a legal representative) as a market participant that holds water rights. His chapter points to some practical challenges for the judicial system in coping with such innovations, and he also suggests that the treatment of risk at a time of impending scarcity caused by climate change ought to incorporate some form of 'emissions tax' on emitters to support adjustment by water users who will be adversely affected by climate change. In line with a number of other chapters, this study also highlights the significance of constitutional arrangements in shaping the sorts of local legal interventions that are possible. The combination of political agency theory and the institutional limits of constitutionality support the views expressed by other authors that any sense of an 'ideal' instrument isolated from on-the-ground institutions and dynamics is deceptive.

The human tragedy that can arise from weak water laws and institutions is highlighted by Ke Jian in his chapter ('Drinking water security in China: a critical justice issue'), which focuses on rural drinking water. He indicates that 0.3 billion rural people who are surface water dependent are under threat from water contamination. In common with the chapters that discussed the rapid evolution of China's legal governance arrangements for natural resources generally, Ke Jian highlights the clash between the development imperative at the local government level and the firm commitments to sustainability that have emerged at a national level. However, in the area of water pollution (reflecting its critical need status), the protection of this natural resource has received strong support, particularly with the establishment of protective standards for drinking water sources in 2008. Also as reflected in other chapters on developments in China, the need for strong citizen rights for civil and administrative relief is highlighted. To some degree civil rights in relation to water pollution have advanced further than the general environmental rights outlined by other authors on China, with no-fault liability principles being established for water pollution claims, and with legal aid being authorized for such claims. It seems that the legislative structure for good governance of water has advanced in China, and that its effectiveness will depend upon citizen activism and the integrity of government authorities to deliver equitable access to this vital resource.

Linking Local and International Legal Innovations

A great deal of environmental law scholarship is concerned with the creation of new international agreements, conventions, or protocols. The final chapters of the book (coupled with many of the earlier ones) demonstrate the deficiency of shaping international arrangements without a great deal of consideration of how they interact and how they will be implemented at state or even regional level. This mirrors earlier observations in several chapters in this book that good environmental governance requires a great deal more than a proliferation of theoretically useful instruments, and that increasingly, concern has to shift to the challenges of implementation and coordination 'on the front line'. This is likely to require significant changes in scholarship and policy creation practice, for it demands more detailed consideration of the trade-off between interests and objectives, evaluation of the resources and capabilities of the institutions that are intended to implement and the people who are intended to adjust to these instrumental directives, and a concern for the integration of arrangements to ensure seamless and low transaction cost implementation. If such matters are left to the art of muddling through, as so often seems to be the case, then international public law arrangements will increasingly prove to be a weak link in the total system of governance of natural resources.

The necessity for detailed pragmatic thinking about international arrangements is well illustrated by the discussion of a potential World Environmental Organization 'The quest for a World Environment Organization: reflections on a failing debate as an input for future improvement' by Nils Goeteyn and Frank Maes. Based upon evaluation of a variety of criticisms of the United Nations Environment Programmme (UNEP), and proposals for a World Environment Organization as a replacement, these authors suggest that much of the thinking is not well suited to a consideration of the practical differences between the two structures in terms of goals, resourcing and operations. In doing so, they raise some fundamental questions about international natural resource governance, notably the absence of a consensus about the vision for such a governance regime (and therefore the institution charged with its implementation) and the significant problems of political economy that exist at an international level. It is interesting to note, incidentally, the extent to which choice theory concerns recur at local, state and international levels in the creation of effective governance arrangements. Nils Goeteyn and Frank Maes' recommendation that institutional reform needs to be preceded by a more fundamental resolution of the purposes and priorities of the proposed institution, and greater concern to clarify the vision and guiding principles (and by implication issues of resourcing), is one that could be usefully applied to many initiatives. The failure to move beyond high-minded rhetoric to practical action is all too frequently reflected in the need for courts and administrators to fill the gap that is left by insufficient consideration of requirements for legal implementation.

The challenge of intersecting instruments is illustrated by Michèle Morel in the chapter 'Human rights law, refugee and migration law, and environmental law: exploring their contributions in the context of "environmental migration" '. In this chapter the author considers four different branches of international law that could be relevant to people who are forced by environmental circumstances to relocate from their homes. The chapter considers the respective role and operation of international legal instruments concerned with human rights, refugees, migration and environmental law. It highlights that whilst there is potential for an intersecting network of rights and obligations that might cover dislocation issues in different ways, there is no integration between these. The chapter suggests that there is a lack of political will to address this problem of disintegration and mis-coordination. The development of an integrative framework seems possible, but only if this lack of commitment is addressed.

The absence of real political will to give effect to high-minded international arrangements, and the impact that this has on less advantaged societies, is well illustrated by Zhou Chen in a detailed discussion of the impediments to the transfer of technologies that could materially assist in the implementation of international agreements on climate change. The chapter 'Climate change: legal impediments to technology transfer' traces the range of arrangements pursuant to the United Nations Framework Convention on Climate Change (UNFCCC) to facilitate the transfer of climate-protective and climate-adjusting technologies to countries and industries where the use of this technology could assist in the achievement of international aspirations to alleviate adverse climate change. The chapter demonstrates once again the clash between private economic interest and the public ecological interest, and the impediments to adjusting private interests even to the strongest public good needs. As was demonstrated in consideration of water allocation and pollution, in China and other jurisdictions the existence of strong private property rights serves as a significant impediment to realignment to a more sustainable regime of resource use. With the advent of international agreements to support private trade, notably the Trade-related Aspects of Intellectual Property Rights (TRIPS) regime to protect intellectual property monopolies, the ability of developing economies to take 'one-off' steps to overcome their limited access to advanced technologies is substantially reduced. This suggests a further dimension to the property rights/sustainability/social justice discourse that has been contributed to by John Page and Ann Brower, Ke Jian, John Dellapena and Alex Gardner in earlier chapters. A further dimension is the clash of principles and instruments when private market competitive principles which support the many gains that come from relatively unfettered free enterprise collide with the need to ensure collaboration and the suppression of economic self-interest to achieve adjustment to the ecological challenges that threaten many people (including future generations). This challenge is one that is repeated in many ways throughout this book. One would have to suggest, on the basis of the issues that have been raised, that our governance mechanisms have failed to find principled ways of handling this fundamental challenge. Zhou Chen suggests that corporate social responsibility is a relevant consideration, but without a governance regime that strengthens this and requires private enterprises to consider the broader social impacts of their accepted competitive practices, social responsibility will be insufficient to ensure that the international community has the basic tools needed to protect the common interest of mankind in its shared atmosphere.

The final chapter brings many of these considerations back to the level of the African farmer seeking to eke out a living by farming on publicly owned farmland. Robert Kibugi's exploration of the *shamba* system of land management ('Implementing stewardship in Kenyan land use law: the case for a sustainability extension') demonstrates how international agreements, in this case a series of African Union treaties, have embedded a practical concern for the capacity of the resource-dependent least privileged to achieve improved economic outcomes whilst exercising a stewardship ethic. The key to this multi-level outcome is extension, a targeted approach to ensuring that these resource users have the appropriate knowledge and attitudes to be able to manage their farming in a more sustainable manner. What is perhaps most illuminating about this example is that it shows how legal arrangements can embed a framework that does have concern for the least powerful individuals, and for the resources that will also be needed for future generations. This front-line innovation brings together a number of the proposals that have been proposed in a more abstract manner in other chapters. It integrates a practical concern for the natural resource that is to be exploited with a consideration of what changes social systems need to undergo to enable behaviour change, and it uses the law as a mechanism to enable a number of non-law interventions that can have an on-the-ground effect. Whilst undoubtedly still experimental, this example draws a clear line from international high-minded principles down to the everyday lives of the people whose behaviour will determine whether the public goals of resource management will be achieved.

IMPLICATIONS FOR ENVIRONMENTAL LAW SCHOLARSHIP

These chapters provide an overview of the key developments relevant to legal scholarship on the environment. In doing so, they perhaps cause us to reflect on whether our methods and our training are sufficient to meet the challenges that environmental governance will face and is already facing. Do we really have the methods and skills needed to integrate legal scholarship with ecological and social science? Are our fledgling lawyers sufficiently confident and imbued with the necessary jurisprudential values and skills to ensure that the unique contributions of legal culture and norms are 'heard' in the evolution of legal governance of the environment? Are we as a profession being sufficiently strong in highlighting our justified scepticism about the latest instrument or instrumental fashion?

Some important directions are suggested by this book.

It is clear that our scholarship will have to expand further, so that we can marry to good doctrinal approaches a new set of methods to provide comprehensive and sophisticated governance solutions to a world that is increasingly in need of them. This will involve moving to a systems framework, and deepening our thinking about instruments and institutions. This can only be done if we can draw upon the knowledge that exists in economics, social sciences and the biophysical natural sciences, but without submerging the law's concern for social justice and the lawyer's learned scepticism about simple solutions to complex problems.

The issue of property rights and responsibility is closely intertwined with the issues of political economy and public choice, and the risk of marginalizing the underprivileged (at both a personal and national level). There is a serious jurisprudential and practical challenge in understanding how to harness the entrepreneurial power and economic capital that comes with private property, at the same time as ensuring that the public interest is not swamped by these same forces. It is hard to see that any other disciplinary group will tackle these challenges if lawyers do not, but at the present time it is difficult to see where a set of unifying principles might come from to resolve these fundamental tensions that inevitably make themselves felt in natural resource governance.

The issue of 'practicality' also emerges as a concern for the law. We have enough examples of high principles being embedded in laws, conventions and national constitutions that are not efficiently translated into on-the-ground implementation. We know that unless this gap is bridged, true sustainability will not be achieved however many new doctrinal improvements are achieved on paper. Many of the chapters have signalled directions through which this translation might occur. Participative governance enabled by technology, co-regulation, consumer action, citizen standing and the support of government agencies, or capacity development through extension, are all illustrative of ways in which well-conceived and actively implemented law can make a significant difference.

This book illustrates that environmental law scholars have many reasons to be proud of the contribution that they and other lawyers have made and are continuing to make to the advance of sustainable and equitable use of scarce natural resources. However, the chapters also clearly show that the outcomes fall far short of the ideal, and that for our profession the challenge is not only about the work we deliver. It is clear that to meet the challenges we face, we too will have to continue to change, and probably at an accelerating pace. This is no small task for a profession that is generally considered to be intrinsically conservative and slow to change.

But above all, the chapters in this book suggest that this is a challenge that we can, and must, meet.

Acknowledgements

The chapters in this book were the subject of a rigorous process for competitive selection and peer review, and of editorial review. Particular thanks are due to the peer reviewers and the editors, who contributed significantly in ensuring not only a high standard of content but also who assisted their scholarly colleagues to ensure that all the ideas within the papers were presented to a consistently high standard.

Paul Martin (Chief Editor)
Li Zhiping
Qin Tinbao
Anel Du Plessis
Yves Le Bouthillier

PART I

The architectural design of environmental governance

1. Instruments for environmental governance: what works?

Michael G. Faure

1.1 INTRODUCTION

I would like to thank the Academy for the great honour of inviting me to speak at the colloquium to my distinguished colleagues and subsequently contributing to this volume. Apparently a keynote speaker is supposed to present two rather than one keynote speech. However, since I was also to present a paper on environmental criminal law in China with two Chinese colleagues, I was afraid that three times Faure would have been too much for the audience.

If I were to give two lectures, I would probably have structured it as follows: first, I would have presented (on the basis of legal and economic scholarship) what theoretical assumptions exist about the functioning of various instruments intended to reduce environmental harm and to promote sustainable development. The second lecture would have considered the empirical evidence of the extent to which the theoretical assumptions, on which much of our environmental governance is based, do work in practice. Since the organisation agreed that I would only give one keynote presentation, I will integrate the two approaches and briefly look at what theory tells us about how environmental law should work and spend most of my time at looking at the empirical evidence.

My contribution hence does not deal directly with doctrinal environmental law, but I give some insights into the empirical evidence about the effectiveness of environmental law. To a large extent, this evidence is not provided by lawyers. When making environmental law and choosing environmental instruments, environmental lawyers have many ideas and perhaps hopes for environmental law in promoting sustainable development. But do we actually know how effective the chosen instruments are? In other words: what do we know empirically?

Even though environmental lawyers are probably the lawyers most interested in research on the effectiveness of law and policy, empirical legal work in this domain remains relatively limited. One reason is that much of this empirical material on the effectiveness of environmental legal instruments is the result of research not by lawyers but by economists or other social scientists. These results are often published in journals not directly read by lawyers and in a language (for example using mathematics) which is difficult for lawyers to understand. Moreover, much of this empirical research will not deal with the effectiveness of environmental law generally, but will look at the effect of one particular instrument on one specific environmental parameter (such as CO_2 concentrations) in one particular country or even region. Results are hence often very instance-specific.

My argument is not that environmental lawyers should necessarily do more empirical research ourselves.[1] My message is rather that the results of these empirical studies are relevant for scholars of environmental law and policy since they may allow us to fine-tune environmental instruments, based on proven effectiveness in practice.

The goal of my contribution is therefore twofold. I first would like to present some empirical results concerning the effectiveness of various environmental policy instruments. So much has been published that I could easily fill the entire volume with that. This overview will hence necessarily entail a great degree of 'cherry picking' of studies to give the reader the flavour of the empirical work. My second goal is to present some thoughts on how to interpret these empirical results. A central consideration is that in order to provide such interpretation, one obviously needs some theoretical backing for the conclusions that are drawn.

The remainder of this chapter is structured as follows. First, I present a few general studies on what determines environmental quality. Next, I will discuss a few studies related to particular environmental policy instruments, mainly liability rules, regulation and market-based instruments. Then, I will turn to the enforcement of environmental law and conclude by highlighting a few opportunities and challenges posed by the empirical research.

1.2 LAW AND ENVIRONMENTAL QUALITY

Starting at a very general level, it may be interesting to address the question 'to what extent does environmental law play a role in determining environmental quality'? Interesting empirical research has been undertaken using the concept of the 'Environmental Kuznets Curve'. This concept is named after the Nobel prize winner Simon Kuznets who explored the relationship between income inequality and income level in a country (Kuznets 1955). Various scholars have shown empirically that economic development leads to environmental degradation. There is a turning point in economic development, where individual income levels increase and a demand for higher environmental quality emerges, suggesting increased economic welfare goes hand in hand with environmental improvements. The interesting question is to identify when a nation reaches that turning point. This is relevant to determining whether China (for example) has already reached the point where a social demand for environmental protection emerges.

Empirical studies which look at the relationship between per capita income and environmental indicators show roughly that environmental pollution first rises as income increases, but that, after a turning point, pollution levels will typically fall (Selden and Song 1995). A recent empirical study shows indicative evidence for China comparing the scale of economic activity and environmental quality across a broad set of environmental indicators for various Chinese provinces (Shen and Hashimoto 2004).

The policy conclusion from these studies seems to be that the best way for a nation, such as China, to promote environmental protection is to promote economic growth because higher income levels go hand in hand with increased environmental protection (Esty and Porter 1998 and 2000). This suggests the somewhat worrying conclusion (for environmental lawyers) that environmental law can only to a limited extent influence environmental quality, since it is to a large extent dependent upon factors such as economic welfare.

Dan Esty from Yale Law School has in many joint papers with Michael Porter examined empirically to what extent a nation's regulatory regime influences environmental quality. The findings of this powerful research are that economic development and environmental protection go hand in hand with improvement in a country's institutions, particularly the environmental regulatory regime (Esty and Porter 2005). The empirical evidence hence suggests that a country can benefit environmentally not only from economic growth, but also from developing the rule of law and strengthening its governance structures (Esty and Porter 2005, p. 424).

An important policy conclusion from this empirical literature is hence that, even though the Environmental Kuznets Curve indicates a pivotal relationship between economic growth and higher environmental quality, the lesson is not that environmental law does not matter. On the contrary, Esty and Porter show convincingly that strengthening the regulatory structure also encourages the promotion of environmental quality.[2]

1.3 SPECIFIC INSTRUMENTS

Turning now to more specific instruments, we can address the question to what extent empirical evidence shows that these instruments have the effects they are supposed to have.

1.3.1 Liability Rules

A first instrument, very popular in environmental law, is the use of liability rules. They are supposed to have a preventive effect and deter potential polluters.[3] Much research is devoted to the question of whether environmental liability should be determined using negligence or using a strict liability rule. The economic literature has often proposed strict liability for reducing environmental pollution, since this would provide potential polluters with optimal incentives for accident reduction.[4] Empirical research, for example by Alberini and Austin (2001), has confirmed that the imposition of strict liability in state environmental policies reduced unintended pollution releases. However, the same authors also found the remarkable result that, in states with strict liability, a greater spill severity and frequency could be found. This was associated with smaller production units with thus reduced assets.

This phenomenon was not found in states using a negligence-based liability approach. At first sight, this surprising finding of more severe pollution under strict liability than under negligence rules seems to be contrary to the assumption from the literature that strict liability would provide stronger incentives for prevention. However, the economic literature also indicated that strict liability could lead to perverse results if polluters were potentially insolvent, meaning that the losses could be higher than their assets (Shavell 1986; Cooter 1984). Alberini and Austin hence found that under strict liability firms organize themselves in smaller production units with limited assets. This confirms the assumption in the literature that strict liability is efficient only if a remedy for the insolvency problem can be found. The normative conclusion from this empirical research is that, if a serious insolvency risk exists, the introduction of strict liability should be accompanied with solvency guarantees, such as compulsory insurance.[5] Otherwise, strict liability may have the effect of driving polluters to reduce the assets that are exposed to liability, rather than investing in pollution control.[6]

An interesting effect of environmental liability was discovered as a result of the enlargement of the European Union to the East. Potential buyers of property in Central and Eastern Europe could be held liable, retrospectively, for cleaning up sites they purchased that were contaminated in the past. Research showed that this retrospective liability limited the possibilities for privatisation in those countries, since potential investors were scared away by the risk of having to pay for the pollution of the past (Bluffstone and Panayotou 2000).

Specific empirical research has also been devoted to the compensation mechanisms for an oil spill. Hendrickx shows that clean-up operations have become expensive, more particularly as a result of pressure from environmental groups and public opinion. However, he also found that, for a high proportion of spills, polluters could not be identified. He suspects that, as a result of the stricter liability facing the tanker owner, they might have improved their skills at concealing their identity (Hendrickx 2007). This indicates that imposing stricter liabilities upon polluters unavoidably comes at a price: the stricter the liability, the more polluters have incentives to avoid liability, for example by avoiding detection or by organizing insolvency to avoid liability by bringing their polluting activities into smaller business units. These perverse effects should hence be taken into account in designing policy.

1.3.2 Regulation

An impressive amount of literature is devoted to the effectiveness of environmental regulation. A theoretical starting point for evaluating regulation is a paper by Shavell. This indicates that since government will often have better information on optimal abatement techniques and because insolvency problems can limit the effectiveness of liability rules, a liability suit for environmental damage might never be brought,[7] and thus regulation may be a more effective way to control environmental pollution than private law instruments (Shavell 1984a and 1984b; Wittman 1977). There is substantial empirical evidence of the relative effectiveness of safety regulation in controlling environmental harm. Dewees demonstrated that in North America the quality of the environment has improved substantially as a result of regulatory efforts, more so than in response to legal action in tort (Dewees 1992a and 1992b). Dewees, Duff and Trebilcock hold that regulatory efforts to improve the environment have been met with considerable success when measured by the reduction of emissions. However, they stress that, while environmental regulation is a determining factor in pollutant emissions and ambient concentrations, other non-regulatory factors such as economic growth and even the weather also influence environmental quality (Dewees, Duff and Trebilcock 1996, pp. 307–23).

An impressive amount of research is devoted to the fact that notwithstanding any beneficial effects of regulation, regulation entails the danger that it may not be welfare improving, and that it may serve the interests of particular groups in society. The application of this interest group theory of regulation has been strongly advocated by the public choice school. Maloney and McCormick were probably the first to show that industry will try to change the content of environmental regulation to its advantage (Maloney and McCormick 1982). They argue that industry, realising that environmental regulation is unavoidable, will cooperate with the development of the regulation and try to shape it to achieve strategic advantage. A classic example is the introduction of so-called 'grandfather clauses' in permit-based regulation. These stipulate that the regulation will be less applicable to firms or products which are already in the market. Nash and Revesz showed that regulations with grandfather clauses are likely to delay the introduction of new, clean plants and keep inefficient plants operating longer than they otherwise would (Nash and Revesz 2007). There is ample evidence that the grandfathering of emission rights under the European Emission Trading Scheme seriously reduced industry incentives for pollution abatement (Endres and Ohl 2005; Peeters and Deketelaere 2006; Faure and Peeters 2008).

As far as China is concerned, there is empirical evidence that environmental regulation does not always follow the road to optimality. Da Zhu and Jiang Ru showed that the Environmental Impact Assessment Law of 2003 lacked effective implementation in China. Non-environmental ministries evaded the act or organised planning environmental assessments on their own without the participation of the State Environmental Protection Administration (SEPA) (Da Zhu and Jiang Ru 2008). Bureaucratic politics and rising tension between various ministries prevented the implementation of efficient environmental regulation, in this case related to environmental impact assessment.

Public choice theory predicts that if it were possible to organise a countervailing power against industry lobbying, competition between various pressure groups could emerge, the result of which might be closer to the optimum than when government is only lobbied by pressure groups representing industry interest (Becker 1983). Binder and Neumayer present some powerful empirical evidence of this in the environmental arena (Binder and Neumayer 2005). They provide a systematic test of the relationship between the strength of environmental NGOs and air pollution levels. Environmental NGOs exert a statistically significant impact on sulphur dioxide (SO_2), smoke and heavy particulates concentration levels. The finding is based on a cross-country time series regression analysis. This recent paper provides important empirical backing for something environmental lawyers have long advocated: that public participation and NGO influence will effectively help to achieve lower pollution levels around the globe!

1.3.3 Command and Control versus Market-based Instruments

A substantial amount of literature compares the traditional command and control approach to regulation with incentive-based mechanisms, referred to as economic or market-based instruments. From this literature, it is impossible in general to compare regulation with market-based instruments. The superiority of the one or the other is very dependent upon the specific context, the type of pollutant regulated, institutional design etc. It is not difficult to point to research showing that a regulatory approach can lead to significant improvement, for example reduced waste water emissions, and that it can encourage the implementation of less polluting production techniques in the long run (Stephan 1988). As long as command and control approaches are designed with one eye on cost saving, incentive-based systems are not necessarily superior (Oates, Portney and McGartland 1989). I provide below some success stories of market-based instruments, concerned with reducing emissions, but that does not imply that similar results could not have been achieved with a regulatory approach.[8]

1.3.4 Taxation

There is a long tradition of using so-called Pigovian taxes to provide incentives for emission reduction. Those interested might review recent overviews[9] or global conferences on environmental taxation, both of which sources provide evidence of successes from environmental taxation.[10] To mention a few: in the Netherlands water pollution by 14 industries responsible for 90 per cent of total water pollution decreased by 50 per cent between 1969 and 1975 and by another 20 per cent by 1980. Half of this reduction was due to an effluent charge (Dewees, Duff and Trebilcock 1996, pp. 326–7). Comparative research by Bongaerts and Kraemer of water pollution charges in France, the Netherlands and Germany came to the conclusion that effluent charges provide a strong incentive to invest in water pollution abatement. The authors argue that the effect is especially strong in Germany, where charges are reduced by 50 per cent for emitters who meet the emission standard.[11]

One should not become overly enthusiastic. There is evidence that special interest groups can also be active when it comes to designing a taxation system. It is for example remarkable that pollution permits are being introduced on a large scale in the US, but that taxation systems have traditionally been more popular in Europe than in the US. Nobel prize winner Buchanan has argued (together with Tullock) that this should not come as a surprise. Firms will generally prefer emission standards or emission trading (especially when emission rights are grandfathered) to taxes. Standards can serve as a barrier to entry for new firms, raising the profits of existing firms. Taxes, on the other hand, do not preclude entry and represent an additional cost to existing firms on the market (Buchanan and Tullock 1975). It should come as no surprise that interest groups representing industry will oppose taxation and that as a result charges are rarely introduced 'in the textbook form'.[12]

As a result of such considerations, there is a lot of evidence of inefficient environmental taxation. Not surprisingly, the likelihood of these inefficiencies increases the greater the power of the interest group. For example recent research shows that whereas a general tax to internalise externalities created by the power generating sector could create important welfare gains, a Belgian regulation is structured in such a way that independent power producers escape most of the air pollution tax (Pigano, Prost and Van Rompuy 2000). In the Netherlands a perverse energy tax was introduced in 1996. The larger the energy use, the lower the tax would be. This tax therefore gave incentives to increase the use of energy. The main concern of the policy-maker was to increase the competitiveness of Dutch industry rather than serving any ecological goal (Faure and Ubachs 2002 and 2005). Similarly, O'Connor reports on the pollution charges on air emissions, waste water discharges, noise, solid waste and radioactive wastes introduced in China at the end of the last century. Charge rates were set slightly above the average operating costs of pollution control facilities in order to provide incentives for compliance. In practice, they were not indexed to inflation, as a result of which their real value eroded over time, resulting in weak incentives for pollution reduction. Efforts to raise the charge met, not surprisingly, with strong opposition from industry (O'Connor 1998, pp. 96–7). Considerations of political acceptability may hence explain the introduction of efficient taxation systems (O'Connor 1998, p. 108).

I should also mention that although earlier research on environmental taxation in China was rather sceptical of its effectiveness, due to political pressure not to increase the tax rate, more recent research indicates that China's discharge fee programmes have had a positive influence on pollution levels.[13]

Similar problems arise with market-based instruments, particularly pollution charges in developing countries. For developing countries, market-based instruments like taxation would arguably, at least on paper, be the most suitable instruments, since they could be implemented at lower costs than command and control regulation (Blackman 2009, p. 101). However, others have argued that implementing market-based instruments is only possible where a reliable institutional and administrative structure is available (Bell and Russell 2002). These conditions will often not be met in developing countries. The empirical evidence seems to confirm this point: in those countries where a basically sound institutional structure is available, environmental taxes may work effectively. Blackman showed that under Colombia's discharge fee programme pollution loads dropped significantly not so much because of incentives provided by the discharge fees, but rather because of incentives created through the programme for regulatory authorities to improve permitting, monitoring and enforcement (Blackman 2009).

1.3.5 Emissions Trading

Since the 1980s, American research has overwhelmingly shown the effectiveness of trading in pollution rights. Research by Hahn and Hester demonstrates that the trading programmes under the Clean Air Act have led to considerable cost savings (Hahn and Hester 1989). This SO_2 cap and trade programme has recently been identified as a 'living legend' of market effectiveness. The total annual health benefits associated with SO_2 emission reductions under the programme are estimated to be more than $50 million per year in 2010 (Burtraw and Palmer 2004, p. 47).

Recently emissions market attention has shifted from the US to Europe. Europe chose emission trading as an instrument to implement the Kyoto Protocol to address the challenges posed by climate change.[14] Too many studies to be mentioned here have addressed the effectiveness of the EU emission trading scheme.[15] The case of the European ETS is interesting, showing the difficulties of interpreting empirical research. Europe chose with Directive 2003/87 of 13 October 2003 to grandfather emissions rights for free to existing industry. The private interest theory of regulation, mentioned above, can explain why emission trading with grandfathering was chosen instead of an environmental tax. Grandfathering serves the interests of industry better than costly taxation measures (Rodi 2005) .

Also not surprising is that grandfathering may lead to over-allocation of emission rights.[16] As a result of this over-allocation in early 2007 the price of allowances dramatically dropped below €1. This low price for allowances provides evidence of over-allocation by the European Member States.[17] It is more difficult to answer the question whether this necessarily makes the whole EU ETS ineffective in driving emission reductions. One may be tempted to argue that this is the case: why would any company invest in emission abatement if a ton of CO_2 emission rights could be purchased at a price of lower than €1 as the marginal costs of pollution abatement are undoubtedly higher. However, Kuik and Oosterhuis convincingly argue that over-allocation could partly be the result of investments in technological and other innovations which did drive emissions reductions. They show that the EU ETS led to additional abatement of between 50 and 200 million tons. They show that the emission trading scheme played a key role in long-term decisions by companies to develop innovative technologies, notably in the steel industry. The mere fact that the price of a ton CO_2 dropped below €1 (at the beginning of 2007) does not necessarily mean that the ETS had no incentive effect. Quite the reverse may be true: the demand for emissions dropped after the introduction of the EU ETS precisely because it had the desired effect of reducing those emissions (Kuik and Oosterhuis 2008).

One has to be very careful in interpreting results of empirical research: the price of one ton of CO_2 falling below €1 does not necessarily mean that the EU ETS is ineffective; one has to interpret this with due regard for the context.

1.3.6 Combinations

One thing is clear from the empirical studies discussed so far. There is not one optimal instrument of environmental policy. The key concern is to find an optimal combination of instruments to achieve environmental goals at the lowest cost.

The empirical literature on market-based instruments shows that it is rare for a market-based instrument alone to lead to improved environmental quality. Usually effective economic instruments are used in combination with more traditional command and control instruments. An important argument to support this combined use of traditional command and control and modern economic instruments has been presented by Bruno Frey. He argues that economic instruments could lead to 'crowding out' of environmental action driven by moral motives. By creating the opportunity of payment for an emission right or an environmental tax, the spontaneous willingness of industry to act in an environmentally conscious way could be 'crowded out', and reduced (Frey 1997a and 1997b). Recently, Goeschl and Perino found evidence that taxes for carbon dioxide (CO_2) emissions do crowd out intrinsic motivations, whereas emission standards are neutral (Goeschl and Perino 2009). For this reason it may be important to combine market-based instruments with traditional regulatory instruments where 'crowding out' may be less of a risk. Other combinations and systems-based design, have also been used successfully.

1.4 ENFORCEMENT

No matter what type of instrument is chosen, an effective enforcement and sanctioning system is always necessary.[18] The deterrence hypothesis was developed in the seminal work of Gary Becker (Becker 1968). A potential polluter will make a rational calculus of the costs and benefits of complying with environmental regulation and will only comply when the expected costs of a violation are higher than the potential gains. This expected sanction consists on the one hand of the probability of being inspected, prosecuted and sanctioned and on the other hand of the sanction imposed.

European data on detection and prosecution of environmental crime show that the likelihood that a violation will end up in court and be sanctioned is extremely low. For the Flemish region in Belgium, based on data from the environmental inspectorate, it was found that the average probability of being apprehended and prosecuted for a violation is less than 1 per cent. Only one in a hundred firms that are in violation will be detected and prosecuted (Faure and Svatikova 2009). This follows from the fact that the probability of being inspected is very low,[19] and from the fact that many detected violations are not prosecuted. In the Flemish region the prosecutor dismissed 62 per cent of violations identified by the environmental inspectorate (Faure and Svatikova 2010; Ponsaers and De Keulenaer 2003). Similar data come from the UK: On average the prosecution rate for pollution incidents is less than 5 per cent (Bell and McGillivray 2006, pp. 295–6). However, serious incidents have a much higher prosecution rate.[20]

Similar rather depressing data can be presented for the sanctions imposed if the case gets to the court. A study on the fines imposed by the courts of appeal of Ghent in the Flemish region in the period 1990–2000 found that an average fine of €5000 was imposed both in first instance and on appeal (Billiet and Rousseau 2003, p. 131). A later study found average fines imposed for violations in the textile sector of €2869 in first instance and €7165 on appeal (Billiet and Rousseau 2003, p. 131). For the Netherlands, average fines imposed through the criminal system ranged from €1351 to €2342 (Schoep and Schuyt 2008).

If one looks at these average fines imposed by criminal courts in Western Europe and multiplies this by the probability of being detected and prosecuted of about 1 per cent, this suggests that expected sanctions for the Flemish region vary from €87.7 (Rousseau 2007b, p. 9) to €176 (Rousseau 2007a, p. 10) to €181 (Rousseau 2008, p. 9). The risk-weighted value of the regulatory sanction is low relative to the cost of compliance.

However, here again one has to interpret numbers with caution. One could argue that not all cases are prosecuted before a criminal court, but that does not necessarily mean that nothing happens. In some legal systems, prosecutors can propose a financial penalty for the perpetrator and deal with the case themselves, to avoid the high administrative costs of the criminal prosecution. This may add something, but probably not a lot, to the strength of the sanction.

A second point is that there may be other costs than the sanctions imposed by the courts that could deter potential violators, for example a conviction could lead to 'shaming' and a loss of reputation for entrepreneurs.[21]

A third reason why the low prosecution rates of environmental violations in Western Europe should be interpreted with caution is that the prosecutor could engage in regulatory dealings (Fenn and Veljanovski 1988), whereby the prosecutor agrees to dismiss the case after evidence of compliance by the firm. Some argue that this so-called 'soft approach' in many cases leads to compliance (Billiet and Rousseau 2005).

There may be a fourth reason why firms comply notwithstanding low expected sanctions under the criminal law.[22] Companies base their *ex ante* decision about compliance on their subjective perception of the probability of being detected and prosecuted and of the sanctions that can be imposed. They may not be aware of the low expected sanction in reality. The Belgian economist Rousseau found strong empirical backing for this hypothesis. When firms had been obliged to pay a monetary sanction during the previous two years, they were on average more likely to be in violation in a second period than firms that had not been prosecuted and fined in the first period. Those who overestimated the expected fine complied. Firms that had been recently fined had a more accurate impression of true expected sanctions and, being aware that they were low, were not deterred (Rousseau 2007c and 2007a). This has an important policy implication: fining a polluter with a too low fine can have a perverse effect: firms will be informed about the low expected sanction. Those who do not experience low sanctions may be more induced towards compliance. It seems that it is better not to seek a fine if too low a fine is likely to be awarded, since otherwise one might destroy potential perpetrators' subjective perceptions that fines are higher than they actually are.

The European experience with low expected sanctions for environmental crime may be different from the US where strict sentencing guidelines apply, to which the judge should in principle adhere.[23] However, Barrett found in a study on the application of sentencing guidelines for environmental crime 'that the sentences imposed in the majority of cases reflected the reluctance of judges to impose significant incarceration for violations of environmental laws' (Barrett 1992). Some studies suggest that these sentencing guidelines led to negative outcomes in terms of deterrence. If judges consider the guidelines to be unreasonable, this results in lenient sentencing of environmental criminals. According to some American scholars, significant violations are sentenced too leniently, which may undermine the deterrent value of environmental enforcement thus trivializing environmental law itself (Babbitt, Cory and Kruchek 2004).

1.5 OPPORTUNITIES AND CHALLENGES

This overview of empirical research shows that many studies, even though they originate from scholars who are not lawyers, provide insights into the effects of environmental legal instruments. One reason for presenting this material was to show the opportunities this empirical research provides for us environmental lawyers. However, there are a few rules of thumb that ought be followed when using this empirical research.

A first rule of thumb is to interpret the research results with care within their particular context. For example, in considering the effectiveness of market-based instruments in developing countries there exists, as discussed above, different and at first blush seemingly contradicting research. A sceptic of empirical research could hold that anyone can find some empirical research to back up his own position. The key consideration is that much of this research is context specific, which raises the question 'why?' For example, the fact that market-based instruments worked well in Colombia but not in other developing countries should cause scholars to pay sufficient attention to the specific institutional context of that country.

It may be misleading to specify the results of a particular instrument without consideration of the entire environmental law context. For example, studies pointing to the effectiveness of market-based instruments often show that it was often not the market-based instrument itself that led to higher environmental performance, but that the introduction of the instrument led to better environmental awareness and enforcement by agencies.

Context specificity is also important when looking at a particular country case study. At the first IUCN Academy of Law meeting I attended at Pace University, the Indian lawyer Mr Mehta was welcomed with a standing ovation when he gave a keynote speech to this distinguished audience. The introduction to the famous casebook on environmental law in India by Divan and Rosencranz (2001) indicates that Mr Mehta was the originator of more than thirty decisions of the Supreme Court of India related to environmental cases. Recent research by economists has proven that environmental public interest litigation and the resulting decisions of the Supreme Court in India have led to a substantial reduction in pollution levels, particularly improving ambient air quality in Delhi (Raja and Xavier 2005a, 2005b and 2007). A straightforward policy conclusion following from this Indian case therefore seems to be that environmental public interest litigation is an effective instrument in reducing pollution levels in developing countries. Such a conclusion would however be unjustified. Even in India, many scholars hold that the judicial activism by the Supreme Court is desirable and effective, but only as a second-best solution, given that the executive power fails to provide adequate protection (Mijin Cha 2005; Rajamani 2007). Many authors in India are also critical of this judicial activism and argue that it violates the separation of powers (Dam 2003–04, p. 608 and p. 612; Anant and Singh 2002). Third, environmental public interest litigation may have generated beneficial effects in India because in that country the judiciary has a long-standing reputation for independence and decision-making in the public interest. The Indian solution may not be possible in countries where the judiciary is not of the same quality and the danger exists that problems of corruption and lacking capacity may limit the effectiveness of the judiciary as well as the legislative and executive branches of government.

A third rule of thumb is that one needs academic honesty in using empirical research. There is a hard to resist tendency among academics to interpret empirical research in a way that fits their established beliefs. Thus for sceptics of market-based instruments like emission trading, the European experience could give rise to the argument that the emission trading scheme was ineffective, since the price of an allowance dropped below €1. As I showed above, this would be a wrong interpretation of the ETS. The low price may well be the result of substantial investments made in anticipation of the ETS, as a result of which there was indeed less demand for allowances.

A fourth rule of thumb is that the results of empirical research also need to be interpreted within a specific theoretical context. For example, the fact that in some cases, strict liability laws were associated with more pollution incidents than negligence laws and that they fuel a tendency to organize in smaller business units should not be misinterpreted as an argument against strict liability for environmental pollution. The theoretical literature warns that strict liability may lead to under-deterrence if an insolvency risk emerges. That is not an argument against strict liability, but rather it suggests the need to manage solvency risk as well as setting a different level of penalty.

Many more examples have been given above, pointing in the same direction: empirical research does provide opportunities and useful information for environmental lawyers, but it has to be handled with care. There are many good reasons for doing empirical research, but it is a challenge to interpret the results within the right context.

1.6 CONCLUDING REMARKS

In the introduction, I indicated that I wanted to show that empirical research holds important lessons for us environmental lawyers, even if it is not always easily accessible because of the language or the journals in which it is published. A lot of empirical material is already known and read by environmental lawyers. This can only become more important in the future. It is indeed crucial for any policy instrument, be it command and control or market-based, that the policy maker has clear ideas on the effects of the instruments chosen in practice. This requires *ex ante* consideration of the available empirical research since the choice of a particular instrument is often based on assumptions about its effects that may be merely theoretical. Good legal policy also requires serious *ex post* evaluation studies to examine whether a particular instrument or policy was indeed able to achieve the goals expected by the legislator.

I have provided a *tour d'horizon* of many environmental policy instruments and realize that I could not be complete. My chapter has involved 'cherry picking' many domains where interesting research exists that is worth further exploring.

One possible conclusion, looking at the many studies discussed, is that the empirical research does not necessarily point in the direction of strongly favouring either command and control or market-based instruments. Rather it shows that the effectiveness of the instruments depends to a large extent upon the particular design. Some studies point at the relative effectiveness of environmental taxation in providing incentives for emission reductions. At first blush, this could be understood. Command and control is dependent upon public enforcement, which may (at least in Western Europe) be weak, giving rise to low expected sanctions *ex ante*. However, studies equally show that for taxation instruments the tax rate is not always efficiently set. Taxation has been shown to be effective only where an effective monitoring and enforcement system applies. In that respect, command and control and market-based are not that much different: both will need effective monitoring and enforcement systems. Strong laws and efficient institutions are a fundamental requirement regardless of instrument choice.

The studies show that it may not be possible to argue that one particular instrument is 'best' or 'optimal'. In most cases, a combination of instruments may be indicated. An important point for further research is to look for 'optimal mixes' of policy instruments. These may also to a large extent depend upon country-specific characteristics. It is not surprising to notice that important differences exist between Europe and the US, and perhaps with Asia as well. To some extent these differences (for example regarding instruments chosen but also enforcement styles) may be due to institutional characteristics or differences in environmental problems. Many studies show that, in practice, optimal instruments are often not introduced simply because of insufficient political acceptability. The reason why the US made more use of emission trading and Europe of environmental taxation, and why initially emission rights in Europe were allocated through grandfathering, is the relative power of interest groups. The recent study by Binder and Neumayer showing that the influence of the civil society has a positive impact on environmental quality gives empirical insights into an issue that has long concerned environmental lawyers. If one wishes governments to make effective environmental regulation in the public interest, it is important to have environmental NGO involvement to provide a counterweight for lobbying industry.

I started this contribution with a reference to the important research by Esty and Porter. They showed that environmental quality does to a large extent depend upon economic growth. The most important lesson for those who want improvements in environmental quality therefore still remains: fight poverty and increase income levels. However, at the same time, their (and other) research also shows that environmental quality is higher in legal systems with a decent regulatory and institutional framework. Therefore, it does pay to examine, based on empirical research, which environmental instruments may in particular contexts be most effective in remedying environmental pollution. In other words: environmental law does matter!

NOTES

1. The prerequisites for doing decent empirical analysis are indeed not that easy to meet. For details, see Van Velthoven 2009.

2. This is also argued by Binder and Neumayer 2005.
3. See for example Monti 2001.
4. The basic paper is of course Shavell 1980, but see for example also the application in Pozzo 1996.
5. As suggested in the literature. See for example Jost 1996 and Polborn 1998.
6. For an overview of the literature concerning the incentive impacts of environmental liability see also Earnhart 2004.
7. For example, because the damage can be widespread, victims may believe damage is caused by a natural cause, no victim may be identified, long latency periods may exist, as well as problems of causation.
8. For an overview of the literature see Stewart 2000; Stewart 1988 and Ackerman and Stewart 1988.
9. See for example the contributions in Harrington, Morgenstern and Sterner 2004.
10. The most recent volume (containing the papers presented at the Ninth Global Conference on Environmental Taxation in Singapore in 2008) is Lye, Milne, Ashiabor, Kreiser and Deketelaere 2009.
11. Bongaerts and Kraemer 1987. They also argue that it is difficult to disentangle the separate effects of charges and emission standards.
12. See in that respect especially Hahn 1989.
13. See more particularly Wang and Wheeler 2005.
14. See, for the costs of climate change, the interesting recent overview by Tol 2009.
15. See for example the contributions in Douma, Massai and Montini 2007.
16. See for example Baldwin 2008.
17. See for example Woerdman, Clo and Arcuri 2008.
18. See, on the importance of enforcement of market-based instruments (particularly emissions trading), Peeters 2006a and Peeters 2006b.
19. As was also established by Billiet and Rousseau 2005, p. 19.
20. Of on average 63 per cent. On this targeting by the Environment Agency in the UK, see Faure and Svatikova 2009, p. 16.
21. See generally on the importance of this shaming notion Braithwaite 1989.
22. This phenomenon has been referred to in the literature as the Harrington Paradox, following research by Winston Harrington, who established that given low expected sanctions, one would expect more environmental criminality than can be observed in practice (Harrington 1988 and Harford and Harrington 1991).
23. For an economic critique of these sentencing guidelines see Easterbrook 1983.

REFERENCES

Ackerman, B. and Stewart, R.B. (1988), 'Reforming Environmental Law: The Democratic Case for Market Incentives', *Columbia Journal of Environmental Law*, 13, 171–99.

Alberini, A. and Austin, D. (2001), 'Liability Policy and Toxic Pollution Releases', in *The Law and Economics of the Environmen*t, Cheltenham, UK and Northampton, MA, USA: Edward Elgar, pp. 92–115.

Anant, T.C.A. and Singh, J. (2002), 'An Economic Analysis of Judicial Activism', *Economic and Political Weekly*, 4433–9.

Babbitt, C.J., Cory, D.C. and Kruchek, B.L. (2004), 'Discretion and Criminalization of Environmental Law', *Duke Environmental Law and Policy Forum*, 15, 1–64.

Baldwin, R. (2008), 'Regulation Lite: The Rise of Emissions Trading', Law Society Economy Working Papers, www.lse.ac.uk/collection/law/wps/wps.htm.

Barrett, J.J. (1992), 'Sentencing Environmental Crimes under the United States Sentencing Guidelines: A Sentencing Lottery', *Environmental Law*, 22, 1421–49.

Becker, G.S. (1968), 'Crime and Punishment: An Economic Approach', *Journal of Political Economy*, 76 (2), 169–217.
Becker, G.S. (1983), 'A Theory of Competition among Pressure Groups for Political Influence', *Quarterly Journal of Economics*, 371–400.
Bell, S. and McGillivray, D. (2006), *Environmental Law*, 6th ed., Oxford: Oxford University Press.
Bell, R. and Russell, C. (2002), 'Environmental Policy for Developing Countries', *Issues in Science and Technology*, 63–70.
Billiet, C. and Rousseau, S. (2003), 'De hoogte van strafrechtelijke boetes: Een rechtseconomische analyse van milieurechtspraak (1990–2000) van het Hof van Beroep te Gent', *Tijdschrift voor Milieurecht*, 120–34.
Billiet, C. and Rousseau, S. (2005), 'De zachte rechtshandhaving in het bestuurlijke handhavingspoor: de inspectiebeslissing en het voortraject van bestuurlijke sancties. Een rechtseconomische analyse', *Tijdschrift voor Milieurecht*, 2–33.
Binder, S. and Neumayer, E. (2005), 'Environmental Pressure Group Strengths and Air Pollution: An Empirical Analysis', *Ecological Economics*, 55, 527–38.
Blackman, A. (2009), 'Columbia's Discharge Fee Programme: Incentives for Polluters or Regulators?', *Journal of Environmental Management*, 90, 101–19.
Bluffstone, R.A. and Panayotou, T. (2000), 'Environmental Liability and Privatisation in Central and Eastern Europe: Towards an Optimal Policy', *Environmental & Resource Economics*, 17, 335–52.
Bongaerts, J. and Kraemer, R.A. (1987), 'Water Pollution Charges in Three Countries: Control through Incentives', *European Environmental Review*, 12–19.
Braithwaite, J. (1989), *Crime, Shame and Reintegration*, Cambridge: Cambridge University Press.
Buchanan, J. and Tullock, G. (1975), 'Polluters' Profits and Political Response: Direct Controls versus Taxes', *American Economic Review*, 65, 139–47.
Burtraw, D. and Palmer, K. (2004), 'SO_2 Cap-and-trade Programme in the United States. A "Living Legend" of Market Effectiveness', in W. Harrington, R.D. Morgenstern and T. Sterner (eds), *Choosing Environmental Policy. Comparing Instruments and Outcomes in the United States and Europe*, Washington: Resources for the Future, pp. 41–66.
Cooter, R. (1984), 'Prices and Sanctions', *Columbia Law Review*, 84, 1343–523.
Da Zhu and Jiang Ru (2008), 'Strategic Environmental Assessment in China: Motivations, Politics and Effectiveness', *Journal of Environmental Management*, 88, 615–26.
Dam, S. (2003–04), 'Green Laws for Better Health: The Past that was and the Future that may be – Reflections from the Indian Experience', *Georgia International Environmental Law Review*, 16, 608–12.
Dewees, D. (1992a), 'The Comparative Efficacy of Tort Law and Regulation for Environmental Protection', *Geneva Papers on Risk and Insurance*, 446–67.
Dewees, D. (1992b), 'Tort Law and the Deterrence of Environmental Pollution', in T.H. Tietenberg (ed.), *Innovation in Environmental Policy*, Aldershot, UK and Brookfield, US: Edward Elgar, 139–64.
Dewees, D.N., Duff, D. and Trebilcock, M. (1996), *Exploring the Domain of Accident Law: Taking the Facts Seriously*, Oxford: Oxford University Press.
Divan, S. and Rosencranz, A. (2001), *Environmental Law and Policy in India: Cases, Materials and Statutes*, 2nd ed., New Delhi: Oxford University Press.
Douma, W.T., Massai, L. and Montini, M. (eds) (2007), *The Kyoto Protocol and Beyond: Legal and Policy Challenges of Climate Change*, The Hague: TMC Asser Press.

Earnhart, D. (2004), 'Liability for Past Environmental Contamination and Privatization', *Environmental & Resource Economics*, 29, 97–122.
Easterbrook, F. (1983), 'Criminal Procedure as a Market System', *Journal of Legal Studies*, 12, 289–332.
Endres, A. and Ohl, C. (2005), 'Kyoto, Europe? An Economic Evaluation of the European Emissions Trading Directive', *European Journal of Law and Economics*, 19, 17–39.
Esty, D.C. and Porter, M.E. (1998), 'Industrial Ecology and Competitiveness', *Journal of Industrial Ecology*, 2, 35–43.
Esty, D.C. and Porter, M.E. (2000), 'Measuring National Environmental Performance and its Determinants', in M.E. Porter and J. Sachs (eds), *The Global Competitiveness Report 2000*, New York: Oxford University Press, pp. 60–75.
Esty, D.C. and Porter, M. (2005), 'National Environmental Performance: An Empirical Analysis of Policy Results and Determinants', *Environment and Development Economics*, 10, 391–434.
Faure, M. and Peeters, M. (eds) (2008), *Climate Change and European Emissions Trading: Lessons for Theory and Practice*, Cheltenham, UK and Northampton, MA, US: Edward Elgar.
Faure, M. and Svatikova, K. (2009), 'Criminal or Administrative Law to Protect the Environment? Evidence from Western Europe', Working Paper.
Faure, M.G. and Svatikova, K. (2010), 'Enforcement of Environmental Law in the Flemish Region', *European Energy and Environmental Law Review*, 19 (2), 60–79.
Faure, M. and Ubachs, S. (2002), 'Environmental Taxation in the Netherlands: A Dutch Treat?', in L.A. Kreiser (ed.), *Critical Issues in International Environmental Taxation: Insights and Analyses for Achieving Environmental Policy Goals through Tax Policy*, Chicago: CCH, pp. 301–29.
Faure, M. and Ubachs, S. (2005), 'Harmful Tax Measures and Greying of Taxation in the Netherlands: What Went Wrong?', in H. Ashiabor, K. Deketelaere, L. Kreiser and J. Milne (eds), *Critical Issues in Environmental Taxation: International and Comparative Perspectives*, vol. II, Richmond: Richmond Law and Tax, pp. 521–32.
Fenn, P. and Veljanovski, C. (1988), 'A Positive Economic Theory of Regulatory Enforcement', *Economic Journal*, 98, 1055–70.
Frey, B.S. (1997a), *Not Just for the Money: An Economic Theory of Personal Motivation*, Cheltenham, US and Lyme, US: Edward Elgar.
Frey, B.S. (1997b), 'Morality and Rationality in Environmental Policy', *Journal of Consumer Policy*, 22, 395–417.
Goeschl, T. and Perino, G. (2009), 'Instrument Choice and Motivation: Evidence from a Climate Change Experiment', Working Paper.
Hahn, R.W. (1989), 'Economic Prescriptions for Environmental Problems: How the Patient Followed the Doctor's Orders', *Journal of Economic Perspectives*, 3 (2), 95–114.
Hahn, R.W. and Hester, G.L. (1989), 'Where did All the Markets Go? An Analysis of EPA's Emissions Trading Programme', *Yale Journal on Regulation*, 6, 109–53.
Harford, J.D. and Harrington, W. (1991), 'A Reconsideration of Enforcement Leverage when Penalties are Restricted', *Journal of Public Economics*, 45, 391–5.
Harrington, W. (1988), 'Enforcement Leverage when Penalties are Restricted', *Journal of Public Economics*, 37, 29–53.
Harrington, W., Morgenstern, R.D. and Sterner, T. (eds) (2004), *Choosing Environmental Policy: Comparing Instruments and Outcomes in the United States and Europe*, Washington: Resources for the Future.

Hendrickx, R. (2007), 'Maritime Oil Pollution: An Empirical Analysis', in M. Faure and A. Verheij (eds), *Shifts in Compensation for Environmental Damage*, Vienna: Springer, pp. 256–7.

Jost, P.J. (1996), 'Limited Liability and the Requirement to Purchase Insurance', *International Review of Law and Economics*, 16, 259–76.

Kuik, O. and Oosterhuis, F. (2008), 'Economic Impacts of the EU ETS: Preliminary Evidence', in M. Faure and M. Peeters (eds), *Climate Change and European Emissions Trading: Lessons for Theory and Practice*, Cheltenham, UK and Northampton, MA, US: Edward Elgar, 208–22.

Kuznets, S. (1955), 'Economic Growth and Income Inequality', *American Economic Review*, 49, 1–28.

Lye, L.H., Milne, J.E., Ashiabor, H., Kreiser, L. and Deketelaere, K. (eds) (2009), *Critical Issues in Environmental Taxation: International and Comparative Perspectives*, vol. VII, Oxford: Oxford University Press.

Maloney, M.T. and McCormick, R.E. (1982), 'A Positive Theory of Environmental Quality Regulation', *Journal of Law and Economics*, 25, 99–123.

Mijin Cha, J. (2005), 'A Critical Examination of the Environmental Jurisprudence of the Courts of India', *Albany Law Environmental Outlook Journal*, 10, 197–228.

Monti, A. (2001), 'Environmental Risk: A Comparative Law and Economics Approach to Liability and Insurance', *European Review of Private Law*, 1, 51–79.

Nash, J.R. and Revesz, R.L. (2007), 'Grandfathering and Environmental Regulation: The Law and Economics of New Source Review', New York University School of Law, Public Law and Legal Theory Research Paper Series, Working Paper 007-03, http://ssrn.com/abstract=965840.

Oates, W.E., Portney, P.R. and McGartland, A.M. (1989), 'The Net Benefits of Incentive-based Regulation: A Case Study of Environmental Standard Setting', *American Economic Review*, 79, 1233–44.

O'Connor, D. (1998), 'Applying Economic Instruments in Developing Countries: From Theory to Implementation', *Environment and Development Economics*, 4, 91–110.

Peeters, M. (2006a), 'Inspection and Market-based Regulation through Emissions Trading: The Striking Reliance on Self-monitoring, Self-reporting and Verification', *Utrecht Law Review*, 2 (1), 177–95.

Peeters, M. (2006b), 'Enforcement of the EU Greenhouse Gas Emissions Trading Scheme', in K. Deketelaere and M. Peeters (eds), *EU Climate Change Policy: The Challenge of New Regulatory Initiatives*, Cheltenham, UK and Northampton, MA, US: Edward Elgar, pp. 169–87.

Peeters, M. and Deketelaere, K. (eds) (2006), *EU Climate Change Policy. The Challenge of New Regulatory Initiatives*, Cheltenham, UK and Northampton, MA, US: Edward Elgar.

Pigano, A., Prost, S. and Van Rompuy, J. (2000), 'Alternative Environmental Regulation Schemes for the Belgian Power Generation Sector', *Environmental & Resource Economics*, 16, 121–60.

Polborn, M. (1998), 'Mandatory Insurance and the Judgment-proof Problem', *International Review of Law and Economics*, 141–6.

Ponsaers, P. and De Keulenaer, S. (2003), 'Met strafrecht tegen milieudelicten? Rol en functie van bijzondere inspectiediensten in de strijd tegen milieucriminaliteit', *Panopticon*, 250–65.

Pozzo, B. (1996), 'The Liability Problem in Modern Environmental Statutes', *European Review of Private Law*, 4, 112–29.

Raja, A.V. and Xavier, F. (2005a), 'Efficiency and Strategic Behaviour: The Case of Mass Torts', Working Paper, Department of Economics, University of Hyderabad.

Raja, A.V. and Xavier, F. (2005b), 'Economic Efficiency and Public Interest Litigations (PIL): Lessons from India', paper presented at the first annual conference of the Asian Law and Economics Association, Seoul National University, Seoul, South Korea.

Raja, A.V. and Xavier, F. (2007), 'Regulatory Failure and the Economic Efficiency of Public Interest Litigation', unpublished manuscript.

Rajamani, L. (2007), 'Public Interest Environmental Litigation in India: Exploring Issues of Access, Participation, Equity, Effectiveness and Sustainability', *Journal of Environmental Law*, 19 (3), 293–321.

Rodi, M. (2005), 'Legal Aspects of the European Emission Trading Scheme', in B. Hansjürgens (ed.), *Emissions Trading for Climate Policy, US and European Perspective*, Cambridge: Cambridge University Press, pp. 199–221.

Rousseau, S. (2007a), 'The Impact of Sanctions and Inspections on Firms' Environmental Compliance Decisions', Working Paper, Center for Economic Studies, Katholieke Universiteit Leuven, No. 2007-04.

Rousseau, S. (2007b), 'Economic Empirical Analysis of Sanctions for Environmental Violations: A Literature Overview', Working Paper series, Katholieke Universiteit Leuven, No. 2007-03.

Rousseau, S. (2007c), 'Timing of Environmental Inspections: Survival of the Compliant', *Journal of Regulatory Economics*, 32, 17–36.

Rousseau, S. (2008), 'Evidence of a Filtered Approach to Environmental Monitoring', available from the author: Sandra.Rousseau@econ.kuleuven.be.

Schoep, G.K. and Schuyt, P.M. (2008), *Feiten en percepties van de sanctionering van milieudelicten en delicten betreffende de volksgezondheid*, Leiden: University of Leiden.

Selden, T.M. and Song, D. (1995), 'Neoclassical Growth, the J-curve for Abatement, and the Inverted U-curve for Pollution', *Journal of Environmental Economics and Management*, 29, 162–8.

Shavell, S. (1980), 'Strict Liability versus Negligence', *Journal of Legal Studies*, 9, 1–25.

Shavell, S. (1984a), 'Liability for Harm versus Regulation of Safety', *Journal of Legal Studies*, 13, 357–74.

Shavell, S. (1984b), 'A Model of the Optimal Use of Liability and Safety Regulation', *RAND Journal of Economics*, 15, 271–80.

Shavell, S. (1986), 'The Judgment-proof Problem', *International Review of Law and Economics*, 6, 43–58.

Shen, J. and Hashimoto, Y. (2004), 'Environmental Kuznets Curve on Country Level: Evidence from China', Graduate School of Economics and Osaka School of International Public Policy, Discussion Papers in Economics and Business, paper 04-09.

Stephan, G. (1988), 'Economic Impact of Emissions Standards: A Computational Approach to Waste Water Treatment in Western Europe', in D. Bös, M. Rose and C. Seidl (eds), *Welfare and Efficiency in Public Economics*, Berlin: Springer, pp. 401–22.

Stewart, R.B. (1988), 'Controlling Environmental Risks through Economic Incentives', *Columbia Journal of Environmental Law*, 13, 153–69.

Stewart, R.B. (2000), 'Economic Incentives for Environmental Protection: Opportunities and Obstacles', in R.L. Revesz, P. Sands and R.B. Stewart (eds),

Environmental Law, the Economy and Sustainable Development, Cambridge: Cambridge University Press, pp. 171–244.

Tol, R.S.J. (2009), 'The Economic Effects of Climate Change', *Journal of Economic Perspective*, 23 (2), 29–51.

Van Velthoven, B.C.J. (2009), 'Empirics of Tort', in M. Faure (ed.), *Tort Law and Economics*, Cheltenham, UK and Northampton, MA, US: Edward Elgar, pp. 453–98.

Wang, H. and Wheeler, D. (2005), 'Financial Incentives and Endogenous Enforcement in China's Pollution Levy System', *Journal of Environmental Economics and Management*, 49 (1), 174–96.

Wittman, D.A. (1977), 'Prior Regulation versus Post Liability: The Choice between Input and Output Monitoring', *Journal of Legal Studies*, 6, 193–211.

Woerdman, E., Clo, S. and Arcuri, A. (2008), 'European Emissions Trading and the Polluter Pays Principle: Assessing Grandfathering and Over-allocation', in M. Faure and M. Peeters (eds), *Climate Change and European Emissions Trading: Lessons for Theory and Practice*, Cheltenham, UK and Northampton, MA, US: Edward Elgar, pp. 128–50.

2. Does (property) diversity beget (landscape) sustainability?

John Page and Ann Brower

2.1 INTRODUCTION

Streams of scholarship as diverse as ecology and political science suggest that a more diverse system is a more stable system. The pluralist school of interest group politics observed that diverse and vibrant interest groups are the core of a policy system (for example, Truman, 1951), and it is well accepted that diverse interest group activity is vital to a stable democracy.[1] Community ecologists (MacArthur, 1955; Odum, 1963) have long hypothesised that 'diversity begets stability' (Tilman et al, 1994), though the hypothesis has its critics (May, 1973) and is far from proven (Givnish, 1994). But ecologists report 'high confidence' in the cumulative finding that a broad range and variety of species that respond differently to disturbance can stabilise ecological systems after a shock, such as a hurricane, fire, or biological invasion (Hooper et al, 2005). As such, more biological diversity in ecosystem function is associated with systems that are more resistant to change and more resilient after a change.

There are three metaphorical variants of the hypothesis that biological diversity begets ecosystem stability. Paul and Anne Ehrlich (1981) present a 'rivets hypothesis' that likens each species in a system to a rivet on an airplane. Losing a few rivets might not cause the plane wing to fall off because other similar rivets will compensate, but eventually the crippled plane will crash. The redundancy (or driver-passenger) hypothesis suggests that each system has a certain number of 'driver' species that maintain ecosystem functions, while the rest of the 'passenger' species are redundant. Remove a redundant passenger species, and the system remains stable; but remove a driver species, and the system teeters (Walker, 1992). The idiosyncratic hypothesis says that diversity affects stability, but in an unpredictable way (Lawton, 1994).

This chapter is an exploration of the question: does diversity in property rights arrangements beget landscape sustainability? In a landscape fragmented by multiple owners and multiple parcels, sustainability is enhanced by a plethora of ownership types – less than fee simple interests that transgress, transcend and supersede parcel boundaries. This rich, multi-dimensional mosaic of varied and overlapping interests creates a system of checks and balances that forms a sustainable landscape, one that is resistant to shock and resilient after an unforeseeable change. On a landscape scale, we focus on three facets of sustainability – legal, economic and political – that serve as driver rivets for overall landscape sustainability, including aesthetic and ecological factors. We first explore the diversity of property across landscapes, then examine three case studies in California, New England (USA), and the New Zealand's South Island high country selected to illustrate the question. We conclude that the case studies suggest a positive relation between property diversity and landscape sustainability. But this chapter is an exploration of the proposition, not a test of a formal hypothesis. We make no claim to prove a thesis, but do hope to propose a new line of scholarly inquiry.

2.2 THE DIVERSITY OF PROPERTY

The history of property is one of constant change. As a social institution, property has conformed to, and been transformed by, social and economic exigency.[2] While such change often appears incremental, property remains dynamic. The mantra that property rights must be secure, certain, and stable can, but should not, be misconstrued as a prescription for stagnation. As we face the consequences of centuries of 'full throttle industrialization' (White, 2008), the contemporary challenge for property is to adapt to pressing environmental imperatives and re-formulate a theoretical framework that enhances the sustainability of landscapes.[3]

A 'mosaic'[4] of property rights, claims and uses builds on this dynamic of change inherent in property. The image of a property mosaic is that of a diverse, overlapping, and interconnected system of property types and uses: private, public, and common; exclusive and shared; competing and co-existing. This mosaic offers the potential for property to develop a new paradigm for an environmental age, a holistic and multi-dimensional metaphor that enables use over dominion; context as well as individual rights; inclusion over exclusion; and stewardship over exploitation.

By examining three geographically diverse landscapes, we describe three mosaics of property rights, claims and uses, in varying stages of construction, transformation, or de-construction. The three stages serve to illustrate our line of inquiry, and make plain the observation that property mosaics interact with different types of challenges to landscape sustainability (political, economic, legal, ecological, aesthetic). The community of 'The Sea Ranch' in Sonoma County, California, is the setting for the construction (from a relatively blank slate) of a diverse mosaic of property interests. In the Northern Forests of New

England, a pre-existing mosaic has been re-invented out of economic necessity, while in the high country of New Zealand's South Island, a statutory mosaic of property tenures is being dismantled and devolved into simpler, more unitary property arrangements. All three landscapes are visually imperious. In selecting them, we invoke Carol Rose's theory that because property is more readily 'seeable' in such landscapes, property becomes *obvious* rather than *oblivious* (Rose, 1994a). Thus to 'see' property in its obviousness is to begin to see property in context, not in abstract isolation, and to recognise its complexity and connection.

2.3 THE PROPERTY MOSAIC

The mosaic is the metaphorical antithesis of the private/public dichotomy in property law. It substitutes complexity for simplicity, and competition and co-existence of uses, for singular use. Formerly dominant, the distinctiveness of the public/private divide is today far from clear.[5] Private property rights are burdened with public restraints, while public and private rights commingle in public lands (Brower et al, 2009). We have moved from seemingly transparent dichotomies to translucent blends. This progression has not passed unobserved.[6] Eric Freyfogle notes 'the sharp rise in property that is subject to shared-use arrangements' (Freyfogle, 2007, p. 144) and predicts that healthy landscapes of the future will 'everywhere … be made up not of two types of land – private and common – but a wide variant that blends the two'. (Freyfogle, 2003, p. 174) Joseph Sax posits that the consequence of 'viewing land through the lens of [an economy of nature is to] reduce the significance of property lines' (Sax, 1992–3, p. 1446).

The disintegration of the public/private divide represents the collapse of a dated dichotomy. In its place is the opportunity for property to articulate a revised narrative that enhances sustainable landscapes. At the heart of this narrative is a renewed emphasis on *use* rights rather than obsolete notions of *dominion or possession*. Use rights place property rights in context, as mere 'sticks' [7] in a greater whole. Use rights also invite the corollary that because a simultaneous plurality of uses is theoretically possible, ideally they should be compatible and sustainable rather than 'resource-intensive [with] short-term orientation' (Bosselman, 2008, p. 15). Across landscapes, a multiplicity of uses and interests pre-disposes greater sharing transcending parcel boundaries and mosaic layers. This trans-boundary overlap creates checks and balances that constrain an owner's ability to act unilaterally, thus enhancing landscape sustainability. Individually, use rights may be privately exclusive, vested in a community, or exercizable by the unorganised public at large (Rose, 1986). Importantly, use rights de-couple property and possession, without necessarily derogating from the need for security critical to property rights. Logically, secure title should not require a universal right to exclude, but rather valid, long-term tenure, including exclusivity of use, not possession.

Use rights also enable the notion of *stewardship*, another key emphasis, by removing the all-consuming spatial inherency of dominion to fill the void.

> [W]e should embrace a notion that landowners are stewards, with clear rights to use but only limited rights to degrade and consume. Perhaps we need to apply more broadly the idea that all of nature remains in a sense in public hands, with private owners receiving only prescribed rights to use. (Freyfogle, 2007, p. 141)

If the extremes of William Blackstone's 'despotic dominion' can be less polarising, duties (as a consequence of rights), especially environmental duties or obligations of stewardship, may gain traction. Aldo Leopold saw 'stewardship' in terms of his highly quoted 'land ethic', a responsibility that was the concomitant of the right to exploit.

> We abuse land because we regard it as a commodity belonging to us. When we see land as a community to which we belong, we may begin to use it with love and respect. … [t]hat land is a community is the basic concept of ecology, but that land is to be loved and respected is an extension of ethics. (Leopold, 1966, p. x) [8]

Another important emphasis is the recognition that property rights are not exclusively private, that the component parts of any mosaic may include private, public, or common property,[9] or blends thereof. The curious myopia (Rose, 1998–9, p. 155) that all property is private, obfuscates the plurality of different types of property interests, and reflects an historical tendency for private property to demonise its alternatives as inefficient or primitive.[10] By being so 'oddly oblivious', we tend to overlook the values of other types of property, and their capacity to shape environmental norms. For example, Carol Rose cites with approval the 'great bodies of law about common property' based on 'an ethic of moderation, proportionality, prudence, and responsibility to others' (Rose, 1994b, p. 27). Such norms have enormous implications for an environmental paradigm of property. By being cognisant of property types other than private property, we re-legitimise the place and role of public and common property, and enable diversity in lieu of monotony.

Lastly, property as a social institution must re-discover its inherent *sociability*,[11] the measure by which it contributes to community and social cohesion. Certain property jurists claim that property can only be justified where it serves a public good (e.g. Freyfogle, 2007). Such 'public good' may have been served in an expanding industrial age by rights of untrammelled exploitation, or the commerce of navigable waterways (discussed in Sax, 1969–70), but in an environmental age, the common 'good' is sustainability. The stark notion of property as commodity ignores the 'personhood' or collective values[12] historically recognised in property, and focuses on individuals exercising control over external things. Such a paradigm is one-dimensional and narrow. As Australian property academic Margaret Davies observes, 'a more modern understanding of property insists upon its relational dimension ... property concerns individuals and communities: how they are formed, how they live together, and how they use their resources' (Davies, 2007, p. 2; Sax, 1984). The multi-dimensional mosaic re-inserts social factors such as place and community into what is predominantly a commoditised equation.

2.4 THE SEA RANCH, SONOMA COUNTY, CALIFORNIA

Our first case study is The Sea Ranch, a 4000 acre (1619 hectare) planned residential community along ten miles of Northern Californian coastline. Devised as an 'open' and 'exploratory' architectural experiment (Lyndon, 2009, pp. 81–2), The Sea Ranch was 'born in the era of Rachel Carson and Ralph Nader, the rise of ... awareness of environmental concerns, [and] the introduction of the term ecology' (Lyndon and Alinder, 2004, p. 29). Its founding ideals were visionary, with landscape architect Lawrence Halprin aiming for:

> [a] feeling of overall 'place', a feeling of community in which the whole was more important than the parts ... if the whole could link buildings and nature ... then we could feel that we had created something worthwhile which did not destroy, but rather enhanced the natural beauty we had been given. (Lyndon and Alinder, 2004, p. 19)

Before the developer Oceanic Properties bought the family owned 'Rancho del Mar' in 1963, the property mosaic was simple, a large, privately owned sheep ranch, with a singular use and a history of ranching, farming and timbering. Any public interest in the landscape comprised the dormant public trust in the wet sands of the beach, and the meandering California State Highway 1. The purchase by Oceanic Properties merely substituted one private owner for another, leaving the simple property pattern intact for the short term.

In 1965 as the development plans gathered pace, a residents' association was formed in which common property in the development was vested. The original design was heavily influenced by the 'establishment of large stretches of commons that would preserve the dominance of the natural setting' in an effort to share the landscape rather than having it 'sequestered in separate private ownerships' (Lyndon and Alinder, 2004, p. 19). Common property also served an environmental function, 'large areas of commonly held land ... would ensure the perpetuation of the coastal ecology' (Lyndon and Alinder, 2004, p. 19). The private/public dichotomy was overlaid by a deliberately constructed mosaic in the form of open space common property. Its intent was to enhance the aesthetics and ecology of the landscape, but it also served a social function.

> Throughout Sea Ranch, the land held in common, particularly the commons in the coastal meadows became a focal point of shared interest. Management of this treasured asset was expressed as a community responsibility, not a task for individual property owners looking out for their own parcels … That no one citizen exclusively owned a piece of the natural resource – the resource that is the very foundation of the community – … defied conventional development wisdom and cemented a bond of common interest … (Sexton, 1995, p. 35)

The residents' association was also charged with enforcing a 'declaration of covenants, conditions and restrictions', title restrictions that regulated building materials and design, but more importantly imposed a strict landscape plan where houses were clustered to mimic the coastal landscape of ridgelines, pastures and hedgerows. Moreover private property interests diversified, splitting between the interest of Oceanic Properties as developer, and the individual interests of private dwelling owners. Unitary property arrangements were evolving into pluralistic patterns.

As the 1960s ended, another interest was added to the mosaic: an assertive awakening of the public trust interest in beach access, and the preservation of coastal vistas. This was both an ironic and tumultuous period for The Sea Ranch, a community conceived in environmental idealism, but stymied from further expansion by wider conservation concerns about coastal development. Many started to see Sea Ranch as an enclave of private privilege, groups such as 'Californians Organized to Acquire Access to State Tidelands' (COAST) complained of The Sea Ranch locking up ten miles of access to publicly owned tidelands. In 1968 COAST sponsored an unsuccessful county initiative to force coastal access through almost every mile of the property. A deal with Sonoma County Supervisors, in which 100 acres of public park[13] were traded for public access rights over the ten miles of coastline, attracted academic (as well as community) criticism in the early 1970s.[14] Eventually the public interest in coastal access prevailed, with the passage of Proposition 20 that established regional and state-wide Coastal Commissions.[15] The planning powers of the North Central Coastal Commission effectively halted The Sea Ranch for eight years through its blanket refusal of building permits. This moratorium was described as 'like a civil war' (Lyndon and Alinder, 2004, p. 29) between those residents who supported the Coastal Commission's demands for public access paths along the entire strip, and those favouring the status quo.

The traumatic stalemate was one in which the state ultimately held the trump card. In 1980 the impasse ended when the State of California entered the mosaic legislatively, in the process asserting all Californians' interest in the

Table 2.1 The constructed Sea Ranch mosaic, 1965–81

1960s mosaic	Post 1980 mosaic
Latent public trust	Public trust asserted by common law, enabled by statutory access easements
Private rights for exclusive housing	Public interest in scenic vistas asserted by statute – height limitations and corridors
Communal interest of The Sea Ranch Association, collective of private rightholders	Private rights for exclusive housing, negotiated with State of California
	Communal interests of The Sea Ranch Association – enforcing aesthetic covenants

beach and unimpeded coastal vistas.[16] The specific state bill ended the planning powers of the North Central Coastal Commission in return for the guarantee of five dedicated access easements with parking, a near halving of the number of house sites,[17] and scenic corridors from State Highway 1. The compromise formalised public rights to access and coastal prospect, and imposed public restraints on private property rights.

The Sea Ranch demonstrates the construction of a mosaic from relatively simple property arrangements in the early 1960s, to a complex inter-connected mix of public, private and common property post 1980.

Broadly, the increasing plurality of property rights and uses resulted in a shift from a 'look-but-don't-touch' landscape, to one with greater public access and entitlement. The mosaic's implications for landscape sustainability are arguable from both political and legal perspectives. It is likely that the communal and architecturally visionary covenants from 1965 would have created an aesthetically and ecologically sustainable[18] landscape, even without public involvement in the mosaic (Sexton, 1995, pp. 32–6). But the political controversy that arose threatened to make Sea Ranch economically unsustainable by imposing a development moratorium until a compromise was found. In the end, the political unsustainability of a 'look-but-don't-touch' inaccessible landscape forced a compromise solution that was likely more aesthetically sustainable; specifically the scenic corridors preserving public prospect from State Highway 1, and the significant downsizing of the development.[19] Legally, given public rights to tidelands in US public trust doctrine,[20] it was necessary to add the public interest to the property mosaic, in the form of statutorily mandated access easements. The contentious status of access rights across The Sea Ranch noted in 1972 was unsustainable (Dyer, 1972, pp. 571, 573). Public property rights in expressly dedicated access paths enhanced the legal sustainability of the landscape by replacing uncertainty with legal certainty.[21]

Theoretically, The Sea Ranch mosaic incorporates many attributes of an environmental property paradigm. The public/private dichotomy was supplanted by multiple property rights and uses, public, private and common; property structures were designed to integrate community and social cohesion (a sense of the 'whole' rather than an aggregate of sequestered housing lots[22]); stewardship was articulated in terms of 'lightly living with the land' (Lyndon and Alinder, 2004, p. 287); and the shared nature of the coastal landscape emphasised co-existing use rights, not assertions of dominion. Thus private exclusive housing rights adjoined communal use of meadows and community infrastructure, while public rights to the beach, access paths and coastal vistas were enshrined by statute and common law. The blurring of property lines predicted by Sax in his 'economy of nature' came to pass. 'Fences enforcing property lines are discouraged ... Where houses are very close together, fences are considered necessary for privacy and for screening cars, but not for demarcating property lines. An intentionally fuzzy line is desired for the boundary between individually owned and community property' (Sexton, 1995, p. 36).

The constructed property mosaic is inherent in The Sea Ranch, and never far from any description of it. In praising the architectural merits of the Hedgerow Houses in 2004, Lyndon and Alinder impliedly invoke the mosaic, describing the housing cluster as

> a model for quiet, thoughtful delineation of common boundaries ... the long row of simple board fence at the property line is made as a common face for the public realm, and not as an individuated expression of the private properties beyond it. It speaks of continuity and public purpose ... the ensemble creates a place of real distinction – a place that shows respect for the private worlds of each house, as well as for the common realms of street and meadow. (Lyndon and Alinder, 2004, p. 55)

2.5 THE NORTHERN FOREST OF NEW ENGLAND, USA

Comprising 26 million acres (10.5 million hectares) spreading across 450 miles (726 kilometres) in four states in the north-eastern corner of the United States (New York, Vermont, New Hampshire, and Maine) (Trombulak, 1994, p. 12), the Northern Forest has long served New England as a productive forestland ecosystem and a popular site for a holiday home (Klyza and Trombulak, 1994, p. 1). The mixed conifer and hardwood forest has a history of producing both high value hardwood timber (Carr, 1994, p. 57), prized for furniture and floorboards, and non-timber forest products such as the famous maple syrup. This mix of uses in the earliest colonised corner of the US – between extractive timber, non-extractive forest products, and recreation – constructed an ecologically, aesthetically and economically sustainable landscape. The demand for and revenues from forestland recreation and maple syrup mandated against clear-cutting vast swathes of forest, and the relatively dense population of forestland in-holdings (1.8 million residents in 1994) (Carr, 1994, p. 53) in the rural landscape enforced the mandate. If there were no demand or revenue from non-timber forest products and no non-timber felling population with observant eyes interspersed between the timber dominated landowners, then large private timberland owners could have, and perhaps would have, treated the land in an unsustainable manner. Further, they could have 'cut and run' with relative impunity.

But in the 1980s, the landscape stability started to change. The Northern Forest had long been 80 per cent privately owned (Klyza and Trombulak, 1994, p. 1), and a majority of that privately owned land was owned by New England based timber firms. But since the 1950s a few larger timber firms, such as Diamond International, had been aggregating land from hundreds of individual small forest landholders (Reidel, 1994, p. 94). The seemingly stable ownership mosaic began to shift in December 1982 when British financier Sir James Goldsmith undertook a hostile takeover of Diamond International Corporation timber company and its 976 000 acres across the four states for \$660 million.[23] In less than a year, he sold most of the corporation and was left with most of the land, which he then sold in 1987 to a French communications and financial holding company (CGE). Then the state of New Hampshire and The Nature Conservancy attempted to buy back land, but New Hampshire refrained from the purchase. In 1988, a real estate development firm bought all 90 000 acres of CGE land in New Hampshire for some vacation home subdivision and some forest products (Klyza, 1994, pp. 39–42). By the end of the 1980s, a very few corporations owned a significant chunk of the Northern Forest landmass. The simplified property mosaic (from multiple and diverse small forest land owners to consolidated few large corporate owners) meant that the landscape was tipping towards subdivision.

This purchase galvanised state, regional, and national attention to the changing ownership and deteriorating sustainability of the Northern Forest landscape. Environmental groups such as The Wilderness Society and the Sierra Club sparked fears of subdivision, loss of recreational access, and loss of the forest's wild character; their proposed solution was federal acquisition to create a legally, aesthetically and ecologically sustainable landscape (Klyza, 1994, pp. 39–42). Economic sustainability was more questionable. But the environmental groups' subdivision fears were far from groundless. They were based on rising land prices representing high demand for vacation homes, coupled with a high supply of land for sale because of declining timber prices and a series of takeovers symbolised by Goldsmith's. Further, a trio of factors made it hard for New England timber to compete with foreign sources like Canada, South America, and south-east Asia: the globalisation of capital, US and state forest regulations on private land becoming more stringent, and the state and federal tax structure (Klyza, 1994, pp. 36–41). Indeed the price of lumber stagnated, being the same in 1990 as it was in the early 1950s; timber imports soared, with Canadian timber constituting 30 per cent of wood consumption in the early 1980s; wood technology changes meant that less wood was needed and fewer people were employed to supply it; finally forestry was moving from the northwest US to the south-eastern US (Klyza, 1994, pp. 37–8). By the late 1980s, the previous economic driver of the Northern Forest landscape – hardwood forestry – had all but disappeared (Carr, 1994, pp. 62–7).

In short, by the late 1980s the old property mosaic no longer supported an economically sustainable landscape and people all around the country were concerned. By 1987, land ownership had shifted on a large scale from New England timber companies to overseas entrepreneurs and financiers. This attenuated the connection to forestry, and deepened the growing disparity in values of land uses. Timber and non-timber forest products could no longer keep pace with subdivision and second home development. By this time the forestry land use was far less valuable than the second home land use for the Northern Forest, all of which is within a day's drive of both Boston and New York City (Fairfax et al, 2005). This disparity threatened to tip the dominant use of landscape from forestry to second homes. Thus the loss of economic sustainability in the landscape threatened aesthetic and ecological sustainability (Klyza, 1994, pp. 37–8).

In the late 1980s and early 1990s, handwringing by a broad array of interest groups gave way to a flurry of state and federal studies of what to do. The flurry included the Governors' Task Force led by Mollie Beattie, the Vermont Commissioner of Forests and Parks, and the US Forest Service-led Northern Forest Lands Study. This resulted in significant differences of opinion between the state-led and federally led studies. Eventually, after the dust cleared, the studies gave rise to a federally coordinated, large scale mixed programme designed to change the disparity in values of land uses (Reidel, 1994, pp. 93–111). This intervention asserted the state and the national interest in the Northern Forest landscape, just as California had done at The Sea Ranch a decade earlier. The state and federal involvement deliberately increased the complexity of the property mosaic by creating new forms of ownership and public–private partnerships.

The Northern Forest story also echoes the Sea Ranch story in the fact that asserting the national interest meant establishing a governance body. Senator

Patrick Leahy (D-VT and chair of Senate Agricultural Committee) secured federal funding to establish the joint federal and state Northern Forest Lands Council to direct the response to the landscape sustainability crisis (Reidel, 1994, pp. 93–111). The response eventually included a range of policy instruments designed to respond to issues of economic sustainability by addressing the disparity in values of land uses between subdivision and timber. The response included the following instruments: easement purchases, state and federal land acquisition, tax and fiscal incentives, and joint ownership schemes (involving land trusts) (Reidel, 1994, pp. 93–111).

Hence the 1980s and 1990s witnessed a transformation of the socio-economic landscape of the Northern Forest. And this socio-economic change meant that the physical landscape changed much less than many in the mid 1980s feared that it would. The property mosaic changed from a predominance of fee-simple private ownership to a mosaic marked by the proliferation of less than fee simple interests such as easements, covenants, and partnerships. The state and federally led changes increased fee simple public ownership only slightly, but greatly increased less than fee simple public property rights, re-invigorating other layers of mosaic.

The intention of the state and federal intervention was to re-construct the Northern Forest property mosaic in order to create a landscape that would be sustainable into the future. Before the 1980s, it was a sustainable landscape with a diverse and pluralistic property mosaic; but land ownership aggregation had decreased the diversity and threatened the sustainability. This thus created the need for deliberate reconstruction of mosaic layers and reconfiguration by the state and federal governments.

Table 2.2 The transformed Northern Forest mosaic

Pre 1980s	Post 1990s
80% privately owned	Still mostly privately owned
	More interconnectivity
Mostly fee simple ownership	Public–private partnerships
Fewer encumbrances	More encumbered fee simple title
	Easements
	Covenants
	Partnerships with land trusts
	More enduring mechanisms for a coordinated response to shocks to the mosaic

As a result, most observers agree that the Northern Forest landscape is more economically sustainable (Perschel, 1994, pp. vii–viii), after the reconfiguration of the property mosaic. It is no longer on the verge of collapse and subdivision as in 1980s, but is still vulnerable. Now that the coordinated (state, federal, non-profit) response mechanisms are in place, the landscape stands ready to respond to future changes, shocks, and crises. In ecological systems, resistance to shock and resilience after a crisis are key factors in ecosystem stability (Berkes and Folke, 1998; Holling, 1986; Westman, 1985). In landscapes, the Northern Forest story suggests that a simple property mosaic (as in the 1980s) leaves a system vulnerable and not resistant to shock; greater diversity in the mosaic enhances the system's resilience after the crisis, and resistance to future shocks. It further suggests that in landscapes dominated by private ownership, aesthetic and ecological sustainability depend utterly on socio-economic sustainability.

2.6 THE HIGH COUNTRY OF NEW ZEALAND'S SOUTH ISLAND

We conclude with a landscape mosaic in the process of deliberate deconstruction. If Garrett Hardin (1968, p. 1243) recognised a tragedy of the commons in 1968, and Eric Freyfogle (2003) a tragedy of fragmentation in 2003, then the high country of New Zealand's South Island is an ongoing tragedy of mosaic destruction.

From 1948 to 1992, 10 per cent of the New Zealand landmass, some 2.4 million hectares on the eastern slope of the Southern Alps, was owned by the Crown and leased to sheep graziers for exclusively grazing purposes. Although pastoral tenure had been utilised since the 1870s, the Land Act of 1948 introduced a new and distinctive tenure (Maclachalan, 1966) for the high country, a perpetually renewable 33 year lease that gave runholders exclusive rights of pasturage, but no right to freehold, and no right to the soil. In this deliberate allocation of property rights, the Crown retained the residual bundle, splitting 'sticks' to create a pragmatic statutory mosaic. Effectively section 66 of the Land Act 1948 established a partnership between the Crown (with its interests in soil conservation, riparian protection, and the land's ultimate disposal) and the pastoral lessees (with their interest in a viable grazing industry). The former relied on the prohibition on freeholding, the latter on secure tenure and low pasturage rents. More broadly, pastoral tenure existed amidst pockets of freehold, and diverse other Crown tenures, a legally sustainable landscape mosaic, anchored around the absence of any right to freehold in the dominant pastoral lease.

However, like the Northern Forest, economic circumstances changed over time, and the once stable landscape became increasingly unsustainable economically. Wool prices had been unreliable for decades,[24] and sheep grazing was no longer the most profitable land use.[25] Restrictions designed to ensure industry viability in 1948 had become an economic straitjacket. Recreationists desired access to pastoral high country land,[26] and conservationists wanted sheep off fragile grasslands above 1000 metres (Brower, 2008, p. 32). Politically, the shift in governmental policy favouring neo-liberalism shunned the ownership of public lands (Swaffield and Brower, 2009, pp. 165–6). By the early 1990s these economic and political pressures converged to undermine the political sustainability of the landscape, even though it remained legally sustainable.

A land reform process known as 'tenure review' commenced informally in the early 1990s, and culminated in the passage of the Crown Pastoral Lands Act in 1998. Tenure review aimed to phase out pastoral leasehold tenure progressively, replacing it with a resuscitated public/private dichotomy: private freehold title on more agriculturally productive land at lower altitudes, and the retention of high country land in Crown ownership as public conservation land. Cash equalisation payments were supposed to address any discrepancy in value that arose from the land-swap. Perceived as a 'win-win' outcome for farmers and the environment, tenure review became an exit strategy from pastoral leases by way of a transfer of wealth and resources from the Crown to farmers, at taxpayers' expense (Brower, 2008). Importantly for the thesis of this chapter, tenure review institionalised the polarisation of property ownership patterns, re-invigorating the public/private divide, and vesting freehold title to most developable land in former pastoral runholders with fewer encumbrances, such as access easements or conservation covenants.

Until 1992, the high country mosaic was one of public–private partnership, one space with two layers. Tenure review created two spaces of one layer each, unshackling the fetters on land use, and carving up the landscape with a blunt knife. What were in 1992 80 Crown-owned parcels of average size of 5938 hectares, on which runholders could only engage in extensive sheep grazing, have so far been subdivided into at least 865 parcels, of which a large majority (at least 550) are smaller than 50 hectares. These 865 parcels are now in private ownership following tenure review, ready and waiting for development (see Table 2.3). So far only 20 per cent of these parcels have been sold by 40 of the new landowners, but the tenant farmers turned real estate agents have grossed over $134 million from these sales of privatised land (see Table 2.4) (Swaffield and Brower, 2009, p. 170; Brower, 2010). Table 2.3 documents the physical transformation of the high country landscape to date, while Table 2.4 documents the economic transformation. While the proliferation of owners may appear a superficial victory for diversity, it is a de-pauperation of ownership types because each has only one layer, simplicity in lieu of diversity.

Table 2.3 Transformation of high country landscape measured by parcel size[1]

Size of parcel (in hectares)	Number of pastoral lease parcels, by size, that completed tenure review between 1992 and 2009	Number of freehold parcels, by size, on former leases after tenure review privatisation and subdivision
0–50 ha	0	550
51–100 ha	0	47
101–500 ha	1	137
501–1000 ha	5	39
1001–5000 ha	38	87

Note: [1] Swaffield and Brower (2009, p. 170).

Table 2.4 The most lucrative gross revenues from private land sales post-tenure review

Name of lease	Gross sales revenue	Total parcels sold	Total hectares sold
Hillend	$26,200,000.00	36	2665.0
Closeburn	$17,696,000.00	25	2442.3
Alphaburn	$10,100,000.00	1	193.0
Eastburn-Waitiri	$9,700,000.00	2	1809.9
Mataura Valley	$9,000,000.00	1	4357.0
Mt Rosa	$7,521,000.00	21	53.1
Queensberry Hills	$7,347,500.00	20	1791.7
Wentworth	$6,607,000.00	16	3889.7
Ben Ohau	$6,149,000.00	10	3707.1
Cairnmuir	$5,466,000.00	15	4106.4
Bendigo	$4,685,000.00	13	623.8
Pukaki Downs	$4,665,000.00	4	582.6

The proliferation of pricey parcels in the high country means the formerly stable pastoral landscape is giving way to golf courses, viticulture, and residential subdivision. Figure 2.1 illustrates the subdivision and transformation of Hillend Station, on the shores of Lake Wanaka in the south of the South

Island. Until 1998, Hillend stretched over 3651 hectares from the edge of Wanaka township into the Cardrona Valley. The dashed white line on the map traces the former boundary of Hillend Station's 3651 hectares. Legally and managerially, it was one parcel of land owned by the Crown and leased to the runholder, with the land use limited to grazing and extensive pastoralism. Subdivision was expressly prohibited. The 1998 tenure review agreement privatised about 2700 hectares, with 717 under covenant that prevents subdivision, and shifted 991 to public conservation land under full Crown ownership (Brower, 2008, pp. 11–14). With the public/private divide solidified, the Hillend runholder-turned-landowner sought consent to subdivide and develop. The solid thin white lines depict the parcels of Hillend in 2009 (Swaffield and Brower, 2009, p. 170).

What these property lines do not indicate is the amorphous (and latent) public interest in or desire to protect iconic landscape vistas, particularly

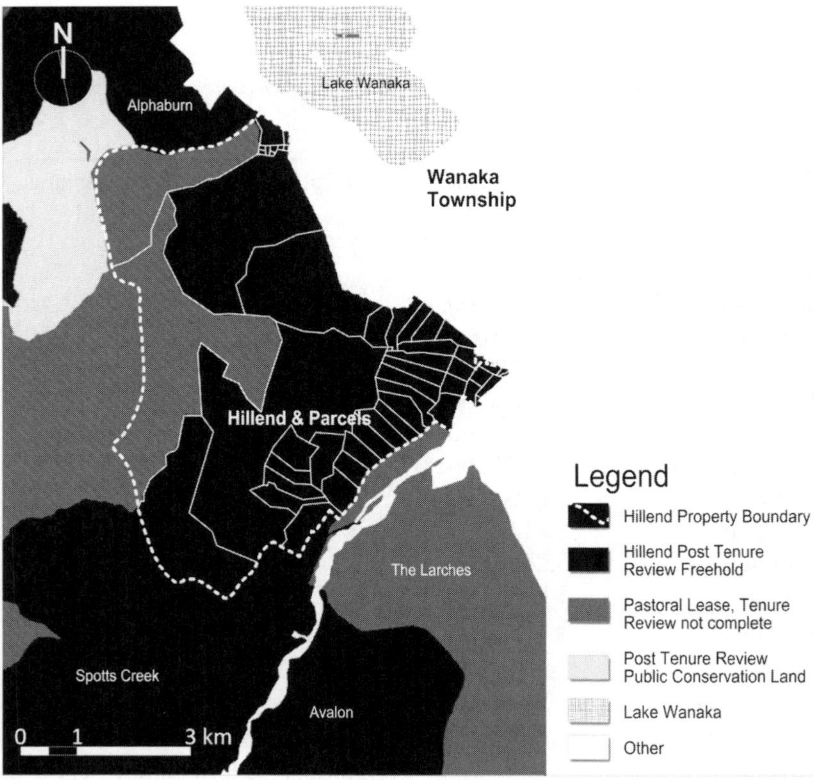

Figure 2.1 Map of Hillend Station subdivision

Table 2.5 The deconstructed New Zealand high country property mosaic, 1948–98 and continuing

1948	Now
Partnership between Crown and farmers	Interconnectivity reduced
Runholders held a limited bundle of sticks:	All freehold or Crown ownership
Exclusivity of pasturage	Public vs private divide distinct
No right to freehold	Freehold owners hold full bundle of sticks, includes development rights
Crown held residual rights:	Public access to new high altitude conservation lands
Including development rights	
De facto public access rights	

vulnerable from intensive land subdivision at lower altitudes or lakesides. This dormant public desire was briefly awakened in 2006–07 when then Land Information Minister, David Parker, announced a moratorium on tenure review of pastoral leaseholds within 5 kilometres of lakes. The moratorium was momentary, the defeat of Parker's government in November 2008 was quickly followed by a reversal of the ban in August 2009. The legal weakness of the New Zealand 'public desire' to protect scenic values in the High Country stands in contrast to the stronger public trust doctrine in the US that bolstered beach access (and coincidentally scenic corridors) at The Sea Ranch.

A legally sustainable landscape, crafted to simultaneously ensure the viability of the sheep industry and ameliorate land degradation, was imposed by the 1948 Land Act on the high country landscape.[27] It remained legally sustainable into the 1990s, but politically and economically, the high country landscape became less viable. The policy response was to deconstruct and simplify the property arrangements through tenure review, so as to disentangle private from public interests in land. This left high country landscape values vulnerable to subdivision and global development pressures, absent Crown restrictions on land use. As a consequence, the high country landscape became less sustainable, particularly in the lower altitude and lakeside lands. The removal of the enforced grazing monopoly left these lands open to residential subdivision, condominium development, and other intensive land uses.

Moreover, the revival of the public/private divide has diminished the theoretical attributes of the environmental paradigm of property. Private fee simple title has come with high fences, keep-out signs, and vigorous assertions of dominion. Shared use and landscape context are overwhelmed by the primacy of private property's right to exclude, while environmental values and concerns are largely quarantined on the public side of the divide.

2.7 DISCUSSION

Property rights, claims and uses, their configuration, and their respective simplicity or complexity, have potential implications for landscape sustainability. The greater the diversity of property types and property instruments, the more intricate the connections, and the plurality of uses, the more property assumes the appearance of a mosaic.

In landscapes where the mosaic is constructed from unitary origins, or where a failing mosaic is transformed into another more viable configuration, we have observed that some forms of landscape attributes have become more sustainable. At The Sea Ranch, the legal sustainability of a northern Californian coastal landscape was enhanced by more, not less complexity in the mosaic. In the Northern Forest, public–private partnerships and added complexity have sustained the economic landscape. Conversely, in the New Zealand high country, the devolution of a statutory mosaic into dichotomous property arrangements has weakened landscape values.

Gary Becker (1983, pp. 371–400) observed in relation to interest group politics that more interest group diversity and competition begets more optimal policy.[28] Analogy and observation from the three case studies suggest likewise for property, and its role in the environmental governance of landscapes. The greater the diversity of property rights, claims, and uses in a given landscape, the greater the propensity for its stability and sustainability. That the mosaic exhibits many of the attributes of an environmental paradigm of property adds theoretical corroboration to the proposition.

2.8 CONCLUSION

To conclude, we return to the biodiversity and community ecology metaphors with which we started. It seems that in landscapes of mixed public and private ownership, a diversity of property rights arrangements might indeed serve as the Ehrlichs' (1981) rivets in the landscape. More types of rivets and more complex rivets were associated with more ecologically, politically, aesthetically and economically sustainable landscapes in all three of our case studies. The Sea Ranch is a story of diversifying and increasingly complex rivets to enable political sustainability by creating a tenable public–private balance. New Zealand's high country is a story of removing the one 'driver' rivet of Crown ownership via pastoral lease and the wings falling off the plane immediately.

Instead of species and biological niches as the rivets, this chapter sees property interests as the rivets. But interest can be proprietary or social. Social awareness of landscape sustainability and threats to it can then incite state intervention in landscapes, which, in privately owned landscapes, inherently increases the diversity and complexity of the property mosaic. By concentrating and reducing the diversity of ownership (as in the Northern Forest), levels of social awareness of the landscape risk falling similarly. Hence social awareness, state intervention, and diversity of property interests are co-related variables. This correlation bears future investigation.

It is the Northern Forest that best translates the rivet hypothesis into the realm of land ownership and landscapes. Ownership of the Northern Forest had been simplifying for decades before the Goldsmith takeover; hundreds of redundant rivets in the form of small landowners had been slowly dropping off and were replaced by one singular driver rivet, Diamond International. With a crescendo of public concern, and to avoid the proverbial plane crash, NGOs, state and federal authorities reconstructed the system's rivets to create more diversity, complexity and redundancy. That in turn seems to have created a landscape system that is more resistant to drastic shocks and more resilient to inevitable shocks. In short, in systems of mixed public and private ownership, we echo community ecologists' hypothesis that property diversity does seem to enhance landscape sustainability.

This new line of inquiry into the relation between property rights and landscape sustainability is exciting. It is clearly applicable to policy, inherently interdisciplinary, and ultimately quantitatively measurable. The question also has the unique advantage of having a 50 year legacy in the ecology literature, so legal landscape scholars can draw on ecologists' many and various methods of examining, measuring, and modelling the thesis. Ultimately it has the potential to transform the means of environmental governance towards the end of sustainability in all its forms.

Of course diversity in ownership in landscapes is also called fragmentation, which is not positively correlated with sustainability. Fragmentation without overlapping interests in a multi-layered mosaic can lead to gridlock in which cooperation and sharing is impossible. This type of gridlocked system is neither resistant to change nor resilient after a shock. Both the Northern Forest and the Sea Ranch experienced gridlocked systems, requiring federal or state intervention to force co-operation. But fragmentation within a multi-layered mosaic in which rights, interests and desires overlap spatially, rendering parcel boundaries immaterial, can lead to greater landscape sustainability through the creation of checks and balances. Hence two-dimensional fragmentation is neither resistant nor resilient, but a multi-dimensional and interlocking property mosaic within a landscape can be resistant, resilient and consequentially sustainable.

NOTES

1. Although later political scholars showed the naïveté of much of pluralism, as summarised in McFarland. (2004, p. 15); and elaborated in Lowi (1969).
2. Joseph Sax (1992–3, p. 1446) describes property as 'continuously adjust[ing] to reflect new economic and social structures'.
3. The capacity for paradigm shift in property has precedent. Eric Freyfogle describes the evolution of American property law and its adaptation from a settled agrarian society to an industrial/capitalist economy in the late 19th century (Freyfogle, 2003). More broadly, the development of Anglo property law reflects the profound changes in English society from feudal times. For an Australian perspective on the adaptation of property law, see Buck (2006).
4. American scholars Sally Fairfax et al (2005, p. 272) articulate this increasing complexity of property claims and uses in terms of the 'mosaic' image. They argue that the mosaic at its 'best [may] ... represent a new, collaborative, and sophisticated approach that can approximate the elusive win-win model so frequently touted in conservation circles.'
5. There is debate as to whether the divide was ever as distinct as sometimes claimed (Freyfogle, 2003).
6. For example Courtney White (2008, pp. 3–4) calls for a 'simultaneous effort ... to increase economic and ecological resilience' through her preferred 'watershed model', a 'collaborative conservation model' with mosaic-like qualities. See also Arnold (2002).
7. The term 'bundle of rights' was reputedly first used in John Lewis, *A Treatise on the Law of Eminent Domain in the United States* 57 (1888), *cited in* Goldstein (1998).
8. For a wider discussion on environmental ethics, see Flourney (2003); and Rose (1994b).
9. Common property, while the most obscure (and overlooked), is perhaps the most instructive form of property in conceptualising the mosaic.
10. For example the proponents of the enclosure movement in 18th century England dismissed commoners as economically inefficient, and contrary to the dominant discourse of improvement.
11. Carol Rose (1986) describes property's socialability as an under-rated attribute.
12. Margaret Radin (1993) divides property into fungible or personal property, the latter having non-market or 'personhood' values.
13. Gifted by Oceanic Properties with the intention of providing the sole public access, later expanded to 140 acres.
14. This was described as one of several 'instances in which developers and other private owners of littoral frontage have unknowingly or intentionally blocked existing means of public access', thereby exercising 'individual exclusive rights of access so as to effectively deny the public any right of access or use' (Dyer, 1972, pp. 571, 573, 585–6).
15. Calif. Coastal Zone Conservation Act of 1972 (Proposition 20), codified as Cal. Pub. Res. Code SS 27000 *et seq.*
16. Known as the Bane Bill of 1980. The Act also created the Californian Coastal Commission, and had state-wide implications for coastal zone land management and recreational access to beaches. It was the first of its kind in the US.
17, The number of housing lots was reduced from 5200 to 2300. Also sites for low-income housing were mandated.
18. 'What has emerged [at The Sea Ranch] is a landscape with much more vegetation than when Oceanic arrived. In addition to the large-scale plantings, the forest has expanded of its own accord. Invasion of the meadows is no longer kept in check by grazing' (Lyndon and Alinder, 2004, p. 73).
19. Sexton (1995, p. 47) argued the loss of condominium sites diminished the original cluster model of Lawrence Halprin.
20. In California the common law includes *Kimball v Macpherson* 46 Cal. 104 (1873); while *Long Beach Land & Water Co. v Richardson* 70 Cal. 206 (1886) notes that a private littoral owner's rights of access is not exclusive of public rights to use the same tidelands. See generally Welby (1986–7).

21. 'Public access to the coast ... throughout the state, is the one paramount goal that the initiative achieved. It is important symbolically and should have existed all along. Within Sea Ranch this was delivered in a compatible and reasonable manner that has not ... negatively impacted the community significantly' (Sexton, 1995, p. 47).
22. The vision of Lawrence Halprin was of a 'social community for people of like minds, with a love of nature ... for whom "living lightly on this land" would be a governing principle. We decided to imagine the entire ranch as a community of people and design holistically. We would cluster buildings densely as in a farm village, by doing so we could leave at least half the land open for nature, undisturbed. The large common areas around which the buildings would be grouped were to remain open forever and form the matrix of the community' (Lyndon and Alinder, 2004, p. 287).
23. Lyndon and Alinder (2004, p. 287).
24. Swaffield and Brower (2009, p. 164).
25. Runholders could obtain special recreational licences to validate activities such as ski-fields, and, at lower altitudes and lakesides, viticulture and land subdivision were profitable.
26. New Zealanders generally assumed that access to high country runs was available under a 'custom' permitting traditional access to outdoor areas. However, runholders increasingly relied on so-called 'trespass rights' to assert claims of exclusivity of possession. Despite certain orthodoxy, the right to exclusive possession in pastoral leases was not clarified until 2009 in a decision by a single judge of the NZ High Court in *NZ Fish & Game Council v Commissioner of Crown Lands* [2009] CIV 2008-485-2020 (unreported); see generally Page and Brower (2007).
27. The policy rationales behind the Land Act can be traced back to the 1920 Sadd Royal Commission on the Southern Pastoral Lands, and the 1946 Royal Commission on the Sheep Industry; see generally Page and Brower (2008).
28. See generally: Becker (1983, pp. 371–400). For a study focused on interest groups and environmental policy, see Binder and Neumayer (2005, pp. 527–38).

REFERENCES

Arnold, C.A. (2002), 'The Reconstitution of Property: Property as a Web of Interests', *Harvard Environmental Law Review*, **26**, 281–364.

Becker, G.S. (1983), 'A Theory of Competition among Pressure Groups for Political Influence', *Quarterly Journal of Economics*, **98**(3), 371–400.

Berkes, F. and C. Folke (1998), 'Linking Social and Ecological Systems for Resilience and Sustainability', in F.F. Berkes, C. Folke and J. Colding (eds), *Linking Social and Ecological Systems: Management Practices and Social Mechanisms for Building Resilience*, Cambridge: Cambridge University Press, pp. 1–27.

Binder, S. and E. Neumayer (2005), 'Environmental Pressure Group Strengths and Air Pollution: An Empirical Analysis', *Ecological Economics*, **55**(4), 527–38.

Bosselman, K. (2008), *The Principle of Sustainability: Transforming Law and Governance*, Surrey, UK: Ashgate.

Brower, A. (2008), *Who Owns the High Country?* Nelson, NZ: Craig Potton Publishing.

Brower, A. (2010), 'High Country Carve-up', *Architecture New Zealand.*

Brower, A., J. Page, A. Kennedy and P. Martin (2009), 'The Cowboy, the Southern Man, and the Man from Snowy River: The Symbolic Politics of Property in Australia, the United States and New Zealand', *Georgetown International Environmental Law Review*, **21**(3), 455–94.

Buck, A.R. (2006), *The Making of Australian Property Law*, Annandale, NSW: Federation Press.

Carr, T. (1994), 'The Northern Forest Economy' in C.M. Klyza and S. Trombulak, *The Future of the Northern Forest*, Hanover, NH: University Press of New England.
Davies, M. (2007), *Property: Meanings, Histories, Theories*, New York: Routledge – Cavendish.
Dyer, D.G. (1972), 'California Beach Access: The Mexican Law and the Public Trust', *Ecology Law Quarterly*, **2**, 571–611.
Ehrlich, P. and A. Ehrlich (1981), *Extinction – The Causes and Consequences of the Disappearance of Species*, New York: Ballantine Press.
Fairfax, S.K., L. Gwin, M.A. King, L.S. Raymond and L.A. Watt (2005), *Buying Nature: The Limits of Land Acquisition as a Conservation Strategy, 1780–2004*, Cambridge, MA: MIT Press.
Flourney, A.C. (2003), 'In Search of an Environmental Ethic', *Columbia Journal of Environmental Law*, **28,** 63–118.
Freyfogle, E.T. (2003), *The Land We Share: Private Property and the Common Good*, Washington, DC: Island Press.
Freyfogle, E.T. (2007), *On Private Property: Finding Common Ground on the Ownership of Land*, Boston, MA: Beacon Press.
Givnish, T. (1994), 'Letter: Does Diversity Beget Stability', *Nature*, 371**,** 113–14.
Goldstein, R.J. (1998), 'Green Wood in the Bundle of Sticks: Fitting Environmental Ethics and Ecology into Real Property Law', *Boston College Environmental Affairs Law Review*, **25**(2), 347–430.
Hardin, G. (1968), 'Tragedy of the Commons', *Science*, **162**(3859), 1243–8.
Holling, C.S. (1986), 'Resilience of Ecosystems; Local Surprise and Global Change', in W.C. Clark and R.E. Munn (eds), *Sustainable Development of the Biosphere*, Cambridge: Cambridge University Press.
Hooper, D.U., F.S. Chapin III, J.J. Ewel, A. Hector, P. Inchausti, S. Lavorel, J.H. Lawton, D.M. Lodge, M. Loreau, S. Naeem, B. Schmid, H. Setälä, A.J. Symstad, J. Vandermeer and D.A. Wardle (2005), 'Effects of Biodiversity on Ecosystem Functioning: A Consensus of Current Knowledge', *Ecological Monographs*, **75**(1), 3–35.
Klyza, C.M. (1994), 'Problems, Politics, and Alternatives', in C.M. Klyza and S. Trombulak (eds), *The Future of the Northern Forest*, Hanover, NH: University Press of New England.
Klyza, C.M. and S. Trombulak (1994), 'Introduction', in C.M. Klyza and S. Trombulak (eds), *The Future of the Northern Forest*, Hanover, NH: University Press of New England.
Lawton, J.H. (1994), 'What do Species Do in Ecosystems?' *Oikos*, **71**(3), 367–74.
Leopold, A. (1966), *A Sand County Almanac with other Essays on Conservation from Round Rive*r, New York: Oxford University Press.
Lowi, T. (1969), *The End of Liberalism*. New York: WW Norton.
Lyndon, D. (2009), 'The Sea Ranch: Qualified Vernacular', *Journal of Architectural Education*, **63**(1), 81–9.
Lyndon, D. and J. Alinder (2004), *The Sea Ranch*, Princeton, NJ: Princeton Architectural Press.
MacArthur, R. (1955), 'Fluctuations of Animal Populations and a Measure of Community Stability', *Ecology*, **36**(3), 533–6.
Maclachalan, R.J. (1966), 'Land Administration in New Zealand', in J.B. Brown (ed.), *Rural Land Administration in New Zealand*, Oxford: Oxford University Press.
McFarland, A. (2004), *Neopluralism: The Evolution of Political Process Theory*. Wichita, KS: University of Kansas Press.

May, R.M. (1973), *Stability and Complexity in Model Ecosystems*, Princeton: Princeton University Press.
Odum, E.P. (1963), 'Relationships between Structure and Function in the Ecosystem', *Ecology*, **12**, 108–19
Page, J. and A. Brower (2007), 'Property Law in the New Zealand High Country: Statutory not Common Law Leases', *Waikato Law Review*, **15**, 48–63.
Page, J. and A. Brower (2008), 'Property Law in the New Zealand High Country: Part II', *Waikato Law Review*, **16**, 73–87.
Perschel, R. (1994), 'Foreword', in C.M. Klyza and S. Trombulak (eds), *The Future of the Northern Forest*, Hanover, NH: University Press of New England.
Radin, M.J. (1993), *Reinterpreting Property*, Chicago: University of Chicago Press.
Reidel, C. (1994), 'Political Process of the Northern Forest Lands Study', in C.M. Klyza and S.Trombulak (eds), *The Future of the Northern Forest*, Hanover, NH: University Press of New England.
Rose, C.M. (1986), 'The Comedy of the Commons: Custom, Commerce, and Inherently Public Property', *University of Chicago Law Review*, **53**(3), 711–81.
Rose, C.M. (1994a), 'Seeing Property', in C.M. Rose (ed.), *Property and Persuasion: Essays on the History, Theory, and Rhetoric of Ownership*, Boulder, CO: Westview Press.
Rose, C.M. (1994b), 'Given-ness and Gift: Property and the Quest for Environmental Ethics', *Environmental Law*, **24**, 1–32.
Rose, C.M. (1998–9), 'The Several Futures of Property: Of Cyberspace and Folk Tales, Emission Trades and Ecosystems', *Minnesota Law Review*, **83**(1), 129–82.
Sax, J. (1969–70), 'The Public Trust Doctrine in Natural Resource Law: Effective Judicial Intervention', *Michigan Law Review*, **68**, 471–566.
Sax, J. (1984), 'The Rights of Communities: A Blank Space in American Law', Boulder, CO: Natural Resources Law Center Occasional Papers Series.
Sax, J. (1992–3) 'Property Rights and the Economy of Nature: Understanding *Lucas v. South Carolina Coastal Council*', *Stanford Law Review*, **45**(5), 1433–55.
Sexton, R. (1995), *Parallel Utopias: The Quest for Community*, San Francisco: Chronicle Books.
Swaffield, S. and A. Brower (2009), 'Globalisation, Contest and Paradox in a Continuing Cultural Landscape: Land Reform in the New Zealand High Country', *Danish Journal of Geography*, **109**(1), 161–79.
Tilman, D., J. Downing and D. Wedin (1994), 'Does Diversity Beget Stability' *Nature*, **367**, 363–65.
Trombulak, S. (1994), 'A Natural History of the Northern Forest', in C.M. Klyza and S. Trombulak (eds), *The Future of the Northern Forest*, Hanover, NH: University Press of New England.
Truman, D. (1951), *The Governmental Process*, New York: Alfred A. Knopf.
Walker, B.H. (1992), 'Biodiversity and Ecological Redundancy', *Conservation Biology*, **6**(1), 18–23.
Welby, L. (1986–7), 'Public Access to Private Beaches: A Tidal Necessity', *UCLA Journal of Environmental Law and Policy*, **6**, 69–104.
Westman, W.E. (1985). *Ecology, Impact Assessment, and Environmental Planning*, New York, NY: John Wiley and Sons.

3. Creating next generation rural landscape governance: the challenge for environmental law scholarship

Paul Martin, Jacqueline Williams and Amanda Kennedy[1]

3.1 INTRODUCTION

The pursuit of sustainability in most countries is characterized by a continuous stream of bad news about the trajectory of the state of our natural resources (Millennium Ecosystem Assessment Board 2005; World Resources Institute 2006; IUCN 2009) alongside government or private sector announcements of new investment schemes, market or regulatory arrangements and other initiatives which are intended to stem this tide of loss (OECD 2008; Snape and de Souza 2006; Better Regulation Task Force 2005; Eliadis et al 2005; Weber and Hemmelskamp 2005). Australia shares this characteristic of documented loss (Beeton et al 2006; NLWA 2002; Prime Minister's Science, Engineering and Innovation Council 2002) alongside significant but eventually insufficient preventative or remedial action (Australian National Audit Office 2008; Commonwealth of Australia 2008; Murray-Darling Basin Authority 2009; Martin et al 2007). Australia is the principal case study for this chapter though the concepts are applicable in most if not all jurisdictions. There are seeds of hope in the efforts that are made by many volunteers, governments, private citizens, agency staff, activists, scientists, landowners and philanthropists and others who struggle to leave to the next generation an intact natural inheritance (Wentworth Group 2002; Standing Committee on Heritage and the Environment 2001; Martin and Werren 2009), but their efforts are simply insufficient to stem the tide of losses.

The facts suggest that we need far more investment in conservation and rehabilitation of landscapes, but they also suggest that the ability to obtain this investment from traditional sources is limited (Allen Consulting Group 2001; National Farmers Federation and Australian Conservation Foundation 2000; Ferraro and Pattanayak 2006; Lee and Neves 2009). It is unlikely that there will be sufficient human or financial capital available to do all that we ought

(Australian National Audit Office 2008; Martin and Werren 2009; Prime Minister's Science, Engineering and Innovation Council 2002). It is vitally important to ensure that our natural resource governance systems manage to secure far greater resources for conservation and restoration, and manage to:

1. Shift the patterns of resource use transactions within society into preferred paths, which will require changing the decisions of many people (Pahl-Wostl 2002; Doran 2001; Gill 2004; Verbeek 2005). This includes shifting away from harm-doing, as well as encouraging financial and human investment to support conservation and rehabilitation.
2. Minimize the investment required to achieve this change in transacting patterns. This includes minimizing the opportunity costs of conservation and restoration, innovating in how we invest, and minimizing the amount of public funds that are required (Better Regulation Task Force 2005; Eliadis et al 2005; Weber and Hemmelskamp 2005; Bapna and McGray 2008; Regulation Taskforce 2006; Gunningham and Sinclair 2004); and
3. Ensure social equity in how governance power is exercised (Adger et al 2004; Douthwaite et al 2004; Farrington and Baumann 2000). This includes ensuring that the costs and benefits of resource governance are shared equitably (Martin and Shortle 2009), and that the approach advances the social inclusion aims of society more broadly.

This will require that instruments and institutions are behaviorally powerful, with low transaction costs, well coordinated and just; and that they garner increased resources for sustainability investment.

Following the 2010 United Nations Year of Biodiversity it is appropriate to illustrate the urgent need for institutional innovation by biodiversity regulation in Australia, which mirrors international problems with the effectiveness and efficiency of strategies used to protect declining landscapes. In Australia environmental groups and scientists rightly point to the continuation of land clearing within farming landscapes as evidence that regulation is not sufficiently effective (Martin et al 2007; Accad et al 2006; Auditor-General 2006; Productivity Commission 2007); as they do for other countries (Inoguchi et al 2005; FAO 2008; Finley-Brook 2007). Farmers, economists and others point to the fact that the same regulations are excessively costly and that the costs are not fairly allocated (Martin and Shortle 2009; Sinden 2004; Nelson et al 2004; Davidson et al 2006; ALGA 2005; Sherrard and Tate 2006; Pizer and Kopp 2003). Advocates of market solutions point to the theoretical potential for biodiversity banking to bridge the gap (Ginn 2005; Walker and Walmsley 2008; Booth 2007; Carroll et al 2007), but critics argue that these approaches may simply be a politically expedient way of sacrificing those habitats with the greatest commercial value (Burgin 2008; Gibbons and Lindenmayer

2007). The contest between market solutions, self-regulation or deregulation, traditional regulation and community or social change programs generates heat, but sheds little empirical light on which are the most effective ways to achieve the governance goals that we have outlined above (Eliadis et al 2005; Martin et al 2007; Faure 2009).

Competing sides of these debates may be simultaneously right. The governance structures that we use to address these challenges are demonstrably far from optimal. Unacceptable levels of resource degradation and financial loss, and unfairness in the distribution of cost and benefit, exist notwithstanding a myriad of laws, conservation investments, market experiments, voluntary programs and genuine commitment on all sides; we are getting too little gain at too high a cost. Social mechanisms, market mechanisms and legal mechanisms may all be simultaneously essential and intrinsically inefficient as they are currently used. There is ample evidence that many of the natural resource governance methods we manage to use combine high cost, inequitable distribution of costs, and insufficient behavioral effectiveness (Martin et al 2007; Martin and Shortle 2009).

In this chapter we intend to suggest some research directions towards improving the behavioral cost-effectiveness and equity of rural natural resource governance mechanisms.

3.2 CONCEPTS AND DEFINITIONS

In order to prevent confusion about uses that may not be common across disciplines, the following terms are defined for the purposes of this chapter.

Natural resources governance This refers to the instruments and institutions used by government in the exercise of its powers and responsibilities to protect the public good in natural resources. It also refers to the architecture of the relationship between these, including jurisdictional arrangements and the linkages between different instruments and programs.

Instruments The mechanisms used to shift the pattern of transactions within a social system through which resources are consumed. Notable among these are financial or other incentives, regulation, persuasion, and the fostering of environmental service markets.

Institutions Institutions are the arrangements of rules and organizational structures that shape patterns of transacting within a society. Whilst for the purposes of this chapter we are mostly concerned with institutions of government, a key consideration is the interaction between government and private institutions.

Landscapes In this chapter landscapes is shorthand for the combination of natural ecosystems and production systems within a defined area. This involves multiple tenures, often of different types. Landscapes contain many different natural values and resources.

Transactions A transaction occurs when a decision gives rise to a flow of resources or information. The interaction between man and man, or man and his environment is through transactions. An altered pattern of transactions is the key indicator of the effectiveness of a natural resource management (NRM) strategy.

Multi-attribute approaches Many natural resource governance arrangements focus on particular sub-components of the landscape, such as biodiversity, water, carbon or food and fiber. A multi-attribute approach attempts to deal with a number of these sub-components in a unified manner, to better mirror the interdependence of elements within systems.

3.3 SCOPING THE CHALLENGE

In Australia, almost 62% of the total landscape is managed for agriculture (Commonwealth of Australia 2009b) and with it large areas of ecological significance, in particular biodiversity hotspots (Commonwealth of Australia 2009a).

The two maps shown in Figures 3.1 and 3.2 reveal an overlap between farmland and biodiversity hotspots. Whilst not apparent from these maps, the form of 'hotspot' farming that is most common is grazing. This is not accidental. What both farmers and nature seek is areas where landscape, water and climate conditions support the growth of vegetation, and the resulting diversity of species opportunities. The intersection with grazing rather than other uses reflects that over time biodiversity does decline more rapidly on intensively farmed land. That it is essential that conservation and rehabilitation are effective on private rotationally grazed lands is a clear implication. This critical grazing/farming/biodiversity relationship holds true for many parts of the world perhaps other than those countries that have been intensively farmed for many centuries.

Equally important in all countries is the systemic aspects of the relationship between public and private lands, and between production and conservation issues. This is illustrated for Australia in relation to ecological connectivity and biodiversity, and the relationship between production and environmental management of water.

Connectivity across landscapes is a critical consideration in the survival of ecological communities (Soule et al 2004). Fragmentation of management across public and private lands results in many conservation challenges. These

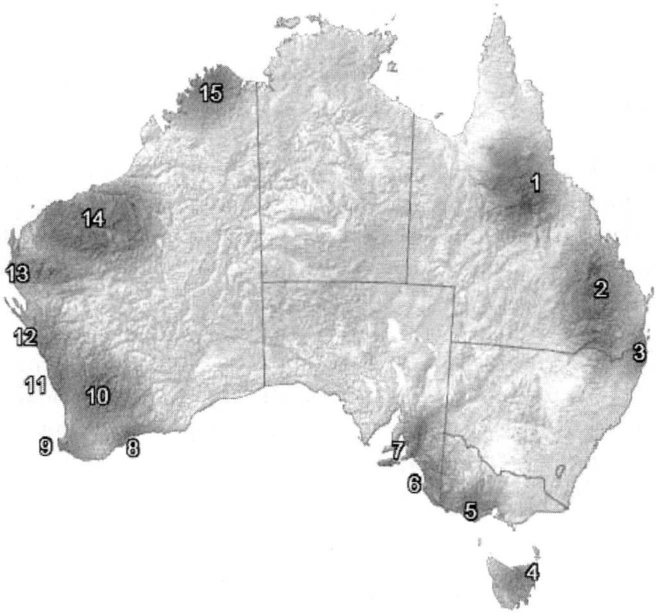

Source: Commonwealth of Australia 2009a.

Figure 3.1 Australia's biodiversity hotspots

not only include difficulties in accessing food or maintaining a viable breeding population, but also challenges that can arise from management regimes on private lands. This is more apparent with species whose habitat requirements span land tenure boundaries, such as the mosaic of habitat types required for threatened bird species like the Red Goshawk, Powerful Owl and Marbled Frogmouth (Queensland Government Commonwealth of Australia 1997) and internationally, iconic species such as the elephant in Africa (Osborn 1998; Sitati and Walpole 2006) or the snow leopard in Asia (Singh 2002). The impacts of farm dogs upon koalas in Australia (NSW Department of Environment and Climate Change 2008) or of farming on wetland bird habitats in South East Asia (Li et al 2009) are illustrative of the difficulties that arise when landscapes are not managed in an integrated manner for ecological as well as production outcomes.

It is not only for the sustainability of fauna that coordinated management is essential. There are many situations where the conservation of pockets of fauna is not likely to be feasible unless private lands are managed in ways that are in sympathy with public environmental purposes. An illustration is the

Source: Commonwealth of Australia 2009b.

Figure 3.2 Australia's land use

recognition by the New South Wales Government that private land management agreements are required to ensure the survival of the Gang Gang Cockatoo, the Glossy Black Cockatoo, the Plains Wanderer and the Koala (NSW Department of Environment, Climate Change and Water 2009).

A related concern is the management of invasive species. The problem is illustrated by the invasion of plants from farmland into conservation zones (such as lantana and blackberry) and the impact of feral animals such as rabbits, foxes, wild dogs and cats that predate upon or compete with populations which are being conserved (Gong et al 2009). What is less frequently acknowledged is the traffic of environmental and production hazards from conservation areas into farmland. Feral dogs predating on sheep and cattle are a significant concern in some farming areas (NSW Government 2006) as is the increase in feral pig populations in Northern Australia (Johnson 1999). Internationally similar problems with weeds and animals are well documented (Pimental et al 2000). The impacts of fire spreading between private and public tenures are another source of ongoing cost, conflict and ecological harm (Volunteer Fire Brigades Victoria 2007; Suyanto 2007; Suyanto et al 2004).

With the onset of climate change, issues of landscape connectivity have become more important, and will become increasingly so (Hannah et al 2002). In order for many species of flora and fauna to survive, it is essential that they can move over time across the landscape (Soule et al 2004; Archer and Beale 2003). It is also likely that climate-exacerbated problems of weeds and invasive fauna will require integrated management across landscapes (Australian Government 2008; van Klinken et al 2008). Fragmented management makes that far less likely.

The sustainable use of water is an equally powerful illustration of the need to connect public (conservation) and private (production) governance. Here the intrinsic connections are over large spans of time and space, when considering interconnectivity of surface and ground water, and production and ecological demands. As has been found in the Murray-Darling Basin the consideration of both groundwater and surface water is crucial in determining what constitutes a sustainable modified hydrological system and the availability of water for irrigation and other uses (Connell 2007). The challenges of managing interconnectivity feature significantly as impediments to the implementation of the National Water Initiative (National Water Commission 2009; Murray-Darling Basin Commission 2008). As in Australia, internationally issues of salinity demonstrate the importance of managing connectivity across tenures of different types, sometimes over very large distances (Jehangir and Ali 1997; Bellamy et al 2002).

Ecological science is increasingly concerned with the management of systems, as well as components of systems (Burgman et al 2009; Gunderson and Holling 2002; Rammel et al 2007; Liu et al 2007). Production uses of landscapes are also increasingly focused on management of systems rather than discrete properties or processes, as is evident from the submissions to the Australian Senate Inquiry into Food Production in Australia (Parliament of Australia 2009) and international experiences in Europe (Piorr and Muller 2009), the Americas (Harvey et al 2007; Tiessen and Stewart 2008) and Asia (Sharma and Xu 2007). Interconnectivity is increasingly seen as an important aspect of management to achieve ecological, social and economic outcomes from landscapes (Williams and Gascoigne 2003; Mander et al 2007; Scherr and McNeely 2008; Gordon et al 2010). All of these things speak of the fundamental importance of coupling public and private management, and there are many attempts to do so through national and regional programs.

3.4 CHALLENGES OF RESOURCE GOVERNANCE LAW

Whilst the energies of environmental lawyers are often directed towards regulation to control harmful actions like polluting or destruction of habitat, the role of the law in natural resource governance is far broader than 'traditional' command and control regulation. Table 3.1 is indicative of the range of instrumental strategies, legal aspects of these strategies, the behavioral mechanism in use and the allocation of costs. Virtually all sustainability strategies rest upon legal foundations, implying that law reform to advance sustainability must address many aspects, including property rights, civil action, and administrative law (as well as the more obvious policed controls). Further, the table indicates that the law reflects a variety of behavioral theories, though these are often not overt, and that there is an inevitable issue of social equity in the allocation of costs and benefits.

What the table also implies is that the underlying role of the law is as a tool to implement social change strategies, all of which are concerned with shifting the patterns of transacting within the social and economic system that

Table 3.1 Range of instrumental strategies

Instrument type	Some legal aspects	Behavioral mechanism?	Who bears the cost?
Markets	Property rights Theft Trading rules	Market entrepreneurship 1. Arbitrage or 2. Improve resource access or value	Consumer of resource bears the cost of consumption
Private Regulation	Civil action Contract Deception	Avoidance of third party harm or 'neighborly' negotiation of interests	Offending party bears costs of avoidance of harm. Affected neighbor may bear costs. Both bear negotiated costs
Public Regulation	Penalties Enforcement Administration	Compliance, focused on least cost to avoid the risk	Regulator bears the costs of enforcement. User bears the cost of compliance
Incentives	Authority Contract Public accountability	Administrative entrepreneurship to • Win grants • Satisfy requirements	The granting agency plus grant applicants
Education	Authority Constraints	Civic responsibility	Volunteers

Source: Authors.

drives our consumption of resources. As we have documented earlier in this chapter, notwithstanding an enormous investment in legal instruments, it is clear that neither the law nor any other mechanism has been a sufficiently effective catalyst for change to these underlying patterns.

Conclusions from our previous studies over the last decade have led us to conduct a program of research focused on developing an understanding of the limits of available instruments and some directions that could help to systematically improve the effectiveness of sustainability laws. This background research includes a number of empirical studies of regulatory arrangements, transaction and institutional structures, and case studies of the implementation (and outcome) of regulatory and market instruments. Without attempting to reprise these studies, some key aspects are worth highlighting, as they underpin the proposals that follow. Whilst the jurisdictional basis of our studies is Australia, we believe (based on discussions with international colleagues, and reading the literature) that the conclusions are relevant in most jurisdictions.

In relation to regulation, some of the conventional wisdom about regulatory instruments is contestable. We cannot find strong *ex-post* research evidence that market instruments are intrinsically more effective than regulation (even if this is strongly indicated by *ex-ante* economic modeling) (Martin et al 2007). This is in part because the success of any form of instrumental intervention is a function of complex and dynamic contexts and because any instrument operates within an overall strategy, where 'operational' considerations such as the institutional energy and resources that are committed to make it work are material variables (Eliadis et al 2005; Faure 2009). Thus, a conceptually ideal market or regulatory instrument has a substantially increased likelihood of success if its implementation is supported by substantial investments by competent agencies. Analysis focused on the instrument as the causal explanation of sustainability outcome must be, in our view, misleading because of the number and complexity of the variables that this ignores (Faure 2009; Martin and Verbeek 2002). To illustrate in the case of water markets, the move from riparian, to administered, to market systems has occurred alongside massive investments in hydrological science, significant innovations in water use technology and large amounts of government adjustment (Eliadis et al 2005; Faure 2009; National Water Commission 2009; Hussey and Dovers 2007, Dovers and Wild River 2003). Even if one can make a meaningful judgment that the final outcomes are more efficient and sustainable than what would have prevailed under the riparian system, it is drawing a long bow to suggest that this is causally the result of the instrument choice. When one considers the fact that the goals of policy are multi-dimensional and heterogeneous (Leach and Scoones 2000; Naylor 2009), the difficulty of making a claim that any form of instrument is empirically demonstrated to be better than any other is apparent.

What is perhaps more useful for legal policy-makers to consider is what is necessary to make legal instruments more effective. In this light, there are factors that require careful consideration in the design of instrumental strategies. One of these is the political economy (Eliadis et al 2005). The evidence that conflict and politics, and the institutional settings within which these are resolved (or not), is pivotal in determining the success of instrumental strategies is strong (Faure 2009; Martin et al 2008). Unfortunately the political economy literature is often retrospective and descriptive, but it does suggest the need for instrumental design processes that consider political risk, potential conflicts and the institutional context as core concerns rather than as extrinsic to the challenges of creating 'efficient, effective and fair' instruments.

Interacting with this, our research highlights the potential of transaction costs to frustrate the effectiveness of instruments, which costs often arise from a combination of institutional path dependence and the dynamics of politics (Martin and Shortle 2009; Martin et al 2008). Our work has suggested that having a large number of environmental laws (including environmental property right laws) is a source of transaction costs that frustrate the achievement of the intention of those same laws (Martin and Verbeek 2002). One consideration is the extent to which the complexity of legal architectures dis-empowers those who want to implement voluntary sustainability programs, including environmental management systems under ISO 14001. This also highlights that, in considering the effectiveness of legal arrangements, it is no longer reliable to assume a clear boundary between state-derived rules (statute and regulation) and industry-derived rules (under contracts, industry standards and increasingly under state-delegated powers). State and private rules now interact, and often do not align towards the achievement of the strategic goals of sustainability that they ostensibly promote (Martin et al 2007). Co-regulation exists *de facto* even whilst we continue to debate its reliability in theory (Moss and Walmsley 2005; Latzer et al 2007; Sorsa 2009). To us this suggests that it is necessary for environmental law scholarship to move from a focus on individual instruments towards a focus on total institutional architectures, married to a consideration of pragmatic challenges such as the links to budgetary processes and organizational capabilities to implement intended arrangements (Martin and Werren 2009). Far more attention should be given to streamlining the laws that exist, and facilitating their implementation even whilst debating the need for new laws and market instruments, if the total effect is to be the achievement of intended goals (Martin et al 2007; Martin and Verbeek 2002).

To create laws that work systemically legal scholars will need to learn from system theorists in sociology, ecology and economics. Their studies point to the need to design interventions that achieve change at multiple points within the social/economic and ecological systems that are being managed. The destruction of ecologies is usually the result of the interaction of multiple resource-consumption activities carried out by many people, and harm occurs in various ways at different points within ecosystems. For example, the destruction of species is frequently the result of generalized habitat loss coupled with specific harms to particular species, with the harmful actions perhaps being carried out at a distance from the place where the species exists. The 'driver' of the harm might be international consumption patterns, warfare, or might be abetted by financing or market-channel arrangements that stimulate the harm. To merely pass a law that designates a species as protected from direct harmful action is hardly addressing the problem (Burgman et al 2009).

This points to the need to design instrumental strategies that target many different transactions by various actors, and to ensure that we intervene to protect or restore multiple ecological assets at the same time. Our experience is that it is possible to design such interventions, but the methods required are new to legal scholarship (Martin and Verbeek 2002; Martin and Verbeek 2006). This in turn points to the need for regulatory design and review processes that truly encourage the design of environmental laws that deal with systems rather than spots within systems. However conventional regulatory review processes like benefit/cost assessment and even regulatory risk assessment are far from sufficient to the task. For example, they pay little more than lip-service to the realities of agency implementation where most regulatory and market failings seem to arise; and the dealing with the embedded social justice implications of any conservation (Martin et al 2007).

Implementation capacity is often a function of government and private market economics. Most legal scholars would in principle agree that to pass a strong law will not be meaningful if the agency charged with its implementation then proceeds not to allocate the resources to do so. However, few analyses of intended regulation focus upon the pragmatic issues of funding for implementation, which is a prerequisite for action. In many countries, including Australia, the funds needed to implement even the existing sustainability initiatives are sadly lacking. The combination of ageing population and the increasing costs of responding to climate change, coupled with the self-generating effects of prior ecological harm, suggests that the economic shortfall will increase. Under these conditions, the design of legal arrangements needs to encompass a deeper concern for the question 'how will we pay for the conservation and restoration we need?' which includes asking 'who will pay to implement the laws we pass?'. Without this being part of environmental legal scholarship, we stand the risk of creating increasingly unrealistic legal regimes (Martin and Werren 2009; Martin et al 2008).

This suggests some concerns that we ought embrace within our legal scholarship. A central question is how to design legal instruments that are behaviorally effective at low cost (Martin 2005). Another is to find new and more effective ways of ensuring fairness is designed into our legal instruments (Martin et al 2008). A third is the need to better integrate three often separate dimensions of legal scholarship: environmental law doctrine, jurisprudence and legal philosophy, and legal institutions. This in turn highlights the need to bring together distinct disciplinary perspectives but within a framework that respects the unique norms and knowledge of the legal discipline.

Overall our prior studies indicate that to meet the challenges outlined the next generation of natural resource governance will need to be characterized as:

1. Economically efficient;
2. Institutionally coordinated;
3. Behaviorally effective; and
4. Trans-tenure.

This requires resource management arrangements that:

1. Respect system interconnectivity;
2. Respect private rights;
3. Re-shape private resource use transactions; and
4. Facilitate public conservation transactions.

In order to optimize:

1. Economic production from natural resources;
2. Within the constraints of water and land capacity;
3. Fairness in the allocation of costs and benefits; and
4. Restoration of landscapes to produce public goods.

3.5 THE CENTRALITY OF INSTITUTIONAL INNOVATION

The institutional impediments to such an ideal are significant. To overcome the tyranny of increasing ecological challenges encountering decreasing economic capacity to use traditional instruments, sustainability will require significant innovation. However, the institutional arrangements that are in place are not attuned to significant and rapid adaptation. It is not only law-making and parliament and the courts that are limited in their flexibility. Williams (2007) found that regional resource management institutions in Australia lack essential attributes. In part this is a result of the institutional complexities and tensions of a federated multi-level approach to resource management. This reflects the problems of instrumental fragmentation and complexity discussed earlier. Many such issues can be traced to constitutional structures that were put in place for reasons unrelated to the environment, at a time when challenges of the type we face could never have been anticipated. These frameworks for resolving resource management conflicts predispose society to government arrangements that are complex, slow to change, and limited in the mechanisms for innovation that they can adopt. In reality, the options available to cope with sustainability challenges are limited by the institutions that we have to implement them. 'Second best' solutions are often the only ones that our historical institutions will allow us to consider as feasible.

Our largely publicly funded approach to natural resource management approaches will require significant change, if there are to be sufficient resources invested in conservation and rehabilitation (Martin and Werren 2009). Current mechanisms have proven to be incapable of winning sufficient resources from the public purse, or from private sources by leverage from the public purse, to achieve their purposes. Hampered also by insufficiently supportive private taxation arrangements, they face a future of an increasing deficiency of funds (Martin et al 2007). This speaks of the need for a different structure and skills, new investment instruments and commercial capacities and relationships.

It also suggests the need for a more thorough understanding of the risks that policies themselves may fail. As discussed above, even theoretically good laws can fail politically because they cannot be enacted or because of the strength of political opposition to implementation. They can also fail because they are unsuited to the problem or do not fit the context, or because of impediments like transaction costs. Further, the history of the outcomes of natural resources policy suggests that environmental laws can create adverse effects (Martin et al 2008). The possibility of such spillovers has not always been considered when new legal regimes are created, with sometimes catastrophic consequences.

We can illustrate this with water markets in Australia. Australia has implemented to a large degree the economic theory of market efficiency in water, by creating water entitlements that are able to be owned or traded without being tied to riparian land (or indeed any land title). The relevant laws embed prohibitions on anti-competitive arrangements that can restrict regional trade, and also incorporate 'water buybacks' as the means to bring over-allocation under control. However, the implementation of these sustainability and efficiency measures has resulted in significant unexpected harms to a range of interests, including the environment. Rural communities claim that water buybacks and reallocation undermine the viability of some local industries and towns (Crase et al 2009). Spillover risks can also arise from unexpected interactions. In the Lower Goulburn and Murray River, tradable water arrangements have triggered claims that significantly higher summer flows (compared to pre-water-market conditions) may increase siltation and reduce river water quality, and ultimately harm irrigation and urban water supplies (Frontier Economics 2007). Whilst 'risk-based regulation' has been widely discussed, it is clear from such examples that the legal treatment of risk is not yet as sophisticated as it needs to be.

Taken together, the discussion above suggests that whilst it is important to continually propose and refine environmental law doctrines, better doctrines will not be sufficient to deliver better outcomes from environmental law. What is needed is a natural resource governance system which (compared to traditional models):

1. Is behaviorally effective, which in part requires that it achieves realignment of private incentives and public controls;
2. Is inexpensive in the form of costs to those regulated, economic loss, and government cost; and
3. Creates conditions for improved private investment in sustainability.

Such an improved legal governance approach would require better legal instruments, but it also requires:

1. Reducing the number and improving the coordination of institutional structures;
2. Reducing the transaction costs of regulatory frameworks and eco-service markets, by integration and streamlined design;
3. Creating credible co-regulatory structures between industry and government, including reliable monitoring metrics and methods;
4. Assisting to improve private incentives for good stewardship, through performance certification and marketplace promotional support; and
5. Providing mechanisms to better allocate private and public investment to better environmental performers.

There are many fledgling innovations that could contribute to such a reform program, but without the 'glue' of good scholarship, targeted at effective legal architectures and instruments, it is hard to imagine that they will result in a sufficiently improved suite of laws and governance arrangements to markedly improve the prospects of sustainability.

3.6 SOME SEEDS OF GOVERNANCE INNOVATION

There are many innovations in natural resource governance in Australia that could contribute to advancing the cause of sustainability, if we could better align our legal instruments to other aspects of natural resource governance (Weber and Hemmelskamp 2005). We illustrate this with four related developments: consumer-led sustainability brands, industry/government co-regulation, new sustainability institutions and innovation in policy instruments. With each of these there are clear indications of a potential to contribute to more efficient natural resource governance, but also unresolved questions about the best means to realize this potential. In all cases innovation in legal arrangements may hold the key to this realization of potential.

1. Consumer and producer-led voluntary responsibility schemes. The variety of schemes indicates the goodwill that can be harnessed, but is also disconcerting as it illustrates how fragmentation inhibits society's ability to create market incentives for sustainable production. Over 60% of Australia is managed for agriculture, with farmers investing an annual average of $3.3 billion in on-farm NRM (Australian Bureau of Statistics 2008) and $314 million in water-related management activities (Australian Bureau of Statistics 2006). However, a misalignment of formal natural resource management and informal arrangements limits the national capacity to exploit this private effort (Williams 2007). Two impediments are the absence of reliable data about actions and outcomes from both public and private land activities, and the absence of a mechanism to translate private good practice into relief from regulatory 'red tape' (Beeton et al 2006; Australian National Audit Office 2008; Primary Industries and Natural Resource Management Ministerial Councils 2006). Environmental Management Systems (EMS) and other environmental assurance programs struggle in the market place (Grains Council of Australia 2006; Pahl 2007; Bhaskaran et al 2007; Keogh 2006; Kristiansen and Chang 2006; Gunningham 2007). There are reasons to believe that industry innovation in standards, certification or recognition systems, coupled with the power of the 'green consumer dollar', could provide an important complement to regulatory reform. However, unless there are mechanisms to overcome fragmentation, and to properly integrate industry with government programs, this opportunity will continue to elude us.
2. Experiments in co-regulation (including self-regulation). Co-regulatory arrangements have existed in different forms for many years. An example is the development of Corporate Social Responsibility (CSR), which is used as a voluntary framework based on self-regulation instruments through which corporations can: manage their social and environmental impacts; exercise power and authority in the development of CSR standards globally through inter-firm cooperation, and as a mechanism to transform business culture through the development of co-regulatory

instruments between corporations and their stakeholders (Albareda 2008). In the rural sector in Australia, food safety co-regulation is practiced (Australian Government AQIS 2010) and is well exemplified in the red meat industry, where a number of accreditation and reporting schemes have been developed over the last decade, such as the National Livestock Identification System (NLIS); the Livestock Production Assurance (LPA); the National Vendor Declarations (NVD), and the National Feedlot Accreditation Scheme (NFAS), an industry self-regulatory quality assurance scheme (Productivity Commission 2009). What has emerged in recent times is increased interest in the use of environmental co-regulation to reduce the transaction costs of regulation and also to provide recognition for the endeavors of industry to self-manage its public responsibilities (Better Regulation Task Force 2005; Aalders 2002; Australian Law Reform Commission 2002; Sparrow 2000). The institutional requirements for effective co-regulation are still far from well-defined (Moss and Walmsley 2005; Segerson and Miceli 1998; Priest 1998). If co-regulation is to be effective, then it is likely to require effective accountability mechanisms, which are not well-developed for sustainability, but have been demonstrated in the commercial sector. Mechanisms that may be adapted include independent financial audit or audit of quality standards. Other possible innovations include prescribed mandatory or voluntary codes of conduct under 51AE of the Trade Practices Act 1974 (Hockey 1999) or coupling industry codes with Certification Schemes under trademark legislation, a mechanism that has been used to give industry quality or origin certification strategies legal strength (Australian Wool Innovation Ltd 2008). Legal recognition of industry codes has been institutionalized in the state of Queensland. An industry or non-government process can now be accredited as satisfying the requirements for a statutory Land and Water Management Plan. Cotton Australia's Best Management Practice system is now recognized for this purpose (Wallace 2008).

3. New institutional alignments. Catchment management has evolved from its incarnation in the mid 1980s as a mechanism for community participation in government natural resource management (Australian National Audit Office 2008; Causley 2000). Catchment management authorities are heavily involved in community consultation and program development, with a focus on landscape-scale sustainability. In parallel (or in some cases in competition) has been the development of private sector institutions with similar purposes. Some are groups of landowners, whilst others combine philanthropy and volunteer efforts to attempt to achieve public good objectives. Intersecting with both government and private institutions is the growth in not-for-profit and for-profit corporate programs for the environment (Landcare Australia Limited 2010).

With each of these institutions come funding and works programs, which intersect with the programs of government agencies. Whilst all programs are laudable, the proliferation of institutions, plans and programs suggests that there are transaction impediments generated by complexity, and that important efficiencies of scale, scope and learning are foregone under current arrangements.

4. A fourth aspect of governance innovation is the explosion of policy instrument concepts, notably the advent of markets for tradable rights to exploit the environment (OECD 2006), and market-like instruments used by government (Gunningham and Sinclair 2004; OECD 2006; Anderson 2001). An important aspect is the link between science and instrumental reform, though this is not a simple matter of making science the core of regulatory designs (Martin et al 2007; Brunner et al 2005). There has been substantial technical research into particular instruments (notably economic modeling of market instruments, and surveys of regulatory cost). What have been less deeply examined are the empirical questions about the achieved benefit/cost and distributional effects of instruments when they are applied in different contexts (Eliadis et al 2005; Martin et al 2007; Faure 2009). We have discussed this issue above, suggesting that whilst there is a great deal of instrumental innovation, our understanding of the behavior of people in response to instruments (within the real-world context) significantly lags our understanding from broad economic or regulatory theories.

These four developments in natural resource governance offer enormous promise, but for each, delivery on that promise is hampered by institutional constraints and gaps in essential knowledge. There are many lenses through which these issues might legitimately be viewed. Economics in its different guises, political science, sociology, natural resource management and ecological theory and many other disciplines all have useful things to say about such matters. However, as natural resources governance is largely implemented through the workings of the legal system, the cost-effectiveness of regulation is an appropriate focus for discussing how to convert these potentials into realized improvements.

3.7 CRITICAL REFLECTION AND 'SMART REGULATION'

Many of the chapters in this volume indicate that it is vitally important for legal scholars to be self-reflective and self-critical if we are to advance scholarship, and the achievement of the underlying sustainability goals of that scholarship. The discussion above highlights many reform opportunities that could help to make law more effective at lower cost. The term 'smart regulation' refers to *an emerging form of regulatory pluralism that embraces flexible, imaginative and innovative forms of social control which seek to harness not just governments but also business and third parties* (Gunningham et al 2005). The concept speaks of the value of combining a variety of instrumental and institutional arrangements in a creative and coordinated manner. There has been attention to the application of the concept in various settings (Jacobs 1999), and it resonates with other themes such as reflexive regulation (Fiorino 2004; Gunningham and Sinclair 2004); regulatory innovation (Weber and Hemmelskamp 2005; Sparrow 2000; Stewart 2001) and participatory approaches to resource governance.

Our synthesis of prior studies indicates that the insufficient outcomes and high costs of natural resource governance approaches are partly a function of our inability to create systemic legal solutions to coupled ecological/social system problems. Natural resource management interventions provide 'spot' responses rather than the sustained management of integrated systems (Burgman et al 2009). They also rely on targeting only some of the transactions that shape the way in which the economic system interacts with natural systems. The mechanisms used are fragmented and too often compete in their approach or purposes.

Rules and programs are required by government institutions for administration and implementation. Each structure involves fixed costs, even ignoring the costs of carrying out their functional purpose (Martin et al 2007; Martin and Verbeek 2000). There are too many rules, too many policies and too many institutions involved for natural resource governance (at least in Australia) to achieve its goals at the lowest possible cost. The clearest illustration of the structural problem is when resource governance complexity requires coordinating bodies to be formed to span government agencies ostensibly charged with similar sustainability objectives. Regional NRM bodies in Australia are a good example (Williams 2007), where the desired outcomes of landscape scale change and sustainable human communities involve coordination of government, industry and community sectors, with high transaction costs and questionable success (Yee and Rolfe 2005). The jurisdictional complexity of coordinating natural resource management is well illustrated through the deliberations and activities of the Primary Industries and Natural Resource Management Ministerial Councils (Australian Government 2009) in their efforts to coordinate state and territories' natural resource management policies and practice.

Many interventions have high transaction costs due to design, and the inefficiencies of the total (fragmented) resource governance system. This leads to high costs imposed on some people, and excessive regulatory and administrative costs imposed on all (Sinden 2004; Maser and Heckathorn 1987; Australian Government 2006). These transaction costs also inhibit effectiveness (Martin and Shortle 2009; Martin et al 2008; Bromley 1991; Colby 1995; Stavins 1995; Allen Consulting Group 2006).

A matter that should be of concern is the over-allocation of the costs of inefficiency upon those who 'do the right thing'. The well-intentioned minority invest the time and money to identify and comply with their legal obligations, and often go further. They participate in regional natural resource planning, committees and workgroups. It is they who go to the trouble and cost of putting in applications for approval of activities that their less concerned peers ignore. It is the same category of people who turn up for tree-planting work groups or who set aside part of their properties for wildlife corridors. Only the concerned few implement environmental management systems, conservation reserves, and obtain environmental accreditation. Institutional complexity and poor coordination add to the transaction costs borne by this important minority (but not by the less socially engaged majority).

There is a hidden transfer of value from ethical to exploitative individuals within this dynamic. Public choice and political economy theories suggest that regulatory complexity is ripe to be politically exploited by the less scrupulous (Lemieux 2004; Stavins 2004; Driessen 2003). Complexity provides an opportunity to obfuscate and confuse implementation, and to support political claims for deregulation that reduces protection of the environment. Regulatory cost also impacts upon the environmental budgets of government (though we have not found any study that has disaggregated the effect of transaction costs of institutional complexity from overall regulatory costs).

'Smart regulation' speaks of instruments that are sophisticated and precisely targeted. Many of the issues in environmental law are about risk, but the legal instruments we develop are a naive reflection of commercial risk strategies. In the governance of natural resources risk, the cutting edge is 'risk-based regulation', a limited reflection of the richness of risk concepts that could be applied (Sparrow 2000; Hutter 2005; Shapiro and Glicksman 2003).

Many issues of sustainability have risk characteristics: exposure of things that are valued to uncertain hazards, with uncertain impacts, and uncertain capacity to recover. However, most environmental instruments, including market instruments, translate this into relatively simple versions of tradable entitlements or controlled practices. This is illustrated by carbon emission markets and regulation. There remains significant uncertainty about: how carbon and other emissions impact on the environment; the specific nature of these impacts; the extent, nature and timing of consequences; and the ability of those affected to adjust or recover (Garnaut 2008). However, through political process and technical analysis the instruments that are proposed have emerged in the form of non-contingent market instruments (emissions markets), regulation, or taxes. The uncertainty of science is dissolved in the translation into law and policy. We can only (at this stage in the development of climate policy) conjecture what policies might arise if we were to consider possibilities for climate risk insurances, sophisticated risk-management structures, risk pooling and other contemporary risk management mechanisms (Econosearch 2006; Hutter 2005).

Next generation resource governance will require laws that facilitate integrated management of many interconnected elements. It will have to address landscape management spanning public and private tenures encompassing a range of ecosystems, with varied environmental attributes. Whether action is driven by the public or the private sector ought to depend upon the nature of the particular issues (not presumptions of role).

The essential requirements for greater success in doing this will involve reliably changing the patterns of the many private transactions that shape ecosystems. Unlike conventional governance proposals, such as broad-scale application of market or regulatory archetypes, the approach (and therefore the legal arrangements) will have to reflect the social, economic and ecological system conditions and dynamics, on a landscape scale.

To overcome the insufficiency of resources the arrangements will have to maximize the total of both public and private resources available to conserve and restore natural resources, whilst reducing the opportunity costs of doing so. This implies significant economic entrepreneurship, alongside social and environmental innovation. To do this requires engaging commercially minded entrepreneurs in pro-ecology actions, not merely those who are publicly minded.

Information is the feedstock of decisions, but information flows (other than scientific or management data and public relations) are rarely a core focus of natural resource management. Transaction costs which impede effective governance are frequently related to information deficiencies, suggesting that more effective governance arrangements require a coherent information strategy. The role of the law in shaping information flows has been addressed in corporate governance, but has not been a focus in natural resource management. This is clearly demonstrated in the recent Australian State of the Environment Report (Beeton et al 2006), which found issues of lack of consistency with resource condition indicators and data to determine the state of the natural resource base.

Governance arrangements will not work effectively unless economic and managerial capacities are readily available for implementation. This implies that capability building within the governance system is essential to a more effective approach. This is not a question of writing new legal doctrine, it is a matter of making the effectiveness of institutions for implementation a more central focus of environmental lawmakers. Designing law focused on implementation capacity of not only legal institutions but also other government and private institutions, and those being targeted by the laws, is extending the ambit of conventional legal scholarship but is a potentially vital component of truly smart regulation[2] (Nelson et al 2004; Cary et al 2002; House of Representatives Standing Committee on Environment and Heritage 2001).

It is hard to see how environmental regulation can be 'smart' and effective when the legal architecture is fragmented, confusing and internally inconsistent. However, such characteristics are the norm in many jurisdictions (Martin and Verbeek 2000). Efficiency requires that the instruments and institutions of government should be realigned and simplified. Further, if environmental law is to be effective, there needs to be an emphasis on creating synergy between private market sustainability programs and public regulation. The evidence that complexity and misalignment can generate excessive transaction costs and impede implementation of environmental governance arrangements is strong. Streamlining the jurisdictional and administrative arrangements that sit behind environmental law should be a higher priority than it is. Environmental lawyers should be as concerned with reducing the number of laws as they are with creating new ones, or developing new doctrines.

Our relationship with the environment is shaped by many transactions throughout the social/economic system. Individual transactions are carried out by actors with differing motivations and capacities, responding to individual drivers and contexts that can be idiosyncratic (May and Winter 2001; OECD 2001; Dovidio et al 2006; Bartel 2005). This requires that the instruments and their implementation strategies be tailored to be behaviorally effective for the many different actors, goal and the context being managed. This will require alignment and coordination of incentives and sanctions, which implies making markets and regulation, government incentives and private philanthropy work together (the essence of smart regulation). However it also implies behavioral sophistication in understanding the issues, and in designing integrated strategies. A behavioral research orientation is generally absent from mainstream environmental law development.

3.8 DEVELOPING AND TESTING A NEXT-GENERATION APPROACH

Whilst smart regulation describes desirable outcomes from more creative and inclusive design processes, it does not propose the processes through which this may be created. The aim of the proponents of smart regulation is to stimulate the search for more sophisticated regulatory designs, rather than to develop these processes. Coupled ecological/transacting systems analysis approaches can be readily applied to this endeavor, providing new methods to pursue the smart regulation goals. Proposed methods (described in the publications earlier referenced) for legal institutional and policy scholarship that will engage with the challenges of creating smart regulation that change systems of resource use include:

1. Behavioral systems approaches to better understand the potential responses of those whose actions are to be regulated, and also to design the patterns of transacting that will reshape resource consumption;
2. Transaction cost analysis, related to these systemic analyses, which help in refining the efficiency and performance of the instruments and institutions that are intended to be used for this purpose;
3. Multi-attribute and multi-instrumental design approaches, using these system analyses as the cornerstone for shaping integrated transformational change for resource consumption systems; and
4. The use of risk analysis and management concepts to create innovative instruments that are better targeted, offer lower cost, and which have the potential to be effective with fewer spillover costs than less sophisticated design.

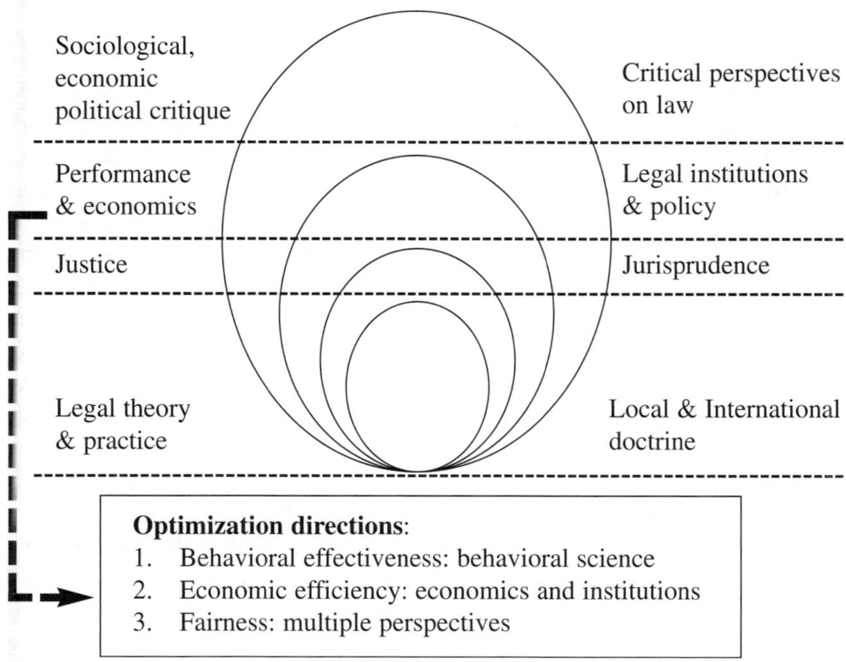

Figure 3.3 Alternative frameworks for legal scholarship

As discussed at the outset of this chapter, our focus is on an outcomes basis for legal policy and research. Resource management laws have not managed to effectively address the systemic ecological, economic and social issues involved in changing natural resource consumption. A more focused approach requires the integration of sophisticated strategic analysis and regulatory design, developing a multi-component change strategy with targeted interventions across the system. To do so at a landscape scale, and to carry the task forward into design and testing of the implementation and monitoring programme, is ambitious.

What is also apparent is that an effective strategy must engage powerful private sector interests who control major resources within the targeted landscape. Many previous natural resource management strategies have focused upon engaging those who are predisposed towards environmental public good activities, or who are likely to respond to relatively small incentives that are administered bureaucratically. A complementary approach is to directly target the economically and politically powerful who can make a substantial difference within the landscape. Our hypothesis from research on tax-leveraged conservation investment (Martin and Werren 2009) is that this target group will respond to instruments, administrative arrangements and communications differently from the responses of less powerful stakeholders. This is a logical conclusion from the very fact that the rich are better enabled commercially, have different opportunities and networks, and command more assets. This is not intended to suggest that they will be less public-spirited, for there is no evidence that this is the case. However, the strategies that are likely to work with them are likely to differ from those that will work with different community segments.

Our research uses sophisticated methods as the basis for this strategic engagement. The engaged scholarship approach to this research (Bridger and Alter 2006) reflects the deep experience of the US Land Grant universities (particularly Penn State University, which has the largest extension program of any US institution), coupled with methods derived from social marketing (McKenzie-Mohr and Smith 1999). These methods integrate with the behavioral systems approach to understanding regulatory effectiveness that we have previously outlined and with the transactions focused approaches to institutional analysis.

The nature of the engagement is determined by the need to simultaneously address the elements discussed earlier. It will be necessary to develop a refined understanding of stakeholder needs and opportunities; ecosystem and economic system issues; extant institutions and instruments; and interactions between these elements. It will be necessary to work in parallel on designing more effective private and public investment and incentives structures; co-regulatory arrangements; and institutional coordination.

As implementation (including capacity development) will involve a range of institutions and people, it will be necessary to develop an understanding of capacity issues, including capacities to support the necessary transformational change. All of these elements will have to be developed in such a way that they do reflect the particular conditions within the economic, social and environmental systems that are involved.

As all elements will have to be tailored for local implementation and require local resourcing (including strong private sector engagement), at the core of the engagement is the need to ensure that we have the active support of strong industry players who control (directly or indirectly) significant parts of the landscape and substantial resources. Success also requires engagement with committed government agents with sufficient control over data and information resources, regulation, and regional natural resource management governance arrangements. The final targets for engagement in the research are powerful political stakeholders, representing both the formal political process and more informal interests whose support can materially impact on the efficiency and effectiveness of the required transformations.

3.9 CONCLUSION

This chapter has suggested a broadening of the scholarly enquiry of environmental law, in order to better shape such laws to meet the increasing demands upon them to be both more behaviorally effective, and to be more economically efficient. We have proposed that to meet these challenges will require a scholarship that is more deeply engaged with some other disciplinary perspectives than has traditionally been the case. We suggest that it is not enough to become comfortable with economics as an informing perspective. It is also necessary to incorporate what is useful from the behavioral and political sciences, and to better understand ecological sciences, if we are to craft a clear paradigm for the design of behaviorally efficient environmental law and institutions. As a profession, it is essential to have a more overt theory of behaviorally efficient law in order to adopt a truly scientific approach to improving legal doctrine. Such a scientific approach requires a disciplined process of theorizing and theory articulation, followed by experimentation and experiment evaluation, leading to re-theorizing based on what has been learned.

This is no small challenge, but it is one for which environmental lawyers are equipped to take a lead. A strength of our profession is the ability to see beyond today's challenges, and to propose ambitious approaches to address tomorrow's. However, to succeed will require a significant effort from a lot of scholars. We look forward to taking this journey with colleagues from within the Academy, and also from other disciplinary groups.

NOTES

1. Australian Centre for Agriculture and Law, University of New England, Australia.
2. Insufficiency of knowledge and resources has been experimentally demonstrated by Moxnes to be an important element in the incapacity of primary producers to manage ecosystems sustainability (Moxnes 2000).

REFERENCES

Aalders, M. (2002), *Drivers and drawbacks: Regulation and environmental risk management systems*, London: Centre for Analysis of Risk and Regulation at the London School of Economics and Political Science, DP 10.

Accad, A., V.J. Neldner, B.A. Wilson, and R.E. Niehus (2006), *Remnant vegetation in Queensland: Analysis of remnant vegetation 1997–1999–2000–2001–2003, including regional ecosystem information*, Brisbane: Queensland Herbarium, Environmental.

Adger, N.W., K. Brown, J. Fairbrass, A. Jordan, J. Paavola, S. Rosendo, and G. Seyfang (2004), *Governance for sustainability: Towards a 'thick' understanding of environmental decision making*, Norwich UK: Centre for Social and Economic Research on the Global Environment.

Albareda, L. (2008), 'Corporate responsibility, governance and accountability: From self-regulation to co-regulation', 8 *Corporate Governance* 4, p. 430.

ALGA (2005), *ALGA submission to ministerial review*, Canberra: ALGA.

Allen Consulting Group (2001), *Repairing the country: Leveraging private investment*, Sydney: Business Leaders Roundtable.

Allen Consulting Group (2006), *Transaction costs of water markets and environmental policy instruments: Final report*, Melbourne: Productivity Commission.

Anderson, R.C. (2001), *The United States experience with economic incentives for protecting the environment*, Washington, DC: National Centre for Environmental Economics.

Archer, M., and B. Beale (2003), 'National parks have Achilles heel: study', available from http://www.abc.net.au/science/articles/2003/09/16/947138.htm (accessed 24 December 2009).

Auditor-General, NSW (2006), *Regulating the clearing of native vegetation: Follow-up of 2002 performance audit*, Canberra: New South Wales Audit Office.

Australian Bureau of Statistics (2006), 'Natural resource management on Australian farms, 2004–05, Australian Bureau of Statistics, Canberra.

Australian Bureau of Statistics (2008), '462.0 – Natural resource management on Australian farms, 2006–07', Australian Bureau of Statistics, Canberra.

Australian Government (2009), 'Primary Industries and Natural Resource Management Ministerial Councils', available from http://www.mincos.gov.au/ (accessed 29 January 2010).

Australian Government (2008a). *Australian 2020 summit final report: Future directions for rural industries and rural communities*, Canberra: Australian Government.

Australian Government (2008b), *Overview of the report implications of climate change for Australia's national reserve system: A preliminary assessment*, Canberra: Australian Government.

Australian Government (2006), *Rethinking regulation: Report of the taskforce on reducing regulatory burdens on business – Australian government's response*, Canberra: Australian Government.

Australian Government AQIS (2010), 'Co-regulation import schemes implemented by AQIS', available from http://www.daff.gov.au/aqis/import/general-info/co-reg (accessed 29 January 2010).

Australian Law Reform Commission (2002), *Securing compliance: Civil and administrative penalties in Australia*, Sydney: ALRC, ALRC Discussion Paper 65.

Australian National Audit Office (2008), *Regional delivery model for the natural heritage trust and the national action plan for salinity and water quality*, Canberra: Australian National Audit Office.

Australian Wool Innovation Ltd (2008), 'What the woolmark brand means to your business', http://www.wool.com/Design-and-Market_Woolmark.htm (accessed 20 December 2008).

Bapna, M., and H. McGray (2008), *Financing adaptation: Opportunities for innovation and experimentation*, Washington, DC: World Resources Institute.

Bartel, R.L. (2005), 'When the heavenly gaze criminalises: Satellite surveillance, land clearance regulation and the human-nature relationship', 16 *Criminal Justice* 3, p. 322.

Beeton, R.J.S., K.I. Buckley, G.J. Jones, D. Morgan, R. Reichelt, and D. Trewin (2006), *Australia state of the environment 2006: Independent report to the Australian Government Minister for the Environment and Heritage*, Canberra: Australian Government.

Bellamy, J., H. Ross, S. Ewing, and T. Meppem (2002), *Integrated catchment management: Learning from the Australian experience for the Murray-Darling Basin*, Canberra: CSIRO.

Better Regulation Task Force (2005), *Routes to better regulation – A guide to alternatives to classic regulation*, http://www.brc.gov.uk/downloads/pdf/routes.pdf (accessed 8 February 2006), London: Better Regulation Taskforce, 62.

Bhaskaran, S., M. Polonsky, J. Cary, and S. Ferdandez (2007), 'Environmentally sustainable food production and marketing opportunity or hype?', 108 *British Food Journal* 8, p. 677.

Booth, D. (2007), *Land trusts and biodiversity*, Charleston, SC: Surge Publishing.

Bridger, J.C., and T.C. Alter (2006), 'The engaged university, community development, and public scholarship', 11 *Journal of Higher Education Outreach and Engagement* 1, p. 163.

Bromley, D.W. (1991), *Environment and economy*, Oxford: Blackwell.

Brunner, R.D., T.A. Steelman, L. Coe-Juell, C.M. Cromley, C.M. Edwards, and D.W. Tucker (2005), *Adaptive governance: Integrating science, policy, and decision making*, New York: Columbia University Press.

Burgin, S. (2008), 'BioBanking: An environmental scientist's view of the role of biodiversity banking offsets in conservation', 17 *Biodiversity and Conservation* 4.

Burgman, M.A., T. Walshe, L. Godden, and P. Martin (2009), 'Designing regulation for conservation and biosecurity', *The Australasian Journal of Natural Resources Law and Policy* 13, p. 93.

Carroll, N., J. Fox, and R. Bayon (eds.) (2007), *Conservation and biodiversity banking: A guide to setting up and running biodiversity credit trading systems*, Environmental Markets Insight Series. Abingdon, Oxford: Earthscan Publications Ltd.

Cary, J., T. Webb, and N. Barr (2002), *Understanding landholders' capacity to change to sustainable practices: Insights about practice adoption and social capacity for change*, Canberra: Department of Agriculture Forestry and Fisheries.

Causley, I.R. (2000), *Co-ordinating catchment management: Report of the inquiry into catchment management*, Canberra: House of Representatives Standing Committee on Environment and Heritage.

Colby, B.C. (1995), 'Regulation, imperfect markets and transaction costs: The elusive quest for efficiency in water allocation', in *Handbook of environmental economics*, D. Bromley (ed.), Massachusetts: Blackwell Publishers, pp. 475–502.

Commonwealth of Australia (2009a), 'Australia's 15 national biodiversity hotspots'. available from http://www.environment.gov.au/biodiversity/hotspots/national-hotspots.html (accessed 24 December 2009).

Commonwealth of Australia (2009b), 'Land use – Australia', available from http://www.anra.gov.au/topics/land/landuse/index.html#use (accessed 24 December 2009).

Commonwealth of Australia (2008), *Caring for our country business plan 2009–10*, Canberra.

Connell, D. (2007), *Water politics in the Murray-Darling Basin*, Sydney: The Federation Press.

Crase, L., S. O'Keefe, and B. Dollery (2009), 'Water buy-back in Australia: Political, technical and allocative challenges', Paper presented at the 53rd Australian Agricultural and Resource Economics Society Conference, Cairns, Australia.

Davidson, A., S. Beare, P. Gooday, P. Kokic, K. Lawson, and L. Elliston (2006), *Native vegetation: Public conservation on private land – cost of forgone rangelands development in southern and western Queensland*, ABARE research report.

Doran, J. (2001), 'Intervening to achieve co-operative ecosystem management: Towards an agent based model', 4 *Journal of Artificial Societies and Social Stimulatio*n 2.

Douthwaite, B., J.M. Javier, M. Ekboir, S.S. Twomlow, and J.D.H. Keatinge (2004), 'The concept of integrated natural resource management and its implications for developing evaluation methods', in *Natural resource management in agriculture: Methods for assessing economic and environmental impact*, B. Shiferaw, H.A. Freeman, and S.M. Swinton (eds.), Oxfordshire, UK and Cambridge, MA: CAB International.

Dovers, S. and S. Wild River (eds.) (2003), *Managing Australia's environmen*t, Sydney: Federation Press.

Dovidio, J.F., J.A. Piliavin, D.A. Schroeder, and L.A. Penner (2006), *The social psychology of prosocial behaviour*, Mahwah, NJ: Lawrence Erlbaum Associates.

Driessen, D.M. (2003), *The economic dynamics of environmental la*w, Cambridge, MA: MIT Press.

Econosearch (2006), *Adoption of new land management practices through conservation insurance*, Unley, SA: Econosearch for the Australian Government National Action Plan for Salinity and Water Quality.

Eliadis, P., M.M. Hill, and M. Howlett (eds.) (2005), *Designing government: From instruments to governance*. Montreal: McGill–Queen's University Press.

FAO (Food and Agriculture Organization) (2008), 'Timore-leste national action program to combat land degradation', Dili, November 2008.

Farrington, J., and P. Baumann (2000), *Decentralised natural resource management: A review of the theoretical issues*. London: Overseas Development Institute.

Faure, M. (2009), 'Instruments for environmental governance: What works?', paper presented at the IUCN International Academy for Environmental Law Conference, Wuhan, China.

Ferraro, P.J., and S.K. Pattanayak (2006), 'Money for nothing? A call for empirical evaluation of biodiversity conservation investments', 4 *PLoS Biology* 4, http://www.plosbiology.org/article/info%3Adoi%2F10.1371%2Fjournal.pbio.0040105.

Finley-Brook, M. (2007), 'Indigenous land tenure insecurity fosters illegal logging in Nicaragua', 9 *International Journal of Energy, Environment, Economics* 4, p. 850.

Fiorino, D.J. (2004), 'Flexibility', in *Environmental governance reconsidered: Challenges, choices and opportunities*, R.F. Durant, D.J. Fiorino and R. O'Leary (eds.), Cambridge, MA: The MIT Press, pp. 393–425.

Frontier Economics (2007), *The economic and social impacts of water trading: case studies in the Victorian Murray Valley*, Kingston, ACT: RIRDC.

Garnaut, R. (2008). *The Garnaut climate change review – final report*, Melbourne Australia: Cambridge University Press.

Gibbons, P. and D.B. Lindenmayer (2007), 'Offsets for land clearing: No net loss or the tail wagging the dog?', 8 *Ecological Management and Restoration* 1, p. 26.

Gill, N. (2004), 'Politics within and without – the origins and development of a rangelands Landcare group', 42 *Australian Geographic Studies* 2, p. 135.

Ginn, W.J. (2005), *Investing in nature: Case studies of land conservation in collaboration with business*, Washington, DC: Island Press.

Gong, W., J. Sinden, M. Braysher, and R. Jones (2009) *The economic impacts of vertebrate pests in Australia*, Canberra: Invasive Animals Cooperative Research Centre.

Gordon, L.J., C.M. Finlayson, and M. Falkenmark (2010), 'Managing water in agriculture for food production and other ecosystem services', 97 *Agricultural Water Management* 4, p. 512.

Grains Council of Australia (2006), *Market signals for environmental and other assurances in the supply chain*, Canberra: Grains Council of Australia.

Gunderson, L.H., and C.S. Holling (2002), *Panarchy: Understanding transformations in human and natural systems*, Washington, DC: Island Press.

Gunningham, N. (2007), 'Incentives to improve farm management; EMS, supply-chains and civil society', *Journal of Environmental Management* 82.

Gunningham, N., R. Kagan, and D. Thornton (2005), 'General deterrence and corporate behaviour', *Law and Policy* 27, p. 262.

Gunningham, N., and D. Sinclair (2004), *Voluntary approaches to environmental protection: Lessons from the mining and forestry sectors*, Canberra: Australian National University.

Hannah, L., G.F. Midgley, T. Lovejoy, W.J. Bond, M. Bush, J.C. Lovett, D. Scott, and F.I. Woodward (2002), 'Conservation of biodiversity in a changing climate', 16 *Conservation Biology* 1, p. 264.

Harvey, C., F. De Clerck, D. Tobar, and F.L. Sinclair (2007), 'Patterns of tree cover and animal diversity within pasture-dominated landscapes of Mesoamerica: Managing the matrix to meet the dual goals of conservation and food security', Paper presented at ESA/SER Joint Meeting, San Jose, California.

Hockey, J. (1999), *Prescribed codes of conduct: Policy guidelines on making industry codes of conduct enforceable under the Trade Practices Act 1974*, Canberra: Treasury.

House of Representatives Standing Committee on Environment and Heritage (2001), *Public good conservation: Our challenge for the 21st century. Interim report of the inquiry into effects upon landholders and farmers of public good conservation measures imposed by Australian governments*, The Parliament of the Commonwealth of Australia.

Hussey, K., and S. Dovers (eds.) (2007), *Managing water for Australia: The social and institutional challenges*, Victoria: CSIRO Publishing.

Hutter, B.M. (2005), 'The attractions of risk-based regulation: Accounting for the emergence of risk ideas in regulation', London: ESRC Centre for Analysis of Risk and Regulation, London School of Economics, DP 33.

Inoguchi, A., R. Soriaga, and P. Walpole (2005), 'Approaches to controlling illegal forest activities: Considerations from South East Asia', Working Paper Series No. 7, http://www.asiaforestnetwork.org/pub/pub59.pdf.

IUCN (2009), IUCN Red List, available from http://www.iucnredlist.org/ (accessed 24 December 2009).

Jacobs, S.H. (1999), *Smart regulation: A regulatory strategy for Canada*, Canada: External Advisory Committee on Smart Regulation.

Jehangir, W.A., and N. Ali (1997), *Salinity management alternatives for the Rechna Doab, Punjab, Pakistan. Volume Six – resource use and productivity potential in the irrigated agriculture*, International Irrigator Institute Lahore: Report R21–6.

Johnson, C.N. (1999), 'Feral pigs: Pest status and prospects for control', Cooperative Research Centre for Tropical Rainforest Ecology and Management Cairns.

Keogh, M. (2006), 'Editorial', 3 *Farm Policy Journal* 4, p. 4.

Kristiansen, P., and H. Chang (2006), 'Selling Australia as "clean and green" ', *The Australian Journal of Agricultural and Resource Economics* 50, p. 103.

Landcare Australia Limited (2010), 'Landcare Australia', available from http://www.landcareonline.com.au/ (accessed 29 January 2010).

Latzer, M., N. Just, F. Saurwein, and P. Slominski (2007), *Regulation remixed: Institutional change through self and co-regulation in the mediamatics sector*, Vienna: Austrian Academy of Sciences, Research Unit For Institutional Change and European Integration (ICE).

Leach, M., and I. Scoones (2000), *The institutional dynamics of community-based natural resource management: An entitlements approach*, Brighton, UK: Institute of Development Studies, University of Sussex.

Lee, D.R., and B. Neves (2009), 'Rural poverty and natural resources: Improving access and sustainable management', ESA Working Paper 09-03, ftp://ftp.fao.org/docrep/fao/012/ak422e/ak422e00.pdf.

Lemieux, P. (2004), 'The public choice revolution', 27 *Regulatio*n 3, p. 22.

Li, Z.W.D., A. Bloem, S. Delany, G. Martakis, and J.O. Quintero (2009), *The status of waterbirds in Asia: Results of the Asian waterbird census: 1987–2007*, The Netherlands: Wetlands International.

Liu, J., T. Dietz, S.R. Carpenter, C. Folke, M. Alberti, E. Moran, A.N. Pell, P. Deadman et al (2007), 'Complexity of coupled human and natural systems', *Scienc*e 317, p. 1513.

Mander, U., H. Wiggering, and K. Helming (2007), *Multifunctional land use: Meeting future demands for landscape goods and service*s, Berlin: Springer.

Martin, P. (2005), *Towards a heuristic framework for choice and mix of instruments in natural resource management*, Armidale, NSW, Australia: UNE.

Martin, P., R.L. Bartel, J.A. Sinden, N. Gunningham, and I. Hannam (2007), 'Developing a good regulatory practice model for environmental regulations impacting on farmers', Land and Water Australia, http://products.lwa.gov.au/downloads/publications_pdf/EF071346.pdf.

Martin, P., and J. Shortle (2009), 'Transaction costs, risks and policy failure', in 10th Global Conference on Environmental Taxation, Lisbon, Portugal.

Martin, P., and M. Verbeek (2006), *Sustainability strateg*y, Sydney: Federation Press.

Martin, P., and M. Verbeek (2002), *50,000,000 Australians? Is sustainability possible?* Canberra: Land and Water Australia, TPF2.

Martin, P., and M. Verbeek (2000), *Cartography for environmental law: Finding new paths to effective resource use regulation*, Land and Water Research and Development Corporation.

Martin, P., and K. Werren (2009), 'Discussion paper: An industry plan for the Victorian environment?' Victorian Department of Sustainability and the Environment.

Martin, P., J. Williams, and C. Stone (2008), *Transaction costs and water reform: The devils hiding in the details*, Cooperative Research Centre for Irrigation Futures.

Maser, S.M., and D.D. Heckathorn (1987), 'Bargaining and the sources of transaction costs: The case of government regulation', 3 *Journal of Law, Economics and Organisation* 1 (Spring), p. 69.

May, P.J. and S.C. Winter (2001), 'Motivation for compliance with environmental regulations', 20 *Journal of Policy Analysis and Management* 4, p. 675.

McKenzie-Mohr, D., and W. Smith (1999), *Fostering sustainable behavior: An introduction to community-based social marketing*, Washington, DC: Academy for Educational Benefit.

Millennium Ecosystem Assessment Board (2005), *Living beyond our means: Natural assets and human well-being*, Washington, DC: Millennium Ecosystem Assessment.

Moss, W., and R. Walmsley (2005), *Controlling the sale of invasive garden plants: Why voluntary measures alone fail*, Sydney: WWF.

Moxnes, E. (2000) 'Not only the tragedy of the commons: Misperceptions of feedback and policies for sustainable development', *System Dynamics Review* 16 (Winter), p. 325.

Murray-Darling Basin Authority (2009), *The Basin Plan*, available from http://www.mdba.gov.au/basin_plan (accessed 24 December 2009).

Murray-Darling Basin Commission (2008), 'Murray-Darling Basin Commission e-letter no.80 August 2008', Murray-Darling Basin Commission Canberra.

National Farmers Federation and Australian Conservation Foundation (2000), *National investments in rural landscapes*, Canberra.

National Water Commission (2009), *Australian water reform 2009: Second biennial assessment of progress in implementation of the national water initiative*, Canberra: Australian Government.

Naylor, R.L. (2009), 'Managing food production systems for resilience', in *Principles of ecosystem stewardship*, C. Folke, G.P. Kofinas and F.S. Chapin (eds.), New York: Springer.

Nelson, R., T. Webb, and I. Bryon (2004), *Socioeconomic indicators for natural resource management: Capacity to change and adopt sustainable management practices in Australian agriculture*, Canberra: Australian Bureau of Agricultural and Resource Economics.

Nelson, R., F. Alexander, L. Elliston, and A. Blias (2004), *Natural resource management on Australian farms*, Canberra: ABARE.

NLWA (2002), *Australians and natural resource management 2002*, Canberra: NLWA.

NSW Department of Environment and Climate Change (2008), *Recovery plan for the koala (phascolarctos cinereus)*, Sydney: NSW Department of Environment and Climate Change.

NSW Department of Environment, Climate Change and Water (2009) 'Recovery strategy: Establish management agreements with public authorities CMA's and land managers/owners', available from http://www.threatenedspecies.environment.nsw.gov.au/tsprofile/pas_recovery_strategies_details.aspx?type=establish+management+agreements+with+public+authorities+cmas+and+land+managers/owners (accessed 24 December 2009).

NSW Government (2006), 'Pest management in NSW National Parks: FACT SHEET'.

OECD (2008), *Environmental performance reviews: Australia*, OECD.

OECD (2006), OECD/EEA database on instruments used in environmental policy, 2006, available from http://www2.oecd.org/ecoinst/queries/index.htm (accessed 6 November 2006).

OECD (2001), 'Improving the environmental performance of agriculture: Policy options and market approaches', OECD Publishing, http://213.253.134.43/oecd/pdfs/browseit/5101171E.PDF.

Osborn, L. (1998), 'Elephant/Human conflict around Maputo elephant reserve', University of Cambridge.

Pahl, L.I. (2007), 'Adoption of environmental assurance in pastoral industry supply chains – market failure and beyond', *Australian Journal of Experimental Agriculture* 47, p. 233.

Pahl-Wostl, C. (2002), 'Agent-based simulations in integrated assessment and resources management', paper presented at the International Environmental Modelling and Software Society Conference, Lugano.

Parliament of Australia (2009), Inquiry into food production in Australia: Submissions received 9 December 2009, available from http://www.aph.gov.au/SENATE/committee/agric_ctte/food_production/submissions/sublist.htm (accessed 24 December 2009).

Pimental, D., L. Lach, R. Zuniga and D. Morrison (2000), 'Environmental and economic costs of non-indigenous species in the United States', *Bioscienc*e 50, p. 53.

Piorr, A., and K. Muller (eds.) (2009), *Rural landscapes and agricultural policies in Europ*e, Heidelberg: Springer.

Pizer, W.A., and R. Kopp (2003), 'Calculating the cost of environmental regulations', Resources for the Future Discussion Paper.

Priest, M. (1998), 'The privatization of regulation: Five models of self-regulation', *Ottawa Law Revie*w 29, p. 233.

Primary Industries and Natural Resource Management Ministerial Councils (2006), Communiqué: April, Vol. 2006 MINCOS.

Prime Minister's Science, Engineering and Innovation Council (2002), *Sustaining our natural systems and biodiversity*, Canberra: Department of Education Science and Training.

Productivity Commission (2009), *Performance benchmarking of Australian and New Zealand business regulation: Food safety*, Melbourne: Productivity Commission.

Productivity Commission (2007), *Annual review of regulatory burdens on business: Productivity commission draft research report*, Melbourne: Productivity Commission.

Queensland Government and Commonwealth of Australia (1997), 'Systemic vertebrate fauna project', Forests Taskforce Department of Prime Minister and Cabinet Barton ACT.

Rammel, C., S. Stagl, and H. Wilfing (2007), 'Managing complex adaptive systems – a co-evolutionary perspective on natural resource management', 63 *Ecological Economic*s 1, p. 9.

Regulation Taskforce (2006), *Rethinking regulation: Report of the taskforce on reducing regulatory burdens on business*, Canberra: Regulation Taskforce.

Scherr, S.J., and J.A. McNeely (2008), 'Biodiversity conservation and agricultural sustainability: Towards a new paradigm of "ecoagriculture" landscapes', 363 *Philosophical Transactions of the Royal Society Biological Science*s 1491, p. 477.

Segerson, K., and T.J. Miceli (1998), 'Voluntary environmental agreements: Good or bad news for environmental protection?', *Journal of Environmental Economics and Management* 36, p. 109.
Shapiro, S.A., and R.L. Glicksman (2003), *Risk regulation at risk: Restoring a pragmatic approach*, Stanford, CA: Stanford University Press.
Sharma, E., and J. Xu (2007), 'Land-use, landscape management and environmental services in the mountain mainland Asia: Introduction', 48 *Tropical Ecology* 2, p. 129.
Sherrard, J., and A. Tate (2006), *Carrying the greenhouse load for the nation: Australia's farmers miss out on billions*, Sydney: Cambiar Pty Ltd.
Sinden, J.A. (2004), 'Do the public gains from vegetation protection in north-western New South Wales exceed the landholders' loss of land value?', 26 *The Rangeland Journal* 2, p. 204.
Singh, J. (2002), 'Transboundary stakeholders: Developing cross-border conservation linkages for the snow leopard', paper presented at the 2002 Snow Leopard Survival Strategy Summit, Seattle, Washington.
Sitati, N.W., and M.J. Walpole (2006), 'Assessing farm-based measures for mitigating human-elephant conflict in Transmara district Kenya', *Oryx* 40, p. 279.
Snape, J., and J. de Souza (2006), *Environmental taxation law: Policy, contexts and practice*, United Kingdom: Ashgate.
Sorsa, K. (2009), *Self regulation and co-regulation in value chain – reviewing retail, food and chemical industry examples*, Helsinki, Finland: National Research Institute of Legal Policy, Research Communications No. 100.
Soule, M.E., B.G. Mackey, H.F. Recher, J.E. Williams, J.C.Z. Woinarski, D. Driscoll, W.C. Dennison, and M.E. Jones (2004), 'The role of connectivity in Australian conservation', *Pacific Conservation Biology* 10, p. 266.
Sparrow, M.K. (2000), *The regulatory craft: Controlling risks, solving problems, and managing compliance*, Washington, DC: The Brookings Institute.
Standing Committee on Heritage and the Environment (2001), *Public good conservation: Our challenge for the 21st century*, Canberra: Australian Government.
Stavins, R.N. (2004), *Introduction to the political economy of environmental regulations*, Washington, DC: Resources for the Future.
Stavins, R.N. (1995), 'Transaction costs and tradeable permits', *Journal of Environmental Economics and Management* 29, p. 133.
Stewart, R.B. (2001), 'A new generation of environmental regulation?', *Capital University Law Review* 29, p. 21.
Suyanto, S. (2007), 'Underlying causes of fire: Different forms of land tenure conflicts in Sumatra', 12 *Mitigation and Adaption Strategies for Global Change Journal* 1, p. 67.
Suyanto, S., G. Applegate, R.P. Permana, N. Khususiyah, and I. Kurniawan (2004), 'The role of fire in changing land use and livelihoods in Riau-Sumatra', 9 *Ecology and Society* 1, p. 15.
Tiessen, H., and J.W.B. Stewart (2008), *Applying ecological knowledge to landuse decisions*, Sao Paulo, Brazil: Inter-American Institute for Global Change Research.
van Klinken, R.D., V.A. Osten, F.D. Panetta, and J.C. Scanlan (eds.) (2008), *Proceedings of the 16th Australian Weeds Conference*, Brisbane, Queensland: Queensland Weeds Society.
Verbeek, M. (2005), *Instrument examples*, pers. com, 24 December 2009.
Volunteer Fire Brigades Victoria (2007), *Inquiry into the impact of public land management practices on bushfire in Victoria: Submission to the*

environment and natural resources committee, Mt Waverley: Volunteer Fire Brigades Victoria.

Walker, J., and R. Walmsley (2008), 'Biobanking: Certainty for developers, new hope for threatened species', 46 *Law Society Journal* 8, p. 53.

Wallace, C. (2008), 'Queensland's cotton industry all sewn up', Brisbane: Queensland Government.

Weber, M., and J. Hemmelskamp (eds.) (2005), *Towards environmental innovation systems*, Berlin: Springer.

Wentworth Group (2002), *Blueprint for a living continent*, Australia: WWF.

Williams, J. (2007), 'Success attributes of regional NRM systems in Australia', University of Queensland.

Williams, J., and H. Gascoigne (2003), *Redesign of plant production systems for Australian landscapes*, Canberra, ACT: CSIRO.

World Resources Institute (2006), 'Earth trends: Environment information', available from http://earthtrends.wri.org/ (accessed 24 December 2009).

Yee, S., and J. Rolfe (2005), 'Institutional choices for natural resource management: Judging efficiency of NRM bodies', paper presented at the International Conference on Engaging Communities, Brisbane, Australia.

PART II

Governance innovation in China

4. Constitutionalism and the environment: the evolution of environmental governance in China's Socialist Market Economy

Kishan Khoday[1]

4.1 INTRODUCTION: ECOLOGICAL CHANGE AND CONSTITUTIONALISM

The launch of China's new Socialist Market Economy policy in 1992 turned out to be a historic event for China and the world. The dramatic shift from a centrally planned, inward-looking state to a globally expansive market-based super power unleashed a new era of development. It has opened up an expanded role for the private sector and set the stage for China's re-emergence at the center of the world economy (Hart-Landsberg and Burkett, 2005, p. 52). Almost twenty years later, China stands as the world's second-largest economy with annual per capita GDP nearing US$7,000 and a foreign currency reserve upwards of US$2 trillion, the world's largest. In the coming decades China is also expected to surpass the US to become the world's largest economy, with the implications of China's rise going well beyond the economic realm and already "opening the way for a multi-polar era in world politics" (Drezner, 2007, p. 1).

China's growth rate already accounts for almost 20% of world GDP growth, second only to the US contribution. It is also the world's leading destination for foreign direct investment (WEF, 2006). Along with its increasingly important role as a manufacturing base for the world, China has also become a major consumer, in terms of materials needed for the manufacturing of export goods to the world and personal consumption by a burgeoning middle class. China now consumes 26% of the world's crude steel, 32% of the rice, 37% of the cotton, and 47% of the cement. "Only US consumption has a larger impact on the environmental and social health of the planet" (Starke, 2006, pp. 5–7).

China's dramatic transformation has helped pull more people out of extreme poverty at a faster rate than at any time in human history. While the impressive nature of China's growth has left many in awe, there is now serious concern for the challenges of sustainability. China is at a juncture of natural resource scarcity and rapidly declining environmental quality. The signs of stress are evident; the climate is changing, severe storm and flood events in China are increasing in frequency, deserts are spreading, food and water security are serious concerns and toxic pollution is taking a steady toll on public health and welfare (State Council of China, 2010).

The launch of China's socialist market economy policy in 1992 also set a new balance between State and society, with a much greater role for the private sector and greater acknowledgement of citizen rights. Ecosystem services such as clean air and water, productive land and natural resources, are increasingly recognized by citizens as being public goods central to achieving human development (see UNDP, 2002b and UNDP, 2009). Recent years have seen a rise in environmental consciousness, with environmental issues being seen through the lens of human rights and the rule of law, alongside an increase in the number of environment-related protests by communities, and increasing use of the courts.

Ecological change is now a key driver of change, with increasing calls for the rule of law to serve as a force to balance growth and sustainability. As noted by UN environment leader Achim Steiner, "decoupling growth from environmental degradation is the number one challenge facing governments in a world of rising numbers of people, rising incomes, rising consumption demands and the persistent challenge of poverty alleviation" (UNEP, 2010). Ecological change has become an existential threat, with fundamental risks to the continuity of China's development model. China now faces the existential threats of ecological change and the need to adapt its State policies and development paradigms to ensure sustainability in the interests of future generations.

Constitutionalism is defined here as an organic and dynamic process by which the fundamental principles, policies and systems of the State evolve to address changing power dynamics and drivers of change within a given society, with these evolving principles, policies and systems representing a nation's basic social and political culture and setting certain fundamental norms to guide the State and its citizens in the process of development. Other drivers of change exist alongside constitutionalism, such as class struggles from an emerging middle class, farmer's land rights, migrant labor rights, etc.

As China marks twenty years since the launch of its socialist market economy policy, it has experienced a shift away from the old Cultural Revolution slogans that "Man Must Conquer Nature" and "Battling with Nature is Boundless Joy" to a new "Ecological Civilization" principle established in 2007 by the National People's Congress (NPC). This concept was first raised at the seventeenth Communist Party Conference in 2007, and was reaffirmed in 2008. It embodies a vision to recast modern development to align with traditional Chinese principles on the balance of humans and nature.

This has been coupled with China's first-ever National Human Rights Action Plan issued by the State Council in 2009. Section 1 (7) on Environmental Rights states that the goal is to uphold "the principle of harmonious development between man and nature and the rational exploitation and utilization of natural resources ... to create an environment favorable for human existence and sustainable development and build a resource-conserving and environment-friendly society to guarantee the public's environmental rights" and to strengthen "the rule of law in the sphere of environmental protection to safeguard the public's environmental rights and interests".

Environmental sustainability is now at the center of development discourse in China and is driving debate on ways to adequately re-calibrate the relationship between humanity and nature. In addition to environmental impacts being a market externality, ecological harm is now eroding the foundations of human security. The ability to achieve and sustain a certain quality of life for current and future generations is under threat. The capacity to deal with ecological change is quickly becoming a universally valued capacity, without which rights to development, human security and human development stand in jeopardy (Dasgupta, 2001, p. 5). As one of the greatest challenges faced by humanity, ecological crisis calls for nothing short of a new "social contract with nature" – a transformative vision of the balance between humans and nature and a new paradigm of progress to shape and sustain the future of development. Two key dynamics of this process are explored below.

A shift in foundational principles Ecological change is catalyzing new thinking and debate on fundamental principles and development paradigms which lie at the foundation of the socialist market economy and the modern State. This shift is expressed in China's ecological civilization paradigm and in increased emphasis within State policies on integrating traditional Chinese concepts about the balance between humans and nature with modernist principles of development.

Rule of law and human rights Ecological change is catalyzing public demands for the rule of law and rights-based approaches as a check and balance on the State; and reforms to basic State policies and systems to institutionalize new conflicts between State, society and the private sector. This includes systems to manage vertical conflicts between the State and citizens, which are expressed in public demands for greater access to information, participation and justice, and horizontal conflicts between the national centers of power in the prosperous eastern region, and the natural resource-rich but less well-off western provinces like Tibet and Xinjiang.

The last twenty years have seen a process of social and cultural change in China, with the emergence of ecological change as a common concern across society. As elaborated further below, new principles, policies and systems are being launched in China today. These present a historic opportunity to set a common national vision of sustainability and catalyze a new foundation for sustainable human development.

4.2 PRINCIPLES OF THE STATE: REBALANCING HUMANS AND NATURE

4.2.1 Freedom from Nature

In making the connection between ecological change and constitutionalism, this chapter argues for the need to rethink development paradigms and epistemological frameworks that underlie modern society and the State. The concept of development has a long history in China, derived in many ways from Enlightenment worldviews of human progress based on humanity's "freedom from nature"; the ability of modern scientific man to control and efficiently exploit the natural environment for the purpose of industry and economic growth. As noted by Argyrou, before the global environmental movement took shape following the 1972 Stockholm Conference on the Human Environment, the dominant discourse was a long-standing one produced by the West – that the environment was in a "state of nature", "a domain of utility, to be mastered and brought under man's control, compelled to satisfy his needs and administer his happiness. Opponents of this approach were viewed as primitive, traditional and underdeveloped. This was the 'anthropology' of the modernist paradigm" (Argyrou, 2005, p. vii).

In the modernist paradigm, "[n]ature was devoid of a spirit, and was a standing reserve of resources for man to serve his development. Mastery of nature came to be regarded as expression of cultural superiority and the key mark of civilization" (ibid., p. 2). "As noted by Marx, man makes himself and is himself only so far as he re-makes the world around him. The more he changes the world around him, the more he becomes his true self" (ibid.).

The Industrial Revolution became a celebration of mastery over nature. This built on Enlightenment worldviews that "acquaintance with the physical laws of the world, and the accompanying power of unlocking the secrets of nature and adapting nature to man's own ends, are on the whole, lowest among savages, mean among barbarians, and highest among modern educated nations" (ibid., p. 17). Civilization was seen as a triumph over rather than an expression of human nature, just as it was a triumph over external nature. Freedom from nature meant internal freedom (ibid., p. 11). Spreading modern civilization became a core mission of development, with developing countries called upon to "leapfrog across the centuries" (ibid., p. 6).

As described by Weller, the spread of the modernist paradigm of scientific utilitarianism and control of nature entered China in the early twentieth century. Throughout the century, "China reveled in its newfound control of nature", resulting in more and more efficient and productive factories and infrastructure that became symbols of society's victory over nature (Weller, 2006, p. 4). Decades of application of the modernist paradigm led to rapid industrial growth, culminating in national slogans during the Cultural Revolution (1966–76) that "Man Must Conquer Nature" and "Battling with Nature is Boundless Joy" (ibid., p. 49).

In recent decades in the West, this worldview has been transformed and to some extent reversed. This shift has been attributable to social and cultural transformation among globally connected youth, rapid growth of pollution impacts, and a growing sense of resource scarcity. The environment has been transformed in the mind of the West from being in a "state of nature" in opposition to humanity, into a complex ecosystem with a delicate balance in need of protection. This is aptly captured in the Stockholm Declaration, "for the purpose of attaining freedom in the world of nature, man must use knowledge to build, in collaboration with nature, a better environment. To defend and improve the environment ... has become an imperative goal of mankind" (UNEP, 1973, p. 3).

The corpus of global and national policies that followed over the past forty years has been the expression of this "reversed Enlightenment", which in some ways seeks to reverse the Enlightenment's great divide between humans and nature. In the view of some, this results in the potential for an "ontological transformation of the highest order heralding a new 'physics' and a new 'anthropology' and thus a new order of things" (Argyrou, 2005, p. 39).

However, while this paradigm shift took off in the West, developing countries still mired in poverty maintained allegiance to the modernist paradigm of rapid industrialization for the purpose of achieving high civilization. For some it was a time to pause (some for years, some for decades), to reflect on whether the right path is to "take the plunge forward and end up in a matter of decades on the other side of time" in a "modern" industrial civilization. China, with its strong socialist focus on scientific development and the march to modernity, moved rapidly to achieve what is now one of the world's greatest industrial systems. However, as we entered the twenty-first century, China commenced a period of hyper-growth with broad social and cultural change. Some have started to look critically at this progress, reconsidering the nation's "evolutionary uncertainties and one-way determination" (Argyrou, 2005, p. 33). As noted in the 2007 Human Development Report, ecological change now "calls into question the Enlightenment principle that human progress will make the future look better than the past" (UNDP, 2007, p. 1).

4.2.2 The Vision of an Ecological Civilization

Reconsideration of environmental sustainability in China has emerged against the backdrop of China's rapid march to industrialization, its participation in global environmental processes since the 1972 Stockholm Conference, and recently the re-emergence of traditional Chinese worldviews on the balance between humans and nature (Weller, 2006, p. 4).

The 1992 United Nations Conference on Environment and Development (UNCED or the Rio Earth Summit) launched a new paradigm intended to balance the 1972 Stockholm Conference goals of environmental protection with the rush by developing countries towards industrialization – the concept of Sustainable Development. China was the first to publish a national Agenda 21 after the Earth Summit and had passed its first-ever Environmental Protection Law in 1989 in the years leading up to the Summit. As the largest-ever gathering of world leaders, and with engagement with developing countries and civil society organizations around the world, the Earth Summit led to the rapid emergence of environmental consciousness around the world. This included a new engagement with traditional views on the environment from around the world, with a view to crafting a new post-modernist paradigm of the relationship between humans and nature that would have resonance in an increasingly global society.

In China the twenty years since 1992 Earth Summit has seen a growth in attention to sustainability by a burgeoning urban middle class with an increasing global reach and sense of Chinese culture and tradition. Recent years have also seen the rise of non-governmental organizations (NGOs) advocating for victims of toxic pollution in the industrial eastern provinces and for environmental justice in the western provinces of the country. Recent years have also seen the revival of Chinese traditions, including the re-emergence of Chinese traditional concepts of the balance between humans and nature within urban areas and among advocacy groups.

As noted by Weller, while the three dominant traditional Chinese worldviews of Confucianism, Taoism and Buddhism all hold humans at the center, unlike the Western modernist paradigm Chinese traditional worldviews "did not subject a de-animated nature to a ruling humanity" (ibid., p.15). Notwithstanding a continued allegiance to modernist policies, traditional views began to influence thinking about the need to balance development with the sustainability of ecosystems. Traditional worldviews on the environment are now seen as a core element of discourse on recasting China's development paradigms (ibid).

The reworking of modernity and tradition in response to concerns over ecological change is leading to new creative forms of social and political thinking on the future of development in China (ibid., p. 83). Given China's growing influence, this important process has implications globally with a potential synergy of Chinese concepts with global policies. Weller compares this potential "reworking" to Japanese re-working and re-exporting concepts like anime or Japanese corporate management practices during the 1980s (ibid., p. 9). Indeed many developing countries now look to China for potential development models, and will also take inspiration from the unfolding directions of China's principles and policies.

In 2007, in the midst of unprecedented levels of engagement by China within global dialogues on climate change and environmental sustainability, the National People's Congress (NPC) unveiled a vision to mark this historic epistemological transition. The ecological civilization policy is intended to serve as the foundations for the low-carbon, resource-conserving society of the future. The principle of an ecological civilization is a pragmatic response to serious concerns over environmental scarcity and carrying capacity of the type that has contributed to the end of ancient civilizations. It is meant to promote a future in which China is marked by innovation and leadership in crafting new forms of governance, industry and development.

Society's vision of nature and its relation to human progress has always been at the core of the concepts of development and civilization. Just as scientific understanding of nature and the new discoveries and worldviews it brought with it was the basis for Enlightenment thinking, so too might the new reality of ecological change drive new thinking and the evolution of foundational principles of development. Some even see ecology evolving into an overarching lens through which various aspects of development are understood. As noted by Homer-Dixon, "physics was the master science of the 20th century. Ecology will be the master science of the 21st century. A master science is, in part, the dominant scientific discipline of a historical epoch. It is the prototypical science of the time – the discipline that people think of first when they consider science. It's also likely to have produced the most spectacular discoveries and technologies. More importantly, a master science generates and orders the concepts through which society understands itself and its relation to its surroundings" (Homer-Dixon, 2009, p. 1)

Beyond being a sub-set of broader development issues, new principles and policies like the ecological civilization paradigm in China show that the narrative of sustainability is evolving in a way that could indeed re-shape basic principles of development and progress. As noted by Argyrou, "the science of global environmental change can only point to facts, but facts themselves are not enough to explain effective engagement with the world. What is needed above science is something that captivates people's full being – a system of values, a moral story, an ontological master narrative within which the ecological crisis becomes not only visible but also relevant and meaningful" (Argyrou, 2005, p. 48).

The ecological civilization concept is one expression of a new narrative. It calls for a new "social contract with nature" – a transformative vision of the balance between humans and nature and the nature of human well-being. In putting forward this new principle for the nation, China seeks to craft its own path to sustainability – "leapfrogging the technologies, policies and even cultures that now prevail in many western countries" (Narain and Starke, 2006, p. 19). As noted by observers, the government has adopted a "proactive approach to modernizing the state system in general, displaying great flexibility and adaptability in adjusting its institutions and practices". The hope is that this record of agility and adaptability can be applied to the historic challenge of ecological change (Zheng, 2004, pp. xvi–xvii).

Preventing serious disruptions to human well-being requires nothing less than a wholesale transformation of dominant cultural patterns and a redefinition of human development and progress. Some view the process as an "awakening" – a "waking up from the cultural trance of denial in which we are all embedded" (Heinberg, 2007, p. 23). This is not just a matter of intellectual conviction as to the seriousness of ecological change, but involves an "emotional, cultural and political catharsis. The biblical metaphor of scales falling from one's eyes is as apt as the pop culture meme of taking the red pill and seeing the world beyond the Matrix: in either case, waking up implies realizing that the very fabric of modern life is woven from illusion. … The great transition of the 21st century will entail enormous adjustments on the part of every individual, family and community" and a redefinition of their relation to broader society and the planet (ibid).

Already engaged in the exploration of new paradigms and principles, China's future will equally be shaped by new systems of policies and rules aimed at achieving the ecological civilization paradigm through the elaboration of new roles, rights and duties for individuals in society. This process of value creation and setting of new norms in society has led a growing sense of environmental citizenship, with individuals and communities expressing a new sense of respect for nature, an aspiration to participate in decisions that affect the environment, a call for greater sharing of benefits from resource use, and the expectation of effective access to remedy and justice for environmental harm.

4.3 RULE OF LAW AND HUMAN RIGHTS

4.3.1 Environmental Citizenship

As noted above, a key element in achieving the ecological civilization goal will be to establish new policies and rules that can engage a new spirit of environmental citizenship in society; individuals and communities expressing themselves with reference to human rights and the rule of law as a check and balance against the State and the growing role of the private sector in society (Dobson and Bell, 2006, p.1). As the impact of rapid growth continues to take its toll in terms of social health and welfare, a key challenge for China in the coming years will be to craft new policies and systems that can help prevent and manage new conflicts between government, the private sector and civil society.

Increased media coverage of environmental challenges, tens of millions of internet users and bloggers expressing their views, and the rise of thousands of environmental NGOs has meant that citizens not only analyze issues from a rights perspective but also take action on environmental protection from a rights perspective. The country has witnessed a surge of environment-related protests, while about 100,000 administrative lawsuits have been filed annually in recent years alongside an estimated 25% annual growth rate, both strong evidence of increasing rights-consciousness (Diamant, Lubman and O'Brien, 2005, pp. 43–5).

With the goal of achieving an ecological civilization and managing emerging tensions in society, in April 2009 China's State Council issued China's first National Human Rights Action Plan (2009–10). Of significance, Section 1 (7) on Environmental Rights states that the goal of the Action Plan is to uphold "the principle of harmonious development between man and nature and the rational exploitation and utilization of natural resources. China will take an active part in international cooperation in an effort to create an environment favorable for human existence and sustainable development and build a resource-conserving and environment-friendly society to guarantee the public's environmental rights" and to strengthen "the rule of law in the sphere of environmental protection to safeguard the public's environmental rights and interests". This new state policy now represents a key element in implementing the ecological civilization concept through rights-based approaches.

However, despite the visionary aspirations of recent State policies, there remain challenges in moving from principle to action. A key factor is the 1989 Environmental Protection Law (EPL) which established an "environmental responsibility system" (*huanjing baohu mubiao zerenzhi*) based on decentralizing decision-making with broad discretionary decision-making powers given to local government (Chen, Li and Otto, 2002, pp. 150–51). The downside of this broad discretion for local agencies has been that State policies and laws have been treated by local governments as mere guidelines setting the parameters of their administrative discretion, rather than the expression of a broader, objective rule of law framework (ibid., p. 92).

While China has enunciated State principles regarding sustainability, the system has traditionally faced difficulties in delivering on such principles through existing systems. This was summarized as far back as 1994 with the State Council finding that "laws are not complied with, enforcement is weak, and offenses are not prosecuted. Enforcement should become the core of environmental protection work" (ibid., pp. 150–51) A key aspiration has always been to galvanize the public's role in this initiative. Indeed as far back as 1996 the State Council Decision Concerning Environmental Protection called for the establishment of a mechanism to "encourage the public to participate in the work of environmental protection and to report and expose various actions that violate environmental laws and regulations". This signaled a turning point in encouraging both media and citizens to participate in local decisions that impact the environment, but tangible systems for participation were absent until recently (Ma and Ortolano, 2000, p. 74).

While the situation remained dire for many years, hope has risen in recent years through unprecedented innovations in the environmental governance system. As noted below, this includes new systems to increase citizen access to information, participation and justice in decision-making. The hope is that through these systems, local agency decision-making can become infused with trends of ecological consciousness in society and take account of ecological facts towards a more neutral and impartial application of the rule of law (Dobson and Bell, 2006, p. 10).

4.3.1.1 Access to information and participation

One of the promising trends in recent years has been the growth of community organizations and a stronger community voice in decision-making. China's recognition of increased citizen rights to information and participation stems from an appreciation of the mutual benefits of cooperation between environmental non-governmental organizations (ENGOs) and local government. This first took root in 1994 when the National People's Congress (NPC) enacted the Rules for Social Organization, granting legal status to NGOs for the first time. ENGOs were the first to register under the new law, and now form the single largest sector of civil society groups across China (Starke, 2006, pp. 152–3).

However, the effective inclusion of ENGOs in decision-making remained at an embryonic stage, with no clear procedural mechanisms to implement such policies. This changed in 2003 when the NPC enacted China's first-ever Environmental Impact Assessment (EIA) Law, specifically requiring public consultations to be held in relation to the passage of EIAs for development projects, with EIA reports to be published and open for comment prior to the endorsement of projects.

This was followed in 2004 when the State Environment Protection Administration (SEPA) (upgraded in 2008 into the Ministry of Environmental Protection or MEP) issued the Measures for Environmental Protection Administration Permission, which allow parties that are potentially adversely affected by development projects to request a hearing to express their concerns over compliance with EIAs (ibid., pp. 154–5). The participation rules embedded in the EIA Law were a major step in the evolution of environmental governance in China, acknowledging participatory means of environmental governance and the positive role of local communities as a check on agency discretion.

To further extend the nature of the process required to achieve the goal of public participation and scrutiny of decision-making, in March 2006 SEPA (now MEP) published Measures for Public Participation in Environmental Impact Assessment, setting out more detailed procedures governing the participatory approach called for by the 2003 EIA Law (ibid., p. 87). This includes a formal notice and comment process whereby potentially affected citizens are afforded the opportunity to provide input during the drafting of an EIA. Also in 2006, a Law on Public Participation in Environmental Appraisals was released along with a regulation on Public Participation in Environmental Protection. This followed in April 2007, when SEPA passed Measures on Open Environmental Information. Recent years have also witnessed the rise of the All China Environment Federation (AFED), a MEP-affiliated NGO. This serves as an umbrella for local NGOs across the nation and has developed since its inception a specialized focus on environmental rights (Gao, 2009, p. 3).

Taken together these new measures provide for the first time a legal channel for the public's right to information and participation in environmental decisions, and seek to engage public interest and advocacy in environmental matters. They hold the prospect of re-balancing power among citizens and communities on the one hand, and the State and corporations on the other. In doing so, they place new requirements on local government and enterprises to disclose environmental information empowering communities to participate in decision-making and seek judicial remedy. The new disclosure rules, for example, require local Environmental Protection Bureaus (EPBs) to disclose seventeen different kinds of environmental information related to environmental quality, amounts of discharge and records of polluters in the given region.

The coming years could serve as a transformational moment in the evolution of environmental governance in China (Diamant, Lubman and O'Brien, 2005, pp. 420–21). If effectively supported, this could help bring about greater coherence between trends of rapid economic growth and new national principles of environmental rights.

4.3.1.2 Access to justice

Equipped with increased access to information and participation in decision-making processes, citizens and communities are now using their increased voice to challenge the application of policies and decisions. Beyond public protests on environmental issues, which have increased dramatically in recent years across the country, citizens and communities also turn increasingly to seek judicial redress and rule of law. Access to justice is meant to ensure rational use of natural resources and the public good, as called for by China's 1982 Constitution. Access to justice has thus emerged as a force for action by local communities and citizens against the State-industrial complex, including claims of local agency capture by the rapidly growing and influential power of the private sector (Gao, 2009, pp. 1–2).

As in other counties, the bulk of environmental claims in China in recent years have been filed as administrative claims challenging arbitrary decision-making, excessive use of discretionary powers, or breach of required public review processes (Ma and Ortalano, 2000, p. 10). The launch of the Administrative Litigation Law and the Administrative Courts in 1989 were seen as key means of ensuring that agency actions complied with the overarching social and economic rights called for by the Constitution and the balance between private wealth generation and social welfare called for the 1992 socialist market economy paradigm.

Administrative courts were established across the country to hear a variety of administrative cases, including environmental claims. There was a growth in the general administrative law caseload across China during the first decade, with a ten-fold increase from 9,934 cases in 1989 to 97,569 cases by 1999 (Cheung, 2002, pp. 1–2). With regard to environment-related administrative cases, the caseload remained static, with 1670 cases in 1998, compared with 1601 in 2008 (Gao, 2009, p. 14). The total number of environmental civil cases, however, grew (by 1471%) from 96 in 1998 to 1,509 in 2008, while environmental criminal cases grew (by 427%) from 1912 in 1998 to 10,075 in 2008.

Environmental cases have historically been brought to Administrative Review panels managed by local agencies under the Administrative Review Law (ARL) and to general administrative courts managed by the Ministry of Justice under the Administrative Litigation Law (ALL) (Cheung, 2002, p. 4). This two-layer process provides for review of technical, scientific issues in the first instance in Administrative Review panels. This may be followed by review of decisions against principles of administrative due process in administrative courts. The goal of the process is to ensure a level of technical expertise in tribunal reviews before ruling on broader principles of administrative law in the general courts. However, concerns have been expressed about the quality of review processes, while administrative panels and courts have been constrained by a lack of understanding by judges of the science of ecological change and principles of administrative due process (Pring and Pring, 2009, p. xi).

The administrative tribunal and court system launched in 1989 was meant to bring greater access to justice in environmental and other cases, as a check on the abuse of power by local government and the private sector. A key challenge has been the lack of independence of review panels from the government agencies hosting them and a lack of technical expertise on environment issues in tribunals and courts, resulting in a gradual decrease in credibility and trust by the public. Owing to these perceptions, Administrative Review panel caseloads have declined nationally over the years (Cheung, 2002, pp. 1–2).

As a result of these trends, a parallel and new system of specialized environmental tribunals and courts has emerged across China in recent years. Environment tribunals and courts have been increasingly recognized around the world in recent years for their potential in promoting and enforcing environmental rights. Their value lies in their higher levels of expertise, increased public confidence in them, and increased speed in reviewing cases (Pring, 2009, p. xi). Over 350 specialized environmental courts and tribunals have been established in 41 countries (ibid., p. v). The benefits of specialized environmental tribunals include the following (Lin et al, 2009, pp. 9–10):

(i) creating a comprehensive, integrated jurisdiction that deals with a range of environmental matters – a "one-stop shop" for merit appeals, judicial reviews, and criminal and civil enforcement;
(ii) providing a forum for experts in environmental law where they can engage in a free and beneficial exchange of ideas and information;
(iii) enabling the formation of panels of officers with expertise for the purpose of interdisciplinary decision making;
(iv) facilitating the development of specialized knowledge of environmental law and issues;
(v) allowing the adoption of a holistic approach to the resolution of environmental matters, through comprehensive jurisdictions and interdisciplinary decision making;
(vi) furthering the use of innovative practices and procedures, such as public interest litigation, to broaden access to justice;
(vii) encouraging innovative solutions to environmental problems;
(viii) fostering the growth of a coherent and consistent body of environmental precedents and jurisprudence;
(ix) making possible the quick progress of complex environmental cases, thereby boosting the efficiency and reducing the cost of litigation;
(x) relieving other courts of some of their backlogs by taking over cases involving environmental issues and resolving them more efficiently; and
(xi) appealing to the conscience of the public, thereby encouraging adherence to environmental laws and greater participation in programs to protect the environment.

China has made progress in this regard. Following an initial pilot in 1989, a Trial Court of Environmental Protection in Wuhan City, Hubei Province and a further eleven local environmental courts and tribunals were established across China in the period 2002–08 (Lin et al, 2009, p. 14).

- Environmental Protection Tribunal of People's Court of Dongling, Shenyang City, Liaoning Province, 2002
- Circuit Court of Environmental Protection, Shahekou, Dalian City, Liaoning Province, 2004
- Environmental Protection Court of the City of Jinzhou, Shijiazhuang City, Hebei Province, 2004
- Environmental Protection Court of the People's Court of Tiexi, Shenyang City, Liaoning Province, 2006
- Circuit Court of Environmental Protection of Shiping, Liaocheng City, Shandong Province, 2006
- Environmental Protection Trial Court of Intermediate People's Court of Guiyang City, Guizhou Province, 2007
- Environmental Protection Court of the People's Court of Qingzhen, Guiyang City, Guizhou Province, 2007
- Circuit Court of Environmental Protection of Jianye, Nanjing City, Jiangsu Province, 2008
- Environmental Protection Tribunal of Intermediate People's Court of Wuxi City, Jiangsu Province, 2008
- Circuit Court of Environmental Protection of Xinbei, Changzhou City, Jiangsu Province, 2008
- Trial Division of Environmental Protection and Environmental Panels of Intermediate People's Courts of Kunming and Yuxi Cities, Yunnan Province, 2008

Furthermore, according to some reports there has been an escalation of these trends since 2008, with a total of 47 environmental courts and tribunals in place by 2010 (Enlaw, 2010). The surge of local environmental courts and tribunals in recent years has been triggered by increased social mobilization against local government policies and industrial pollution along China's industrial beltway in the east, and increased reference by the State and citizens to the rule of law and environmental rights.

Issues of water pollution and human health are topics of particular concern driving citizen activism through the new tribunals and courts, particularly in industrial pollution hotspots in the east. This followed the landmark environmental disaster in Harbin in 2005 and increased attention to issues of water security and environmental health in the years that followed. For example, the two environmental courts in Guizhou Province were launched in late 2007 to address toxic pollution in Hongfeng Lake, Baihua Lake, and Aha Reservoir, a main source of drinking water for four million people in Guiyang City (Gao, 2009, pp. 3–5).

The three environmental courts in Jiangsu Province launched in 2008 were also in response to water pollution and health risks, following the massive blue algae incident in Taihu Lake in 2007. As in Guizhou and Jiangsu, the establishment of environmental courts in Yunnan was also driven by toxic pollution and health risks, after Yangzong Lake experienced high arsenic levels (ibid.). Because Yunnan is a sub-tropical zone hosting high levels of biodiversity, and a hub of the national green movement, the innovation of environmental tribunals and courts has had traction beyond the initial pilot. Six more environmental tribunals and courts were announced in late 2009 to be set up in coming years.

In addition to the tribunals and courts themselves, the movement towards greater recognition of environmental rights has also led to innovative forms of environmental claims, tailored in a sense to China's strong sense of community rights and social justice. July 2009 was a historical moment for environment rights in China, with the All China Environment Federation (AFED) filing China's first-ever Public Interest Litigation (PIL) environmental cases in the Wuxi Environmental Court and the Qingzhen Environmental Court (ibid.). PIL is a legal mechanism used around the world, whereby a group of citizens claims redress based on a violation of public interests. This has been an important trend in the area of the environment, given that environmental cases involve broad public risks from ecological change and toxic pollution.

In the Wuxi Environmental Court, AFED was successful in settling its pollution case against the Jiangyin Port Container Company, while in Qingzhen Environmental Court, AFED was successful in its claim based upon fifteen years of administrative inaction by the local Bureau of Land and Resources on an environmental issue. The local government was forced as a result of the process to take the requested action (Gao, 2009, p. 6).

The process of establishing environmental courts and tribunals across China has also been an experiment in jurisdiction. Courts in Guiyang, Qingzhen, Wuxi and Yunnan have all taken an integrated approach by including civil, criminal and administrative jurisdiction in the new environmental courts and tribunals. This is distinct from the historic and formal practice in China whereby administrative cases are channeled through the administrative tribunals and courts, civil cases through the civil courts and criminal cases through the criminal courts. Thus environmental cases are driving not just innovation in the use of specialized judicial systems in China but also using the environment courts and tribunals as a channel for a broader shift towards environmental rights and justice (Gao, 2009, pp. 1–2).

4.3.2 Environmental Justice in Western China

Environmental justice is defined here as the mitigation and adaptation of State policies that have a disproportionate environmental impact on a distinct group within society, in terms of pollution effects or exclusion from the benefits of natural resource use. This is regardless of whether this distinction is based on general socio-economic status, ethnic or religious difference, and whether the impact is intentional or not. It includes, but goes beyond, the role of judicial remedies aimed at increased citizen access to justice and via judicial mechanisms. It addresses the role of State policy in preventing and mitigating disproportionate impacts on a distinct group within society, and its complicity in producing them.

In China environmental justice reflects two foundational principles of the State noted in the 1982 Constitution – equal protection under the law, and the duty of the State to ensure rational use of natural resources for the public good. Environmental justice has emerged as an important aspect of the socio-political fabric of China. While China is a unitary rather than a federal State, given China's massive geographic scale and the inherent geopolitical challenges, issues of inter-regional balance and equity have been central to China's constitutional order and its development strategies.

Such issues have risen in priority in recent years as demand for natural resources has risen dramatically, along with resource scarcity. Most of China's remaining natural resources are in western regions inhabited by communities who have historically faced exclusion from the benefits of development. China has been experiencing a surge in demand for oil, gas, minerals and timber. Investments in western China can support social development for local communities, but can also spur inequity and ecological devastation if preventive actions are not taken (Haufler, 2002). The pursuit of expansive western development may drive some to rebel against mainstream development in the absence of effective benefits-sharing mechanisms or channels for local traditions and a voice in decision-making.

Communities whose wealth is overly dependent on the export of natural resources are more prone to conflict than those that have a broader growth base (Collier and Hoeffler, 2000, p. 25). The dynamics of a "resource curse" can occur within countries as well as between countries, with resource-rich provinces often suffering from exclusion and inequity, while distant affluent regions enjoy the benefits of resource use.

4.3.2.1 The western development strategy

Of particular importance to environmental justice claims in China are its "Go West" development policies aimed at connecting "less-developed" minority regions to the benefits of rapid industrialization in the east. This includes the western migration of commerce and industry (often highly polluting), along with the surge of new foreign and national investments into the west, particularly in autonomous regions such as Tibet and Xinjiang. Xinjiang is host to 60% of China's coal reserves, along with a significant share of its oil and gas reserves, which are critical to energizing China's development, while Tibet hosts the source waters of the Yangtze and Yellow Rivers and holds vast copper and minerals reserves.

In 2000, the State Council issued China's Western Development Strategy to support the achievement of a set of development goals by the year 2015. This was in line with China's national "Xiaokang" 2020 Goals for a "Well-Off, Balanced Society". Western China covers nine provinces and autonomous regions, and dozens of municipalities, covering 60% of China, with a population of over 370 million (25% of the national total). The region is increasingly vital to continuing national growth, hosting 80% of China's total water supplies, 50% of China's mineral reserves, and the majority of China's coal and natural gas reserves (State Council of China, 2000).

In Tibet, the Chinese Geological Survey conducted the first-ever large-scale survey of the minerals of the Tibetan Plateau, spanning the autonomous region of Tibet and neighboring Qinghai Province. According to national media reports, the results published in 2007 showed vast metal reserves, identifying 600 potential sites for new mines, with estimated reserves of 30–40 million tons of copper, 40 million tons of lead and zinc and several billion tons of iron ore (*China Daily*, 2007).

Given the risks to local communities, the Geological Survey report also called for the "gradual development of mining in the region", warning that rapid exploitation could "permanently damage the plateau's fragile ecosystem" (ibid.). It called for natural restoration plans as a precondition of industrial development. Owing to their rich natural resources and a surge in investments and commerce under the Western Development Strategy, the autonomous regions of Tibet and Xinjiang are experiencing increasing demands for autonomy, access and benefit-sharing related to new extractive sector investments, and measures to prevent pollution impacts from rapid migration of industry.

Phase 1 of the Western Development Strategy (2000–05) was focused on developing basic infrastructure as a base for commercial and industrial investments in subsequent phases. According to reports, during this period the government invested RMB 1 trillion (approximately US$125 billion) in over sixty projects in transport, water, energy and telecommunications (Xinhua News, 2006a). During this period the west reported an annual average GDP growth rate of over 10%. The region's combined GDP reached RMB 3.33 trillion (US$416.25 billion) by 2006, more than double the RMB 1.66 trillion level at the start of the strategy in 2000. Fixed asset investment grew by 23% annually and local revenue grew by an average of 15.5% (ibid.).

In Tibet, during Phase 1 of the Western Development Strategy (2000–05) the region generated fiscal revenue of RMB 5.25 billion (about US$656 million) and inward investment of RMB 72 billion (about US$9 billion) (*Xinhua News*, 2006b). This included investments in over one hundred infrastructure projects, including the now famous Qinghai-Tibet Railway, the world's highest railway and a major channel for new east-west commerce and movement of commodities eastward.

Based on improved infrastructure, Phase 2 of the Western Development Strategy (2005–15) has focused on increasing financial investment as a base for developing commercial and industrial activities (State Council of China, 2000, p. 5). Phase 3 (2015–50) will see a consolidation of local industrial growth trends and increasing synergy with national development trends by mid-century.

In Tibet, several activities planned for Phase 2 of the Western Development Strategy could be vulnerable to social and environmental risks and could exacerbate these. Climate change is a case in point. Over the next decade, geological hazards in Tibet and other mountain areas of Western China are expected to increase, owing to glacial melting. If current trends continue, water tables will fall, springs and streams will dry up and rivers will have reduced flows. Flooding, debris flow and landslides may threaten new cities and industry. Lack of integration of such risks into development policies will undermine local ecology and society, and threaten the sustainability of any development gains.

The Western Development Strategy calls for the mainstreaming of social and environmental sustainability into development and investment activities (ibid., p. 10). This also reflects cultural norms. In Western China concerns over ecological balance align with local traditions. For example Tibet's sacred text, the Sutta Nipata, argues that since humanity is far more powerful than other species, we have special responsibilities to the environment – a duty to protect the environment – linked to this asymmetry of influence.

4.3.2.2 Unequal protection

There is a strong sense in western China that development policies and the enforcement of law are skewed towards the protection of national over local interests and the protection of corporate interests over citizen rights. Many see the process of development as an affront to the Constitutional principle of equal protection and the goals of equity and harmonious development at the center of the socialist market economy paradigm. Development in western China has often been characterized by observers as the pursuit by the State of a "civilizing mission" to bring the region from a traditional past to the modernist order of scientific development. Central to this has been the efficient exploitation of natural resources and the prioritization of national unitary principles over cultural or legal pluralism. This took shape during the Cultural Revolution (1966–76) with its slogans that "Man Must Conquer Nature" and "Battling with Nature is Boundless Joy".

While the 1982 Constitution calls for equal protection of all citizens under the law, this vision has faced internal contradictions, with issues of environmental justice now standing at the center of the debate. As resource development and industry escalate under the Western Development Strategy, there is a risk that the environment will continue to be seen by local officials and the private sector as being in a "state of nature", "a domain of utility, to be mastered and brought under man's control, compelled to satisfy his needs and administer his happiness". This in many ways remains the "anthropology" of the modernist scientific development paradigm, with alternative visions of human development and nature often seen as primitive, traditional and underdeveloped.

A new social contract between east and west would see a shift in State policy and development principles in line with the vision of an ecological civilization based on goals of environmental justice and equitable access and benefit sharing from local resources. This is more than an academic concern. Given the increasing dependence of China's national economy on the critical energy, water and mineral resources of the west, the achievement of such a policy shift could determine the sustainability of China's hard-won development, the ecological sustainability of the fragile west and the prevention of "resource curse" dynamics.

More inclusive forms of governance would see local communities become part of decision-making processes in a way that accounts for local customs and culture, local benefits from resource development, and local access to remedy from environmental impacts. In this regard, the expansion of systems for citizen rights, such as the expansion of environmental courts and tribunals into places like Tibet and Xinjiang, can serve as an important channel for grievances against local government and private interests. They could become an important mechanism for achieving goals of environmental justice and equal protection under the law, engaging both national principles and local traditions regarding environmental protection and social equity.

4.4 CONCLUSION: SUSTAINABLE DEVELOPMENT AS FREEDOM

As China forges ahead towards becoming the world's largest economy in the coming decades, it faces challenges in maintaining social security and environmental sustainability. Declining environmental quality and natural resource scarcity are causing concern for the sustainability of China's development.

This chapter has argued that the process of ecological change has become a key driver of change in Chinese society, triggering a review of foundational principles of development and the State, and increasing demands for the rule of law and principles of equal protection as means of achieving sustainable development. The new ecological civilization principle enunciated by the National People's Congress is a step in this process. It is a call to rethink the "modernist" paradigms that have been the foundation of Chinese progress over the past decades, and instead engage traditional perspectives on the balance between humans and nature with a view to crafting a new paradigm of progress for the future.

Ecosystem services are increasingly recognized by citizens as being public goods central to achieving human development and the socio-economic rights enshrined in China's 1982 Constitution. Recent years have seen a rise in environmental consciousness, with issues seen through the lens of human rights and the rule of law, with citizen demands for a check on the increasing power of local government and the private sector. The State is adapting to this process through legal systems to engage rights-based approaches to deal with conflicts within society – vertical conflicts between State and citizens over the impacts of toxic pollution on basic health and welfare, and horizontal conflicts between regions over access to and benefits from natural resource development.

Landmark developments have included the passage of an environmental rights component in the 2009 National Human Rights Action Plan, China's first, along with the enactment in recent years of new policies and regulations providing access to information, participation and remedy in environmental matters. A major development in recent years has been the expansion of environmental courts and tribunals across the country, new channels of citizen grievances against the State and opportunities for achieving justice. Equally important have been calls for environmental justice in western China, as the expansion of extractive industry westward poses risks to social and ecological security. Claims of environmental justice in places like Tibet and Xinjiang are increasingly based on constitutional principles of equal protection and the rational use of natural resources for the public good, often in opposition to the practices of local government and corporate power. Attempts at more equitable access to and benefits from local resource development will be critical in preventing resource curse dynamics, the outbreak of conflict over access to resources, and maintaining social and ecological security.

As China approaches twenty years since the launch of its socialist market economy policy, environmental sustainability has moved to the center of development discourse driving political debate on ways to re-calibrate social welfare and market-led growth, principles of progress and the role of the State towards sustaining China's hard-won development results for future generations. As noted in the classic *Development as Freedom* by Amartya Sen, solutions to these problems of "inequality (especially that of grinding poverty in a world of unprecedented prosperity) and of public goods (that is, goods people share together, such as the environment) will almost certainly call for institutions that take us beyond the capitalist market economy" (Sen, 1999, p. 267).

The adaptation and continued evolution of China's basic concepts of development and progress, its socialist market economy policy, and its State policies and legal systems will be a critical task for the future, upholding a future based on citizen rights, equality and the sustainable use of natural resources.

As a new center of creativity and change in the global political economy, the evolution of new policies and systems in China will also provide inspiration to other countries as they seek new models of environmental governance. The evolution of governance in China has been characterized by an approach of moving gradually, summarized by the old Chinese saying, "crossing the river by feeling for stones". As China moves forward, the world will watch with great interest, analyzing the emerging lessons from the evolution of environmental governance in China's socialist market economy.

NOTE

1. Kishan Khoday has served with the United Nations Development Programme since 1997 in Indonesia, China and currently Saudi Arabia. The views and opinions expressed herein are solely those of the author and in no way represent the views of the United Nations, UNDP or its member states.

REFERENCES

Angresano, J. (2005), 'The Development of the Chinese Economy: Success through Avoiding Orthodox Economic Advice', *Journal of Socioeconomics*, 34(4) (Chicago University Press).

Argyrou, V. (2005), *The Logic of Environmentalism: Anthropology, Ecology and Postcoloniality* (Berghahn Books).

Chen J., Y. Li and J.M. Otto (eds.) (2002), *Implementation of Law in the People's Republic of China* (Kluwer International Press).

Cheung, A. (2002), 'Working Paper Series – Administrative Litigation in the PRC: The First Ten Years of Implementation' (City University of Hong Kong).

China Daily (2007), 'Metal Reserves Found on the Roof of World', *China Daily, Beijing* (13 February).

Collier, P. and A. Hoeffler (2000), *Economic Causes of Civil Conflict & Implications for Policy* (World Bank).

Dasgupta, P. (2001), *Human Well-Being and the Natural Environment* (Oxford University Press).

Diamant, N.J., S.B. Lubman and K.J. O'Brien (eds.) (2005), *Engaging the Law in China* (Stanford University Press).

Dobson, A. and D. Bell (eds.) (2006), *Environmental Citizenship* (MIT Press).

Drezner, D. (2007), 'The New New World Order', *Foreign Affairs*, March/April edition (Council on Foreign Relations).

Enlaw (2010), 'Environmental Courts and Tribunals in China', <http://enlaw.znufe.edu.cn/bmgl/wrfz/201006/t20100630_22093.htm>.

Fitzpatrick, P. (2000), *The Mythology of Modern Law* (Routledge).

Gao, J. (2009), *Environmental Public Interest Litigation and the Vitality of Environmental Courts: The Development and Future of Environmental Courts in China* (NRDC Beijing).

Hart-Landsberg, M. and P. Burkett (2005), *China and Socialism: Market Reforms and Class Struggles* (Monthly Review Press).

Haufler, V. (2002), *Case Studies of Multi-stakeholder Partnerships: Policy Dialogue on Business in Zones of Conflict* (UN Global Compact).

Heinberg, R. (2007), *Peak Everything: Waking up to Centuries of Decline* (New Society Publishers).

Homer-Dixon, T. (2009) 'The Newest Science', *Alternatives Journal*, 35(4) (University of Waterloo Press).

Lin, T., C. Wang, Y. Chen, T. Canacho and F. Lin (2009), *Green Benches: What can the People's Republic of China Learn from Environment Courts of other Countries?* (Asian Development Bank).

Ma, J. and T. Ortolano (eds.) (2000), *Environmental Regulation in China* (Rowman & Littlefield).

Narain, S. (2006), 'Foreword', in L. Starke (ed.), *State of the World 2006: The Challenge of Global Sustainability* (Earthscan).

Pring, G. and C. Pring (2009), *Greening Justice: Creating and Improving Environmental Courts and Tribunals* (World Resource Institute).

Sen, A. (1999), *Development as Freedom* (Random House).

Starke L. (eds.) (2006), *State of the World 2006: The Challenge of Global Sustainability* (Earthscan).

State Council of China (2000), *Development Strategy of Western China* (PRC).

State Council of China (2005), *White Paper on Democratic Governance* (PRC).

State Council of China (2010), *Twelfth Five Year Development Plan (2010–2015)* (PRC).

Tennyson, R. and L. Wilde (2000) *The Guiding Hand – Brokering partnerships for sustainable development* (UN Publications).

UNDP (2002a), *Trade & Development: Part 1 Trade and Human Development*, (Palgrave Macmillan).

UNDP (2002b), *China Human Development Report 2002: Making Green Development a Choice* (Oxford University Press).

UNDP (2007), *Human Development Report: Fighting Climate Change – Human Solidarity in a Divided World* (Palgrave Macmillan).

UNDP (2009), *China Human Development Report 2009: Towards a Low-Carbon Society and Economy* (Chinese Academy of Social Science (CASS)).

UNEP (1973), *Declaration on the Human Environment* (UNEP).

UNEP (2010), *Statement on 3 June 2010 by Achim Steiner, UNEP Executive Director, at the Launch of Report on Assessing the Environmental Impacts of Consumption and Production* (UNEP).

UNESCAP (2004), *Export Diversification and Economic Growth: The Experience of Selected Least Developed Countries*, UN Development Papers No. 24 (UNESCAP).

WEF (2006), *World Economic Forum China Summit,* <http://www.weforum.org/site/homepublic.nsf/Content/China+Business+Summit+2006>.

Weller, R. (2006), *Discovering Nature: Globalization and Environmental Culture in China and Taiwan* (Cambridge University Press).

Xinhua News (2006a), 'Western China Development Strategy Bears Fruit' (31 August 2006), *Xinhua News* (Xinhua).

Xinhua News (2006b), 'State Aid Promotes Tibet's Development' (14 April 2006), *Xinhua News* (Xinhua).

Zadek, S., N. Hojensgard and P. Rayhard (eds.) (2001) *Perspectives on the New Economy of Corporate Citizenship* (Copenhagen Centre).

Zheng, Y. (2004), *Globalization and State Transformation in China* (Cambridge University Press).

5. Toward a more effective environmental criminal law in China[1]

Michael G. Faure and Hao Zhang[2]

5.1 INTRODUCTION

There is increasing attention to the role of environmental law in promoting sustainable development and effective environmental governance in China, but so far less has been published (at least in English) on the effectiveness of various enforcement mechanisms that could be used to support material environmental law. The goal of our chapter is to identify how public sanctioning systems (mostly criminal law, but to some extent also administrative law) might be employed in an effective way to induce compliance with environmental legislation. To answer that question and hence to address to what extent criminal and administrative law are able to perform a crucial role in the protection of the environment in China, we will first of all try to explain the structure of environmental criminal law in China (Richter, 2002, p. 78). A difficulty in describing environmental criminal law in China is that the norms can be found in a variety of documents with different legal status, like the Criminal Law, subsidiary criminal law and environmental statutes. Altogether, these provide a wide range of crimes, the formulation of which is in some cases not very precise and clear.

After a description of environmental criminal law in China, the question arises to what extent environmental criminal law in China can be considered as effective. In order to answer that question, we will use recent literature which has argued that an ideal environmental criminal law should make use of a combination of provisions in order to let environmental criminal law play its crucial role in environmental governance (Faure and Visser, 1995, p. 316; Mandiberg and Faure, 2009, p. 447). This literature holds that a combination of provisions is necessary such that a violation of administrative norms should be punished, but also unlawful emissions (concrete endangerment of the environment) as well as serious pollution. The question of course arises as to what extent Chinese environmental criminal law corresponds with this ideal model. Environmental criminal law has been critically reviewed in legal doctrine in China. Hence we will also take into account criticisms formulated in Chinese legal doctrine to evaluate the effectiveness of the protection offered by the criminal law to the environment in China.

Of course, we do realize that an important limitation of our chapter is that we merely review the structure of environmental criminal law as it appears from the texts and hence do not address the actual enforcement of criminal law in China. Enforcement is undoubtedly crucial to guarantee the effectiveness of environmental law (Gunningham and Grabosky, 1998, p. 26). However, it would be wrong merely to focus attention on enforcement and not to address material environmental criminal law at all. It may be true that without enforcement material environmental criminal law will remain a dead letter. But the reverse is true to some extent as well: enforcement may be pointless if the provisions that have to be enforced are simply not able to provide adequate protection to the environment. Hence, within the scope of this chapter, we examine to what extent, at least on paper, environmental criminal law provisions can provide adequate protection of the environment. The enforcement of those provisions in legal practice may be an important point for further research.

Our contribution is structured as follows: after this introduction we first provide a description of environmental criminal law in China (Section 5.2). A critical analysis follows (5.3). Based on this critical evaluation, we will formulate a few obvious suggestions for reform (5.4) as well as a few concluding remarks (5.5).

5.2 ENVIRONMENTAL CRIMINAL LAW IN CHINA

5.2.1 Main Structure and Sources of Environmental Criminal Law in China

As is well known, the dramatic economic development of China has had a severe impact on the environment during the past thirty years. Many consider the application of the relevant environmental laws and regulations as inadequate to deal with the huge environmental problems China is facing. This inadequacy may to a large extent also apply to environmental criminal law. The main problem recognized in legal doctrine in China is that the formulation of the legal texts is running far behind the social needs of China as far as adequate protection of the environment through the criminal law is concerned[3] (Xu and Zhang, 2010, p. 147; Jiang, 2008, p. 84; Wang and An, 2008; Wang, 1996, p. 148).

The norms of environmental criminal law can mainly be found in the Criminal Law of 1997, in subsidiary criminal law and in separate criminal law.[4] In other words, China's current environmental criminal law is the sum of the relevant legal norms concerning the protection of the ecosystem (including the environment and resources) in the Criminal Law (Criminal Law, 1997) and subsidiary criminal law (Richter, 2008, p. 262; Wang, 2004, p. 150; Richter, 2002, p. 78; Yang, 1995, p. 671). The provisions of the Criminal Law expressly stipulate environmental crimes and specific penalties, while the subsidiary environmental criminal law has different forms, whereby they often refer to the provisions of the Criminal Law. The integration of these two main parts constitutes China's environmental criminal law. All of these norms are supposed to play the role of protecting the environment and resources, which is the essence of environmental criminal law in China (Wang, 2004, p. 157).

China adopted the way of penalizing the environmental crimes in the Criminal Law, while not situating the sanctions elsewhere in other regulations. The largest number of provisions on crimes against the environment exists in the Criminal Law of 1997. The Criminal Law of 1997 is essentially a major amendment to the Criminal Law of 1979. The Criminal Law of 1997 contains the main structure of environmental criminal law. The crimes of 'impairing the protection of environment and resources' can be found in section 6 of chapter 6 which is devoted to crimes related to the obstruction of the administration of public order (Richter, 2006, p. 69). The section on crimes of obstructing the administration of public order has the biggest concentration of articles concerning environmental crimes. Other provisions sporadically appear in section 5 on 'crimes against public health' of chapter 6, section 2 concerning 'crimes of smuggling' of chapter 3 'crimes against the socialist market economic order' and chapter 9 of 'crimes of dereliction of duty', with a total of 15 articles of 25 charges, which constitute the main part of environmental criminal law.

The subsidiary environmental criminal law in China can mainly be found in the provisions of the laws and regulations on the environmental and resources protection, such as the Environmental Protection Law and Law on Prevention and Control of Noise Pollution. It consists of a total of 72 laws and regulations.

This combination of environmental criminal law in the Criminal Law and subsidiary environmental criminal law is typical of environmental criminal law in China and also reflects the combination of administrative and criminal law in the fight against environmental offenses.

5.2.2 Environmental Criminal Law

5.2.2.1 General

The provision concerning environmental crimes along with the penalties applicable can all be found in the Criminal Law. As mentioned above, the provisions of subsidiary environmental criminal law make no specific provision in terms of criminal charge, punishment and range of penalty. Therefore the relevant provisions of the Criminal Law constitute the basic framework of environmental criminal law in China.

Chinese criminal law follows the traditional socialist legal theory even though it has been the object of major amendments since 1997. The legal theory of Chinese law requires at least four elements for a crime: a subject, an object, a subjective aspect and an objective aspect (Zhang, 1997, p. 96). These elements are reflected in the formulation of the specific articles. This often leads, as we will show below, to very complex conditions that have to be fulfilled concerning the circumstances in which the environmental crimes have been committed. These conditions may seriously limit the possibilities for these articles to be applied in practice.

As mentioned above, the environmental provisions of the Criminal Law have the largest number of articles. All 25 environmental crimes in the Criminal Law have been listed in an overview provided in note 3.[5]

An examination of the current articles concerning environmental crimes in the Criminal Law reveals a surprising number of articles and a wide variety of aspects covered. As the Chinese Criminal Law divides the chapters on the basis of the social interest protected, most articles included in section 6 on 'crimes of impairing the protection of the environment and resources' are allocated under chapter 6 on 'crimes of obstructing the administration of public order'. This shows that environmental criminal law in China aims to protect the administration of public order instead of focusing on the protection of the environment directly. Most of the articles deal with crimes with respect to the protection of nature and wild life, the so-called 'crime of impairing resources'. Very few are crimes directly penalizing pollution (Wang and An, 2008, p. 148; Richter, 2006, p. 69).

5.2.2.2 Categorization of criminal environmental norms in Criminal Law of 1997

Based on the analysis of current criminal environmental articles, one can notice that the scope of the 15 articles is relatively broad, covering different aspects of damage to the environment and resources. According to Chinese legal theory, the crime's subjective condition should be either intent or negligence, the criminal subject could be either an entity or the common individual and the crime itself could be either behavioral, consequential or circumstantial. We will now follow this categorization and provide an example from each category to show to what extent these provisions can be applied in order to provide adequate protection for the environment.

Behavioral crimes So-called behavioral crime concerns anyone who performs the criminal behavior regulated by the provisions of *Criminal Law*. The following provisions fall under this category:

- Crime of smuggling rare animals and rare animal products (chapter 2, art 151, para 2);
- Crime of smuggling rare plants and rare plant products (chapter 3, art 151, para 3);
- Crime of smuggling waste (chapter 6, art 339, para 3);
- Crime of illegal disposal of imported solid waste (chapter 6, art 339, para 1);
- Crime of illegal logging and the destruction of valuable trees (chapter 6, art 344);
- Crime of practicing favoritism and committing irregularities in quarantine of animal and plant (chapter 9, art 413, para 1).

A feature of this behavioral crime is that as long as the subject performs the behavior stipulated in the specific provisions, the crime is considered as completed. The specific conduct is considered to endanger a protected interest, including both concrete and abstract endangerments (Jiang, 1994, p. 115; Chen, 1992, p. 214; Gao, 1989, p. 160; Liang, 1987, p. 160). However, it is not necessary that any harmful result or consequence should be proven. The punishment is targeted at the behavior and no causality is required by law.

In principle an imprisonment and a criminal fine can be imposed, although the conditions for the application of the sanction are not always very clearly formulated. We may refer to paragraph 3 of article 339 as an example of the explanation of the crime of smuggling waste. Article 339 stipulates that:

> Whoever, in violation of the regulations of the State, has solid waste from abroad dumped, piled up, or treated within the territory of China shall be sentenced to fixed-term imprisonment of not more than five years or criminal detention and shall also be fined … if the consequences are especially serious, he shall be sentenced to fixed-term imprisonment of not less than ten years and shall also be fined.
>
> Whoever, under the pretext of using it as raw material, imports solid waste that cannot be used as such shall be convicted and punished in accordance with the provisions of Article 155 of this Law.

The formulation itself is problematic as the definition of 'especially serious' is not further defined in the Criminal Law, even though this can result in not less than ten years' imprisonment and a criminal fine can be applied. It is very unlikely that a prosecutor could prove that a situation is 'especially serious' and therefore, it is difficult to apply an upper range sentence.[6] Another aspect is that behavior may only be punished if 'in violation of the regulations of the State', which demonstrates that the article is dependent on administrative regulations.

Consequential crime To constitute a criminal offense, a particular result is requested by the law. It includes the following charges and articles:

- Crime of breaching the quarantine of animal and plant (chapter 6, art 337);
- Crime of major pollution incident (chapter 6, art 338);
- Crime of unauthorized imports of solid waste (chapter 6, art 339, para 2);
- Crime of illegal occupation of arable land (chapter 6, art 342);
- Crime of illegal mining (chapter 6, art 343, para 1);
- Crime of destructive mining (chapter 6, art 343, para 2);
- Crime of illegally chopping down trees (chapter 6, art 345, para 1);
- Crime of illegal denudation (chapter 6, art 345, para 2);
- Crime of neglect of duty concerning environmental monitoring (chapter 9, art 408);
- Crime of neglect of duty concerning quarantine plant and animal (chapter 9, art 413, para 2).

Article 338 in chapter 6 details the crime of a major pollution. This article stipulates that:

> Whoever, in violation of the regulations of the State, discharges, dumps or treats radioactive waste, waste containing pathogen of infectious diseases, toxic substances or other hazardous waste on the land or in the water bodies or the atmosphere, thus causing a major environmental pollution accident which leads to the serious consequences of heavy losses of public or private property or human casualties, shall be sentenced to fixed-term imprisonment of not more than three years or criminal detention and shall also, or shall only, be fined; if the consequences are especially serious, he shall be sentenced to fixed-term imprisonment of not less than three years but not more than seven years and shall also be fined.

It's not surprising that the number of articles under this category is almost twice as high as the number of behavioral crimes. The current Criminal Law has a large number of articles which require that a particular result has to be achieved in order for the conditions of criminal liability to be fulfilled (Zhang and Cao, 2004, p. 33).

A second aspect worth focusing on is that most articles in this category have a strong dependence on administrative law, as mentioned above. As a consequence, there is usually criminal liability only if the offender has violated administrative rules.

The penalty under article 338 is another aspect which has been criticized by Chinese lawyers (Jiang, 2008, p. 83; Xu, 2007, p. 149; Li, 2005, p. 36). The sanction provided for in this article is 'imprisonment or criminal detention of not more than three years and/or a fine'. It is striking that this sanction is lower than sanctions for similar offenses against property. Article 345 in this category concerning the crime of illegally chopping down trees specifies the penalty of at most seven years for the serious circumstance, while someone guilty of the similar crime of theft in article 262 could be sentenced to more than ten years and could either be fined or have his or her property confiscated. These differences reflect the reality that current environmental criminal legislation in China emphasizes much more the economic benefits of natural resources and the environment. There is little concern for direct protection of the environment as such (He, 2005, p. 96). Indeed, article 345 of the Criminal Law provides a severe sanction for the illegal chopping down of trees for the simple reason that this activity may endanger forestry activities. Comparing this to article 338 of the Criminal Law, which punishes the causing of a major environmental pollution incident with a maximum of three years' imprisonment, one realizes that Chinese Criminal Law provides better protection to economic interests than to environmental ones.

Circumstantial crimes The third category under this classification is circumstantial crime. In this case the constitution of a crime requires the presence of certain circumstances regulated by law. The legal circumstances in the provisions vary from each other and may include different patterns of behavior, serious results, or the amount of the illegal gain. This category includes the following provisions:

- Crime of illegal transferring the land use rights (chapter 3, art 228);
- Crime of illegal fishing of aquatic products (chapter 6, para 340);
- Crime of killing rare and endangered wildlife (chapter 6, art 341, para 1);
- Crime of illegal acquisition, transport, sale of precious and endangered species of wild animals and their products (chapter 6, art 341, para 1);
- Crime of illegal issuing of tree cutting licenses (chapter 9, art 407);
- Crime of illegal approval of requisition and occupation of land (chapter 9, art 410);
- Crime of illegal sale of use rights of state-owned land at a low price (chapter 9, art 410)

Article 340 provides an example. The article reads:

> Whoever, in violation of the law or regulations on protection of aquatic resources, catches aquatic products in an area or during a season closed to fishing, or uses prohibited fishing gear or methods for the purpose, if the circumstances are serious, shall be sentenced to fixed-term imprisonment of not more than three years, criminal detention or public surveillance or be fined.

The circumstantial crimes mentioned here in the Criminal Law of 1997 all belong to the category of aggravated consequence crimes, which contains a formulation along the lines of 'if the circumstances are serious/especially serious'. As long as serious results are required, the causal relationship between the aggravated consequence and the illegal action has to be proved during the public prosecution. This therefore makes these provisions very hard to apply. The articles here suffer from the same problem as the consequential crimes mentioned above.

Mens rea The Chinese theory on criminal offenses holds that any crime must have a subjective fault (Wu, 2008, p. 1). From the perspective of the state of mind of the criminal, the crimes can be divided into those requiring merely negligence and those requiring intent. The current Criminal Law does not clearly express whether a crime requires negligence or intent and there is still no consensus among Chinese lawyers regarding the required *mens rea*. The categorization here draws on the general theory which has most support in China on this issue and categorizes environmental crimes into two categories: the intentional destruction of the environment and resources on the one hand and environmental crimes caused by negligence on the other hand (Xu, 2007, p. 39).

Environmental crimes are more complex than traditional ones. From a practical point of view, to prove the subjective fault of the offender can be very difficult. So-called intentional crimes to the environment and resources refer to the subjective state of mind whereby someone has acted knowingly, or knows that his/her action would cause harm to society in violation of relevant laws and regulations. This concerns a large number of criminal provisions.[7]

To be very clear: the words intent or negligence are usually not used in the text of the legislative provisions. Whether a particular crime is therefore considered as an intentional one or one requiring merely negligence is determined by legal doctrine and case law. In some cases, however, it is clear that a crime is an intentional one, based on the formulation used in the legislation. An example is the crime of illegal acquisition of timber through illegal logging and deforestation.[8] The formulation reads:

> Those who, in order to make a profit, illegally and intentionally purchase timber from illegal or wanton logging in a serious manner are to be sentenced to less than three years of fixed-term imprisonment or criminal detention or control and, in addition, be sentenced to a fine. They may also be punished by a simple fine. In especially serious cases, those law offenders are to be sentenced to not less than three years and not more than seven years of fixed-term imprisonment and, in addition, be sentenced to a fine.

This is one of the few cases where the legislator clearly requires intent. In all other cases it is not the legislative provision itself that requires the intent, but the interpretation of the provision by legal doctrine and case law.

For example article 341, paragraph 2 of the Criminal Law concerning the crime of illegal hunting is considered to be a crime of intentional environmental harm even though the word 'intent' does not appear in the provision itself. The provision reads:

> Whoever, in violation of the law or regulations on hunting, hunts wildlife in an area or during a season closed to hunting or uses prohibited hunting gear or methods for the purpose, thus damaging wildlife resources, if the circumstances are serious, shall be sentenced to fixed-term imprisonment of not more than three years, criminal detention, or public surveillance or be fined.

As we mentioned, the second category comprises environmental crimes caused by negligence. Compared to the large amount of intentional crimes stipulated in the *Criminal Law*, crimes of negligence or recklessness are relatively few. They only constitute one third of intentional crimes. Crimes of negligence refer to the situation where the criminal behavior has caused a particular consequence and where there is fault on behalf of the perpetrator. The fault is that the perpetrator should have anticipated that his action may cause harm to society. Negligence or recklessness thus constitutes a crime against the environment. Nearly all the crimes in this category are consequential crimes, except for the crime of illegal issuing of tree cutting licenses, which is regarded as a circumstantial crime (but the serious consequence is also one of the circumstances) (Xu, 2007, p. 41).

Negligent crimes are, as we mentioned, fewer in numbers than the intentional crimes.[9] An example of a negligent crime according to Chinese legal doctrine would be the crime of a major pollution incident mentioned in article 338 of the Criminal Law which we referred to above.[10] Richter notes that the required *mens rea* for article 338 is debated, although a majority of authors regards article 338 as a crime for which negligence and lower order recklessness may be sufficient (Richter, 2006, p. 70; Richter, 2002, p. 83).

5.2.3 Subsidiary Environmental Criminal Law

Subsidiary environmental criminal law also plays an important role in practice. It mainly concerns provisions in state regulations aimed at the protection of the environment. These provisions have no specific description of criminal charges, punishment or range of penalty and the majority of them relate to how to apply the corresponding provisions in the Criminal Law. An example is an article in the Environmental Protection Law (Environmental Protection Law, 1989) which stipulates in article 43 that '[i]f a violation of this law causes a serious environmental pollution accident … the persons directly responsible for such an accident shall be investigated for criminal responsibility'.

Another example is article 62 of the Law on Prevention and Control of Noise Pollution (Law on Prevention and Control of Noise Pollution, 1996) which provides that:

> If any person who is in charge of supervision or administration of prevention and control of noise pollution abuses his power, neglects his duty or conducts malpractice for personal gain, the unit to which he belongs or the competent authority at the higher level shall give him administrative penalty. If a crime is constituted, criminal liability shall be investigated according to law.

From the examples above it follows that administrative law and criminal law in China are strongly intertwined. Administrative regulations provide specific duties or prohibitions, but for their enforcement they mostly refer to corresponding provisions in the Criminal Law'. That is why these administrative regulations are considered as 'subsidiary environmental criminal law' since they potentially enlarge the scope of the criminal law. Several reasons are advanced in Chinese legal doctrine for this particular structure of subsidiary environmental criminal law. These reasons relate to the comparative benefits of administrative law. First it is argued that criminal law often only intervenes at a relatively late stage. On the other hand, administrative law allows an intervention at an early stage which could lead to the prevention of environmental harm and thus provide an alternative approach to the Criminal Law (Liu, 2002, p. 91). Second, the current combination approach could keep the unity of the Criminal Law, as the cost of amending Criminal Law is relatively high and this cannot be done frequently (Xie, 2001, p. 78). Third, the approach distinguishes, in one piece of legislation, between criminal and administrative illegality. By adding administrative law to the criminal law, administrative law could fill some of the gaps that exist in the criminal law (Liu, 2004, p. 134). Finally, it is argued that it is in practice not always possible to clearly distinguish between environmental crimes and administrative infringements (Lin, 1981, p. 129). In Chinese legal doctrine, the relationship between both domains has been illustrated as shown in Figure 5.1 (Xu, 2007, p.114).

This figure shows that to some extent administrative and criminal offenses in China are logically connected and that punishment is graduated from administrative to criminal offenses. The connection between the two systems has been examined by Chinese academics (Zhao, 2007, p. 32; Shao, 2004, p. 73; Wang, 1999, p. 8; Wang, 1996, p. 92; Zhang, 1995, p. 115). Legal doctrine suggests that the relationship between administrative environmental law and criminal law can take four different forms:[11]

a. A first possibility is that the state regulations and laws concerning the protection of the environment and natural resources just hold generally

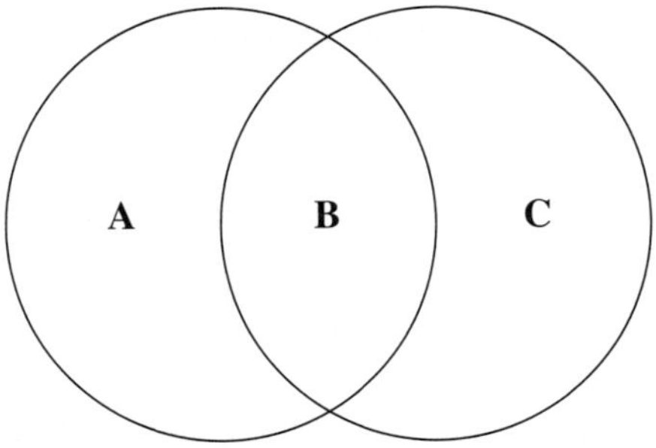

Notes: A: Criminal offenses;
B: Administrative offenses leading to criminal liability;
C: Administrative offences.

Figure 5.1 Relationship between administrative offenses and criminal offenses

that violation may lead to 'criminal responsibility', but neither the sanctions, nor the specific provision of the Criminal Law which would have to be applied is indicated. This general reference to criminal law could take two different sub-forms:

(a) A first possibility is that an administrative environmental law simply stipulates that a particular 'conduct constitutes a crime and can be held criminally responsible'. An example is article 62 of the Law on Prevention and Control of Noise Pollution. This regulates that '… If a crime is constituted, criminal liability shall be investigated according to law'.
(b) A second possibility is that the law holds '[o]ne of the following acts constitutes a crime, in accordance to the relevant provisions of the Criminal Law, to be held criminally responsible'. In that case there is at least an explicit reference to 'relevant provisions of the Criminal Law'. An example is article 48 of Law on Prevention and Control of Radioactive Pollution (Law on Prevention and Control of Radioactive Pollution, 2003) which provides that 'Where administrative authorities who are in charge of supervision or administration of prevention and control of radioactive pollution, in violation of the law and committing one of the following circumstances, extorts property from others with job convenience, seeks other interests or neglects his duties, they shall be given administrative sanctions according to law; If a crime is constituted, they shall be investigated for criminal liability according to law: (i) The admin-

istrative license is granted to an applicant who does not meet statutory requirements; (ii) Fail to perform the statutory obligations of supervision and administration; (iii) Fail to investigate into and deal with irregularities as found."

When it comes to the practical application of these provisions, there are no problems where the violation of the particular environmental statute has a clear corresponding penalty in the Criminal Law. This may be the case if the environmental violation can be qualified as for exmaple theft, deforestation crime, the crime of destruction of cultural relics or the crime of a major pollution incident. The case is more complicated when there is no specific provision in the Criminal Law that could be applied to the specific violation. The crime of marine pollution, for example, is an example of a case where no penalty in the Criminal Law could be applied against such conduct (Fu, 2001, p. 710).

b. The second way of referring to criminal law is more specific, restricting the application of the provision to a particular article in the Criminal Law. For example, paragraph 1 of article 39 of the Mineral Resources Law (Mineral Resources Law, 1996) prescribes that: '[i]n violation of this law, without obtaining the mining permit ... causing great loss to the mineral resources, shall be held criminally liable according to the article 156 of the Criminal Law'.
c. A third way of referring to the Criminal Law is that the administrative environmental law simply refers to a corresponding article in the Criminal Law which could apply *mutatis mutandis* to the environmental administrative violation where similar circumstances are required for the provision to apply. However, it is necessary to distinguish between the expressions 'in accordance with' and 'by analogy with'. According to criminal law principles, if an act constitutes a crime, and a specific article in the Criminal Law could be applied, the term of 'in accordance with' should be used. On the hand, 'by analogy with' refers to the situation where no specific article can be found in the Criminal Law with regard to certain conduct but an article with analogous description of the action and level of sanctions could be applied.

The term 'by analogy with' actually creates an analogous article with the formulation 'to be held criminally responsible by analogy with similar article in the Criminal Law'. Such formulations are rare, but do exist in some regulations. An example is article 57 of the Law on Prevention and Control of Water Pollution (Law on Prevention and Control of Water Pollution, 2008), which provides that 'a violation of the provisions of this Law, causing major water pollution accidents, resulting in heavy losses to public and private property, personal injury, or serious consequences, can be prosecuted in analogy with article 115 or article 187 of the Criminal Law and be held criminally responsible'.

d. The fourth manner is to refer in the administrative environmental law provision to a specific crime in the Criminal Law without explaining the detailed requirements of that crime, but to simply apply the relevant article from the Criminal Law directly. The Law on Prevention and Control of Solid Waste Pollution (Law on Prevention and Control of Solid Waste Pollution, 2004) prescribes for example in article 66 that 'to evade Customs control thus constitutes the crime of smuggling, shall be held criminally responsible'. Paragraph 2 of article 35 of the Wild Animal Protection Law (Wild Animal Protection Law, 2004) stipulates that '[i]n violation of this law, sale and acquisition of national key protected wild animals or their products, with serious circumstances, constituting the crime of speculation and/or crime of smuggling, shall be held criminally responsible in accordance with the relevant provisions of the Criminal Law'.

Looking in particular at models 'b' and 'd' above, one has to be careful to distinguish between the two legislative measures. When applying model b, which restricts reference to a certain article, the prosecutor still needs to take on the burden of proof when charging a criminal offense that the four elements of constituting a crime have been fully satisfied. In Chinese Criminal Law one article sometimes has different charges in different paragraphs in the same article. The reference to a certain article is somehow quite clear for enforcement and at the same time, gives the judges full discretion to choose which charge (paragraph) to apply, whereas the model 'd' indicates the charge (paragraph) directly and the discretion of the judge is limited.

It follows from this brief sketch of the various ways in which violations of administrative environmental laws can be punished by using the Criminal Law that the scope of the articles in the Criminal Law has been substantially expanded through administrative environmental law. From the description above, one can conclude: first, that crimes against the environment and penalties are mainly regulated by the provisions of the Criminal Law and that the administrative laws and regulations provide material requirements that may lead to criminal liability, although they do not contain penalty provisions. Second, the environmental administrative regulations and the crimes and penalties regulated by the Criminal Law are in a relationship of supplementarity with each other (Hu et al, 1992, p. 369).

5.2.4 Administrative Sanctions

While in many cases violations of administrative environmental law can lead to criminal liability under provisions of the Criminal Law, in some cases violations of administrative environmental law (also) constitute administrative offenses.[12] These could hence give rise to the application of administrative sanctions. Chinese legal doctrine regards criminal law and administrative law as an integral system which can provide sanctions and remedies for environmental offenses. From the perspective of preventing environmental crime, it is therefore held that administrative and criminal sanctions can both have a specific value (Shu, 2008, p. 29). Administrative sanctions can be found in various administrative environmental laws, usually under the chapter referred to as 'legal liability'. Depending upon the regulation applicable, a wide range of possible administrative sanctions can be applied.

5.2.4.1 Sanctions

The general regulation concerning the administrative sanctions is the Administrative Penalty Law (Administrative Penalty Law, 1996).[13] Most of the administrative measures that may be taken in case of environmental offenses can be found in the Measures on Administrative Sanctions against Environmental Offences (Measures on Administrative Sanctions against Environmental Offences, 2009), adopted by the Ministry of Environmental Protection. This document mainly focuses on rules and regulations on sanctioning environmental offenses. It concerns for example polluting without a permit or license, violating license conditions and causing pollution and ineffective pollution control method. Depending on the violation, the relevant authority can issue a warning, impose a fine, confiscate illegal gains, order the closing of a polluting plant or stop production, revoke a permit or license, or impose other types of administrative penalties that the state environmental protection laws and regulations provide for (Wang, 2004, p. 163).

Besides the above-mentioned approaches, state regulations on environmental protection with specific priorities have other sanctioning methods, such, as for example, to re-install and use environmentally friendly techniques; pollution control with limited time; ordering the removal of polluting plant or project; confiscating facilities; destroying after confiscation; cancelling production; imposing import quotas; ordering the construction of facilities before the deadline; ordering the transport of hazardous waste back to the exporters; ordering an importer to eliminate pollution; ordering the removal, suspension and closure of a business; ordering the suspension of a business for pollution control; eliminating barriers; mandatory recycling of products and packaging; replanting grass and restoring vegetation; cancellation of mining permits; confiscation of fishing gear; cancellation of a fishing permit; ordering an end to acts of vandalism; setting a deadline for restitution; cancelling the approval of documents; taking remedial measures; ordering a halt to construction; ordering a stop to tilling; administrative detention and so on (Gao, 2008, p. 55; Liu, 1994, p. 17). Some of these measures can be taken separately and some may be combined for sanctioning. Even though, as mentioned above, administrative authorities have in theory the discretion to use a large number of different administrative sanctions, the sanction most used in practice is the administrative fine. In almost every case, a fine will be imposed on the offender. One of the reasons for the frequent recourse to this sanction is that other sanctions, such as the closure of the polluting plant or an order to stop production, can usually only be issued by public authorities above the county level.

The amount of the administrative fine depends on the applicable administrative regulations. In some cases, fines are imposed without any legislative basis. This is debated in the legal doctrine and some hold that the fine constitutes an abuse to increase the income of the state authorities (Liu, 2005, p. 42).

When the fine is compared with other administrative sanctions like ordering the closure of a plant or the revocation of a license, the economic impact of a fine for firms is usually not very great. The regulations generally state that the authority 'may also impose a fine' without specifying the precise amount or the (environmental) principles according to which the fine should be imposed. The paradoxical result is that, on the one hand, the fine is the most used sanction in practice, but that, on the other hand (given the low amount), it is in most cases ineffective in fighting environmental violations.

5.2.4.2 Examples

The newly amended Law on Prevention and Control of Water Pollution, 2008 aims to specify the sanctions against pollution of surface and ground water. Article 75 provides a good example of the sanctioning approach:

> The entitities having set up sewage outfalls within the drinking water source reserves shall be ordered to dismantle those sewage outfalls within the time limit prescribed by the local people's governments at or above the county's level, and a penalty of not less than RMB 100 000 but not more than RMB 500 000 shall be imposed thereon; the sewage outfalls shall be dismantled by force if the entities fail to dismantle them within the time limit, and the charges thus incurred shall be borne by the offenders, a penalty of not less than RMB 500 000 but not more than 1 000 000 RMB shall be imposed thereon and the offenders may be ordered to suspend their operation for rectification.

This law adopted, to some extent, the argument put forward by scholars that the degree of administrative fines should be substantially increased for deterring environmental offences. This is especially clear in article 76 of the Law on Prevention and Control of Water Pollution. This provision, aimed at punishing unlawful emissions, provides that:

> Whoever commits any of the following acts, shall be ordered to stop illegal activities, to take control measures to eliminate pollution and/or to be fined by the environmental protection department of the local people's governments above the county level; if the control measures are not taken within the time limit, the environmental protection authorities can designate another entity which is capable of taking control measures and the costs shall be charged from the offender:
> (1) discharging oil, acid and/or lye into water body;
> (2) discharging or dumping into any water body or directly burying deadly toxic soluble slag, tailings, etc. containing such substances as mercury, cadmium, arsenic, chromium, lead, cyanide and yellow phosphorus;
> (3) washing and cleaning in any water body any vehicles or containers which have been used for storing oil or toxic pollutant;
> (4) discharging or dumping industry waste residues, urban refuse or other wastes into any water body or to pile or deposit solid wastes and other pollutants on beaches and bank slopes below the highest water level of rivers, lakes, canals, irrigation channels and reservoirs;
> (5) discharging or dumping radioactive solid wastes or waste water containing any high- or medium-level radioactive substances into any water body;
> (6) in violation of relevant regulations or standards, discharging waste water and/or hot water containing low-level radioactive material or waste water containing pathogens;
> (7) using seepage wells, seepage pits, crevices or caves for discharging or dumping of waste water containing toxic pollutants, pathogens or other wastes;
> (8) using non-anti-seepage measures, ponds for transporting or storing of waste water containing toxic pollutants, pathogens or other waste.
>
> A fine above 10 000 RMB and no more than 100 000 RMB shall be imposed for any of the situations in paragraph 3 and/or paragraph 6; a fine above 20 000 RMB and no more than 200 000 RMB shall be imposed for any of the situations in paragraph 1, paragraph 4 and/or paragraph 8; for any of the situations in paragraph 2, paragraph 5 and/or paragraph 7, a fine above 50 000 RMB and no more than 500 000 RMB shall be applied.

This article clearly shows a rather differentiated approach by providing different sanctions according to the seriousness of the violation. This is, however, one of the rare cases in Chinese law where such an approach can be found.

The newly amended article above and the Law on Prevention and Control of Solid Waste Pollution allow the imposition of a fine up to 1 000 000 RMB. However, in practice, the average fines in the state regulations were always fixed up to a maximum of 200 000 RMB (Cai and Ye, 2008, p. 120). In reality, the operational cost of a pollution purifying installation would be 100 000 RMB per day and the administrative fine for not operating the plant would merely be around 100 000 RMB. Hence, large-scale factories, such as paper mills would not keep the pollution treatment facilities running from a cost-benefit perspective, which, on the other hand, increases the cost of law enforcement.

Yet another example of the use of administrative fines in regulation is provided by the Law on Prevention and Control of Atmospheric Pollution (Law on Prevention and Control of Atmospheric Pollution, 2000). Article 56 of this law provides that a fine of 50 000 RMB can be imposed for 'discharging of dust, fetor or other gases with toxic substances into the atmosphere without taking any effective measures to prevent and control pollution'.[14] Again this example shows that fines even for serious environmental offenses are not sufficiently high to have any serious deterrent character.

5.3 CRITICAL ANALYSIS

5.3.1 The Model Tested

One way to assess environmental criminal law in China is to examine whether the ideal provisions from the models found in the academic literature (Faure and Visser, 1995, p. 316; Mandiberg and Faure, 2009, p. 447) can also be found in criminal law in China. This literature holds that an ideal criminal law, providing adequate protection for environmental interests, should consist of a combination of provisions that, together, provide adequate protection to the various components of the environment (water, soil, air and natural resources).

A first type of necessary (but not sufficient) provisions is the category of so-called abstract endangerment crimes. These are the types of crimes that punish the lack of respect for administrative duties, such as operating a plant without a license, violating administrative duties, license conditions etc., without an emission or actual harm occurring. It is important to punish non-respect for these administrative duties since they allow intervention in the protection of environmental interest at a very early stage (long before an emission or harm occurs). Since the relationship between the violation and the protected interest is rather remote, this would be the type of violation that could be punished through the administrative law.

In this respect, the approach followed by Chinese law seems to make sense: failure to respect administrative obligations such as the duty to obtain a permit and respect for permit conditions is not criminalized in the Criminal Law. Most of these obligations can be found in administrative environmental regulations. These are mostly enforced through administrative sanctions.

Even though the choice of an administrative sanctioning system may theoretically make sense, questions can be asked concerning its effectiveness. On the one hand, administrative sanctions aim at preventing further harm from occurring or remedying a harm that has occurred in the past. These types of very detailed administrative remedial measures aim at the restoration of environmental harm, and can successfully do so. A problem with these sanctions is, however, that they merely force an offender to do what he already had to do according to the law: for example, installing environmentally friendly techniques or pollution control mechanisms etc. Given that a major problem with environmental violations lies in the fact that the probability of detection can be very low, a polluter who only risks remedial sanctions has little to lose. A sanction should normally be provided that outweighs the low probability of detection of the environmental offense. Thus the sanctions should be higher than the potential benefit to the offender. The deterrent sanction that can be provided through the administrative law is an administrative fine. However, we have indicated that most administrative environmental acts provide for fines of between 500 000 and 1 000 000 RMB, whereas in practice fines are often below 200 000 RMB. It may be that given the low probabilities of detection and the high potential gain from violation, these sanctions can never provide an effective deterrent.

Looking at concrete endangerment crimes, there is in theory a long list of crimes provided in the Criminal Law, but many of these require a certain consequence. As we will show below, these are in practice very hard to prove. That is particularly why crimes punishing, for example, 'causing pollution' were not part of our ideal model of environmental criminal law.

Some of the provisions from the Criminal Law could be qualified as punishing the concrete endangerment of environmental interest such as the crime of smuggling waste (article 339 paragraph 3), or the illegal disposal of solid waste (article 339, paragraph 1).

In this kind of situation the punishment is targeted at the behavior and no causality is required by the law. The prosecutor has the burden of proof that the defendant has committed the act, but does not need to prove the harm and the complex causality relationship between the behavior and a result.

Yet another problem is that some concrete endangerments of the environment are punished, but as an administrative infringement rather than as a crime. This is the case with article 76 of the Law on Prevention and Control of Water Pollution, mentioned above, which punishes unlawful emissions with administrative fines. Even though these are, by Chinese standards, considerable (up to 500 000 RMB), they may not sufficiently deter unlawful emissions of waste water or other substances.

A weakness is, moreover, that not all unlawful emissions into the environment are punished in the same way. Disposal of waste is an example of a concrete endangerment crime found in the Criminal Law, but surprisingly, unlawful emissions of waste water, or unlawful emissions into the air are not directly punished under it. For those violations one is hence dependent upon either subsidiary environmental criminal law or administrative sanctioning systems. Since no corresponding article exists for water pollution or air pollution in the Criminal Law, the applicable sanction will mostly be restricted to an administrative sanction. In that respect we can refer to the comment above that these are usually too limited in amount.

The autonomous crime whereby it would be possible to apply criminal law against cases of serious environmental pollution (for example, in the case where there would be concrete danger to human health) cannot be found in Chinese environmental criminal law. The most serious crime (at least on paper) would be article 338 of the Criminal Law, punishing the causing of major environmental pollution. The problem is not only that causation is required, but also that all of the criminal provisions in the Criminal Law are characterized by a very strong administrative dependence. Even article 338 of the Criminal Law is only applicable when the major environmental pollution accident was caused 'in violation of the regulations of the state'. There is therefore absolute administrative dependence and no independent environmental crime.

5.3.2 Specific Problems

5.3.2.1 Administrative dependence of environmental criminal law

Law and economics scholarship has discussed the trade-offs of using criminal as opposed to administrative law in general (Faure and Svatikova, 2010, p. 60; Ogus and Abbot, 2002, p. 283), as well as applied to the enforcement of environmental law (Bowles et al, 2008, p. 389). A major weakness of environmental criminal law in many legal systems is a (too) strong link between administrative and criminal law. That problem also arises in Chinese environmental criminal law. Most provisions in the Criminal Law only apply when the offender acted 'in contravention of the state law and regulations'. This may seriously limit the possibilities of applying the criminal law (obviously dependent on how this provision is interpreted). In all cases where the offender, for example, complied with the conditions of a permit, there would be no 'violation of the regulations of the state' even if emissions covered by the permit would cause serious environmental harm. As far as article 338 of the Criminal Law is concerned, the fact that the crime of a 'major pollution incident' can only be applied when it occurred in violation of administrative rules has been criticized by Chinese lawyers. Indeed the problem remains that substantial harm could be caused to the environment while still respecting administrative law. These formulations hence seriously limit the possibility for the judiciary to provide autonomous protection for the environment through the use of criminal law.

5.3.2.2 Combining administrative and criminal law

The relationship between criminal law and administrative law is particularly strong in the case of China since administrative environmental law often refers (in different ways) to the Criminal Law as a sanctioning mechanism (Richter, 2006, p. 73). As we explained above, the way in which the administrative environmental acts refer to the provisions in the Criminal Law varies substantially and is, moreover, not always very clear (ibid., p. 73). In some cases, the administrative environmental law mentions explicitly that a particular article in the Criminal Law (for example article 156) will be applicable when a violation of administrative environmental law has taken place. In that case, for all parties involved (potential offenders, the public prosecutor and the judge), the applicable provision is clear and criminal law could thus exercise its deterrent effect and provide adequate protection for the environment.

In other cases, the reference to the Criminal Law is less clear, when administrative environmental law, for example, merely mentions that a violation will be punished 'in accordance with the relevant provisions of the Criminal Law' without specifying which those provisions would be.

Clearly, the subsidiary environmental criminal law in China has a strong dependence on the penalties in the Criminal Law, which leads to the consequence that the application of the administrative laws and regulations against environmental crimes can rarely be witnessed in legal practice, since the connection between administrative laws and the Criminal Law is not that clear. This makes implementation very hard in practice. Still, legal doctrine in China holds that the relationship between administrative and criminal law is necessary since it maintains the integral structure of the sanctioning system, without undermining the unity of the Criminal Law by amending or adding new types of crimes against the environment to the criminal law system (Huang, 2001, p. 75).

5.3.2.3 Consequential crimes

We discussed above that a large number of crimes in the Criminal Law require a certain result, for example chopping down trees, occupation of arable land, causing major pollution etc. It will be very difficult to apply these provisions in practice since they also all require that the action 'results in heavy losses of public or private property or the grave consequences of injuries or deaths of persons'. It is generally known that these kinds of provisions are not practical since they require a causal relationship between a certain action and the resulting damage. Also legal scholars in China are critical of the fact that criminal law can only intervene when a particular behavior has produced certain consequences dangerous to society, without having the possibility of punishing the behavior as such.[15]

This is also the problem with article 338 of the Criminal Law, punishing the crime of major pollution incident. This provision not only requires that the incident was caused 'in violation of the regulation', but also that it caused 'serious consequences'. In this kind of situation not only the illegality, but also the required result, means that the law would only intervene at a very late stage (Richter, 2008, p. 265).[16] In addition, the burden of proof for the public prosecutor would be very onerous. It is therefore highly questionable that 'causing a major environmental pollution accident which leads to the serious consequences of heavy losses of public or private property or human casualties' would result in criminal liability only if state regulations have been violated. This makes the article very hard to apply. In most legal systems, these provisions apply even if the defendant followed the conditions of a license (Heine, 1986, p. 67).

Another aspect of this article which has been widely discussed in legal doctrine in China is the low degree of sanction. Indeed, there is a prison sanction of not more than three years even if serious consequences of death and loss of property occur. This sanction may not be sufficient to prevent such criminal behavior (Dong, 2006, p. 78). Moreover, it is remarkable that this serious crime is only punished with a sanction of three years (and a maximum of seven years), whereas, for example, theft is punished in article 262 of the Criminal Law with imprisonment of ten years and more.

5.3.2.4 Intent

Above we also mentioned that the Chinese Criminal Law is not always very clear as to the required *mens rea*. The difficulty is that this does not always follow from the text of the legislative provisions, but rather from solutions in other legal doctrine or case law. According to these, in some cases intent is required. Legal doctrine holds that a large number of the environmental crimes in the Criminal Law require proof of intent. The intent in most environmental crimes refers to two different aspects: intent towards concrete endangerment and intention towards the illegality of the administrative law, among which proof of knowing illegality would theoretically be one element constituting a crime. In legal practice, the proof of knowing the illegality may pose big problems as the defendant could always argue that he/she does not know the specific regulations (Zhang, 2003, p. 70). The leading opinion is of the view that knowledge of the illegality is not a necessary component of intentional crime as the intention of a harmful result would be regarded as really intentional (Xu, 2007, p. 95). However, as long as acting 'in violation of state regulations' is a condition of criminal liability, knowledge of illegality should necessarily be addressed by the prosecution.

5.2.3.5 Rule of law

From the description above, it has also become clear that in some cases the relationship between administrative environmental law and the criminal provisions in the Criminal Law (the so-called subsidiary environmental criminal law) is not regulated very clearly. In some cases, it has even been held that provisions from the Criminal Law should be applied by analogy to other violations of administrative regulations. The adoption of these provisions has been criticized as it is against the general principle of law concerning the prohibition of analogy (Ma, 2003, p. 11). Under current criminal law, in accordance with the principle of legality, an explanation through analogy is prohibited. The leading opinion holds that the application of criminal law through analogy would result in discretionary decisions by judges and would hence violate the basic rights of defendants (ibid., p. 11). Moreover, in that case, potential wrongdoers can no longer predict the consequences of their actions and may be subject to punishment for unforeseen reasons (Zhang, 2007, p. 48).

5.4 SUGGESTIONS FOR REFORM

Even though one always has to be extremely careful about formulating suggestions for reform, we nevertheless think that it is possible to put forward a few suggestions which may allow criminal law in China to provide more adequate protection of the environment. Moreover, our suggestions are strongly in line with the criticisms formulated in legal doctrine in China.[17]

One obvious and general suggestion would of course be to reformulate the protection awarded through administrative and criminal law more along the lines of the ideal model developed in the literature (Faure and Visser, 1995, p. 316; Mandiberg and Faure, 2009, p. 447). The core of these thoughts is that a variety of provisions is used that, with an increasing intensity of protection of ecological values, provides more adequate protection while, at the same time, loosening the ties to administrative law. Also the sanctioning system should reflect the nature of the endangerment of ecological interests[18] (Richter, 2006, p. 78) and similar protection should be provided to similar ecological interests. For example, it is striking that particular interests are strongly protected in the Criminal Law (such as animals, plants, trees and soil), whereas other values like air or water (that are at least equally important from an ecological perspective) do not receive adequate protection within the scope of the Criminal Law.

The starting point for a reform of environmental criminal law in China should also be that if one wishes to protect ecological values, it is important to reflect on the importance of protecting them through criminal law. For example, it is striking that many environmental crimes in the Criminal Law do not in fact aim directly at protecting the environment as such, but aim merely to protect the economic use that is made of the environment[19] (see, for example, the relatively severe punishments for illegal logging) (Richter, 2006, p. 78).

Were the Chinese legislator to decide that environmental interests deserve at least the same degree of protection as economic interests, this should also be reflected in the way the provisions and sanctions are formulated.

These rather general suggestions lead to more specific recommendations.

First of all, it seems important to clearly punish the abstract endangerment of the environment, for example through illegal activities such as operating a plant without a license. For minor administrative violations, an administrative sanctioning system may of course suffice (as is the case in Chinese law today), but that at least requires that the amount of the sanctions is substantially increased in order to provide an adequate deterrence. Moreover, some seemingly administrative violations may in fact be potentially so harmful to the environment (for example, the operation of a chemical plant without a license) that even this mere abstract endangerment would deserve protection through criminal law.

Second, better and more integrated provisions could be included, aiming not only at the protection of animals, forests and soils, but equally at the protection of other environmental components such as air and water. Here the relationship with administrative law, as explained in Section 5.2, could be somewhat loosened. In this case, it is not merely breach of an administrative obligation which is sanctioned, but an unlawful emission. The emission can potentially cause (concrete) harm to the environment, but it is only punished in case of unlawfulness. However, this unlawfulness concept can be interpreted more broadly than merely a violation of administrative rules. Important environmental components like water and air at least deserve some protection within the Criminal Law.

A third step would also be to include specific provisions for a serious endangerment of the environment. In the latter case, especially when not only the environment is endangered but also human health, criminal law should be able to provide protection, even if the conditions of the permit are complied with. These independent environmental crimes (which of course should only apply on rare occasions) currently do not exist in environmental criminal law in China.

Moreover, one can add detailed suggestions for reform within this general framework.

A first consequence of our suggestions would be that within a new, reformed framework there should no longer be room for environmental crimes where a particular consequence (pollution or serious consequences) needs to be proven. These crimes are very hard to prove in practice, given the causality requirement. By focusing on unlawful emissions, these causation problems are avoided. This would for instance lead to a fundamental rewriting of article 338 of the Criminal Code, aiming at the punishing of 'causing a major environmental pollution accident which leads to serious consequences'. Within a new model, this provision could be rewritten as an independent crime where the condition that this would have to take place 'in violation of the regulations of the state' would be eliminated.

A second point of reform would be that the link with administrative law should be formulated much more clearly. Also Chinese legal doctrine is critical of the way in which in subsidiary environmental criminal law the link with the Criminal Law is regulated. In some cases, the judge has to guess which provision of the Criminal Law may apply in case of a violation of administrative environmental law. It is in the interests of potential perpetrators, but also of the environment, that the applicable provisions be clearly stated in advance.

Third, and strongly related to the points above, is the recommendation to formulate the conditions for criminal liability as clearly as possible, as is required by the so-called *lex certa* principle, following from the legality principle. In some cases, it may be impossible for perpetrators (but hence also for the judiciary) to find out which penalties may be applied for a violation. In such cases, one can criticize this from the rule of law perspective, but it is equally clear that criminal law will also lack a deterrent effect. An effective criminal law needs to signal clearly *ex ante* to perpetrators which sanctions can be expected in case of a particular behavior.

A fourth point would be to link much more clearly the specific conditions of *mens rea* to specific provisions. A simple way to do this is to not require specific intent in case of abstract endangerment crimes, and to distinguish between the situations where someone acted knowingly or negligently in case of concrete endangerment crimes. The applicable sanction could also be differentiated according to the state of mind of the perpetrator. Lack of intent would, in that case, not lead to a dismissal of the case, but merely to the application of a (presumably lower) penalty for a negligent violation.

5.5 CONCLUDING REMARKS

In this contribution, we have critically analyzed environmental criminal law in China. On the one hand, we have provided an overview of the provisions that can be applied to environmental pollution and, on the other hand, we have critically reviewed current environmental criminal law in China, using a theoretical perspective developed in Europe and the US, whereby an ideal model for environmental criminal law was developed.

It became clear that even though the Criminal Law in China has an impressive number of articles that formally deal with environmental pollution, many of these are in fact aiming at the protection of economic interests and less at the protection of the environment as such. Moreover, it equally became clear that the provisions in the Criminal Law often contain very onerous conditions that have to be met in order to be applicable. It is especially problematic that the provision aimed at serious environmental incidents can only be applied if there is proof that this incident caused serious consequences. This puts a very heavy burden of proof upon the prosecutor which may make it extremely hard to apply this provision in practice.

We also noticed that it is complicated to find out the precise scope of environmental criminal law since many material provisions can be found in administrative environmental regulations which refer (in various and sometimes rather vague ways) to provisions in the Criminal Law. Moreover, in some cases (especially those where no provision from the Criminal Law can be applied), administrative sanctions could be applied. However, the statutory limit is very low and the sanctions that would be applied in practice (in particular, administrative fines) are even lower.

We have therefore proposed that China needs to restructure its environmental criminal law in a fundamental way in order to be able to provide adequate protection for the environment. To some extent we have based these recommendations on a model of environmental criminal law developed on the basis of experiences in the EU and the US. The danger of such a 'legal transplant' is that one is assuming that solutions that worked well in the EU and the US will work well in China. In order to avoid making this mistake, one would therefore have to look carefully at the particular institutional features of the Chinese legal system, also as far as enforcement is concerned. For example: the theoretical literature suggests a significant reliance on administrative sanctions for mere breaches of administrative obligations (without emissions taking place). This, however, supposes that administrative agencies are well equipped and able to establish violations in an independent manner, acting in the public interest. If these conditions are not fulfilled, it may be dangerous to rely upon administrative sanctions.

We realize that we have merely looked at one side of the coin: how to formulate an effective environmental criminal law on paper. The other side of the coin is admittedly at least as important: how will enforcement take place in practice and are judges in China willing to apply environmental criminal law against perpetrators (including corporate entities)[20] (Yang, 1995, p. 677)? These questions relating to the practice of environmental law enforcement in China could certainly be the topic of further research. But, as we mentioned in the introduction, if one has a perfect enforcement system but inadequate material provisions, enforcement is pointless. We have merely attempted to take the first step by examining the material environmental criminal law in China and formulating suggestions for reform. If these are implemented, attention should then also be given to the equally important aspect of effective enforcement.

NOTES

1. We are grateful to the participants in the Annual Conference of the Academy of Environmental Law of the IUCN which was held in November 2009 in Wuhan (China) where we presented this paper. We are equally and wholeheartedly grateful to Professor Ping Xu of the Law Department of Beijing Forestry University, who provided us with valuable insights into environmental criminal law in China.
2. Professor Michael G. Faure LL.M is the visiting International Professor of Law, University of Pennsylvania Law School, Professor of Comparative and International Environmental Law, Maastricht University (NL) and Professor of Comparative Private Law and Economics, Erasmus School of Law (NL). Mr. Hao Zhang was a student at the Graduate School of Beijing Forestry University in China at the time of first drafting this chapter and is currently a PhD student at Melbourne Law School of the University of Melbourne in Australia.
3. See for example Wang (1996). He argues that there are to date no specific provisions which define environmental crimes and measure penalties against environmental crimes.
4. The only separate environmental criminal law in China was approved by the Standing Committee of the National People's Congress and enforced in 1988 on the Protection of Rare and Endangered Wildlife, stipulating the killing of rare and endangered wildlife as a kind of crime. The separate environmental criminal law has meanwhile been incorporated into the Criminal Law of 1997 and abolished since the enactment of Criminal Law of 1997.
5. Overview of environmental crimes in the Criminal Law of China:

    - Crime of smuggling rare animals and rare animal products (chapter 2, art 151, para 2);
    - Crime of smuggling of rare plants and rare plant products (chapter 3, art 151, para 3);
    - Crime of smuggling waste (chapter 6, art 339, para 3);
    - Crime of illegal transfer of the land use rights (chapter 3, art 228);
    - Crime of evading the quarantine of animal and plant (chapter 6, art 337);
    - Crime of major pollution incident (chapter 6, art 338);
    - Crime of illegal disposal of imported solid waste (chapter 6, art 339, para 1);
    - Crime of unauthorized imports of solid waste (chapter 6, art 339, para 2);
    - Crime of illegal fishing of aquatic products (chapter 6, para 340);
    - Crime of killing rare and endangered wildlife (chapter 6, art 341, para 1);
    - Crime of illegal acquisition, transport, sale of precious and endangered species of wild animals and their products (chapter 6, art 341, para 1);
    - Crime of illegal hunting (chapter 6, art 341, para 2);
    - Crime of illegal occupation of arable land (chapter 6, art 342);
    - Crime of illegal mining (chapter 6, art 343, para 1);
    - Crime of destructive mining (chapter 6, art 343, para 2);
    - Crime of illegal logging and the destruction of valuable trees (chapter 6, art 344);
    - Crime of illegally chopping down trees (chapter 6, art 345, para 1);
    - Crime of illegal denudation (chapter 6, art 345, para 2);
    - Crime of illegal acquisition of timbers through illegal logging and deforestation (chapter 6, art 345, para 3);
    - Crime of illegal issuing of tree cutting licenses (chapter 9, art 407);
    - Crime of neglect of duty concerning environmental monitoring (chapter 9, art 408);
    - Crime of illegal approval of requisition and occupation of land (chapter 9, art 410);
    - Crime of illegal sale of use rights of state-owned land at low price (chapter 9, art 410);
    - Crime of practicing favoritism and committing irregularities in quarantine of animal and plant (chapter 9, art 413, para 1);
    - Crime of neglect of duty concerning quarantine plant and animal (chapter 9, art 413, para 2).

6. The maximum sentence of imprisonment in Chinese Criminal Law is 20 years. Therefore the

description of 'not less than 10 years' means the imprisonment will be no less than 10 years and no more than 20 years. This applies to all the sentences of imprisonment in the Criminal Law.

7. It concerns more particularly:

   - Crime of smuggling rare animals and rare animal products (chapter 2, art 151, para 2);
   - Crime of smuggling of rare plants and rare plant products (chapter 3, art 151, para 3);
   - Crime of smuggling waste (chapter 19, art 339, para 3);
   - Crime of illegal transfer of the land use rights (chapter 3, art 228);
   - Crime of unauthorized imports of solid waste (chapter 6, art 339, para 2);
   - Crime of illegal fishing of aquatic products (chapter 6, part 340);
   - Crime of killing rare and endangered wildlife (chapter 6, art 341, para 1);
   - Crime of illegal acquisition, transport, sale of precious and endangered species of wild animals and their products (chapter 6, art 341, para 1);
   - Crime of illegal hunting (chapter 6, art 341, para 2);
   - Crime of illegal occupation of arable land (chapter 6, art 342);
   - Crime of illegal mining (chapter 6, art 343, para 1);
   - Crime of destructive mining (chapter 6, art 343, para 2);
   - Crime of illegal logging and the destruction of valuable trees (chapter 6, art 344);
   - Crime of illegally chopping down trees (chapter 6, art 345, para 1);
   - Crime of illegal denudation (chapter 6, art 345, para 2);
   - Crime of illegal acquisition of timbers through illegal logging and deforestation (chapter 6, art 345, para 3);
   - Crime of illegal approval of requisition and occupation of land (chapter 9, art 410);
   - Crime of illegal sale of use rights of state-owned land at low price (chapter 9, art 410);
   - Crime of practicing favoritism and committing irregularities in quarantine of animal and plant (chapter 9, art 413, para 1).

8. Paragraph 3, article 345 of chapter 6, Criminal Law of People's Republic of China.
9. They concern *inter alia*:

   - Crime of avoiding the quarantine of animal and plant (chapter 6, art 337);
   - Crime of major pollution incident (chapter 6, art 338);
   - Crime of illegal disposal of imported solid waste (chapter 6, art 339, para 1);
   - Crime of illegal issuing tree cutting licenses (chapter 9, art 407);
   - Crime of neglect of duty concerning quarantine plant and animal (chapter 9, art 413, para 2);
   - Crime of neglect of duty concerning environmental monitoring (chapter 9, art 408).

10. Again the difficulty is that the fact that in this case merely negligence would be required is based on interpretation in legal practice and does not automatically follow from the reading of the text.
11. Western scholars working on environmental criminal law have also attempted to differentiate the forms of the accessory status of criminal law. See Richter (2006, pp. 74–5).
12. Refer to Figure 5.1.
13. Adopted at the fourth session of the Eighth National People's Congress on March 17, 1996, this law stipulates the main approaches state regulations and laws would follow for administrative sanctions, namely the following: (1) warning; (2) fines; (3) confiscating illegally gained income and property; (4) ordering the suspension of production and operations; (5) provisionally suspending or revoking permits or licenses; (6) administrative detention; (7) other administrative punishments stipulated in laws and administrative regulations.
14. The highest amount of the fine that could be applied is merely 200 000 RMB (when specific conditions mentioned in article 60 are fulfilled).
15. Wang (1996).

16. Richter also argues that the scope of application of article 338 is limited by the fact that the requirements for the damage are high: property, health or life has to be ensured and mere endangerment of these interests is not sufficient.
17. See for example Wang, S.L., who argues that legislative changes are urgently needed in environmental criminal law in China (1996).
18. Also Richter has suggested that endangerments should be criminalized as well and that criminal law should focus less on the results of an action.
19. Typical is also the fact that section 6 of chapter 6 in the Chinese Criminal Law dealing with environmental crimes is part of the chapter in the Criminal Law dealing with 'crimes of obstructing the administration of public order'. There are hence many crimes with respect to the protection of nature and wildlife (the so-called 'crimes of impairing resources'), but fewer crimes penalizing pollution.
20. In a 1995 article, Yang, C. argued that in China 'polluting corporations and their officials are the untouchables' (mainly because of the lack of enforcement of environmental law). It is not clear to what extent the situation has changed since then.

REFERENCES

Administrative Penalty Law (promulgated by the National People's Congress, Mar. 17, 1996, effective Oct. 1, 1996) 1996 Supreme People's Court Gazette 3(47) (P.R.C.).

Bowles, R., M. Faure, and N. Garoupa (2008), 'The Scope of Criminal Law and Criminal Sanctions: An Economic View and Policy Implications', *Journal of Law and Society*, 35(3), 389–416.

Cai, X.P. and H. Ye (2008), 'Huanjing Baohu Falü Zhi Xing Nan de Sikao he Duice' [Difficulties in Enforcement of Environmental Protection Law and its Countermeasures in China], *Zhongguo Gaosein Jishu Qiye* [*Journal of China High Tech. Enterprises*], (2), 120–21.

Chen, X.L. (1992), *Xingfa Zhexue [Philosophy of Criminal Law]*, Beijing: Zhongguo Zhengfa Daxue Chu Ban She [China University of Political Science and Law Press], 214–18.

Criminal Law (promulgated by the National People's Congress, July 1, 1979, revised Mar. 14, 1997, effective Oct. 1, 1997) 1997 Standing Committee of National People's Congress Gazette 2 (P.R.C.).

Dong, B.J. (2006), 'Huanjing Fanzui Lifa Sikao' [Thinking of Legislation of Environmental Crime], *Zhongguo Dizhi Daxue Xuebao (Shehui Kexue Ban)* [*Journal of China University of Geosciences (Social Sciences Edition)*], 6(1), 78.

Environmental Protection Law (promulgated by the Standing Committee of National People's Congress, Dec. 26, 1989, effective Dec. 26, 1989) 1989 Standing Committee of National People's Congress Gazette 6 (P.R.C.).

Faure, M. and K. Svatikova (2010), 'Enforcement of Environmental Law in the Flemish Region', *European Energy & Environmental Law Review*, (19), 60–79.

Faure, M. and M.J.C. Visser (1995), 'How to Punish Environmental Pollution? Some Reflections on Various Models of Criminalization of Environmental Harm', *European Journal of Crime, Criminal Law and Criminal Justice*, (4), 316–68.

Fu, L.Z. (2001), *Huanjing Xingfa Xue* [*Environmental Criminal Law*], Beijing: Zhongguo Fangzheng Chu Ban She [Fangzheng Press], 710–11.

Gao, H.S. (2008), 'Dangqian Huanjing Zhifa zhong Cunzai de Wenti ji Wanshan Duice' [Problems in the Implemention of Environmental Law and its Countermeasures], *Hengyang Tongxun* [*Hengyang Communication*], 58(8), 2008, 55–6.

Gao, M.X. (1989), *Zhongguo Xing Fa Xue* [*Criminal Law in China*], Beijing: Zhongguo Renmin Daxue Chu Ban She [Renmin University of China Press], 160.

Gunningham, N. and P. Grabosky (1998), *Smart Regulation: Designing Environmental Policy*, Oxford: Clarendon Press, 26.

He, Q.J. (2005), 'Xingfa Zhong Huanjing Fanzui Guiding de Quexian Fenxi' [Defect Analysis on the Regulations against Environmental Crimes in China], *Xibei Daxue Xuebao (Zhexue Shehui Kexue Ban)* [*Journal of Northwest University (Social Science Edition)*], 35(6), 96–9.

Heine, G. (1986), 'Aspekte des Umweltstrafrechts im internationalen Vergleich' [Aspects of Environmental Criminal Law in International Comparison], *Goltdammer's Archiv für Strafrecht*, 67–88.

Hu, B.L., D.Y. Cao and Y.H. Yang (eds) (1992), *Huanjingfa Xinlun* [*New Comments on Environmental Law*], Beijing: Zhongguo Zhengfa Daxue Chu Ban She [China University of Political Science and Law Press], 369–84.

Huang, H. (2001), *Xingzheng xingfa bijiao yanjiu* [*Comparative Study on the Administrative Criminal Law*], Beijing: Zhongguo Fangzheng Chu Ban She [Fangzheng Press], 75–6, 79–80.

Jiang, W. (1994), *Fanzui Xingtai Tonglun* [*Research on Criminal Patterns*], Beijing: Falü Chu Ban She [Law Press], 115–16.

Jiang, M. (2008), 'Woguo Xingfa Youguan Huanjing Fanzui de Quexian Fenxi' [Defect Analysis on the Articles concerning Environmental Crimes of the Penal Code in China], *Huzhou Shifan Xueyuan Xuebao* [*Journal Huzhou Normal College*], 30(3), 84.

Law on Prevention and Control of Atmospheric Pollution (promulgated by the Standing Committee of National People's Congress, Apr. 29, 2000, effective Sep. 1, 2000) 2000 Standing Committee of National People's Congress Gazette 3 (P.R.C.).

Law on Prevention and Control of Noise Pollution (promulgated by the Standing Committee of National People's Congress, Oct. 29, 1996, effective Mar. 1, 1997) 1996 Supreme People's Court Gazette 4(72) (P.R.C.).

Law on Prevention and Control of Radioactive Pollution (promulgated by the Standing Committee of National People's Congress, June 28, 2003, effective Oct. 1, 2003) 2003 Standing Committee of National People's Congress Gazette 4 (P.R.C.).

Law on Prevention and Control of Solid Waste Pollution (promulgated by the Standing Committee of National People's Congress, Oct. 30, 1995, revised Dec. 29, 2004, effective Apr. 1, 2005) 2005 Standing Committee of National People's Congress Gazette 1 (P.R.C.).

Law on Prevention and Control of Water Pollution (promulgated by the Standing Committee of National People's Congress, May 11, 1984, revised May 15, 1996 and Feb. 28, 2008, effective June 1, 2008) 2008 Standing Committee of National People's Congress Gazette 2 (P.R.C.).

Li, Z.C. (2005), 'Qianlun Woguo Huanjing Fanzui Guiding de Xianzhuang' [Study on the Articles in Penal Code concerning Environmental Crimes in China], *Senlin Gong'an* [*Journal of Forestry Police*], (4), 36–8.

Liang, S.W. (1987), *Xingfa Xue Jiao Cheng* [*Criminal Law*], Nanjing: Nanjing Daxue Chu Ban She [Nanjing University Press], 160.

Lin, S.T. (1981), *Jingji Fanzui Yu Jingji Xingfa* [*Economic Crime and Criminal Law*], Taibei: Taibei Sanmin Shuju [Sanmin Press], 129.

Liu, G.J. (1994), 'Huanjing Xingzheng Chufa Zhong Cunzai de Wenti yu Duice' [Problems and Solutions in Environmental Administrative Punishment], *Huanjing Baohu* [*Journal of Environmental Protection*], (4), 17–19.

Liu, S.D. (2002), *Kongbai Zuizhuang – Jieding, Zhuiwen, Jiedu* [*Blank Criminal Rules – Defining, Questioning and Analyzing*], Beijing: Renmin Fayuan Chu Ban She [Court Press], 91–8.

Liu, Y.H. (2004), 'Kongbai Xingfa Guifan de Zuixing Fading Jineng – Yi Xiandai Fazhi Guojia wei Beijing de Fenxi' [On the Function of Blank Criminal Rules – Analysis with the Modern Country with the Adequate Legal System as the Background], *Zhongguo Faxue* [*Journal of China Legal Science*], (4), 134–6.

Lu, Z.W. (2005), 'Huanjing Xingzheng Chufa Zhonglei Jieding Jiqi Jiaozheng' [Problems of Types of Administrative Punishment on Environmental Violations and their Resolutions], *Huanjing baohu* [*Journal of Environmental Protection*], (10), 42–5.

Ma, K.C. (2003), *Xingfa Xue [Criminal Law*], Beijing: Gaodeng Jiaoyu Chu Ban She [High Education Press], 11.

Mandiberg, S. and M. Faure (2009), 'A Graduated Punishment Approach to Environmental Crimes: Beyond Vindication of Administrative Authority in the United States and Europe', *Columbia Journal of Environmental Law*, (34), 447.

Measures on Administrative Sanctions against Environmental Offences (promulgated by the Ministry of Environmental Protection, Aug. 6, 1999, revised Dec. 30, 2009, effective Mar. 1, 2010) 2010 Ministry of Environmental Protection Order 8 (P.R.C.).

Mineral Resources Law (promulgated by the Standing Committee of National People's Congress, Mar. 19, 1986, revised Aug. 29, 1996, effective Jan. 1, 1997) 1996 Supreme People's Procuratorate Gazette 5(35) (P.R.C.).

Ogus, A. and C. Abbot (2002), 'Sanctions for Pollution: Do We Have the Right Regime?', *Journal of Environmental Law*, (14), 283–98.

Richter, T. (2002), *Umweltstrafrecht in der Volksrepublik China* [*Environmental Criminal Law in the People's Republic of China*], Freiburg im Breisgau: Max Planck Institute for Foreign and International Criminal Law, 78–136.

Richter, T. (2006), 'Interdependencies between Criminal Law and Oil Pollution Regulation in China', in Michael G. Faure and James Hu (eds), *Prevention and Compensation of Marine Pollution Damage: Recent Developments in Europe, China and the U.S.*, The Netherlands: Kluwer Law International, pp. 61–82.

Richter, T. (2008), 'Transboundary Environmental Crimes: An Analysis of Chinese and European Law', in Michael G. Faure and Ying Song (eds), *China and International Environmental Liability: Legal Remedies for Transboundary Pollution*, Cheltenham, UK and Northampton, MA, USA: Edward Elgar, 253–72.

Shao, D.P. (2004), 'Zhongguo Huanjing Fanzui Lifa Moshi zhi Gouxiang' [The conception of Chinese environmental legislation model], *Guangxi Zhengfa Guanli Ganbu Xueyuan Xuebao* [*Journal of Guangxi Administrative Cadre Institute of Politics and Law*], 19(2), 73–5.

Shu, Z.G. (2008), 'Huanjing Fanzui Shiyong Fei Xingfa Cuoshi Tanxi' [Non-Penalty Measures are Suitable for Environmental Crime], *Guizhou Jingguan Zhiye Xueyuan Xuebao* [*Journal of Guizhou Police Officer College*], 20(3), 29–32.

Wang, C.F. (1996), 'Woguo Chengzhi Huanjing Fanzui Jidai Jiejue de Jige Wenti' [Some Problems that need Solving in Penalizing Environmental Crimes in China], *Zhongguo Faxue* [*Journal of Domestic and Foreign Law*], (1), 92–3.

Wang, J. and S.K. An (2008), 'Huanjing Fanzui de Xingfa Xianzhuang Jiqi Gaijin' [The Current Penal Code Articles on Environmental Crimes in China and its further Improvement], *Yunnan Xingzheng Xueyuan Guanli Ganbu Xuebao* [*Journal of Yunnan Administrative College*], (3), 148–51.

Wang, S.L. (1996), 'The Environmental Criminal Justice in China', Fourth International Conference on Environmental Compliance and Enforcement, available at http://www.inece.org/4thvol1/wang.pdf, accessed 19 August 2010.

Wang, S.Z. (2004), 'Environmental Crime and Environmental Criminal Law in the People's Republic of China', *European Journal of Crime, Criminal Law and Criminal Justice*, 12 (2), 150–65.

Wang, X.M. (1999), *Pohuai Huanjig Ziyuan Fanzui de Dingzui yu Liangxing* [*Conviction and Sentencing of Environmental Crimes*], Beijing: Renmin Fayuan Chu Ban She [Court Press], 8–9.

Wild Animal Protection Law (promulgated by the Standing Committee of National People's Congress, Nov. 8, 1988, revised Aug. 28, 2004, effective Aug. 28, 2004) 2004 Standing Committee of National People's Congress Gazette 6(82) (P.R.C.).

Wu, X.P. (2008), 'Lun Woguo Huaning fanzui Xingshi Lifa de Wanshan' [On the Perfecting of Criminal Legislation of Environmental Crime in China], *Kunming Ligong Daxue Xuebao* (*Sheke Faxue Ban*) [*Journal of Kunming University of Science and Technology* (*Social Science and Law Edition*)], 8(5), 1–5.

Xie, X.W. (2001), 'Woguo Huanjing Fanzui de Lifa Jishu Fenxi' [Analysis of the Legislative Techniques on Environmental Crimes] in *2001 Nian Huanjing Ziyuan Faxue Guoji Yantaohui Lunwenji* (*xiace*) [*International Colloquium on Natural Resources and Environmental Law in 2001* (*2nd volume*)], 78.

Xu, P. (2007), *Huanjing Xingfa Yanjiu* [*Environmental Criminal Law*], Beijing: Zhongguo Fazhi Chu Ban She [China Legal Publishing House], 149–51.

Xu, P. and Zhang, H. (2010), 'Cong Weihai Xingwei Tansuo Huanjing Xingshi Lifa de Moshi' [Analysis of the Environmental Criminal Law Legislation based on Environmental Endangerments], *Zhengfa Luntan* [*Tribune of Political Science and Law*], 28(2), 149–57.

Yang, C. (1995), 'Punishing for Environmental Protection? Enforcement is Used in China', *International and Comparative Law Quarterly*, (44), 671–82.

Zhang, M.K. (1995), 'Xingzheng Xingfa Bianxi' [Differentiating and Analyzing the Administrative Criminal Law], *Zhongguo Shehui Kexue* [*Journal of China Social Sciences Study*], (3), 115–17.

Zhang, M.K. (1997), *Xingfa Xue* [*Criminal Law*], Beijing: Falü Chu Ban She [Law Press], 96.

Zhang, M.K. (2007), *Xingfa Xue* [*Criminal Law*], Beijing: Falü Chu Ban She [Law Press], 48–9.

Zhang, S.J. and W. Cao (2004), 'Huanjing Ziyuan Baohu Faren Fanzui Qianxi' [Analysis of the Juridical Person Offense against the Environment Resource Protection], *Hebei Faxue* [*Hebei Law Science*], 22(7), 33.

Zhang, Z.T. (2003), 'Huanjing Fanzui Guize de Zhuguan Yaojian Fenxi' [The Imputable Subjective Requisites of Environmental Crime], *Xiandai Faxue* [*Modern Law Science*], 25(5), 70.

Zhao, X.Y. (2007), 'Luelun Woguo Huanjing Fanzui de Lifa Zai Wanshan' [Consummating China's Legislation of Environmental Crimes], *Hubei Xingzheng Xueyuan Xuebao* [*Journal of Hubei Administration Institute*], 36(6), 32–5.

6. A feasible approach to environmental public interest litigation: the people's procuratorate as plaintiff

Mei Hong and Yin Yanjie

6.1 INTRODUCTION

Faced with environmental pollution, the environmental administrative organizations in China, such as the Environmental Protection Agency and the Maritime Authority, are able to exercise their executive power. The people's procuratorates,[1] as state organs of legal supervision, are entitled to supervise the environmental administrative organizations' performance of their duties; and to institute criminal and civil litigation against the polluters. For many years, to better safeguard the environmental public interest, local prosecutorial organizations in China have supported the use of environmental public interest litigation in addition to criminal prosecution. In most instances, these actions have been supported or initiated by the people's procuratorates. This chapter looks at this practice, considers its legitimacy, and proposes reforms to ensure its more effective application.

A number of examples have illustrated the use of environmental public interest litigation, all of them civil actions instituted by the people's procuratorates. We discuss later public interest proceedings that have been initiated in Hunan province, Guangdong province, Jiangxi province, and Jiangsu province. Such public interest trials have dealt powerful blows against illegal actions that damage the environmental public interest. In part such actions make up for deficiencies in China's prosecutorial system concerning environmental crimes. However, these separate and partial practices are local and occasional. They represent minor breakthroughs, without systemic improvement in the overall prosecution system.

6.2 BASIS OF PEOPLE'S PROCURATORATES' ENVIRONMENTAL PUBLIC GOOD LITIGATION

Environmental protection is one of China's modern basic state policies.[2] Special administrative organizations such as the Environmental Protection

Agency in China have been established to manage and protect all resources and environment factors, and judicial agencies such as the people's procuratorates have been created to legally supervise the fulfillment of this duty.

The use of environmental public interest litigation instituted by special governmental agencies has become established as part of many modern countries' environmental law. Under such a system, the special governmental agencies, including administrative organizations, such as the Environmental Protection Agency, charged with responsibility for the environment and resources management and judicial agencies, such as prosecuting attorneys charged with safeguarding environmental public interest, can institute civil proceedings in courts.[3] The jurisprudential justification for the use of such civil litigation is as a means for prosecutors to carry out their legal duties. Special administrative organizations such as an Environmental Protection Agency and Marine Authority are required to exercise their administrative authority in ways that reflect their responsibilities to the people and the nation. With regard to environmental damage, it ought to be expected that these organizations shall have the authority to pursue an alternative judicial remedy, where they cannot protect or control the environmental damage through an administrative remedy.[4] Such judicial remedy is essential and is well illustrated by the US Environmental Protection Agency in its practice of instituting proceedings in the district courts to demand prohibition and seek a civil penalty.

It is said in Article 129 of the Constitution of the People's Republic of China (2004) that the people's procuratorates of the People's Republic of China are state organs for legal supervision. As the state legal supervisory organ, people's procuratorates should require administrative organizations to perform their duty when they fail to act in the face of harms of the type they are meant to prevent, or where they abuse their administrative discretion. The people's procuratorates as the state legal supervisory organ, should have the right to demand the performance of their duties. According to the Constitution of the People's Republic of China, the people's procuratorates can institute proceedings in the environmental public interest on behalf of the nation, to clarify the legal duties of environmental harm-doers.

The people's procuratorates may elect to support the prosecution if there is an absence of other plaintiffs able to take effective action, or intervene if the people's courts do not accept or dismiss the actions. This is analogous to environmental prosecutorial responsibilities in other countries, such as the Crown Prosecutor, or the Attorney General. Despite the different setup of prosecutorial organizations in various countries, the prosecuting attorney, as the representative of social public interest, has the power to institute environmental public interest litigation on behalf of the nation according to the Constitution. This reflects the political imperative to safeguard the national and public interest and the social need to provide a public right to protect human rights and procedural justice.

In China there are many reasons why, even though the people's procuratorates have a lawful duty and power to institute environmental public interest proceedings, they may not actively elect to function as the principal plaintiff in environmental public interest litigation. The reasons are as follows: firstly, increased attention to advance prevention and emergency control due to disastrous environmental damage downplays the judicial role of the people's procuratorates as the plaintiff. Secondly, with environmental litigation, there are many complex technical and evidentiary issues, which may act as a disincentive to pursue the action. The identification of environmental damage and the collection of sufficient reliable evidence are often difficult. The degree of scientific uncertainty in a potential environmental litigation needs to be evaluated by professional environmental inspection agencies. Thirdly, the professional staff and the abilities of the people's procuratorates may not necessarily be sufficient to meet the requirements of the potential cases.

According to Mauro Cappelletti, judicial officers or prosecutors should not play a part in environmental public interest litigation. He argues that in order to protect the environment and 'diffusible fragment interests', it is more effective to establish specialized governmental agencies, which are entitled to issue an injunction and sometimes demand compensation for damage.[5] Lv Zhongmei is of the same opinion in relation to the situation in China.[6] She argues that the nature and content of environmental public interest litigation is different from the nature and task of the prosecuratorial organizations, that it is quite feasible for other environmental protection organizations to be the plaintiff in environmental public interest litigation, and that more importantly, action by other agents is more likely to meet the requirements of timeliness and harm prevention in environmental public interest protection.

These opinions represent a persuasive theoretical case, but notwithstanding, it seems there remains a practical need for prosecutorial agencies to be prepared to intervene through litigation. Assuming that the specialized governmental agencies whom these authors believe ought to be responsible for action are by and large the administrative organizations which are expcted to exercise supervision and administrative management, and that national judicial organizations are not included, the situation can and does arise where such agencies are reluctant to perform their duties, or where these agencies lack power, or are caught up in power conflicts that can prevent them acting. Sometimes environmental administrative organizations, as part of local government, may suffer interference due to department interests and regional protectionism, or possibly government–business collusion or other covert deals between administrative organizations and the organizations that cause environmental harm. This raises the question of how administrative power can be supervised or restricted where such agencies fail to act, or fail to act properly. Oversight only by the general public is not necessarily competent to meet the need, and judicial supervision is therefore justified.

Whilst public prosecutors should not be the first choice of plaintiff for conducting environmental public interest litigation, we argue that they are an indispensable and well-qualified plaintiff as part of the system of environmental public interest litigation, and are the last line of defense for maintaining environmental justice. Whilst it is not the main duty of the people's procuratorates to institute environmental public interest proceedings, given their duty of legal supervision of a range of issues on behalf of the public, the existence of a reserve right to act as plaintiff is beneficial to ensure timely prevention and remediation of environmental damage. It also contributes to ensuring indispensable judicial support for the construction of a robust environmental jurisprudence in China. This use of the law can also encourage non-governmental forces concerned about environmental issues (including individuals, groups, and NGOs) to be more active in relation to defects in the operation of responsible government agencies, such as failures to act, a lack of timeliness, or excessive compromise.

6.3 THE HISTORY OF PROSECUTORIAL ORGANIZATIONS' PUBLIC WELFARE LITIGATION

The international history of the involvement of prosecutorial organizations in public interest litigation can be traced back to when the prosecutorial system first appeared. The French agent of the monarch in the twelfth century is considered to mark the beginning of the prosecutorial system. The 'agent of the monarch', as the precursor of the prosecutorial official, was in charge not only of reporting or taking action against feudal lords who trespassed on crown interests, but also when there was conduct such as compounding a felony between plaintiff and defendant or trespassing on crown power or other public interests. This responsibility for the defense of the integrity of public office required that they 'on behalf of the king, listen to private betrayals, make investigations, institute proceedings, support prosecutions and judgments of prosecutorial protest court', and so on (Hong, 2001).

Prosecutors' public welfare litigation was also a characteristic of German public welfare litigation. According to Article 35 of the German Administrative Courts Act, prosecutors in the Federal Administrative Court may, for the sake of the public interest, participate in any litigation in the Federal Administrative Court. The purpose of this role is to use the status and power of prosecutorial organizations to safeguard civil interests, especially those of the general public, against defects in the action of arms of government.

Within the French legal system the public prosecutors are in charge of criminal public prosecution. As they are the representatives of public interests, they have power to institute civil public actions and intervene in civil actions. Chapter 13 of the French Code of Civil Procedure authorizes the prosecutors to pursue any cases concerning national, social, or individual interests in the name of the plaintiff, who is primarily the party concerned, and to intervene in any case closely related to the public interest at any stage of a court action in the name of the party concerned.

In Anglo-American law systems such as England's, the Attorney General, as the representative of the crown, had the power to institute proceedings in cases involving royal interests (including those related to the public interest) in the name of the crown or the royal household. If public interests were claimed as being unlawfully infringed upon, the Attorney General might, at the request of delators, institute proceedings in the name of the Attorney General or *ex officio*. The British environmental public interest litigation set a loose control on the plaintiff's prosecution qualification, but it was only through the Attorney General that anybody could institute an action because the Attorney General was the only one who could represent the public in court to institute proceedings. If the Attorney General did not agree with the individual's prosecution in court, then the court did not have the power to adjudicate the case.

In relation to environmental protection, when the Parliament of Britain realized the traditional law could not effectively control environmental infringement the law was amended. Under these reforms the sufferer of harm as a result of an environmental infringement and the prosecutor could both institute environmental public interest litigation. In America the State and Federal Attorney General have a wide scope to institute environmental litigation. Some environmental regulations enacted by the Federal government, such as the National Environmental Policy Act, 1969, the Clean Air Act (CAA),[7] the Clean Water Act (CWA),[8] and the Noise Regulation Act, Toxic Substances Control Act, and the Solid Waste Control Act, authorize public prosecutors to institute corresponding environmental non-criminal litigation, or support the legal claims of competent administrative authorities or individuals (Puchinski, 1983).

As an example, the 1970 Michigan Environmental Protection Act (MEPA) stipulates that the Attorney General has the right to institute environmental proceedings. 'Any person (or the attorney general) may bring an action for declaratory or injunctive relief against any person for the protection of the air, water, and other natural resources and the public trust from pollution, impairment or destruction.'

From the very beginning of the prosecutorial system in government, the prosecutorial organizations appeared in the name of the government as the representative of public interests. Whilst there are many differences in the setup of prosecutorial organizations and the scope of prosecutorial power around the world, in all of them prosecutorial arms of government institute criminal prosecutions or supervise law enforcement for the purpose of safeguarding the public interest on behalf of the nation. That it is a logical extension of this role for prosecutorial organizations to institute environmental public interest litigation can be supported by the logic of jurisprudence, and by the long history of prosecutorial systems.

6.4 THE PEOPLE'S PROCURATORATES' ENVIRONMENTAL PUBLIC INTEREST LITIGATION

In China, the people's procuratorates have been instituting environmental public litigation litigation for a few years. Whilst there is no explicit legislative stipulation empowering the people's procuratorates to institute environmental public interest litigation, many local prosecutorial organizations have pursued such litigation in order to safeguard environmental public interests. In 2003, the people's procuratorate in Leling, Shandong province, instituted a civil prosecution against a defendant Fan, whose illegal oil refining polluted the environment.[9] In the same year the people's procuratorate in Langzhong, Sichuan province, instituted a civil prosecution against Qunfa Bone-dust Factory's infringement upon the environment.[10] In 2004, the people's procuratorate in Yanjiang District in Ziyang, Sichuan province, sent a prosecutorial notice to eight stone factories in Qingshuihe River Basin for illegal stone processing and stone broth discharge into watercourses, which caused pollution and silting of the waterway.[11] In 2008, the people's pprocuratorate in Wangcheng county, Hunan province, instituted the first environmental public interest proceeding in Hunan province for environmental pollution caused by Changsha Pingtang Cement Co., Ltd and eventually won the case.[12] The people's procuratorate in Haizhu District, Guangzhou city instituted the first environmental public interest proceeding in Guangdong province against Xinzhongxing Rinse Factory.[13] The People's Procuratorate in Yushui District, Xinyu city instituted the first environmental public interest proceeding in Jiangxi province for pollution of the Xiannu Lake.[14] In 2009, the People's Procuratorate in Xishan District, Wuxi city, instituted a proceeding against Li Huarong and Liu Shimi for unlawful tree-felling beside a highway, which damaged the highway environment.[15] These trials dealt powerful blows against illegal actions that damage the environmental public interest. In so doing, they addressed some of the deficiencies in the Chinese public interest judicial and administrative law system. However, there is no denying that such instances are only local and occasional. They are minor breakthroughs but do not create a significant improvement in the system of legal environmental protection overall.

There are many difficulties which inhibit the people's procuratorates from instituting environmental public interest litigation, which have limited the use of this potentially important approach. One important factor is the present law, which has not made explicit the function of the people's procuratorates in instituting environmental public interest litigation, nor clarified the people's procuratorates' right of intervention in support of environmental public interest litigation.

Whilst we have argued above that by implication and long judicial history it ought be expected that the people's procuratorates do have the right to initiate or participate in non-criminal actions in the pursuit of their role, this is not clear from their enabling legislation.[16] Article 5 of the Organic Law of the People's Procuratorates prescribes that people's procuratorates at all levels shall exercise the following functions and powers: (1) procuratorial authority over cases of treason, cases involving acts to dismember the state and other major criminal cases severely impeding the unified enforcement of state policies, laws, decrees and administrative orders; (2) conduct investigations of criminal cases handled directly by themselves; (3) review cases investigated by public security organs and determine whether to approve arrest, to prosecute or to exempt from prosecution; exercise supervision over the investigatory activities of public security organs to determine whether they conform to the law; (4) initiate public prosecutions of criminal cases and support such prosecutions; exercise supervision over the judicial activities of people's courts to determine whether they conform to the law; and (5) exercise supervision over the execution of judgments and organs in criminal cases and over the activities of prisons, detention houses and organs in charge of reform through labor to determine whether such execution and activities conform to the law.

It is obvious that the rights of the people's procuratorates are confined to the criminal field, as scant mention is made of civil or administrative litigation. Secondly, Article 108 of the Civil Procedure Law of the People's Republic of China provides that the following conditions must be met when a suit is brought: (1) the plaintiff must be an individual, legal person or any other organization that has a direct interest in the case; (2) there must be a specific defendant; (3) there must be a concrete claim, a factual basis, and a cause for the suit; and (4) the suit must be within the scope of acceptance for civil lawsuits of the people's courts and within the specific jurisdiction of the people's court where it is filed. In accordance with it, the parties nominated as authorized to institute proceedings are confined to the citizens, legal persons, and other organizations that share a direct interest in the cases. The people's procuratorates are not listed. In addition, Article 2 of the Administrative Procedure Law of People's Republic of China stipulates that in case a citizen, a legal person or other organization's lawful rights and interests are infringed upon by a concrete administrative action by an administrative organ or its personnel, they shall have the right to initiate an action in a people's court in accordance with this law.

Because of the lack of a clear legal standing to commence or join such litigation, it can become difficult for the people's procuratorates which institute environmental public interest litigation to obtain the support of the courts. This will slow down the process of the people's procuratorates advancing public interest litigation. Sometimes actions initiated by the people's procuratorates are rejected by the courts. Sometimes the people's procuratorates have to try to persuade other departments and groups to institute environmental proceedings. In most cases, however, even when faced with environmental damage, they are at a loss.

Affected by the lack of clear legal support for the people's procuratorates pursuing non-criminal action, the setup of the functional departments and issues of human resources, people's procuratorates place more emphasis on criminal rather than civil or administrative action. The practical challenge is illustrated by the practice of the Laoshan district people's procuratorate in Qingdao. Two weeks of field work were used to analyse this example. The procuratorate structure includes departments responsible for arrest, investigation and supervision, public litigation, anti-corruption and bribery, anti-malfeasance and infringement, accusation and appeals, and civil administration. Only the prosecutorial departments concerned with accusation and appeal and civil administration are potentially aligned with the conduct of civil and administrative actions. However, there are only three permanent staff in the relevant department. In the first half of the year 2009 they were involved in twenty appeals. Such a workload makes it unlikely that this department can provide adequate supervision and prosecution of unlawful civil or administrative acts, making it difficult in practice to institute environmental public interest proceedings.

The personnel allocation and caseloads of the people's procuratorates in other districts of Qingdao City are similar. The problem is circular: the lack of specialist resources limits the practice of environmental public interest litigation, and the lack of such cases reduces the incentive to create the specialist resources.

Through our investigation we learned that the lack of prosecutorial funds is another issue that blocks the people's procuratorates from instituting environmental public interest litigation. If a citizen protests against a civil or administrative judgment and appeals to the people's procuratorate, he only needs to prepare an appeal and need not pay litigation costs. With no capital sources from complainants, the people's procuratorate bears the investigation costs themselves from the limited state funding allocated, as well as in dealing with criminal cases. In this context, if the people's procuratorates wish to initiate any environmental public interest litigation, the expenditure including litigation cost is destined to place very heavy pressure on their internal funds. Thus there is little possibility for the people's procuratorates to participate in the environmental public interest litigation under the current financial situation.

6.5 IMPROVING THE LEGISLATIVE ARRANGEMENTS FOR PUBLIC INTEREST LITIGATION

The Chinese environmental public interest litigation system has not fully matured. In many other jurisdictions public prosecutorial bodies have demonstrated a willingness to support the use of civil and administrative remedies to complement criminal prosecution. Chinese people's procuratorates play a limited role in civil and administrative cases involving public interests, especially in cases concerning environmental matters. The establishment of a more robust environmental public interest litigation system is needed in China as part of the long development of democracy and constitutionality. There is a rising clamor for the people's procuratorates, in exercising their function as supervisory organs of government on behalf of public interests, to institute environmental public welfare litigation (Xiao, 2008, pp. 157–63; Jiang and Chang, 2008, pp. 123–8). A number of reforms would better enable and encourage the people's procuratorates to more completely exercise their potential power in instituting environmental public welfare litigation.

It is necessary to revise the Organic Law of the People's Procuratorates to make clear that taking and supporting civil and administrative actions is part of the role of the people's procuratorates. In Article 5, the general principles should clearly stipulate that the power of the people's procuratorates enables civil and administrative prosecutorial work, and that the people's procuratorates have the right to institute environmental public interest litigation on their own behalf or on behalf of other plaintiffs.

Because China has not established an independent environmental prosecution system environmental actions depend on civil, administrative and criminal procedures. It is desirable to revise the three main procedural laws to make clear the people's procuratorates' function and power in environmental public interest litigation. Under Section 1, Chapter 5 of the Civil Procedure Law that deals with parties to litigation, the legislation should state that the people's procuratorates have the right to institute (or to defend) environmental public interest litigation. In Chapter 4 of the Administrative Procedure Law, which deals with participants to an action, it should be stipulated that the people's procuratorates have a right to institute public interest administrative litigation for the purpose of defending public interests, including environmental interests (Ma, 2006, pp. 166–7). Whilst these amendments will provide the standing required for the people's procuratorates to take certain actions, these amendments are not enough. The scope, procedure and approach of the people's procuratorates who institute environmental public interest litigation will also need specific rules. It would be possible for the Supreme People's Procuratorate to enact the Environmental Public Interest Procedure Rule of the People's Procuratorates based on the Criminal Procedure Rule of the People's Procuratorates.

In relation to environmental crimes that have already taken place, it is important that the people's procuratorates do institute criminal and subsidiary civil action. It has been suggested that this requires amending the Criminal Procedure Law to encompass civil liabilities and to improve coordination of criminal law through the amendment of the Civil Procedure Law and Administrative Procedure Law (Cao and Yin, 2007, p. 158).

Some districts have progressed legal and judicial practice in this direction. For example, the people's court and the people's procuratorate in Beilun District, Ningbo City, have jointly established the Interim Provision of the People's Court and the People's Procuratorate in Beilun District of Ningbo City with regard to Instituting Criminal and Subsidiary Civil Action. This provides the local procuratorates with the legal basis to pursue subsidiary civil public interest actions.

In addition to clearly authorizing people's procuratorates' environmental public welfare litigation, it would be desirable to ensure a preferential policy for managing the expense of such litigation. Article 8 of The Payment Means of Expense in Litigation was passed by the State Council of the People's Republic of China on 8 December 2006. It lists situations where there is a free acceptance fee for certain cases. It covers four kinds of cases under the special procedures in civil law where no court costs will be charged against the plaintiff. We propose adding to this list of cost exemptions the conduct of cases concerning the protection of social public interests such as environmental interests. This would better encourage citizens, public interest organizations and the People's Procuratorates to institute environmental public interest litigations and remove another obstacle for public welfare litigation instituted by the people's procuratorates.

NOTES

1. Article 129 of the Constitution of the People's Republic of China states that the people's procuratorates are state organs for legal supervision. Article 130 of the Constitution of the People's Republic of China provides that the PRC establishes the Supreme People's Procuratorate, local people's procuratorates at different levels, the military procuratorates

and other special people's procuratorates. In accordance with the Constitution of the People's Republic of China, the people's procuratorates have the right to exercise procuratorial authority. They exercise this authority over cases endangering state and public security, damaging economic order and infringing citizens' personal and democratic rights, and other important criminal cases; they examine cases scheduled for investigation by the public security agencies, and decide on whether a suspect should be arrested or not, and whether a case should be prosecuted or exempt from prosecution; they institute and support public prosecution in criminal cases; and oversee the activities of public security agencies, people's courts, prisons, houses of detention and reform-through-labor institutions.

2. On 31 December 1983, in the Second National Environmental Protection Conference of China, environmental protection was, for the first time, officially approved as one of the state policies of China.
3. In China, the people's courts are judicial organs exercising judicial power on behalf of the states. According to the Constitution and the Organic Law of the People's Courts of 1979 as amended in 1983, China practices a system of courts characterized by 'four levels and two instances of trials'. The judicial authority of the PRC is exercised by the following people's courts: local people's courts at various levels; military courts and other special people's courts and the Supreme People's Courts. The local people's courts are divided into basic people's courts, intermediate people's courts and higher people's courts.
4. See: Executive Compensation Law of the People's Republic of China.
5. Mauro Cappelletti (1927–2004) was an Italian jurist. He received his doctorate in law from the University of Florence, Italy, and was a Professor of Law at that same institution as well as at Stanford University Law School. In addition, he was Chairman of the Law School at the European University Institute, Florence. For nearly 35 years, Mauro Cappelletti was essentially concerned about fundamental issues like the orality principle, the fundamental guarantees of the proceedings and their social dimension, access to justice either by means of participation or by protection of so-called diffuse interests, alternative ways of guardianship and coexistential justice based on conciliation ways, the judge's role and his responsibility, not to mention, of course, the issues of ideology.
6. Professor L.V. Zhongmei is a dean of Zhongnan University of Economics and Law, China and is one of China's leading environmental law scholars.
7. CAA 302(a): The term 'Administrator' means the Administrator of the Environmental Protection Agency. 303 Notwithstanding any other provision of this chapter, the Administrator, upon receipt of evidence that a pollution source or combination of sources (including moving sources) is presenting an imminent and substantial endangerment to public health or welfare, or the environment, may bring suit on behalf of the United States in the appropriate United States district court to immediately restrain any person causing or contributing to the alleged pollution, to stop the emission of air pollutants causing or contributing to such pollution, or to take such other action as may be necessary.
8. CWA 309 (a)(1) Whenever, on the basis of any information available to him, the Administrator finds that any person is in violation of any condition or limitation which implements section 301, 302, 306, 307, 308, 318, or 405 of this Act in a permit issued by a State under an approved permit program under section 402 or 404 of this Act, he shall proceed under his authority in paragraph (3) of this subsection or he shall notify the person in alleged violation and such State of such finding. If beyond the thirtieth day after the Administrator's notification the State has not commenced appropriate enforcement action, the Administrator shall issue an order requiring such person to comply with such condition or limitation or shall bring a civil action in accordance with subsection.
9. In 2003 the people's procuratorate in Leling, Shandong province, instituted civil prosecution against a defendant Fan whose illegal oil refining polluted the environment. The people's court in Leling supported the litigation according to Article 5, Article 73, and Article 134 of the General Principles of Civil Law. Defendant Fan's factory was asked to be closed down within five days to stop the infringement on the environment and the local residents. This is a good example of successful environmental public interest litigation instituted by the people's procuratorates in recent years in China.

10. In 2002 the People's Procuratorate in Langzhong, Sichuan province, instituted civil public interest litigation against Qunfa Bone-dust Factory's infringement upon the environment. After the trial, the people's court in Langzhong held that the pollutants discharged from the factory made great infringement on the environment and the local residents' lives and adjudicated that the factory should stop the infringement and improve this equipment within one month until they could reach the legal standard.
11. In 2004, the people's procuratorate in Yanjiang Distrct in Ziyang, Sichuan province sent a prosecutorial notice to eight stone factories in Qingshuihe River Basin for illegal stone processing and stone broth discharge into watercourses which caused pollution and silting of the waterway. These factories were required to rectify their plant and report that to the People's Procuratorate. They were warned that civil action would be taken.
12. In 2008, the people's procuratorate in Wangcheng county, Hunan province, instituted the first environmental public interest proceeding in Hunan province regarding environmental pollution caused by Changsha Pingtang Cement Co., Ltd.. With the mediation of the people's court, an agreement was made between the people's procuratorate in Wangcheng county and the factories concerning pollution that stipulated these factories would compensate for the victims.
13. In 2008, the people's procuratorate in Haizhu District, Guangzhou City, instituted the first environmental public interest proceeding in Guangdong province against Xinzhongxing Rinse Factory. The people's court in Haizhu District adjudicated that the defendant should submit 117,000 RMB as compensation for environmental pollution to the plaintiff, which would then be turned over to the state treasury for environmental protection.
14. In 2008, the people's procuratorate in Yushui District, Xinyu City, instituted the first environmental public interest proceeding in Jiangxi province for pollution of the Xiannu Lake. With the mediation of the people's court, an agreement was made between the people's procuratorate in Yushui District and the defendant such that the defendant promised to deal with the environmental problem to achieve zero emission. As a consequence of that prosecution, a further eight harm-doers in the same district promised to undertake pollution treatment.
15. In 2009, the people's procuratorate in Xishan District, Wuxi City, instituted a public interest proceeding against Li Huarong and Liu Shimi for unlawful tree felling beside a highway and a criminal proceeding against their breaking the Forest Law of the People's Republic of China. Under the judgment of the people's court in Xishan District, the two defendants received a criminal penalty and fines and they were required to plant 19 trees and to be responsible for caring for the trees under the supervision of the Agriculture and Forestry Bureau in Xishan District.
16. The authors of this chapter acknowledge funding from the Ministry of Justice PRC's research program on national constitutionality and juristic theory, 'Research on the Function and Legislative Support of People's Procuratorates Instituting Environmental Public Interest Litigation' (Grant No. 09SFB3040).

REFERENCES

Cao, S.C. and G.Z. Yin (2007), 'The Criminal Responsibility Investigation in Criminal Cases', *Review of Civil and Administrative Prosecution* (6), 158.
Hong, H. (2001), *On Prosecutorial Power* (Wuhan University Press), 60–61.
Jiang, W. and T.B. Chang (2008), 'The Innovation and Prefect of Civil Prosecution and Supervision', *Review of Civil and Administrative Prosecution* (7), 123–8.
Ma, H.D. (2006), 'It is Necessary to Set up Public Interest Administrative Litigation System', *Review of Civil and Administrative Prosecution* (4), 166–7.

Fuchinski, B.K. (1983), *American Civil Litigation* (translated by Jiang W. and J.H. Liu) (Beijing Law Press), 67.

Xiao, J.H. (2008), 'Establishing Public Interest Litigation System is an Urgent Subject in Civil Prosecution Legislation Amendment', *Review of Civil and Administrative Prosecution* (7), 157–63.

7. Environmental e-governance in China: insights from government-citizen interaction[1]

Qin Tianbao[2] and Wang Huanhuan[3]

7.1 INTRODUCTION

In what has been labeled the "Information Age", information, predominantly through the Internet and other Information and Communication Technologies (ICTs), is widely and ever freely produced, disseminated and accessible. This, in turn, has had major impacts at the social, economic, cultural and political levels as was anticipated long ago by John Dewey: "Our modern state-unity is due to the consequences of technology employed so as to facilitate the rapid and easy circulation of opinions and information, as so as to generate constant and intricate interaction far beyond the limits of face-to-face communities … The elimination of distance, at the base of which are physical agencies, has called into being the new form of political association" (Dewey (1946), pp. 114–15). Indeed, the impacts of ICTs can be found in almost every realm of modern society with the advent of so many "electronic things" such as e-commerce, e-governance, and e-government.

Environmental governance is also changing as a result of the Information Age. A new environmental governance mode based on ICTs, defined later in this chapter as environmental electronic governance (EEG), is emerging. Many leading countries have pioneered the use of ICTs in varied aspects of environmental governance. For instance, in their decision-making processes, the United States Department of Agriculture and the United States Forest Service have both used the Internet as a major channel to solicit public input for their proposed rules, respectively, the 1997 Organic Labeling Rule and the 2000 Roadless Area Conservation Rule (Zavestoski et al. (2006), pp. 1–26). On a broader spectrum, ICT-enabled energy efficiency measures could contribute to reduced energy consumption.[4] GIS (Geographic Information System), is a type of ICT in a broader context which can be utilized in environmental planning, natural resources management and environmental modeling, to name but a few uses for this technology (Waddell (2002), pp. 297–314; Mallawaarachchi (1996), pp. 169–89; Goodchild (1993), pp. 3–28).

In China, there is increasing enthusiasm for online environmental initiatives, but little systematic evaluation of their actual impact on environmental rulemaking in the current literature. In order to bridge the gap, this chapter aims to draw the contours of electronic environmental governance, the emergence of which is given little attention in China, to find out how and to what extent ICTs exert influence on environmental governance in China, and to analyze possible future scenarios for environmental governance in that country. Given the pivotal roles of government and citizen in environmental protection, the interaction between the two is the focus of this research. The chapter first provides an overview of environmental e-governance in China. Then, environmental e-governance initiated by government is examined through content analysis of portal websites of environmental agencies at national and provincial levels. Citizen-oriented environmental e-governance, categorized into organized, semi-organized and unorganized forms, is explored in the third section. Finally, the chapter analyzes the structural transformation that might happen in future environmental e-governance, the barriers that might impede it and the role that law plays in the advancement of environmental e-governance.

7.2 ENVIRONMENTAL E-GOVERNANCE (EEG) AND ITS EMERGENCE IN CHINA

7.2.1 Scope

For the purposes of the chapter, EEG is used to refer to the rules, behavior and dynamic process by actors, including government, industries, market and civil society, using information and communication technologies for the purpose of protecting the environment and achieving sustainable development involved in environmental protection.

Environmental e-governance could contribute to steering society toward sustainable development for a number of reasons. First, it can facilitate coordination and various formal or informal types of interactions between actors, including political institutions and public-sector organizations, corporations, civil society and international organizations. Second, environmental administration becomes more cost-benefit effective when relying on ICTs such as GIS, remote sensor, shared database, the Internet and so forth. Third, a large range of environmental information become accessible to anyone, regardless of ethnicity, gender, income, region, who has the equipment and basic skills for navigating the Internet or other ICTs almost anytime they want. Fourth, by eliminating geographic barriers, it also has the potential to allow environmental administration to reach out to, and to hear from, people who would not normally participate in person. Citizens are able to post complaints on environmental problems on the Internet or even talk online with the staff of environmental agencies. Detailed, localized, and customized information is made available over the Internet. Citizens' participation, which, for all practical purposes, was almost impossible under traditional environmental governance, can now become a reality.

Therefore, environmental e-governance is more than a new form of environmental governance. It can transform the structures of political and social power, as well as their institutional functioning significantly. In a modern democracy, environmental e-governance is a process though which the public influences environmental legislation, environmental administration, and environmental justice with the help of ICTs. Generating, processing, transmitting and using environmental information are sources of power enabling environmental reform. The conventional power of authorities in environmental protection is partly replaced by informational resources and flows, and processed in new governance arrangements and networks (Mol (2006), pp. 497–514). This is because the new information technologies such as SMS, Bluetooth, tracking systems, email, online community facilities, online forums, groups, BBS, blogs, chat room, instant messages and wireless networks, provide easily accessed, large-scale, high-speed, as well as low-cost information through interactions with a great number of actors engaged in environmental governance. Citizens have many more opportunities than before to influence and participate in environmental policy-making and related processes. Therefore, in environmental e-governance, every actor is likely to become an information supplier and to influence governance, resulting in multi-decentralization of country/state power in environmental administration as a more stable structure.

7.2.2 Features of EEG

As a new but promising form of environmental governance, embodying different values and functions, EEG has the following features not embraced by traditional government with regard to environmental protection:

- It provides abundant tools to solicit citizen input in the environmental rulemaking and implementation process. The public sphere, broadened by the Internet, spurs citizens' interest in environmental problems and protection and facilitates their engagement. In some cases, groups of citizens become strong enough to be at the center of environmental governance due to their deliberation and agreement on the Internet and other ICTs without the limitation of distance.
- It focuses on networking and interaction among social sectors, includ-

ing government, NGOs, citizens and other formal or informal entities. The net-structured relations, i.e. coordination, collaboration and partnership, are in accord with ubiquitous ICTs and their combination.

- Ultimately, there is a virtual political-social structure pertaining to environmental governance concerned with how citizens exert influence on government's environmental decision making and suggesting new ways for the public sector to perform environmental administration. In this context, the emergence of environmental rights is facilitated.

Therefore, if environmental e-governance is a natural development choice in the Information Age, it also has as a consequence the democratization of environmental governance in this century.

7.2.3 Core of EEG

There is a consensus in the current literature regarding ICTs' positive role on democracy (Hague and Loader (1999), pp. 21–5; Snellen (2001), pp. 45–8). By putting information in the hands of citizens, individuals and groups are given the capacity to understand and to challenge the performance of industry and government officials in ways that historically they have not been able to do due to limited access to information (Esty (2004), pp. 115–211). Internet-based public participation may hold the greatest promise for environmental decisions where stakeholders are dispersed and face-to-face interaction is implausible (Zavestoski et al. (2006), pp. 1–26). It focuses on the breadth and the depth of a participatory and direct form of citizen engagement in addressing environmental challenges. The Internet and other ICTs are an ideal way for government to demonstrate its position in environmental governance and for citizens to understand the concern and framework of others. In this way, citizens are provided with more opportunities to participate in environmental protection activity, to communicate their own needs and opinions and to be considered by the authorities. Also, they are likely to become independent actors in environmental governance once they express their environmental concerns or get involved in environmental actions, for instance through environmental movements.

With the continuing environmental degradation and accompanying government deficiency, public *trust* in government generally declines. More practical environmental information, expanded solicitation and acceptance of public comments derived from environmental e-governance are good ways to reverse this situation, resulting in increased trust in government. It can also enhance citizens' access to more environmental information, to be engaged in public sphere, to share experience, knowledge and value with each other and finally to upgrade their ability to understand environmental issues and get involved in environmental governance. In addition, the Internet and other ICTs provide a reflexive open platform in which participants are able to voice diverse demands and need on an equal footing, without political pressure and unconstrained by economic concerns. More environmental information available online and more convenient participation channels spur public interest in participation and thus lead to transparency and accountability in environmental governance.

Compared with electronic systems that provide information, service and tools for the public, businesses and various levels of government, the use of computer networks to expand public involvement in policy deliberation has a more profound impact on the functioning of democratic societies (Carlitz and Gunn (2002), pp. 389–405).

7.2.4 The Emergence of EEG in China

China has assigned high priority to ICTs. It began to focus on telecommunications infrastructure in the early 1980s and has made great strides since then. The number of persons using the Internet in China was estimated to be approximately 460 million by June 2010. This number is expected to continue to increase sharply in the foreseeable future, according to the annual report of the China Internet Network Information Center.[5] As the data of the Ministry of Industry and Information Technology show, the number of mobile phone users approached 814 million in July 2010 and should expand by 17.51 percent annually in the coming years.[6] It is unquestionable that Chinese citizens are increasingly connected by ICTs, a development which is bound to influence social governance profoundly.

China is investing a large amount in e-government, growing at a compounded annual rate of 40 percent or so. Even before the country was fully connected to the global "network of networks", China began to implement programs to facilitate e-government (Zhou (2004), pp. 4–19). In 1993 China started an e-government project called "Golden Projects" (Lan (2004), pp. 317–24). In 1999 it launched the "Government Online Project". Online electronic information exchange, online government procurement bidding, online welfare payments, electronic delivery, information center, electronic document management and publication, electronic tax, and digital identification were implemented across the country (Zhaoxing (1999)).

The Internet and other ICTs have been affecting the way we protect our environment as well. Esty has noted that the breakthroughs in computers and communications technologies as well as the knowledge revolution will change our understanding of environmental problems, the value we put on environmental harm and our thinking about response strategies (Esty (2004), pp. 115–211). The environmental e-governance under way in China can be identified with better monitoring, greater information disclosure, more active citizen involvement and more ecolabelling and certification. More specifically, at least four dimensions of environmental governance are changing with the pervasive application of ICTs. First, the scale and methods of environmental monitoring have changed profoundly. Continuous automatic monitoring and subsequent data analysis performed by ICTs are more and more widely used in environmental administration. Former monitoring procedures such as sample analysis combined with succeeding result release, are becoming obsolete. Second, ICTs are broadly used in environmental planning and resource conservation in the country. In 2008, China launched three additional satellites for environmental protection and disaster control. Third, ICTs' role in energy saving, GHG (greenhouse gas) emission reduction and natural resource preservation are gradually being recognized. Direct impacts such as reductions in paper consumption, application of ICTs in intelligent transport systems, smart production streamlined with less resource input and waste have come into being in recent China. Fourth, citizens' environmental awareness, their rights to know, and public participation are enhanced with the advent of environmental e-governance. More information is posted on government websites, and some interactive tools are even employed. Lay citizens resort to the Internet to promote various environmental petitions.[7] The four categories can be differentiated analytically, but they exist to varying degrees and on varying scales in the real-world context.

While each of these categories is important, we will focus on the fourth one to examine the interaction and coordination between government and citizens. As noted by Donald F. Kettl, governance is the outcome of the interaction of government, the public service, and citizens throughout the political process, policy development, program design, and service delivery. Also, it takes a larger view of social objectives, so it involves the coordination of efforts rather than focusing on an individual practice, or player, or process (Kettl (2002), p. 23).

7.3 GOVERNMENT-ORIENTED EEG IN CHINA

7.3.1 Overview

Given the predominant role of government in governance, government-oriented environmental e-governance is the main component of environmental e-governance in China. Faced with environmental governance in transition, environmental agencies, which exist at the national, provincial, municipal and county levels, are moving rapidly to adopt ICTs to provide information, services and to interact with the public, businesses and other governmental entities. Early in the seventh Five-year Plan from 1986 to 1990, a few ICT application systems and small databases called Dbase II were adopted in the State Environmental Protection Administration (SEPA).[8] In 1992, a project sponsored by the Asian Development Bank – "Construction of environmental management information system in selected cities", generally viewed as a milestone of "informatization" in the environmental agencies, was carried out in the Environmental Protection Bureau (EPB) of Shanghai, Nantong and Dalian, followed by the foundation of Information Centers in the three cities.[9] A similar center was set up in the State Environmental Protection Administration four years later. In between, the application of GIS was enhanced in the sphere of environmental protection. With the help of a World Bank loan, an information network consisting of a Sybase database and UNIX server combined with X.25 web was completed in 27 Environmental Bureaus at the provincial level.[10] The ambitious pace of environmental agencies heading for e-governance apparently accelerated further in the new century. In 2003, a comprehensive information platform developed by the Information Center of the State Environmental Protection Administration was set up to support a portal website of the Administration online, to integrate an environmental government system with office automation, and to share useful information resources.[11] Today, all the provincial environmental agencies except Xizang (Tibet) have portal websites to facilitate environmental governance. Considering the endeavors and enthusiasm so far, one can expect that more resources will be invested in EEG, with environmental agencies taking the leading role.

7.3.2 Content Analysis of Environmental Agencies' Website

In order to investigate government-oriented environmental e-governance in China both quantifiably and quantitatively, one has to explore the content of environmental agencies' websites to gain insight into how they are harnessing ICTs for governance. "Through a portal, the information systems of all departments and agencies can be linked to deliver integrated services in a way that avoids citizens having to understand the complicated internal organizational structures of government" (Holmes (2001), p. 21). A government portal website is not equivalent to government-oriented environmental e-governance, but it is a vital element of the latter. The portal website largely indicates the spectrum and depth of e-service provided by the government. Content analysis of the portal websites of the environmental agencies will shed light on the achievements and shortcomings in terms of environmental e-governance, as well as on the government-citizen relationship in the environmental protection realm. Therefore, we have examined the current national and all provincial websites, that is, the website of the Ministry of

Environmental Protection and 30 other websites of environmental agencies at the provincial level.[12] Several benchmark themes are proposed based on a survey of websites of state environmental agencies in the United States (Beierle and Cahill (2000)):

- Information on environmental provisions: including information on environmental laws and regulations, environmental news, environmental conditions, environmental knowledge as well as environmental information on regulated firms.
- Online consultation: solicit public input concerning draft of environmental laws and regulations, environmental plans, EIA reports and other documents containing decision making over the Internet.
- Online service: including administrative permits, application for administrative reconsideration, application for information dissemination, and document downloads service.
- Interaction: including online survey, online consultation from citizen, online complaints, online discussion and public forum.

7.3.2.1 Environmental information provision

A thorough scrutiny of each website of the 31 environmental agencies reveals that most of the websites perform relatively well on environmental information provision.

Those who are good information providers not only provide comprehensive environmental information at the national level, but also detailed regional and local environmental information, such as regional environmental quality data, annual environmental quality report and the results of the Quantitative Examination System. For instance, the EPB of Hunan province has set up a specific sub-website on biodiversity protection in the Dongting Lake area, the largest fresh water lake in China. Related information, including natural reserves, alien species invasion and species distribution and so forth, are made public via the Internet.[13] Another case in point is the website of the EPB of Jiangsu with the page on Watershed Management, with information on plans, laws and regulations, unified standards, management news on combating water pollution and water resource management.[14] Laggard environmental agencies, such as the EPBs of Qinghai and Guizhou, deal poorly with broad environmental information provision and updates.

It is worth noticing that monitoring data with respect to control and enforcement of discharge permits, together with other environmental information on individual companies, is hard to access over the Internet apart from mandatory information dissemination by regulated firms with illegal pollution emission. The Ministry website is undoubtedly taking the leading role. Early in 2007, SEPA published a 237-page list of more than 6000 industrial polluters on its website, requiring them to install automatic emission monitoring and control systems that are directly connected to local EPBs, and planning for disclosure of this collected data (Mol (2009)). The EPB of Shanxi's website at least releases some firms' environmental information. This ranks it among the good performers, regardless of the authenticity of the information, a topic which is beyond the scope of the research.[15] The government's reluctance to release information is in part due to a poor monitoring system and incomplete pollution data in China.

7.3.2.2 Online consultation

Consultations concerning draft environmental laws and regulations, environmental plans and EIA reports and other documents involving environmental decision making are sometimes solicited via websites by these agencies. Due to the variation in environmental protection levels, large discrepancies exist between the provinces, with those with prosperous economies generally doing better on online consultation. For example, information about the EIA's approval of construction projects is posted on the website of the Zhejiang Environmental Protection Bureau to solicit public review.[16] On the other hand, there is hardly any consultation through the EPB of Nei Mongol's website.[17]

One problem with consultation is that few people take part in it since the governmental websites are not attractive for those who want to get useful and genuine information. The comments from one individual are not shared with others, and therefore there is no space for discussion. Most seriously, the decision maker does not respond to comments from the public. As a result, whether one comment is scrutinized and adopted or not remains veiled to the public. Thus, it often seems that soliciting a viewpoint is no more than one way of dismissing them in favor of scientific accounts. Public trust in environmental agencies generally declines, and the likelihood of future participation diminishes.

7.3.2.3 Online service

Online services ranging from application for an administrative permit to approval of construction projects via environmental agencies' website are primarily serving industries. The EPBs of Beijing and Shanghai are among the best of these service providers for industry. There are still a number of provinces, especially in inland China, which offer poor services. An "Online Application" icon links to a blank page on the websites of the EPBs of Guizhou,[18] Nei Mongol[19] and Ningxia.[20]

An online service titled "Application for Information Disclosure" for the lay citizen is available on each agency's website. This is due to a transparency rule requiring all government environmental agencies and polluting companies to disclose important environmental information to the public. This rule was adopted by the State Environmental Protection Administration in May 2007[21] and is also part of the wider Regulations on Open Government Information issued by the State Council in 2008[22] to open up access to government information. Since then, all the agencies' websites host a special space for online "application for information disclosure". The results from this service are far from satisfying, according to the annual reports concerning environmental information dissemination released by environmental protection agencies. For example, according to the report from the EPB of Tianjin in 2008, no one visited the column on Information Disclosure through the year, and there were no online applications for information disclosure.[23] The situation for other provinces is not encouraging either. However, the situation is different at the Ministry of Environmental Protection where the rate of online application for information disclosure was 89.7 percent in 2008.[24] The reasons for insufficient usage of online services by citizens ought to be examined, considering the broader social context.

7.3.2.4 Interaction

Online surveys, online consultations from citizens, online complaints, online spaces for comments as well as online conversations with agency staff are gradually being adopted across environmental protection agencies. These tools are likely to attract more public engagement via the Internet.

None of the websites is performing well under the interaction theme due to the one-way, closed character of all the interactive tools provided. To be specific, more than half of the agencies are reluctant to post citizens' comments, complaints, survey choice and consultation on their websites. The Internet's potential to facilitate dialogue is being undermined. Even those who have offered web access to the comments of citizens do not allow horizontal communication among citizens. There are, however, exceptions. The EPB of Tianjin's website has a public forum online, but apparently with few discussions.[25]

Some websites, such as those of the EPBs of Nei Mongol and Guizhou, suffer from many deficiencies such as unlinkable icons, blank pages, superficial design or infrequent response by government representatives. As a result, citizens are not given a sufficient opportunity to engage, to develop a symbolic consensus on the necessity and legitimacy of environmental governance. Another example is the EPB of Shanxi's website which received 115 environmental complaints but replied to only a few of them, with many of the replies lacking substantial content, such as "Please call local 12369 Hotline[26] to complain".[27] Furthermore, among the limited number of meaningful replies, nearly all investigation conclusions reject citizens' complaints.

7.3.3 "Untold Stories" of Current Government-oriented EEG in China

To sum up, government-oriented environmental e-governance mainly associated with government portal websites has sprung up in China. Existing efforts to apply ICTs in environmental e-governance have a noticeable effect on the conventional ways to fulfil government's responsibility in environmental protection and to enable lay citizens to play a greater role in environmental rulemaking. However, the results so far suggest that electronic governance led by environmental agencies is in an early and experimental phase. There are still "untold stories" revealed in part by our investigation in the preceding section.

The first is the differences between various levels of governance, revealing a regional gap with respect to environmental protection. Generally, the national websites put the emphasis on information concerning environmental provisions, while regional websites, specifically the municipality and coastal provinces, and environmental agencies, performed better with online service and interaction. These are regions with a prosperous economy and citizens there are clamoring for more participation. As a result, the national websites of environmental agencies and those in coastal provinces are more sophisticated. Those of inland provinces are rigidly designed to meet the basic needs of government, citizens, and business relevant to environmental governance. Any investigation of environmental e-governance in China is inappropriate without taking account of the economic, social and cultural domains underlying this gap.

Second, all but one provincial environmental agency have websites and most provide substantial amounts of information online. However, opportunities for active online interaction between citizens and government, as well as among citizens themselves, are relatively limited. A one-way, closed information flow is no different from traditional information flows based on letters, fax or telephone. By contrast, open and two-way communication processes such as online public forums should be developed and incorporated in environmental e-governance. Otherwise, the conflict and controversy characteristic of environmental regulatory policy-making will not be tempered through the use of the internet as a public participation mechanism (Zavestoski et al. (2006)).

Third, the level of environmental e-governance in China is surprisingly a little better than we assumed, whereas the actual effect of these online governance tools seems not so promising. Much the same effect could easily have been achieved through the annual reports and information disclosure released by environmental agencies. The Annual Report on Information Disclosure of the Ministry of Environmental Protection shows that only 10 percent of all consultations from the public were over the Internet in 2008.[28] Things are even less promising at the provincial level. There were only two cases of online application for information disclosure in 2008, and no online comment is recorded on the website of Hubei Province Environmental Protection Agency.[29] The limited response rate with regard to online surveys also reveals the insufficiency of EEG in China. In addition to low environmental awareness and the inherent deficit in website layout, the unavailability of demand-side analysis inevitably discourages public input and deliberation. There are means to avoid this. For example, websites can be dedicated to the collection and dissemination of public comment on proposed rules similar to the one adopted by the USDA's National Organic Program (Zavestoski et al. (2006)). Additionally, tools like "WAC Track" allow the public to subscribe to a list to be automatically notified twice a week by email of all new postings of the Washington State Department of Ecology in the US (Beierle and Cahill (2000)).

Finally, a "trust crisis" gradually emerges during the government-oriented EEG process. Considering ICTs' role in enhancing public trust, they also have the potential to undermine it. Government-oriented EEG is in many ways a two-step-forward-one-step-backward method of government-citizen trust building. Those who use ICTs, especially the Internet, in all aspects of their lives, have greater expectations of the extent of the government's online service, the speed of information access, interactivity, the spectrum of online service, as well as the security of information (Holmes (2001), pp. 10–11). The current situation of government-oriented EEG is still far from satisfying. More demands and relatively fewer achievements induce greater disappointment on the part of citizens. Also, face-to-face communication is still today the prevailing source of reliance between people due to Chinese traditional culture. The virtual relationship, on the other hand, risks generating panic and suspicion, especially in its earlier phase.

The government failure mainly lies in what is both a hierarchical and at the same time fragmented structure for environmental protection. The pervasiveness of ICTs does provide some hope. Whether a connected government could lead to real sustainable development will depend on the nature of the relationship between the structure of government, an entity obligated to take decisions on a systematic basis and to implement measures and governance based on a dynamic process emphasizing more interaction, collaboration and wide effect. The traditional ways in which government operates, informs and solicits citizen input ought to change into a more dynamic and cooperative structure.

7.4 CITIZEN-ORIENTED EEG IN CHINA

Just as information technology has transformed the environmental agencies' governance process, so the Internet and other ICTs also change the way that lay people are involved in environmental governance. It has spurred the emergence of citizen-oriented e-governance as a counter domain to government-oriented e-governance in China. Rather than the more heavily scrutinized and restricted information dissemination and participation mechanism of government-oriented environmental e-governance, citizens prefer to utilize a commercial network to initiate governance. It is thus not surprising that environmental e-governance motivated by citizens has greater potential to generate localized, autonomous, and effective, even if slightly unstable,[30] contributions to good environmental governance and deliberative democracy in China. The reason for its effectiveness is that lay citizens directly affected by environmental degradation might negotiate with the polluters by means of ICTs' potential for building consensus without the intervention of a third party. The transaction cost is accordingly reduced.

7.4.1 ICTs and Public Sphere

ICTs, and especially the Internet, extend and pluralize the public sphere in a number of ways (Dahlgren (2005)). The use of the Internet by thousands of individuals and groups around the world for political activism as a tool to influence the electoral system and governmental policy has become an important part of the e-democracy equation.[31] The enlarged public sphere, due to large-scale usage of the Internet and other ICTs, not only diversifies the channels through which lay citizens may express themselves, but also makes free dialogue, negotiation, debate and deliberation available everywhere.

Although electronic media might not fully replace face-to-face meetings, well-organized use of ICTs can help to enhance the participation of citizens and to achieve a balanced representation of people's values and concerns, for instance, by representing analytical results appropriately and by supporting discourses between citizens and authorities (Göhring et al. (2004)). With ICTs "in hand", citizens in China, together with the online public sphere they rely on, have gradually grown to become a bold and somewhat independent power for environmental governance.

7.4.2 Current Situation of Citizen-oriented Environmental E-governance in China

Generally, citizen-oriented environmental e-governance takes three forms. Each of these will be analyzed through the use of a case study.

7.4.2.1 Organized citizen-oriented environmental e-governance

Case 1: Green-web (http://www.green-web.org) In September 1999, a group of Internet users set up a web-based environmental NGO called "Green-web" which, in the following ten years, took full advantage of the Internet in terms of its abundant information and diversity to unite environmental volunteers. Online activities are the main expression of this NGO, while it also emphasizes offline environmental protection activities. The Internet-based communicative realm is ploughed to enhance international outreach. It also launched a capacity building program in 2004 to help new grassroot environmental NGOs to build or improve their websites.

Like Green-web, some other web-based environmental groups such as Greener Beijing,[32] The Tibetan Antelope Information Center,[33] Han Hai Sha,[34] and the Green Student Environmental Action Network[35] have mushroomed to raise environmental awareness and enhance public mobilization. Former offline environmental NGOs also have moved rapidly to use the Internet and other ICTs. More than half of them have set up websites with environmental information, bulletin boards and Internet campaigns aimed at publicizing environmental information, setting up discussion groups, mobilizing volunteers, organizing activities and campaigns, and catalyzing offline campaigns.[36] There exists today in China an organized citizen-oriented environmental e-governance domain, where discussion is framed by organizations with generally shared perceptions, values, and goals – and geared toward forms of political intervention. These online or offline environmental non-governmental organizations, especially those that operate both online and on the ground, are relatively influential in linking activists, disseminating environmental information, publicizing their views in the mass media and pressurizing governments and industries to adjust environmentally adverse decisions. They are able to attract attention via the Internet to a varying extent, depending on their scale and influence. However, many web-based environmental NGOs are not legally recognized by the government since they do not register in competent administrative departments. This impedes further development of these organizations and explains why most of the organizations of this kind remain small.[37]

7.4.2.2 Semi-organized citizen-oriented environmental e-governance

Case 2: Xiamen anti-PX Protest In 2007, the Haicang PX (short for "p-xylene", a raw material used in chemical production) Project, with an investment of 10.8 billion RMB, was supposed to be launched in the coastal city of Haicang in south-eastern China. It was projected that it could bring GDP of over 80 million RMB to the city. However, it was halted and had to move away due to the strong protests of the citizens. … In March 2007, more than a hundred Chinese People's Political Consultative Conference members signed a petition to move the project away from

Xiamen on the grounds of the risk it posed to the city. Thereafter, all the reports with respect to the Haicang PX Project were posted on a local online forum and raised a great deal of controversy. A large number of discussion groups on QQ (the most famous and widely used instant message tool in China) were simultaneously set up. Blogs were also used to spread related information. Despite passionate opposition from Xiamen citizens, the government initially decided to still go ahead with the project. A two-day march with more than 15 000 participants took place on June 1 and 2, 2007. SMS was used to disperse information among citizens before and during the march. Finally, the project was moved to a town 160 miles away.

The protest in the above case lasted for nearly a year. During that time,the Internet played an irreplaceable role in information dissemination, deliberation formation and movement support. The deployment of BBS, discussion groups on QQ and blogs, among others, were the key tools used by the environmental movement. These tools provided a real-time and interactive discussion platform for people actively interested in the project They expressed their own viewpoint regarding the project as well as commenting on, criticizing or interpreting others' arguments. In the process, a movement, that was "anti-PX, protect Xiamen", sharing the same values and viewpoint, came into being.

The Xiamen anti-PX protest is an example of a semi-organized citizen-oriented environmental e-governance based on intangible networking devoted to serving real-world movement. Several leading activists, who were also managers or founders of online forums, discussion groups or hot bloggers, played a key part in the organization of the protest. For instance, a famous blogger, Lian Yue, posted a wide range of information on the PX Project and provided useful advice to the protesters. He was considered to be one of the "spiritual fathers" of the movement. This virtual coalition justified its description as a semi-organized feature of citizen-oriented e-governance.

Why are the Internet and other communication tools extraordinarily critical to citizen-oriented environmental e-governance in China? Scott and Street's arguments concerning the impact of the Internet on social movements provide some answers to this question: first, it allows a high degree of co-ordination between movement networks across a broad geographic range without creating fixed hierarchical organizational forms; second, this, in turn, greatly reduce costs, producing a significant impact with few resources; third, the Internet provides activists with "editorial control" over the image they convey, for example enabling them to counter newspaper and TV reports with their own alternative news media; finally, the relative lack of regulation of the Internet at present offers the option of secrecy and of bypassing the state (Scott and Street (2001)).

7.4.2.3 Unorganized citizen-oriented environmental e-governance

Case 3: Suspicious cobalt-60 leakage in Henan On July 10, 2009, a message entitled "Co-60 leaking in Qixian Kaifeng" appeared online. It immediately circulated in various major online forums and received thousands of hits. It said that the Limin Irradiation Plant, located in Qixian Henan province, which uses Co-60 to preserve garlic and chili powers, had a history of accidents due to malpractice. In the last accident, the pipeline used to store radioactive sources broke. The substance was exposed to the air, resulting in direct radiation from Co-60 leaking. The news sparked a widespread panic, spurring an estimated one million citizens to flee the region. Thereafter, citizens began to question the vague attitude taken by the local government during the accident and urged the adoption and implementation of safer protection measures.

Although the message finally proved to be a false rumor after various tests by the Ministry of Environmental Protection, it demonstrated the immense power citizens can have with regard to environmental governance. The above case is only one instance of the unorganized citizen-oriented environmental e-governance stream flows on the Internet. They are categorized as unorganized EEG for a number of reasons. First, the main objective of this e-governance type is to grab the attention of the conventional mass media or government. The Internet is used as a channel to spread information concerning pollution or a severe ecological disaster. Second, major online forums, such as Tianya, Maopu, Baidu Tieba, as well as major news organizations that have gone online, Internet-based news organizations such as 163.com, sina.com, yahoo.com, are used as a platform for the unorganized, incident-based input. Strong reaction and support from a large range of citizens is the prerequisite for further action. Third, the direct reason for exposing the incident online is the restriction of information from local government and the resulting lack of trust by citizens. This also reveals the tension between national and local government when weighing up their priorities in relation to economic development and environmental protection. In order to achieve economic growth and keep a good reputation, local government often intentionally ignores the adverse impact of environmental problems and conceals accidents. This forces citizens to rely on an easy-access and relatively democratic path like the Internet to speak out.

7.4.3 Will Citizen-oriented Environmental E-governance Go Further?

The three forms of e-governance examined above provide an overview of citizen-oriented environmental e-governance in nowadays China. Whether they are organized, semi-organized or unorganized, they exert great influence on the promotion of environmental protection, enhancement of people's environmental awareness and environmental democracy. With its networking capabilities, the Internet and other communication technologies can connect citizens to each other, making it easier to organize and act on shared environmental protection concerns. Consensus can be achieved through the Internet because positions are strengthened by repetition throughout the comment or other process. Hence, it helps to enhance common social values on environmental affairs.

It is worth noting that environmental movement via the Internet is, for now, only influential if other social or political powers are also engaged. The conventional mass media join in when they find something worth reporting on. A petition, which is also supported by scientific evidence or those who wield political power, tends to be accepted easily. Despite the pitfalls, citizen-oriented environmental e-governance will keep growing due to its key role in improving environmental governance and making up for governmental deficiencies in open democracy. The challenge now is to successfully combine citizen-oriented environmental e-governance with conventional power in the public sphere.

7.5 STRUCTURAL ANALYSIS AND FUTURE DIRECTION FOR ENVIRONMENTAL E-GOVERNANCE IN CHINA

ICTs have undoubtedly become an integral part of environmental governance and promise many improvements in the delivery of governmental service and interactive public participation. Internet-based public participation results in authentic democratic expression rather than aggregation of preferences. When two more or less equal powers in environmental governance contend for influence, each of them can have their unique strategy "enhanced" by this new media. This has special significance for ordinary citizens who were historically overlooked in the environmental governance process in China. The new development stems more from citizens' enthusiasm for environmental e-governance rather than efforts by government. The development of government-oriented versus citizen-oriented EEG is uneven, with more financial support for the former. Reflecting a pre-existing consensus reached by an online population that shares a common concern over local environmental problems, the Internet facilitates the establishment of a citizen alliance. Notwithstanding the unstable structure of EEG in China, in our view, ICTs' role in better environmental governance will be strengthened in the foreseeable future.

Environmental e-governance in China, in its government-oriented and citizen-oriented forms, is still at an early and experimental stage. Key actors will reshape the environmental e-governance pattern continuously through dynamic interactions. More transparent, effective and accountable environmental e-governance initiated by government will probably lead to a decrease in semi-organized and unorganized environmental e-governance by citizens; the expansion of citizen-oriented environmental e-governance will also diminish the need for semi-organized and unorganized environmental e-governance. Any structural adjustment inevitably will be deeply influenced by the overall social, political and cultural context.

There is still room for considerable advancement by means of, among others things, adopting laws and regulation concerning citizens' rights to know and public participation to improve EEG in China. Participation and discourse on environmental rulemaking through the Internet is codified in several existing legal documents such as the 2002 Cleaner Production Promotion Act, the 2008 Regulations on Open Government Information, the 2007 Interim Rule on Open Environmental Information, the 2006 Interim Measures on Public Participation in Environmental Impact Assessment, the 2000 Regulation on Management of Information on the World Wide Web, and the 2000 Regulation on Telecommunication. However, they merely provide a skeletal and incomplete legal basis for environmental e-governance. The role that law can play in future environmental e-governance and in possible improvements to the existing framework needs to be further analyzed. At a minimum the following aspects should be incorporated in future legislation: first, the compulsory disclosure of environmental information of industry should be enhanced since only those in breach of the pollution emission standards now have an obligation to do so. Online information disclosure should be legally recognized. Second, the accessibility and accountability of online environmental information disclosure by government ought to be improved by enforceable legal mechanisms such as administrative action. Third, the right of citizens' participation in environmental governance both through online and offline means should be clearly recognized and protected by law.[38]

In conclusion, we do not think that environmental e-governance is a panacea for environmental governance and all problems of sustainability. Instead, only a systematic combination of conventional and electronic environmental governance can put us on a fruitful path to environmental protection and sustainable development.

NOTES

1. The research for this chapter was supported by the Program for New Century Excellent Talents in University (NCET-10-0617), the key project of Key Research Institute of the Ministry of Education (2009JJD820005) and the Post-70s Scholars Academic Development Program of Wuhan University.
2. Professor in Law, Research Institute of Environmental Law, Wuhan University.
3. Lecturer and Post-doctoral Researcher of Law School at Sun Yat-sen University.
4. See, for instance, Erdmann, L et al. (2004), "The future impact of ICTs on environmental sustainability", http://www.ictregulationtoolkit.org/en/Document.3507.pdf, June 21, 2010.

European Information and Communication Technology Association (2009), "ICT for energy efficiency mobilizing ICT to facilitate the transition to an energy-efficient low carbon economy", http://europa.eu/legislation_summaries/information_society/si0007_en.htm, June 21, 2010.
5. CNNIC (2010), "Report on Internet Development in China" (26th edition), http://www.cnnic.net.cn/uploadfiles/pdf/2010/7/15/100708.pdf, August 20, 2010.
6. Ministry of Industry and Information Technology of the PR China, "Main data of communication industries in July 2010", http://www.miit.gov.cn/n11293472/n11293832/n11294132/n12858447/13363671.html, August 25, 2010.
7. For instance, cases in Section 7.4 of the chapter can exemplify the change.
8. Renamed Ministry of Environmental Protection in the institutional reform of the State Council in 2008.
9. Zhou, Anli (2009), "How advanced is intelligent environmental protection?" http://cio.zdnet.com.cn/cio/2009/0826/1444783.shtml, September 12, 2009.
10. *Id.*
11. Conference file of the First National Conference on infomationization of Environmental Protection, http://www.mep.gov.cn/ztbd/gzhy/xxgzh/, February 5, 2010.
12. There are provincial Environmental Protection Bureaus in Beijing, Tianjin, Hebei, Shanxi, Jilin, Hubei, Hunan, Shannxi, Anhui, Fujian, Gansu, Guangdong, Guizhou, Heilongjiang, Henan, Jiangsu, Jiangxi, Liaoning, Qinghai, Shandong, Sichuan, Yunnan, Zhejiang, Shanghai, Hainan, Chongqing, Guangxi, Nei Mongol, Ningxia, Xinjiang Uygur excluding that in Xizang, Macau, Hong Kong and Taiwan.
13. http://www.hbt.hunan.gov.cn/dongt/, August 23, 2009.
14. http://www.jshb.gov.cn/jshbw/rdzt/lyzz/, August 23, 2009.
15. http://www.sxhb.gov.cn/qyxx/index.asp, August 23, 2009.
16. http://www.zjepb.gov.cn/, September 2, 2009.
17. http://www.nmgepb.gov.cn/, September 2, 2009.
18. http://www.gzhjbh.gov.cn/, September 2, 2009.
19. http://www.nmgepb.gov.cn/Common/nmList.aspx?mid=1148, September 2, 2009.
20. http://www.nxep.gov.cn/, September 2, 2009.
21. Rules on Environmental Information Disclosure, SEPA Decision No. 35, 2008.
22. State Council Decision No. 492, 2008.
23. http://www.tjzfxxgk.gov.cn/tjep/ConInfoParticular.jsp?id=14578, September 2, 2009.
24. The total number of applications for environmental information disclosure in 2008 was 68. Ministry of Environmental Protection, "Government Report on Environmental Information Disclosure 2008 (No. 16/2009)", available at http://vip.chinalawinfo.com/newlaw2002/SLC/slc.asp?db=chl&gid=115493, August 30, 2009.
25. http://www.tjhb.gov.cn/guestbook/index.asp, August 29, 2009.
26. Unified hotline for environmental complaints in China.
27. http://www.sxhb.gov.cn/main/Book.asp?ClassID=2, October 3, 2009.
28. *Supra* note 23.
29. http://www.hubei.gov.cn/zwgk/zfxxgk/tjxxgk/tjndbg/200904/t20090409_94769.shtml, August 20, 2009.
30. Its instability lies in the barely institutionalized structure generated by citizen-oriented environmental e-governance analyzed in the following section.
31. Riley, Tomas B. (2003) "E-government vs. e-governance: Examining the differences in a changing public sector climate. International Tracking Survey Report" available at http://www.rileyis.com/publications/research_papers/tracking03/IntlTrackRptMay03no4.pdf.
32. http://www.grchina.org/greenerbeijing.htm)areunregisteredandoperateonly, October 13, 2009.
33. www.taic.org, October 15, 2009.
34. www.desert.org.cn, October 15, 2009.
35. http://www.gsean.org/, October 15, 2009.
36. As one of the biggest environmental NGOs in China, Friends of Nature pays special attention to the potential of the internet. It organizes volunteers, provides online surveys, and offers environmental information in a broad spectrum through its website. See http://www.fon.org.cn/, December 13, 2010.

37 To register or not is a dilemma for environmental NGOs, including online environmental NGOs in China. On the one hand, they can get very little financial support from the government and companies in China without registration, especially when support from funds and development organizations outside China are more and more competitive and less funding is available. They are also faced with an "identity crisis" when operating and cannot access social insurance for their employees if they do not register. On the other hand, registration might bring about more restrictions and interest conflicts due to the current regulation concerning registration of NGOs in China. If an organization wants to register as a non-profit organization, it should make sure there is no other organization with the same characteristics in the same area. Also, it should find a governmental department to be affiliated to. This means more interference and control. However, in a phase when survival is the biggest challenge for environmental NGOs in China, registration is almost the only way for them to expand their operations.

38. The overall statement of the citizen's role in environmental protection is "each citizen has the duty to protect the environment. Also, they have the right to report any infringement of the law." Article 6 of the Environmental Protection Law of the PRC.

REFERENCES

Beierle, Thomas C. and Sarah Cahill (2000), "Electronic Democracy and Environmental Governance: A Survey of the States", RFF Discussion Paper 00-42, Washington, DC: Resources for the Future.

Carlitz, Robert D. and Rosemary W. Gunn (2002), "Online Rulemaking: A Step toward E-governance", *Government Information Quarterly*, 19 (4), 389–405.

Dahlgren, Peter (2005), "The Internet, Public Spheres, and Political Communication: Dispersion and Deliberation", *Political Communication*, 22 (1), 147–62.

Dewey, John (1946), *The Public and its Problems: An Essay in Political Inquiry*, Chicago: Gateway Books.

Esty, Daniel C. (2004), "Environmental Protection in the Information Age", *New York University Law Review*, 79 (1), 1–24.

Goodchild, Michael F. (1993), *Environmental Modeling with GIS*, New York: Oxford University Press.

Göhring, Wolf *et al.* (2004), "Knowledge Discovery, Thematic Maps, and E-discussion as Means for a Sustainable Decision Making in Developing Countries", 18th International Conference, Informatics for Environmental Protection, EnviroInfo 2004, 21–23 October, Geneva.

Hague, Barry N. and Brian Loader (eds) (1999), *Digital Democracy: Discourse and Decision Making in the Information Age*, New York: Routledge.

Holmes, Douglas (2001), *E-gov: E-business Strategies for Government*, London: Nicolas Brealey Publishing.

Kettl, Donald F. (2002), *The Transformation of Governance*, Baltimore, MD: Johns Hopkins University Press.

Lan, Ling (2004), "E-government: A Catalyst to Good Governance in China", KMGov 2004, LNAI 3035.

Mallawaarachchi, T. et al. (1996), "GIS Based Integrated Modelling Systems for Natural Resource Management", *Agricultural Systems*, 50, 169–89.

Mol, P.J. Arthur (2006), "Environmental Governance in the Information Age: The Emergence of Informational Governance", *Environment and Planning*, 24 (4), 497–514.

Mol, P.J. Arthur (2009), "Environmental Governance through Information: China and Vietnam", *Singapore Journal of Tropical Geography*, 30 (3), 114–29.

Scott A. and J. Street (2001), "From Media Politics to E-protest: The Use of Popular Culture and New Media in Parties and Social Movements", in Frank Webster (ed.), *Culture and Politics in the Information Age: A New Politics?* New York: Routledge, pp. 32–51.

Snellen, Ignace (2001), "ICTs, Bureaucracies, and the Future of Democracy", *Communication of the ACM*, 44 (1), 45–8.

Waddell, Paul (2002), "UrbanSim: Modelling Urban Development for Land Use, Transportation and Environmental Planning", *Journal of the American Planning Association*, 68 (3), 297–314.

Zavestoski, Stephen, W. Stuart Shulman and David Schlosberg (2006), 'Democracy and the Environment on the Internet: Electronic Citizen Participation in Regulatory Rule Making', *Science, Technology, & Human Values*, 31 (3), 1–26.

Zhaoxing, X. (1999). "The Chinese Government on Line", Tsinghua University Bulletin, 139.

Zhou, X. (2004), "E-Government in China: A Content Analysis of National and Provincial Web Sites", *Journal of Computer-Mediated Communication*, 9 (4), available online at http://jcmc.indiana.edu/vol19/issue4/zhou.html, last accessed September 15, 2011.

PART III

The intersection of economics and social justice around water laws

8. Global climate disruption and water law reform in the United States

Joseph W. Dellapenna

8.1 INTRODUCTION

We live today on a planet undergoing disruptive climate change (IPCC 2007a). Regardless of cause, a great deal of climate change now seems unavoidable – with potentially disastrous consequences (IPCC 2007b). Farmers in the Northern Hemisphere are experiencing measurably longer growing seasons, which is not always a blessing (Angelo 2010). Climate disruption brings more extreme events – droughts and floods – at more frequent intervals. Even more importantly, global climate disruption also will change the timing and nature of precipitation throughout much of the planet. These changes will make water more available in some areas and less available in others (e.g. Kim and Kaluarachi 2009; Young 2009). Unfortunately, precise prediction of just how these changes will play out remains impossible and might not become clear for decades. We can predict that over the coming century, hotter temperatures and drier air will cause higher rates of evapo-transpiration and drier soils less supportive of plant life without irrigation, while arid regions will become wider. The melting of glaciers and the mountain snowpack will reduce or destroy the storage capacity of these immense reservoirs of fresh water that sustain rivers during the dry months of the year. Global climate disruption will also lead to a rise in sea levels, which in some parts of the world will lead to salt water intrusion into fresh waters that today are widely consumed for human uses. Temperatures, the amount of precipitation, and the depth of snowpacks will vary, up and down, from year to year, yet the long-term trends are clear: in many areas with large populations, the availability of water will decrease substantially. Much human-built infrastructure for managing water will become obsolete.

The foregoing points allow us to predict, even without precise foreknowledge, that climate disruption will cause more stress for already stressed water management regimes (Dellapenna 1999, 2010). These changes will challenge environmental governance, for water is one of the central, perhaps the central, resource for ecosystems, human societies, and human individuals. How we govern water goes a long way to define how we govern the environment generally. Yet the emerging climate disrupt renders obsolete existing arrangements for water management even in regions where water historically has been plentiful. Pressure for water law reform at the national and international levels was already felt in many parts of the world long before the impact of climate disruption because of the growth in water demand fueled by population growth and changing patterns of use (Marks 2009; Dellapenna 1997). Designing correct legal reforms, however, will not be easy. Too much legal response can produce as much social turmoil as inadequate legal response certainly will. Suggestions for responses to the need for water law reform, whether arising from climate disruption, population growth, or other causes, range from muddling through by doing what we are already doing to radical reforms such as the introduction of markets as the best response to the massive uncertainty in water management.

I have written elsewhere in some detail about the problems of relying on markets for coping with climate disruption (Dellapenna 2008a). I have also written at some length about the challenges posed by climate disruption to the international law applicable to water resources (Dellapenna 2008b). Here, I focus on how to reform existing water law regimes in order to create the capacity to respond to the global climate disruption. While my discussion draws upon the experience with legal regimes in the United States and possible reforms there, the variety of state legal regimes for water in the United States provides examples of the three possible paradigm approaches. While recognizing that legal systems within the United States and elsewhere often involve hybrid systems that blend elements of each paradigm, studying these pure paradigms provides useful information for water managers and water law systems worldwide.

8.2 MODELS OF PROPERTY IN WATER

Adaptations to global climate change necessarily will center on the management of water resources given its importance to human survival and thriving. Water is found nearly everywhere, but, being variable in quantity and quality, it is often in the wrong place, or at the wrong time, or the wrong amount, or too impure. Usable water therefore is a scarce and valuable commodity. Yet if large-scale importation from far away remains impractical, water truly will remain a strictly regional resource with a vengeance. The resulting stresses might overcome the concerns that have made it impossible in many areas of the world to build new large dams (World Commission on Dams 2000). Such problems will also require reconsideration of laws allocating water among users to enable appropriate adaptation to the changing situation.

Water allocation law is primarily a matter of state law in the United States. The vastly differing experiences of different communities in the United States regarding water led to very different approaches to property rights in water (Dellapenna 2009c). As a result, three distinct bodies of water allocation law arose in the United States, each with its own characteristics that render it more or less suitable for adaptation to global climate disruption. To the east of Kansas City, people traditionally considered water to be readily available at little or no cost. Although there might be serious human-induced problems with water quality, shortages historically were rare and short-lived. In this setting, the states applied riparian rights, which treat raw water as a species of common property (Dellapenna 2009a, 2009b). To the west of Kansas City, people considered water to be scarce, or at least misplaced. Therefore, the right to use water in the west was treated as private property under appropriative rights (Dellapenna 2009c). Finally, in the second half of the twentieth century, water users in the eastern United States began to experience recurring and intensifying shortages. This led about half of the eastern states to change from riparian rights to a third model, which has come to be called regulated riparianism and treats water as public property (Dellapenna 2009d). Despite numerous variations in detail in each state, the state laws all fall within one or another of these models.

The correspondence between modern forms of American water law and the several types of property is more than a simple curiosity. In light of the work done in recent decades on the theory of property, the correspondence of forms of water law to theoretical models enables us to predict with some certainty whether existing forms are adaptable to changing circumstances, or whether an entirely new form must be substituted when water demand or supply changes dramatically (Dellapenna 1999, 2010). Before examining these models of property in water, we must explore the unusual characteristics of water that make simple application of any model of property problematic for water. This discussion is followed by analysis of the suitability of riparian rights, appropriative rights, and regulated riparianism in a world undergoing climate disruption.

8.3 WATER'S SPECIAL CHARACTERISTICS

Water's physical characteristics make recourse to property rules problematic. Tom Robbins captured the peculiar properties of water in a prose poem from his best-known novel:

> Water—the ace of elements. Water dives from clouds without parachute, wings or safety net. Water runs over the steepest precipice and blinks not a lash. Water is

> buried and rises again; water walks on fire and fire gets the blisters. Stylishly composed in any situation—solid, gas or liquid—speaking in penetrating dialects understood by all things—animal, vegetable or mineral—water travels intrepidly through four dimensions, *sustaining* (Kick a lettuce in the field and it will yell "Water!"), *destroying* (The Dutch boy's finger remembered the view from Ararat) and *creating* (It has even been said that human beings were invented by water as a device for transporting itself from one place to another, but that's another story). Always in motion, ever flowing (whether at steam rate or glacier speed), rhythmic, dynamic, ubiquitous, changing, and working its changes, a mathematics turned wrong side out, a philosophy in reverse, the ongoing odyssey of water is virtually irresistible. (Robbins 1976, pp. 1–2)

The following discussion of the characteristics of water may strike some as belaboring the obvious, yet they must be discussed expressly because all too often legal regimes applicable to water simply ignore them. Foremost of these characteristics is water's critical importance to human life and thriving. Water is more essential to life itself than anything other than breathable air; a person can go longer without food than without water, as many a hunger-striker has demonstrated. And, as a Turkish businessman once commented, "Countless millions of people have lived without love, but none without water." Water serves innumerable other purposes, human and non-human, which makes denying its use to particular persons, at least for survival needs, impossible to sustain under law. This point is made most clearly in Islamic law, which recognizes a right to quench one's thirst – which must be honored by the owner of land on or under which water is found so long as the owner's own immediate needs have been met (al Bukhari 870).

Nearly as central as water's importance is its ubiquity – water is found nearly everywhere and in nearly everything. Water is our more nearly universal solvent, a characteristic that makes it extremely useful, but also means that water is extraordinarily heterogeneous. Water not only is one of the few substances that appears in all three forms (gaseous, liquid, and solid) in nature, but it is also never found in nature without contaminants. Pure water is a manufactured product. Yet water is stable enough to be used and reused repeatedly, despite other uses and transformations. Water, moreover, is in constant motion, moving through a continual cycle that returns it to each place and form where it is now found. Thus water is endlessly renewable, and is used repeatedly as it moves through its cycle. Yet, because at any given moment in any given place water is finite, it can be exhausted or polluted to the point of being rendered unusable.

Water, in short, is a common pool resource, one that inevitably passes into and out of one's control; in this sense, water cannot be owned. Of course, water can be owned in a fairly normal way in small quantities ("This bottle of water is mine."), and economists create elaborate market models for water management that at least in theory function effectively (e.g. Posner 2007,

§3.12). Yet such market models have never played a large role in managing large sources of raw water. In fact, because of water's continual movement and its importance for human survival and thriving, water generally has been treated as a free good. Users seldom pay for water when they remove it from a natural source, and even public delivery systems seldom charge for the water itself, as opposed to the services of extracting, purifying, delivering, and carrying away water after its use (Gleick *et al.* 2002, pp. 29–40). Water therefore has long been considered to be the quintessential "public good" (Dellapenna 2009a, §6.01(b)). What is a public good and why that is significant for water as property thus requires careful consideration (Kaul, Grunberg and Stern 1999).

"Public goods," as distinguished from private goods, share two qualities: indivisibility and publicness (Rawls 1972, pp. 266–74). Because public goods are indivisible, or "non-excludable" as contemporary economists say, one cannot simply divide them among users or buy as much as one wants. Because the goods are public, or subject to "open access" as contemporary economists say, one cannot keep others from accessing and enjoying the goods as long as anyone can access and enjoy them. A public good therefore is one that all within the relevant public must enjoy more or less equally, or no one can enjoy it at all. Perhaps the best example of a public good is the blue sky. That it is a public good raises an important problem: if you invest in improving the blueness of the sky (say by reducing your emission of pollutants), others who invest or pay nothing will enjoy the benefits of your investment. You cannot exclude them from enjoying the good. These people are "free riders" – those who enjoy the fruits of investment in public goods without sharing the costs. Free riders can seriously inhibit investment unless the government (or some other institution) is able to ensure that all (or nearly all) pay for the benefits they receive. The market simply won't work; regulation will. As Nobel Prize-winning economist Ronald Coase famously demonstrated, while a private-property market system is a most efficient mechanism for allocating resources to particular uses when it works, the system fails if there are significant barriers to the functioning of a market (Coase 1960).

If water is a public good, then water, like other public goods generally, must be a free good as far as markets are concerned because consumers cannot realistically be excluded from enjoying the good. Water, in some settings, is a private good. We have all bought bottled water. This does not dispose of the question of whether raw water, water in its natural condition, is a public good. Few things in this world are strictly indivisible and public. While water is not indivisible and public in the strictest sense (unlike a blue sky), even economists who embrace the extreme of market fundamentalism use water metaphors when discussing what they concede are public goods: "common pool resource"; "spill over effects"; and so on. Still, some economists prefer to consider water to be "common goods" rather than "public goods" (e.g. Ostrom 1990). Common goods differ from public goods in that, while the goods are shared among a group of common owners, the goods can be exhausted and not everyone in the universe has equal access to the goods. In other words, public goods are "non-rivalrous," but common goods are "rivalrous." Because of these features, the consumption of common goods by one person reduces other persons' ability to consume the same good. Common goods exhibit some measure of subtractability and excludability – qualities that, economists tell us, do not apply to true public goods. Nevertheless, it is possible for many consumers to benefit jointly from the resource as long as there are means for excluding others from using the resource.

If we take the idea of common goods seriously, there are very few true public goods. Even a lighthouse, sometimes presented as the paradigm of a true public good, is not used by everyone in the world, but only by those on ships coming within range of its light (Coase 1974), perhaps leaving only the blue sky as a true public good. And when the number of "common users" numbers in the thousands or hundreds of thousands, the distinction between public goods and common goods hardly matters. In such settings, at least, common goods are just public goods for which there is a limited group of co-owners. From a legal point of view, the most central managerial problems regarding public goods are precisely the most central managerial problems for common goods: how can we cover the costs of maintaining or enhancing the resource when a significantly large group of people have access to, and the legal right to use, it without direct charge for their uses. This problem leads directly to the "tragedy of the commons" (Hardin 1968).

The peculiar characteristics of water – its critical importance, its ubiquity, its heterogeneity, its renewability, its commonality, and its vulnerability – combine to make markets unworkable for raw water. A person (natural or corporate) can own bottles of water but not a river or an aquifer, nor, given the reality of transaction costs that arise from attempts to market a share of a river or an aquifer, can one readily market a right to use a portion of a river or an aquifer. I have written elsewhere in detail on why markets fail for water (Dellapenna 2000, 2008a). Here, I address the laws that govern the allocation of water without regard to the possibility of markets. What determines whether institutional arrangements serve to achieve the optimum use of a resource is how society accords to particular individuals or to collectivities the power to determine how a resource is used. This depends not just on the qualities of the goods themselves, but on the social relations created or confirmed by law regarding rights to use the good: is the good subject to individual decisions by everyone with legal access to the goods (common property), or to individual decisions by persons with sole legal access to some share of the goods (private property), or to collective decisions by all interested persons acting through a collective management mechanism (public property). Each form of water law has been applied by one or another state of the United States: riparian rights (common property); appropriative rights (private property); and regulated riparianism (public property).

8.4 RIPARIAN RIGHTS (COMMON PROPERTY)

"Riparian rights" take their name from the Latin word *ripa*, meaning a riverbank. Today, the term "riparian rights" also extends to lakes and other water bodies, although historically rights pertaining to lakes and other large bodies of water were called "littoral rights" (from the Latin *litus*, meaning "shore"). The doctrine of riparian rights provides a rule for the allocation of water to particular uses among users with lawful access. Today, states applying riparian rights do not rely solely on "pure" riparian rights (Dellapenna 2009d, §§9.01 to 9.02(d)), with regulations at least of particular aspects of water usage. Still, about half of the states east of Kansas apply traditional riparian rights to disputes relating to the allocation of water among users.

Land abutting or underlying a body of water is termed "riparian land" (Dellapenna 2009b, §7.02(a)). As the name suggests, riparian rights are based on the premise that the right to use water is a natural attribute of riparian land, dependent on the natural availability of water to the land. Many courts and scholars assert that at one time the doctrine of riparian rights required the protection of the "natural flow" of a watercourse, under which only domestic uses of water (use of water to meet immediate survival needs) were allowed to alter materially a water source in quantity or quality. In fact, there is very little evidence that courts ever actually enforced the "natural flow rule." Instead, courts embraced the "reasonable use rule," under which a riparian landowner is entitled to make any use the landowner chooses so long she does not transgress the equal right of other riparian landowners to use the water. Although "natural flow" language continues to appear in cases invoking riparian rights today, the courts always end up applying the reasonable use theory (Dellapenna 2009b, §7.02(c)).

In one of the few recent cases that could be cited for natural flow rule, *Dimmock v. City of New London*,[1] the court found a violation of riparian rights from the mere diminution of the level of water in a pond, but the court also denied an injunction through a balancing of the equities, while suggesting that only nominal damages would be recoverable. Complicating the interpretation of the *Dimmock* precedent is the fact that the city of New London was not exercising riparian rights because it was exporting the water out of the watershed of origin.

Today, apart from a preference for domestic uses, the only real restrictions on water uses under riparian rights are that no use is legal if it "unreasonably harms" another riparian use and that the use must be on riparian land (Dellapenna 2009b, §§7.02 to 7.03(e)). The reasonable use rule thus is a common property system, under which all who own land contiguous to a surface water body are co-owners of the right to use the water. (Many courts apply an analogous rule to groundwater, turning on the ownership of overlying land (Dellapenna 2009e).) As co-owners, they are left pretty much to their own individual judgment to decide whether, when, and how to use the resource. A court will intervene in the riparian owners' decisions only when a use by one co-owner interferes directly with a use by another co-owner.

The case of *Harris v. Brooks*[2] is illustrative. That case involved a dispute between a commercial boat rental service operated on land leased on the shore of a small lake and a rice farmer who drew water for his fields from the same lake, when a severe drought made it impossible to satisfy both needs. The Arkansas Supreme Court applied the reasonable use theory to ensure the equal rights of each riparian "as near as may be," while maximizing the social benefit of the use of the water and minimizing the harm to the others consistent with maximizing social benefit. This is not simply a question of stopping one water user, from interfering with or harming another water user for in a case like this, each use necessarily interferes with the other, and whichever prevails necessarily destroys the other (Coase 1960, pp. 3–15). The court adopted a relational test that involves a weighing of the social value of competing uses against each other to determine which is more socially valuable (Dellapenna 2009b, §7.02(d)(2)). In this process, temporal priority has seldom, if ever, been relevant to the resolution of riparian rights disputes (Dellapenna 2009b, §703(d)). In *Harris v. Brooks*, the court ignored that the defendant had been irrigating rice for more than 20 years, while the year of the suit was the first year that the plaintiff operated the boat livery. Ultimately, the court enjoined the rice farmer's pumping whenever the level of the lake level fell below the level at which his pumping would unreasonably interfere with the plaintiffs' use of the lake. The court, however, only discussed how to balance uses against each other in vague terms, leaving us uncertain as to how precisely to perform this calculus. Such balancing requires a polycentric process that requires courts to act not as a disinterested umpire but rather as an actively involved manager.

If the key to cases like *Harris v. Brooks* is the economic value of the competing activities, the court will have to reconsider the result whenever product values change significantly. If the market values of the two products change, or if the rice farmer were to acquire more land and therefore was able to produce more rice by pumping even more water, the court would have to re-evaluate the reasonableness of the competing uses. On the other hand, courts appear to give only minimal, if any, attention to such non-economic questions as the natural characteristics of the stream, general social concerns, or abstract justice. If these or other variables account for the conclusion that the boat livery was a more reasonable use than irrigating rice, then a change in those circumstances would also necessitate reconsideration of the reasonableness of the competing uses. The Arkansas Supreme Court adopted a specific lake level for the rice farmer to stop pumping precisely in order to avoid frequent re-litigation of reasonableness. Nonetheless, the court would have to reconsider its judgment for any truly significant change in the relevant facts.

Courts applying the reasonable use rule sometimes try to avoid such problems by ordering *pro rata* sharing among competing users (Dellapenna 2009b, §7.03(c)). That cannot be done when a *pro rata* share is too small to be of any use or for widely differing uses. In *Harris*, the rice farmer would have to stop pumping during a serious drought, forcing the farmer not to plant rice or the farmer could pump the water and the boat livery would be out of business. The farmer did not suffer a loss in the actual case because the case took two years for the case to reach the state's highest court. By then, the drought had ended. In the future, however, the farmer would have to plant a less water-intensive crop or gamble on the possibility of persuading a trial judge that the circumstances had changed.

Riparian rights thus are seriously problematic for addressing water shortages, and thus for addressing the most serious consequences of global climate disruption. The problems include the vagueness, instability, and unpredictability of the criteria of decision in any water dispute, the lack of a process for managing water during extreme shortages or for protecting public values, and a systematic bias in favor of large users. The only firm rule under riparian rights is that any use on non-riparian land is unreasonable *per se* (Dellapenna 2009b, §7.02(d)(1)). The resulting uncertainties were used to justify shifting from riparian rights to appropriative rights in western states, and shifting to regulated riparianism in eastern states (Dellapenna 2009c, §8.02(b); Dellapenna 2009d, §9.01). There is, moreover, no mechanism for judicially determining and reviewing the rights of all users on a particular watercourse. Even if one could join all water right holders with claims on a particular water source in a single proceeding, courts are ill equipped to consider the unrepresented interests of the public generally. Small users will also find themselves at a severe disadvantage because they are less able to afford to litigate or to organize collectively for litigation. If small users are able to litigate their claims, the balancing process generally strongly favors larger users over smaller users because the economic value of the water to the large user usually will outweigh the economic loss of the small users. While smaller users can effectively aggregate their claims by receiving their water through a public system, this approach is constrained by legal doctrines limiting the riparianness of public systems (Dellapenna 2009b, §7.05(c)). Aggregation also requires submission to yet a different sort of large-scale enterprise.

These problems derive from the nature of riparian rights as common property. All persons owning riparian land are co-owners of the right to use water. Each co-owner has equal rights with every other co-owner, and thus none can dictate how the others are to use the water. Each is free to decide individually when, where, and how to use the water. The result of such a common property system will be a "tragedy of the commons" (Hardin 1968). The tragedy arises because a common property system – a system combining open access with individual decision making – can only function successfully when the common resource is available in greater supply than the aggregate demand for the resource. Otherwise problems arise because each common owner can decide for herself whether to increase the use of the resource regardless of the effect on other common owners (except for direct interference with the uses of the others). Each owner therefore appropriates for herself the whole of each additional increment of use, but the whole group shares equally the cost imposed on the common resource. Consider cows grazing on a common pasture: I obtain the full benefit of each additional cow I add to my herd, but the common owners as a group share the burden of the reduced carrying capacity of the pasture. If each co-owner keeps adding cows, which is rational if we decide only through an individual cost-benefit analysis, we will continue to do so until the pasture is exhausted.

Economists and others have criticized this analysis for oversimplifying how "commons" have functioned in earlier times or in remote areas (e.g. Ostrom 1990). Commons have indeed functioned successfully over extended periods even when use was close to the carrying capacity of the commons, through informal limits imposed by small communities sharing a commons. These examples are irrelevant for describing how a commons functions in a larger society where most persons are strangers to each other, informal sanctions are not effective, and formal law recognizes no real limits on any co-owner's exploitation of the commons. Under these circumstances, typical of states where riparian rights are applied, the tragedy of the commons will fully play itself out. This is more than a theoretical model. Common pool resources have been destroyed over and over again in the past century when the rule of common property was not displaced by a different rule. The tragedy of the commons has played itself out precisely as predicted for (to name just a few examples) fish in the sea (Babcock 2007; Ellis 2007) or public park access (Garvin *et al.* 1997).

Garret Hardin, who coined the term "tragedy of the commons," concluded that only a private property system which concentrates the costs as well as the benefits of resource management decisions on a particular owner could avoid the tragedy of the commons (Hardin 1968). He concluded that appeals to moderation and moral suasion can only be self-defeating because each responsible user soon realizes that, heeding a moral appeal, they reduce their gains with little or no benefit to the common resource because others will take what they do not. Many who agree with an appeal to morality therefore would join in grabbing whatever they can before it is all gone. Experience with riparian rights suggests another problem for commons. When exploitation of a common pool resource requires significant capital investment, the inability of potential investors to keep others from pre-empting an investor's uses will bring about underinvestment in the resource (Rose 1986). Fear of such problems, deriving ultimately from the uncertainty that arises under traditional riparian rights, was invoked to justify rejection of riparian rights in the drier, western third of the United States in favor of a private property system such as Hardin argued was necessary for all commons when demand approaches supply.

To evaluate riparian rights as a system for facilitating adaptation to climate disruption, one need only consider the strengths and weaknesses of riparian rights in operation. While the characteristics of the reasonable use version of riparian rights might provide the flexibility necessary to adapt to climate disruption, the slow, laborious process of litigation between two or a few individuals is ill-suited to adapting water usage to changing supply or demand. Decisions are made by judges who are not versed in hydrology, meteorology, or economics, to name only some of the potentially relevant disciplines. The tragedy of the commons that will result from the lack of an effective mechanism for resolving disputes has already led about half of the states that traditionally followed riparian rights to abandon that system in favor of regulated riparianism, even without fear of climate disruption (Dellapenna 2009d, §9.03). That process will most likely only accelerate as the effects of climate disruption become more widely felt. Nor would a reversion to the natural flow theory help – it would only freeze out consumptive uses at a time when some communities will desperately need new sources of water for consumptive uses.

8.5 APPROPRIATIVE RIGHTS (PRIVATE PROPERTY)

In the United States, the climate generally becomes drier as one goes from east to west, with truly arid regions between the Rocky Mountains and the mountains of the Pacific coast, with predictable consequences for the law of water allocation (Dellapenna 2009c, §8.01). When settlers from the eastern United States ("Anglos") reached this region, they needed water for mining and irrigation, and later for industrial and municipal uses. They concluded that their needs for water could not be satisfied under riparian rights, whether in its natural flow version or in its reasonable use version. Furthermore, the newcomers generally were trespassers on the public domain, often before any effective government was in place. The prospectors who suddenly re-peopled

California after the discovery of gold at Sutter's Mill in 1848 did not carefully analyze the legal needs of western states. The Yankee intruders swept away Spanish-Mexican law and the law derived aboriginal practices, relying on the only law with which they were familiar – the common law of the eastern United States (Reid 1997). Yet, regarding land and water, the two most important material factors in their lives, the common law was useless.

The land itself was deemed to belong to the federal government (the "public domain") and, under riparian rights, the right to use water belonged to the owner of the land. Because the "forty-niners" would not wait for the establishment of a regular government and the comprehensive land surveys necessary before they could buy the land from the government, they simply trespassed on the land and took what water they needed. The miners sought to bring order to their lives through "vigilance committees," giving rise to vigilante law and creating a national mythology of violent disputes, blood feuds, and sudden death. Vigilante law was based upon the most elementary notion of justice – first in time, first in right (Hundley 1992, pp. 67–73). If someone were found on another person's mining claim, the new occupant would hang if he could not justify his presence. Government, when finally organized, could only ratify the customs of the miners.[3] The mining camps applied the same principles to water as they did to land. Again, organized governments had to follow the customs of the miners.[4]

Successive mineral rushes to other western territories brought California prospectors who had failed to strike it rich there – and the customs of the California mining camps came with them (Dellapenna 2009b, §8.02). In some states, these customs blended with misunderstood principles of Spanish-Mexican law, while farmers, particularly if they got there first, tended to apply riparian rights. Eventually, nearly everywhere across the West, appropriative rights displaced riparian rights. After 150 years, the miners' rule has been developed into a complex system of water administration found, in various forms, in every appropriation state (Goplerud 2009a). In the Plains States and along the Pacific Coast, vestigial riparian rights remained, but usually with little actual impact on how water is managed (Dellapenna 2009b, §§8.03, 8.04).

Appropriative rights provide a private property approach to water allocation under which water rights are defined as to quantity, time, place, and manner of use, and most importantly according to their priority relative to other uses.[5] Like traditional riparian rights, appropriative rights have serious problems, even without reference to global climate disruption (Gaffney 1969). Appropriative rights exhibit more uncertainty than the principle of first in time, first in right suggests. The earliest priority dates predate the modern administrative machinery. Despite legal procedures designed to put these claims on record, the earliest, and hence most valuable, rights to use water still have not been quantified on some watercourses (Goplerud 2009b).

Prescriptive, abandoned, or forfeited rights can also create gaps in the official record (Goplerud 2009c). A more serious problem arises, however, from the rule of temporal priority than gaps in the water rights records. Appropriative rights actually encourage waste and other bad practices because the "first in time, first in right" principle leads water users to seek to capture the rents from unappropriated waters. Appropriative rights reward the use of water before it is needed, or even if it will never actually be needed (Neuman 1998). In order to capture rents, appropriators use as much water as they can. Withdrawing water, a cost to society, is a private gain to an appropriator, creating ownership of the right to use the water in the future. This requires water users to invest real social capital to divert, store, and apply the water to establish ownership. Capital moves from socially productive uses to the capturing of sub-marginal resources. As a result, excessive diversion capacity is the rule under appropriative rights, yet for most appropriations of water, there is inadequate investment in post-diversionary aspects of water development, especially in measures to save water.

Appropriators thus live in an environment where it is smart to over-irrigate or otherwise to waste water. Much of the water shortage in the west would disappear if appropriators had to start paying a realistic price for water and the shortage would greatly abate if appropriators simply started thinking in terms of a zero price, instead of, as now, regarding the price as negative because of the gain they realize by piling up a "history" of use. The introduction of conditional rights made it even easier to "capture" rents – by establishing an intent to appropriate water that might take many years before completion of the works necessary to put the water to use.

Even if all appropriators were careful only to appropriate as much water as they actually need, the legal regime violates two of the most fundamental economizing principles: (1) marginal productivity; and (2) pooling of risk (Gaffney 1969, p. 140). Under the rule of "first in time, first in right," appropriators are senior and junior to one another along a scale from the very first person to begin to use water to the person who began to use the water most recently. When there is not enough water to meet all water rights, the most junior appropriator must drop out and lose everything before the next senior appropriator loses anything.[6] Senior appropriators are protected by exaggerating the risk to junior appropriators. A junior appropriator may lose all access to water, including marginal units of higher productivity than some marginal units protected for the senior appropriator. There is no pooling of risk whatsoever. Water rights derive from a larger common supply, but each water right is defined in a way that changes in the aggregate variability of supply beyond the natural variability and that distributes these risks unequally.

The impact of appropriative rights on efficient use of water does not end with denial of marginal utility. When administered by large irrigation districts, appropriated water may be applied to rationally defined service areas. When claimed by individuals or small districts, however, service areas from any given source are generally scattered. The farther one is from a source, and the more convenient it is to others, the greater the motive to get there first to preclude them. So, typically, the first claimants on a source are scattered; soon the supply is fully claimed, and the included dry lands can never get water from this source.[7] They can, however, find other, more remote, sources. The results need not be imagined, they may be observed throughout the West: canals ("ditches") crisscross states carrying water in opposite directions as appropriators exercise their rights. Recent legal innovations to protect areas of origin have had only limited impact on this problem.

Even more than for riparian rights, appropriative rights favor large users. To make an appropriation, water must be used "beneficially" (Neuman 1998). The amount of water that one can use beneficially is a function of, among other things, the amount of land or the size of the factory that one owns. Appropriative rights thus tend to distribute publicly owned water to those who already own the most (Gaffney 1969, p. 138). Traditionally, no effort was made to protect the public interest in those publicly owned waters or to distribute the fruits of their use among the disadvantaged of society. Many appropriative rights states have now enacted statutes requiring consideration of the public interest in evaluating applications to make a new appropriation (Goplerud 2009a, §15.03(c)(3)). Such statutes, however, do not preempt existing water rights and thus have little practical effect in the many water basins in which most or all available water has already been appropriated. Whether in today's economy distributive equity favors protecting endangered species and providing water for other public values rather than for irrigation is a hotly debated question, illustrating the difficulty of reaching a proper balance between the public interest and private need (Cosens 2008).

These rather serious problems could perhaps be dealt with fairly easily if markets could be made to work under appropriative rights. But there never has been a market for appropriative rights to any significant extent (Dellapenna 2000, 2008a). Appropriative rights then create a rather peculiar form of private property, one that rather than ensuring free transferability and efficient use of the resource, effectively freezes uses in place – unless the state intervenes directly and dramatically to transfer the water to other uses (Dellapenna 2009a, §§6.01(b)(2), (b)(3)). Small-scale transfers of water rights among users who are making similar uses at more or less the same place are the only ones that regularly occurred under appropriative rights without state intervention (Dellapenna 2004).

The foregoing problems make appropriative rights even less capable than riparian rights of responding to the changes induced by global climate disruption. A rigid freezing of water use in wasteful patterns that disregard fundamental principles of marginal utility and pooling of risk is the opposite of what is necessary when water use patterns need to be adjusted to a new reality. Sustaining appropriative rights in regions where it already exists will be difficult or impossible, and major efforts are underway to subvert the regime through a pretense of markets that are not really markets (Dellapenna 2009a, §6.01(b)(3)). Drawing on appropriative rights to replace riparian rights would face additional impediments in states with numerous and well-developed water use patterns. To understand why requires some attention to the experience of the Pacific coast states, from Alaska to California, and the high plains states, from North Dakota to Texas, that adopted appropriative rights to replace an earlier system of riparian rights (Dellapenna 2009c).

In the transition from predominantly riparian rights states to dual systems recognizing both appropriative rights and riparian rights, legislatures generally chose to preserve actual uses under riparian rights as of the effective date of the first appropriative rights statute. Although most of these transitions happened when existing water uses were relatively few, they produced a dual system that combined the worst features of both bodies of law. Mississippi attempted to do the same in 1956 (Dellapenna 2009c, §§8.05 to 8.05(b)). The attempt failed and 29 years later Mississippi abandoned appropriative rights in favor of regulated riparianism. Appropriative rights failed in Mississippi because innumerable consumptive uses of water were established in 1955, and claiming an appropriative right would only concede priority to an opponent claiming a pre-existing riparian right. The best that an appropriator could hope would be that the appropriative use would be balanced against the complaining riparian's use, which brings us full circle back to the reasonable use version of riparian rights (Dellapenna 2009c, §8.04(b)). More likely, if an acute water shortage were to develop, an appropriator would simply find no water to apply to the appropriation because riparian rights would be held to be senior rights as against the appropriation. As a result therefore, eastern states making a sharp departure from the more or less pure riparian rights uniformly have not gone to appropriative rights, but to regulated riparianism.

8.6 REGULATED RIPARIANISM (PUBLIC PROPERTY)

Hawaii and about half of the states east of Kansas City have now developed administrative permit systems to replace traditional riparian rights based on riparian principles that are best described as a system of public property (Dellapenna 2009d). The new system is called "regulated riparianism." The transition from extremely limited regulatory intervention to more or less comprehensive regulation often occurs incrementally, resulting in disagreement over when to date the emergence of a true regulated riparian system. It remains debatable even today whether certain states have in fact moved from relying largely on unregulated common law riparian rights to a regulated riparian system. The following states have enacted regulated riparian systems at the approximate date indicated: Alabama (1993); Arkansas (1957); Connecticut (1982); Delaware (1959); Florida (1972); Georgia (1977); Hawaii (1987); Iowa (1957); Kentucky (1966); Maryland (1933); Massachusetts (1985); Michigan (2006); Minnesota (1973); Mississippi (1985); New Jersey (1965); North Carolina (1973); New York (1979); Virginia (1989); and Wisconsin (1957). Four other states (Arizona, Illinois, Nebraska, and South Carolina) apply regulated riparianism to groundwater without applying it to surface waters. The Delaware Basin Water Commission and the Susquehanna Basin Water Commission also operate a limited sort of regulated riparianism in parts of Pennsylvania. The following summary description of regulated riparianism is based upon its common core of principles as found in actual regulated riparian statutes and articulated in the Regulated Riparian Model Water Code of the American Society of Civil Engineers (Dellapenna 2003). No state has a system precisely like the one described here or in the Model Code, although several come very close. The Model Code includes detailed commentaries explaining the various provisions and exhaustive references to actual regulated riparian statutes.

The most fundamental departure from traditional common law riparian rights under regulated riparianism is that generally no water is to be withdrawn from a water source without a time-limited permit from the state within which the withdrawal occurs (Dellapenna 2003, §6R-1-01). The permits determine water rights, not the riparian nature of the use, yet the new system of law remains within the riparian tradition because the criterion by which permit applications are evaluated is whether the proposed use is "reasonable" (Dellapenna 2003, §§2R-1-01, 2R-2-20, 6R-3-01, 6R-3-02). The criterion of "reasonable use" is applied very differently than at common law in that an administering agency decides before a use begins whether it is reasonable, both in terms of general social policy and in terms of the effects of the proposed use on other permitted uses (Dellapenna 2003, §§6R-2-01 to 6R-2-08, 6R-3-02, 6R-3-05). Water users gain a significant advantage because they know – for the duration of the permit – whether their use is reasonable; they cannot be caught unaware by a judicial decision that wipes out their investment without a penny of compensation. Permits therefore allow potential investors to gauge whether their investments can be profitable and inform potential investors about the proper scale of the investment.

The administering agency is to subject the permit to conditions designed to protect other lawful users and public values (Dellapenna 2003, §7R-1-01). The statutes often provide preferences for certain classes of uses (Dellapenna 2003, §§6R-1-02, 6R-3-04). Temporal priority has only a strictly limited role in the permit process (Dellapenna 2003, §§6R-1-03, 6R-3-02). Uses on non-riparian land are no longer unreasonable *per se*; often one of the principal motives for enacting a regulated riparian statute is to authorize the use of water on non-riparian land (Dellapenna 2003, §2R-1-02). Finally, permits generally are issued only for a period of time (three to twenty years) (Dellapenna 2003, §7R-1-02). The Regulated Riparian Model Water Code sets twenty years as the duration of the permits. Upon expiration of a permit, the continued reasonableness of the use is re-examined, introducing a desirable flexibility into the development, use, and protection of water resources.

Regulated riparian statutes include elaborate judicial enforcement provisions (Dellapenna 2003, §§5R-4-01 to 5R-5-03), provide for hearings within the agency (Dellapenna 2003, §§5R-1-01 to 5R-1-03), and judicial review of agency decisions (Dellapenna 2003, §§5R-3-01 to 5R-3-03). Courts generally have been very deferential in reviewing agency decisions under regulated riparian statutes. Hawaii's Supreme Court, however, has invoked the public trust doctrine to justify taking a "close look" at agency decisions, at least regarding the protection of ecological values.[8] The Model Code also supports alternative dispute resolution and the administrative resolution of disputes between permit holders (Dellapenna 2003, §§5R-2-01 to 5R-2-03). Such provisions are not generally found in actual regulated riparian statutes.

While users are sometimes required to pay fees for permits based on the amount of water they use, the fees are not payment for the water itself (Dellapenna 2009d, §9.03(a)(5)(C)). Statutes that set uniform fees regardless of the amount of water used clearly do not charge for the water being used. Even if the fee is variable, however, it is set according to the presumed ability of the user to pay, rather than according to the value of the water or the value that could be created through use of the water. The Model Code breaks new ground in this respect, requiring water use fees that, to some extent at least, reflect the use value of the water (Dellapenna 2003, §4R-1-08). Charging for water use is intended to provide economic incentives for the efficient use of water in a setting where markets are not likely to be effective. Such fees can be varied by class, with the fees going into the general funds of the state.

Regulated riparian statutes also include extensive provisions for protecting and implementing the public interest in water resources (Dellapenna 2009, §§9.05(b) to 9.05(d)). At a minimum, these statutes provide for long-term planning (Dellapenna 2003, §§4R-1-02 to 4R-1-04). The Model Code would establish a particularly comprehensive statewide data system (Dellapenna 2003, §4R-2-03). The administering agency also is usually given broad discretion to plan for and to deal with crises brought on by extreme water shortages, even including suspending permits in whole or in part (Dellapenna 2003, §§7R-3-01 to 7R-3-07). The agency can incorporate permit conditions based on its plans or as necessary to protect the public interest (Dellapenna 2003, §7R-1-01).

The transition to regulated riparianism is easily justified on the basis of the state's police power to regulate water withdrawal and use in order to protect the public health, safety, and welfare (Dellapenna 2009d, §9.04(a)). Still, fear of the political (if not the legal) repercussions of such transformation of traditional water rights has led many state legislatures to exempt from the permit requirement large classes of users (usually agricultural) who were using water when the new statute came into effect, thus introducing a significant temporal element (Dellapenna 2009d, §9.03(a)(3)). A more sophisticated solution would be to guarantee existing users an initial permit, but thereafter subjecting to renewal on the same terms as any other permit, limiting the temporal preference to a single permit cycle (Dellapenna 2003, §6R-1-03). Existing users who refuse to apply for a permit within a short period of time after the new regulated riparian system comes into effect are conclusively presumed to have abandoned their claim of water right. There is some evidence, however, that administering agencies prefer to use temporal priority or *pro rata* sharing as the allocation method least likely to provoke litigation or other difficulties for the agency (Dellapenna 2009d, §9.05(d)). Such an approach sabotages the entire scheme of regulated riparianism. Thus far, no clear way to prevent such sabotage has emerged.

Today, the main threats to the availability of water in eastern states, as to both quantity and quality, are not pollution or withdrawal, but the man-made physical and ecological transformation of water sources and the lands on or in which the sources are found. Global climate disruption is only the most extreme instance of such changes. Regulated riparian statutes address these problems through mandated planning and protections for the public interest, including requirements for the agency to define and protect minimum flows, whether an historic average low flow, the amount necessary for the preservation of certain kinds of wildlife, or the amount necessary to protect human health or well-being. The Model Code in particular requires protection of the biological, chemical, and physical integrity of the water source, defined in terms of federal and other relevant legal standards (Dellapenna 2003, §§3R-1-01 to 3R-2-05).

While regulated riparianism scores well for balancing flexibility in water usage with the protection of public values compared to appropriative rights and traditional riparian rights, both important dimensions of adaptation to global climate disruption, regulated riparianism still has unsolved problems. Actual regulated riparian statutes usually do not provide for the transfer of water rights or permits between users (Dellapenna 2009d, §9.03(d)). The Model Code charges the administering agency to encourage market transfers of water, but there seems to be little reason to think a market would function better under regulated riparianism than under appropriative or riparian rights (Dellapenna 2003, §§1R-1-07, 7R-2-01 to 7R-2-04, 7R-3-05, 9R-1-01, 9R-1-

02). In practice, the agencies free up far less water through the periodic renewal process than theory suggests because the agencies prefer to tighten conditions on existing uses rather than to deny renewal outright (Dellapenna 2009d, §9.03(a)(4)). Non-renewal of permits probably will remain an infrequent and cumbersome device unless the state is willing to create a good deal of investment insecurity.

Another problem that could impact on the ability to adapt to global climate disruption is that regulated riparian statutes might not provide adequate security for investment in water facilities. If the duration of a permit is too short, leaving too little time to recover the initial cost of a project before the permit expires, private actors will be reluctant to invest in water facilities. Additional uncertainty could arise from the administering agency's power to modify permits in light of water emergencies, typically unforeseen water shortages. In the actual operation of regulated riparian systems, however, neither investment nor transfer insecurities seem to have caused difficulty (Dellapenna 2009d, §9.03(a)(4)). Administering agencies have been, if anything, too sensitive to the fears of large institutional investors in water. Administering agencies seldom flatly refuse to renew a permit, although new and more stringent conditions are sometimes attached at the time of renewal. Instead, authorities in eastern states generally have consulted with major water users in crafting responses to water emergencies and have not made their own expert determinations regarding the matter. The cost of imposing an elaborate administrative system might also be substantial (Dellapenna 2009d, §9.05(a)(5)(D)). Because of these costs, states sometimes limit their regulated riparian system to certain water basins or other areas of the state where the competition for water is most intense (Dellapenna 2009d, §9.03(a)(1)).

8.7 CONCLUSION

Water law can either impede or facilitate the adaptation of societies to global climate disruption. None of the three models of water law found in the United States – riparian rights, appropriative rights, and regulated riparianism – guarantees that societies will strike the perfect balance between the public interest and private need, between flexibility for society and certainty for the individual, that will enable optimal adaptation. Yet given the increasing failure of traditional riparian rights (a common property system) to cope with the needs of modern societies, and the only slightly better performance of appropriative rights (as close to a private property system as we are likely to see), and the general failure of markets as a water management tool (as opposed to state water management masquerading as a market), there seems little choice but to move to a regulated riparian system (a public property system). Regulated riparianism is not perfect, but it appears to be best suited to coping with the enormous challenges that will face societies during the coming century – at least unless some better system is devised.

NOTES

1. *Dimmock v. City of New London* (1968), *Connecticut Reports*, 157: 9–20, *Atlantic Reporter (2nd series)*, 245: 569–74.
2. *Arkansas Reports*, 225: 436–48, *Southwestern Reporter (2nd series)*, 283: 129–36.
3. *Jennison v. Kirk* (1878), *United States Reports*, 98: 453–62, at p. 457.
4. *Irwin v. Phillips* (1855), *California Reports*, 5: 140–47.
5. *State* ex rel. *Cary v. Cochran* (1940), *Nebraska Reports*, 138: 163–78, *Northwestern Reporter*, 292: 239–48.
6. *State* ex rel. *Cary v. Cochran*, note 5.
7. *State* ex rel. *Cary v. Cochran*, note 5.
8. In re *Water Use Permit Application by Kukui (Molokai), Inc.* (2007), *Hawai'i Reports* 116: 481–510, *Pacific Reporter (3rd series)*, 174: 320–49; In re *Water Use Permit Applications* (2000), *Hawai'i Reports* 94: 97–198, *Pacific Reporter (3rd series)*, 9: 409–510.

REFERENCES

al Bukhari, Muhammad ibn Isma'il (870), *Les traditions islamiques* (O. Oudas and W. Marçais trans. and eds., 1906 ed.).

Angelo, Mary Jane (2010), "Corn, Carbon and Conservation: Rethinking U.S. Agricultural Policy in a Changing Global Environment", *George Mason University Law Review*, 17: 593–660.

Babcock, Hope M. (2007), "Grotius, Ocean Fish Ranching, and the Public Trust Doctrine: Ride 'em Charlie Tuna", *Stanford Environmental Law Journal*, 26: 3–75.

Coase, Ronald H. (1960), "The Problem of Social Cost", *Journal of Law and Economics*, 3: 1–23.

Coase, Ronald H. (1974), "The Lighthouse in Economics", *Journal of Law and Economics*, 17: 357–76.

Cosens, Barbara (2008), "Farmers, Fish, Tribal Power, and Poker: Reallocating Water in the Truckee River Basin, Nevada and California", *Hastings West-Northwest Journal of Environmental Law and Policy*, 14: 1243–93.

Dellapenna, Joseph W. (1997), "Population and Water in the Middle East: The Challenge and Opportunity for Law", *International Journal of the Environment and Pollution*, 7: 72–110.

Dellapenna, Joseph W. (1999), "Adapting the Law of Water Management to Global Climate Change and Other Hydropolitical Stresses", *Journal of the American Water Resources Association*, 35: 1301–26.

Dellapenna, Joseph W. (2000), "The Importance of Getting Names Right: Myth of Markets for Water", *William and Mary Environmental Law and Policy Review*, 25: 317–77.

Dellapenna, Joseph W. (ed.) (2003), *The Regulated Riparian Model Water Code*, Reston, VA: American Society of Civil Engineers (ASCE Stdd. 40–03).

Dellapenna, Joseph W. (2004), "Special Challenges to Water Markets in Riparian States", *Georgia State University Law Review*, 21: 305–38.

Dellapenna, Joseph W. (2008a), "Climate Disruption, the Washington Consensus, and Water Law Reform", *Temple Law Review*, 81: 383–432.
Dellapenna, Joseph W. (2008b), "International Water Law in a Climate of Disruption", *Michigan State Journal of International Law*, 17: 43–94.
Dellapenna, Joseph W. (2009a), "Introduction to Riparian Rights", in Amy K. Kelly (ed.), *Waters and Water Rights*, 1, Newark, NJ: LexisNexis (2009 edn), ch. 6.
Dellapenna, Joseph W. (2009b), "The Right to Consume Water under 'Pure' Riparian Rights", in Amy K. Kelly (ed.), *Waters and Water Rights*, 1, Newark, NJ: LexisNexis (2009 edn), ch. 7.
Dellapenna, Joseph W. (2009c), "Dual Systems", in Amy K. Kelly (ed.), *Waters and Water Rights*, 1, Newark, NJ: LexisNexis (2009 edn), ch. 8.
Dellapenna, Joseph W. (2009d), "Regulated Riparianism", in Amy K. Kelly (ed.), *Waters and Water Rights*, 1, Newark, NJ: LexisNexis (2009 edn), ch. 9.
Dellapenna, Joseph W. (2009e), "The Reasonable Use Rule", in Amy K. Kelly (ed.), *Waters and Water Rights*, 2, Newark, NJ: LexisNexis (2009 edn), ch. 22.
Dellapenna, Joseph W. (2010), "Global Climate Disruption and Water Law Reform", *Widener Law Review*, 15: 409–45.
Ellis, Jaye (2007), "Fisheries Conservation in an Anarchical System: A Comparison of Rational Choice and Constructivist Perspectives", *Journal of International Law and International Relations*, 3: 1–40.
Gaffney, M. Mason (1969), "Economic Aspects of Water Resources Policy", *American Journal of Economics and Sociology*, 28: 131–44.
Garvin, Alexander *et al.* (1997), *Urban Parks and Open Spaces,* Washington, DC: Urban Land Institute.
Gleick, Peter H., Gary Wolff, Elizabeth L. Chalecki and Rachel Reyes (2002), *The New Economy of Water: The Risks and Benefits of Globalization and Privatization of Freshwater*, Oakland, CA: Pacific Institute.
Goplerud, C. Peter III (2009a), "The Permit Process and Colorado's Exception", in Amy K. Kelly (ed.), *Waters and Water Rights*, 2, Newark, NJ: LexisNexis (2009 edn), ch. 15.
Goplerud, C. Peter III (2009b), "Adjudication of Water Rights", in Amy K. Kelly (ed.), *Waters and Water Rights*, 2, Newark, NJ: LexisNexis (2009 edn), ch. 16.
Goplerud, C. Peter III (2009c), "Administration, Protection, and Termination of the Water Right", in Amy K. Kelly (ed.), *Waters and Water Rights*, 2, Newark, NJ: LexisNexis (2009 edn), ch. 17.
Hardin, Garrett (1968), "The Tragedy of the Commons", *Science*, 162: 1243–8.
Hundley, Norris, Jr. (1992), *The Great Thirst: Californians and their Water, 1770s–1990s*, Berkeley, CA: University of California Press.
IPCC (2007a), *Special Report: Working Group I, Fourth Assessment Report: The Physical Basis of Climate Change*, Cambridge, UK: Cambridge University Press, available at http://www.ipcc.ch/publications_and_data/ar4/wg1/en/contents.html.
IPCC (2007b), *Special Report, Working Group II, Fourth Assessment Report: Impacts, Adaptation, and Vulnerability*, Cambridge, UK: Cambridge University Press, available at http://www.ipcc.ch/publications_and_data/ar4/wg2/en/contents.html.
Kaul, Inge, I. Grunberg, and M. Stern (eds) (1999), *Global Public Goods: International Cooperation in the 21st Century*, New York, NY: Oxford University Press.
Kim, Ungtae and J.J. Kaluarachi (2009), "Climate Change Impacts on Water Resources in the Upper Blue Nile Basin, Ethiopia", *Journal of the American Water Resources Association*, 45: 1361–78.
Marks, Susan J. (2009), *Aqua Shock: The Water Crisis in America*, New York, NY: Bloomberg Press.

Neuman, Janet C. (1998), "Beneficial Use, Waste, and Forfeiture: The Inefficient Search for Efficiency in Western Water Use", *Environmental Law*, 28: 919–96.
Ostrom, Elinor (1990), *Governing the Commons: The Evolution of Institutions for Collective Action*, Cambridge, UK: Cambridge University Press.
Posner, Richard A. (2007), *Economic Analysis of Law*, New York, NY: Aspen Publishers (7th ed.).
Rawls, John (1972), *A Theory of Justice*, Oxford, UK: Clarendon Press.
Reid, John Phillip (1997), *Law for the Elephant: Property and Social Behavior on the Overland Trail*, San Marino, CA: Huntington Library (paperback ed.).
Robbins, Tom (1976), *Even Cowgirls Get the Blues*, Boston, MA: Houghton-Mifflin.
Rose, Carol M. (1986), "The Comedy of the Commons: Custom, Commerce, and Inherently Public Property", *University of Chicago Law Review*, 54: 711–81.
World Commission on Dams (2000), *Dams and Development: A New Framework for Decision-Making*, London, UK: Earthscan Publications, available at http://www.dams.org/report
Young, Charles A. (2009), "Modeling the Hydrology of Climate Change in California's Sierra Nevada for Subwatershed Scale Adaptation", *Journal of the American Water Resources Association*, 45: 1409–23.

9. The legal protection of Ramsar Wetlands: Australian reforms

Alex Gardner

INTRODUCTION: ENVIRONMENTAL WATER FOR WETLANDS AND WATERFOWL

The Ramsar Strategic Plan 2009–2015 identifies 'the inadequate availability of water to wetlands' as the first of a number of key issues causing continued deterioration and loss of wetlands and their services (Ramsar Convention on Wetlands, 2008, para. 20). Water that sustains wetlands and their services is termed 'environmental water'. Frequently, the inadequate flow of such water is the direct result of demands for water abstraction for human consumptive use, particularly for irrigated agriculture. Another key issue is 'the impacts of a changing and increasingly extreme and unpredictable climate' (Ramsar Convention on Wetlands, 2008, para. 20).

These issues are testing Australia's management of wetlands of international importance that it is obliged to protect under the Ramsar Convention on Wetlands of International Importance, especially as Waterfowl Habitat (1971). Some of the Australian Ramsar listed wetlands are also the habitat of migratory birds that are to be protected under bilateral international legal obligations, such as the China-Australia Migratory Bird Agreement (CAMBA 1988). Australia faces huge challenges in implementing these international obligations because of a dramatic decline in the flow of environmental water to a number of wetlands, as was recently acknowledged by the Australian Government (Australian Government, 2008, p. 15). The scale of those challenges is well illustrated by the critical situation facing the 'Lower Lakes' of the Murray-Darling Basin (MDB). The MDB features an extensive network of inland river, wetland and groundwater systems that range over four states and one territory in the south-east of Australia.[1] These water systems eventually form into the Murray River, which flows into the Lower Lakes before venting to the sea on the South Australian coast. The Lower Lakes are listed as a Ramsar site and are also the habitat of a number of CAMBA listed migratory species of birds. They have also been the source of irrigation and domestic water supply, have supported riverine fisheries, and have been a prominent area for tourism and recreation. While a system of barrages held the level of the lakes artificially stable for decades, it dropped suddenly in 2006–09 because of declining inflows. The dramatic decline in freshwater levels not only threatened all of the ecological and human beneficial use values; it threatened to expose sulfidic soils to acidification that could further degrade the ecosystem (Paton et al., 2009; Government of South Australia, 2010, Part 1).

The Macquarie Marshes in central New South Wales are another example of a Ramsar listed and CAMBA protected wetlands in the MDB, which are also confronting the decline of environmental water flows causing a degradation of the wetlands that is impacting on the waterfowl (Australian Government and New South Wales Government, 2010, pp. 14–15 and 40).[2] The flow of water in Australia's inland rivers is notoriously variable. However, the declining environmental water flows are caused by a pattern of irrigation development, over-allocation of water access rights, subsequent severe drought and emergent climate change (Australian Government and New South Wales Government, 2010, pp. 46–7; Chartres and Williams, 2006, p. 19).

The problems of water resource scarcity in the MDB are bigger than how to manage Ramsar wetlands; there are questions of how to meet the newly defined 'critical human needs': Water Act 2007 (Cth), s. 86A(2). The particular environmental concern is that the Commonwealth Scientific and Industrial Research Organization (CSIRO) has recently projected a median 2030 climate outlook that depicts a 12% decline in the average total surface water availability and, under current water sharing arrangements, predicts that most of the impact of climate change will be borne by the environment rather than by consumptive water users (CSIRO 2008, pp. 5–6). Thus, it is now accepted that there need to be reductions in the allocations of water for consumptive use.

What does Australian law provide in respect of water sharing arrangements, and how will its laws be administered to meet its international environmental obligations to provide environmental water flows to these Ramsar wetlands and migratory waterfowl? In particular, can the law deliver the necessary reductions in allocations of consumptive use water to provide environmental flows to these important wetlands stressed by climate change? This chapter considers these questions in three stages. First, it begins with an overview of Australia's international legal obligations under the Ramsar Convention, then outlines Australia's constitutional framework for addressing them. Next, it reviews the operation of the Environment Protection and Biodiversity Conservation Act 1999 (Cth) in relation to the environmental approvals of water resource management actions in the MDB that impact on the performance of Australia's Ramsar obligations. Finally, it explains the Australian national water policy and water resources law reforms that impact on environmental water flows, including (i) the reformed water access entitlements for consumptive uses, (ii) the new regimes for water resources planning to provide legally secure environmental water allocations; and (iii) the facility of water trading to recover water for environmental flows. The Conclusion considers how this legal framework is responding to the impact of climate change on the performance of the international legal obligations.

9.1 INTERNATIONAL OBLIGATIONS AND CONSTITUTIONAL FRAMEWORK

Australia has international obligations defined in the Ramsar Convention and the CAMBA;[3] that is, in the text of the formal agreements. There are also guidelines adopted by the Ramsar Conference of the Parties, which have recently shown great concern for the provision of environmental water. What are these obligations and the principles enunciated in the guidelines and how are they to be implemented under Australia's federal constitution?

9.1.1 The Convention on Wetlands of International Importance ('Ramsar Convention')

There are two essential obligations for a party to the Ramsar Convention (Farrier and Tucker, 2000). First, there is a commitment to designate suitable wetlands within its territory for inclusion in a 'List of Wetlands of International Importance' (the 'List') and an accompanying obligation to 'promote the conservation of wetlands included in the List' (Ramsar Convention on Wetlands, 1971, Articles 2 and 3(1)). Secondly, there is a general commitment to promote 'as far as possible the wise use of wetlands in their territory', including by the establishment of nature reserves on wetlands (Ramsar Convention on Wetlands, 1971, Article 4). In respect of both commitments, a party is to consider its international responsibilities for the conservation, management and wise use of migratory stocks of waterfowl. This initial focus of the Ramsar Convention has been criticized as neglecting the broader management of catchments because confined nature reserves on wetlands can be susceptible to threats from a range of activities carried out elsewhere in the water catchment that may affect the quantity and quality of water flows.

The parties to the Ramsar Convention have recognized this issue over the past 15 years. In 2005, the Ninth Conference of the Parties adopted 'An Integrated Framework for the Ramsar Convention's Water-related Guidance' ('Integrated Framework') (Ramsar Convention on Wetlands, 2005), which explains the evolution in the parties' concerns.

> 16. The Convention has addressed water issues indirectly since its establishment in 1971, primarily through resolutions and guidance related to maintaining the

ecological character of wetlands. However, until COP6 in 1996, water for maintaining wetland ecosystem functions and ecological character was treated as an external factor, seen as beyond the scope of the Convention and generally outside the control or influence of wetland managers.

17. The adoption of Resolution VI.23 'Ramsar and Water' by the Contracting Parties at COP6 in 1996 marked a significant step forward, for the first time making explicit the recognition that:

    a. water resources management is dependent to a large degree on the hydrological functions of wetlands; and
    b. wetland ecosystems need a certain amount of water allocated for maintenance of ecological character, in order to maintain these hydrological functions.

The conference resolution IX.1 explained:

4. Over-abstraction of water from wetlands, from the water catchments in which they occur, and pollution of the water which feeds them, can all lead to significant changes in wetland ecological processes. These usually lead to changes in the physical and chemical habitat templates and a resulting, generally irreversible, loss of biodiversity. No amount of careful land management or vegetation management can mitigate these changes. Wetland ecosystems need water, in the right amount, at the right time, and of the right quality.
5. The key message here is: '*No water, no wetlands*' [emphasis added].

The Conference resolution also emphasizes the importance of wetlands to the protection and wise use of water resources.

The Integrated Framework establishes the foundation for understanding a suite of guidelines intended to provide guidance for agencies and organizations responsible for the management of wetland ecosystems to engage in the water allocation debate. Those guidelines enunciate a set of seven principles, led by the goal of sustainability: '[a]dequate water has to be provided to wetlands to sustain the functioning of ecosystems, respecting their natural dynamics for the benefit of future generations' (Ramsar Convention on Wetlands, 2005, para 52). The guidelines address, among other things, the integration of planning and management frameworks at various scales from regional to river basin to local catchment level. They include:[4]

- Resolution VIII.1: Allocation and management of water for maintaining the ecological functions of wetlands; and
- Resolution IX.1: Management of groundwater to maintain wetland ecological character.

Finally, the Integrated Framework document moots the possible preparation of guidance on 'managing water-related aspects of wetlands under conditions of climate change and desertification' (Ramsar Convention on Wetlands, 2005, para. 57, Box 2).

9.1.2 The Australian Constitutional Framework[5]

In Australia, the management of water resources and environmental protection is traditionally the responsibility of the States. At federation in 1900, the Commonwealth of Australia Constitution did not give the Commonwealth an express legislative power over natural resources and the environment. It is subsequent judicial interpretation of the Constitution that has recognized the Commonwealth Government's capacity to affect directly and indirectly water resources management through several of its legislative and financial powers.

The State parliaments enjoy plenary legislative power; that is, they can make laws about any topic. Upon federation, the States also inherited the Crown's sovereign title to all land formerly held by the British Imperial Crown. The States legislated to control the access to natural resources by claiming sovereign title to most natural resources and requiring any person who wished to exploit those natural resources to obtain an authorization from the State Government. From the end of the 19th century, the States enacted water resources legislation on this basic model, gradually curtailing the common law rights to water resources and requiring all major water access rights to be held under a direct authorization. In the past 15 years, these early entitlement regimes have been much reformed by the States to create the contemporary water access entitlement regimes.

The States' legislative powers are subject mainly to various limits founded on the Commonwealth Constitution. Principal among those limits is s. 109, by which State legislation is made inoperative by the overriding effect of valid Commonwealth legislation.

Commonwealth legislation will be valid if it pertains to one of the specific topics of legislative power conferred by the Constitution. None of them covers directly water regulation or indeed any natural resources, except for fisheries in Australian waters beyond territorial limits (s. 51(x)). The main potential heads of power are the powers in s. 51 to make laws with respect to: para. (i) interstate and overseas trade and commerce; para. (xx) foreign, trading and financial corporations; and para. (xxix) external affairs. Additional support may be derived from the defence power in para. (vi) and the implied nationhood power. The Commonwealth may also indirectly regulate water resources through its taxation regime (s. 51(ii)) and its financial powers to appropriate money for the purposes of the Commonwealth (s. 81 and s. 83)[6] and to make grants to the States on any conditions the Parliament thinks fit (s. 96). The Commonwealth Parliament has also the power to exercise legislative powers referred to it by a State parliament or parliaments (s. 51(xxxvii)).

In addressing the implementation of international legal obligations, the Commonwealth's legislative power over external affairs is the most pertinent. It authorizes the Commonwealth Parliament to enact legislation to give effect to any international legal obligations that the Australian Government has agreed to be bound by under international law. The width of this power was established in *Tasmania v Commonwealth* (1983) 158 CLR 1 (the *Tasmanian Dam* case), where a majority of the High Court accepted that any international treaty or convention to which Australia is a party, whatever its subject-matter, constitutes an external affair. But the Court maintained two constraints on the power. First, the international agreement must be a *bona fide* one and not just a ruse by the Commonwealth for the purpose of simply assuming power over that topic. Such a situation is unlikely ever to arise. Secondly, and more significantly, the Commonwealth legislation must be in pursuit of the purpose of the convention. The implementing legislation must give effect to the convention in such a manner as to be reasonably capable of being considered appropriate and adapted to the achievement of the convention's purpose or object: *Victoria v the Commonwealth of Australia* (*The Industrial Relations Case*) (1996) 187 CLR 416 at 487–8; applied in *R v Tang* (2009) 237 CLR 1. It is not confined to implementing treaty obligations; it may extend to the carrying out of recommendations adopted pursuant to the convention provided that such recommendations can reasonably be regarded as appropriate and adapted to giving effect to the convention: *The Industrial Relations Case* (1996) at 509. Declarations or recommendations of international agencies that are not made with reference to the implementation of international treaty obligations may not support the enactment of legislation.[7] The external affairs power supports the two Acts discussed below. The interesting question is whether the Ramsar Convention's Integrated Framework guidelines will support Commonwealth action to provide for environmental flows to the wetlands.

There are two particularly relevant limitations on Commonwealth legislative power. Section 100 imposes a restriction on the Commonwealth, namely:

> The Commonwealth shall not, by any law or regulation of trade or commerce, abridge the right of a State or of the residents therein to the reasonable use of the waters of rivers for conservation or irrigation.[8]

So far the High Court has confined this restriction as applicable only to laws that fall within the interstate and overseas trade and commerce power in s. 51(i), including those within s. 98, which provides that '[t]he power of the Parliament to make laws with respect to trade and commerce extends to navigation and shipping, and to railways the property of any State'. In 2009 the

High Court was asked to reconsider this narrow application of the s. 100 restriction, but it declined because the plaintiffs' case was otherwise found not to be within the scope of s. 100: *Arnold v The Minister Administering the Water Management Act 2000 (NSW)* (2010) 240 CLR 242 (*Arnold*). The Court held that plaintiffs' rights to access groundwater were not within the scope of the s. 100 protection of the right to the use of 'the waters of rivers'. In any case, s. 100 only prevents the Commonwealth from '[abridging] the right of a State or of the residents therein to the *reasonable use* of the waters of rivers *for conservation or irrigation*'. In 1901, the reference to 'conservation' was apparently meant to cover the impounding or damming of water (McKay 2006, p. 24). Today, it is arguable that a Commonwealth law which promotes an environmentally sustainable use of river water would not violate this provision, since this would be intended to provide for the 'reasonable use' of the river water.

The second potentially relevant limitation is s. 51(xxxi), which provides that the Commonwealth Parliament may make laws for 'the acquisition of property on just terms from any state or person for any purpose in respect of which the Parliament has power to make laws'. There is no similar limit on the authority of the State parliaments to acquire property and it is State law that generally governs water access rights. However, s. 51(xxxi) was recently at issue in *ICM Agriculture Pty Ltd v The Commonwealth of Australia* [2009] 240 CLR 140, a case in which some agricultural enterprises argued that it was a limit on the Commonwealth using s. 96 grants to fund State actions to reduce groundwater access rights on the transition to a new regime of water access entitlements. A majority of the High Court upheld this argument.[9] However, as discussed below, the plaintiffs failed to convince a majority of the Court that the State laws reducing the water access rights amounted to an 'acquisition of property' by the State.

In summary, the States have the primary constitutional authority to manage water resources and the environmental flows crucial to the ecological health of Ramsar wetlands. Until 2007, Commonwealth influence over water resources management was asserted mainly by the adoption of policy guidelines and the provision of financial assistance; its efforts were directed to promoting cooperative arrangements with the States, especially in the MDB. State law remains the foundation for the water resources entitlement regimes, and the reason for that is constitutional. However, in the last two years, the Commonwealth has begun to define more specific environmental legal limits on the operation of the States' water resource regimes; not by the assertion of authority under its decade old environmental legislation, but by the enactment of its own water resources legislation.

9.2 ENVIRONMENT PROTECTION AND BIODIVERSITY CONSERVATION ACT

The Environment Protection and Biodiversity Conservation Act 1999 (Cth) (EPBC Act) regulates matters of national environmental significance and international obligation, as well as activities in Commonwealth areas. The EPBC Act provides for the protection of Ramsar wetlands and migratory species by:

(1) providing for their identification; by declaring the designation of wetlands for inclusion in the Ramsar Convention List (ss. 17–17A and 326–327)[10] and the listing of migratory species (s. 209);
(2) requiring an environmental assessment and approval of 'actions' that may adversely impact upon them; that is, of actions that may have a 'significant' (implicitly adverse) effect on the ecological character of a declared Ramsar wetland (ss. 16 and 17B) or of actions that may have a significant adverse effect on a listed migratory species (ss. 20 and 20A);
(3) by preparing and implementing plans for their conservation in cooperation with the States and Territories; that is, planning for listed Ramsar wetlands (ss. 328–36) and for listed migratory species (ss. 285–300B) – the Commonwealth must make plans for wetlands and migratory species within Commonwealth areas but is only bound to cooperate with the States or Territories to prepare and implement such plans for wetlands and migratory species within a State or Territory, which is most of them; and
(4) providing for a Commonwealth administered permit system to regulate the killing, taking, trading, keeping or moving of members of a listed migratory species in a Commonwealth area (ss. 211 ff) – only the States and Territories will regulate such activities within their territories.

Brief comment will be made on (3) conservation planning and on (2) environmental approval of activities that may impact on environmental flows to Ramsar wetlands. Both Commonwealth functions are to be performed consistently with the Ramsar Convention and the 'Australian Ramsar management principles' (ss. 334–5; Environment Protection and Biodiversity Conservation Regulations 2000 (Cth), reg 10.02 and Schedule 6).

There is a Commonwealth program of Ramsar management planning but there has been little formal Ramsar management planning completed, possibly because the Commonwealth is allowing the process to be driven by the States.[11] The Macquarie Marshes seems to be an isolated beneficiary of this statutory facility (Australian Government and New South Wales Government,

2010). These plans may identify management measures to address the impacts of actions that individually or cumulatively endanger the ecological character of a Ramsar wetland, including changes to water regimes (Environment Protection and Biodiversity Conservation Regulations 2000 (Cth), reg 10.02 and Schedule 6), but the plans themselves cannot provide for the allocation of water to environmental flows. Other instruments do that, particularly State and Territory water entitlements and plans, as discussed below.

The scope of the operation of the environmental assessment and approvals provisions is particularly dependent on two elements of the statutory regime: the definition of 'action' and the meaning of 'significant'. The EPBC Act, s. 523 defines 'action' to mean the physical activity that is subject to the Commonwealth's environmental approval. A Commonwealth, State or Territory governmental decision to grant an authorization for a person to take an action is not itself an action (s. 524). Thus, State and Territory decisions to authorize water allocations will not be subject to a Commonwealth environmental approval.

There could still be numerous actions involving works or activities for the taking and use of water resources that could be 'actions'. The question becomes whether their impact will be 'significant'. Actions taken within a catchment that may have a significant impact downstream may require assessment: Environment Protection and Biodiversity Conservation Regulations 2000 (Cth), reg 10.02 and Schedule 6, s. 3.01. Indeed, assessment and approval will be required even for actions taken by third parties, provided they are within the contemplation of the proponent of the action. For example, the impacts of irrigated agriculture were required to be assessed in the proposal to construct and operate an irrigation water supply dam.[12] The problem, however, has been the disregard of actions that are, by themselves, likely to have only a very small effect on a very large problem. The Federal Court has refused to require the Minister to assess proposals to mine and export coal because the emissions of greenhouse gases from the combustion of that coal would be a very small contribution to the overall problem of global warming: *Anvil Hill Project Watch Association Inc v Minister for the Environment & Water* [2008] FCAFC 3. This approach has been applied by the Minister in determining whether an action relating to water resources would require assessment and approval for its impact on a Ramsar wetland.[13] Even the Commonwealth Government's environmental significance guidelines state that a significant impact on the ecological character of a declared Ramsar wetland means that it will result in 'a substantial and measurable change in the hydrological regime of the wetland, for example, a substantial change to the volume, timing, duration, and frequency of ground and surface water flows to and within the wetland' (Australian Government 2006, p. 15). This approach does not assess the cumulative effects of many actions.

A further aspect of environmental assessment of water resources proposals has been reliance on a proponent's promises that the proposed water resource extraction would make the environmental effect downstream no worse because of offsetting measures and existing regulatory requirements. This was the approach taken in the assessment of the Sugarloaf Pipeline proposal, by which water is to be extracted from the upper catchment of the Goulburn River in the southern MDB and piped over the Great Dividing Range to supplement the public water supply to metropolitan Melbourne.[14] This decision may also illustrate that the Federal Environment Minister would not use the EPBC Act approval process to require increased provision of environmental water. That task is left to the water resources legislation.

9.3 WATER RESOURCES LAW REFORMS AND ENVIRONMENTAL FLOWS

The reform of Australian water resources law since the inception of national water reform policy in 1994 has been guided by the twin themes of:

- the transition to a new water access rights regime centred on proprietary 'water access entitlements' that are tradable in regulated water markets; and
- the establishment of statutory water resources planning to secure environmental sustainability and to provide the foundation for the proprietary access entitlements.

These reforms have been achieved principally by the reform of the State-based entitlement regimes that operate at the local or area management level. Environmentally sustainable levels of consumptive use of a water resource mean not only limiting of the grant of new access licences in a fully allocated resource, but also reconceptualizing water access entitlements as subject to ongoing definition under a water plan. Two essential elements of water planning are: (i) to determine the environmental water allocations and to define a 'consumptive pool' of water in which long-term individual access entitlements are issued; and (ii) to provide for periodic determinations of the amount of water that is actually available to be taken by those entitlement holders.

Much of the conceptual development of the State entitlement regimes has come from addressing the significant challenges of managing the water resources of the MDB. Cooperative arrangements for the management of the MDB have been developing since federation and have, in recent decades, been recorded in the Murray-Darling Basin Agreement – an intergovernmental agreement between all of the MDB governments (Commonwealth, State and

Territory) (Gardner et al., 2009, ch. 7). The initial management focus was on sharing water for consumptive use, but, over the decades, the focus has expanded to include whole of catchment measures to address water quality and protection of water dependent ecosystems. The most significant recent reforms include provisions for environmental flows.

To understand the effect of these reforms, we will review the:

- nature of the water access rights, especially the new 'water access entitlement';
- effect of the local or area management planning under State law;
- Water Act 2007 (Cth) provisions for a 'Basin Plan' to set sustainable diversion limits; and
- provisions for trade of environmental water and the Commonwealth Environmental Water Holder.

9.3.1 Water Access Rights

There are now two basic forms of water access rights: landholder rights (including native title rights) and access rights held under a specific grant of authority in the form of a licence or 'water access entitlement'. The volumes of water taken in exercise of landholder rights are generally small and used for watering stock and domestic or indigenous cultural purposes. All larger extractions of water for commercial or public water supply purposes require a specific grant of authority (typically called a water licence) from the relevant State government.

The old form of access licences specified the entitlement to take water initially in terms of purposes to which the water would be applied and subsequently in fixed maximum annual volumes, which could be varied temporarily by executive government order in times of scarcity. These licences were of limited term but renewable. They were also typically appurtenant to land and not separately transferable from the title of the pertinent land. Importantly, they were mostly not issued on the basis of a water plan, so there was no careful evaluation of water resource availability and no environmental water allocation to limit the allocations to consumptive use. In the MDB, this old regime prevailed during the period of perceived abundance of water and led to significant problems of over-allocation and overuse.[15]

The water law reforms have seen these old licence rights transformed into perpetual and tradable 'water access entitlements' (WAE), separated from land title and clearly specifying the volume of water that may be extracted from time to time in accordance with a plan. The essence of the new WAEs is that they only give the holder a 'share' of the water that is determined under the plan to be available for consumptive use from time to time, usually on an annual basis. The share has a nominal volumetric entitlement, but the annual allocation reflects what is available. There may also be different classes of shares in a consumptive pool with different levels of priority, which will affect the volume actually accorded by annual allocations.

Legislating the share concept was a fundamental reform. It changed the presumption that a water access licence was an entitlement to a maximum volume that only could be varied in times of scarcity by the exercise of extraordinary powers to a presumption that the legal entitlement was only to a share of the water that was available in the climatic circumstances of the time. This makes sustainable water management much easier to achieve politically.

9.3.2 Area Management Planning for Environmental Flow

The two central objectives of the national water policy in relation to environmental water allocations (EWA) are to (Australian Government, 2004, para. 23(iii) and (iv)):

- make statutory provision for *environmental and other public benefit outcomes*, and
- complete the return of all currently over-allocated or overused systems to *environmentally sustainable levels of extraction.*

9.3.2.1 Statutory provision for EWAs

To give effect to this first objective, the national water policy (Australian Government, 2004, para. 35) provides that an EWA defined in a water plan is to:

(i) be given statutory recognition with at least the same degree of security as water access entitlements for consumptive use and be fully accounted for;
(ii) be defined as water management arrangements under plan rules or held as a water access entitlement; and
(iii) when held as a water access entitlement, it may be tradable on the temporary market if that is consistent with the defined outcomes.

In respect of the statutory recognition of EWAs, one could ask:

- is there a legal duty to make an EWA,
- to make it at a certain level, and
- to make it in priority to the allocation and delivery of water to consumptive purposes?

No State maintains legislation to this effect for every water source in the State (Gardner et al., ch. 16). New South Wales experimented with, and resiled from, a statutory duty on the Minister to make EWAs to maintain fundamental ecosystem health in priority to allocating water for consumptive uses. Amendments to the initial legislation provide no certain environmental flow and endorse the technique of providing for EWAs as a residue of water after allocation to consumptive uses.

The Victorian legislation provides a different picture of a similar story, but with a new chapter recently drafted. In 2005, legislation established an 'environmental water reserve'[16] as the means of giving effect to the national water policy principle that EWAs should be given statutory recognition of at least the same degree of security as water access entitlements for consumptive use. The essential objective of the environmental water reserve is that it be maintained 'so as to preserve the environmental values and health of water ecosystems': Water Act 1989 (Vic), s. 4B. However, there are various associated provisions that provide for the assessment of water resources and the creation of EWAs in various ways that ultimately make the content of the environmental water reserve a matter of executive discretion rather than statutory duty. Despite the statutory objective, the Act does not require that an EWA be determined and implemented at any particular level or in priority to the satisfaction of consumptive uses of water (Foerster, 2007). Further, although the legislation authorizes the issue of 'environmental entitlements' to the Environment Minister to form part of the environmental water reserve, the Water Minister has the statutory authority to qualify temporarily environmental entitlements just as much as consumptive use entitlements: Water Act 1989 (Vic), ss. 33–33AAC. In normal water shortages, the qualifications are proportional; that is, equal for all classes of entitlements. However, in circumstances of severe water shortage, the Water Minister may assign different priorities to different classes of entitlement and, in this way, can move environmental water to consumptive use purposes. This power has been exercised.

In August 2010, the Victorian Parliament amended the Water Act to create the Victorian Environmental Water Holder (VEWH), a body corporate with at least three commissioners and its own staff, to hold and manage the various rights and entitlements of the environmental water reserve consistently with the objective: Water Amendment (Victorian Environmental Water Holder) Act 2010 (Vic). The VEWH must prepare plans to guide the performance of its functions and is subject to the power of the State Environment Minister issuing public directions that are consistent with those plans. The VEWH may trade in water access rights and entitlements, but subject to the Environment Minister's consent. The environmental water rights will still be subject to the Water Minister's powers to qualify rights in times of water shortage.

9.3.2.2 Dealing with over-allocated and overused systems

In the development of national water policy, the States have repeatedly agreed with the Commonwealth to provide a better water balance for all over-allocated river systems and groundwater resources, including by appropriate allocations to the environment and adjustment of water access entitlements. Another way to achieve that objective is by the purchase of access entitlements and converting them from consumptive use to EWA purposes (discussed below). This section focuses on the adjustment of entitlements in the conversion of the old form of licences to the new water access entitlements.

In 2004, the States committed to making substantial progress by 2010 in addressing all over-allocated and/or overused surface or groundwater systems (Australian Government, 2004, paras 41–44 and 97). Any significant adjustment issues arising from reduction in water availability to access entitlement holders were to be addressed by consulting affected parties through the planning process on the potential responses. In addition, the Commonwealth committed to negotiating with the States for provision of regional structural adjustment assistance. Thus, the general approach to addressing over-allocation is that reductions of water availability in the adjustment of water access entitlements to establish the new regime is not to trigger a legal entitlement to compensation, though the Commonwealth may assist with the costs of structural adjustment. State legislation has, generally, adopted this approach (Gardner et al., 2009, 16.89–16.107).

The problem of defining 'over-allocation' is the problem of defining 'sustainable yield'. There are difficulties in fashioning practical definitions of these terms. How does one establish that an allocation limit is sustainable? The National Water Commission has found that, in many areas, 'estimates of sustainable yield are based on the current level of entitlements' (Australian Government, National Water Commission, 2007, Part B, p. 30). Despite the CSIRO report on 'Water Availability in the Murray-Darling Basin' and attempts by the National Water Commission to develop national guidelines on the concepts of over-allocation, overuse and sustainable yield, there is still 'no shared national understanding of the definition of over-allocation and sustainable levels of extraction' (Matthews, 2009). This is reflected in the fact that the legislation of the various States provides little, if any, statutory recognition of the problems of over-allocation and overuse, and no State legislation mandates government action to address these problems within a particular time or in a particular way.

9.3.3 Water Act 2007 (Cth) – From the 'Cap' to the Basin Plan

The two significant steps in defining sustainability for the MDB have been the adoption in 1995 of the 'Cap' (a limit on the extractions of water from MDB river systems) and its proposed more comprehensive replacement, the Basin Plan, which is to be made under the Water Act 2007 (Cth). (A draft of the Basin Plan is due for release in November 2011, which could lead to approval of a final Basin Plan in the course of 2012.)

9.3.3.1 The MDB Cap

Defining the limits of allocation across the MDB began with 'the Cap'. It was initially adopted by the Murray-Darling Basin Ministerial Council (the MDB Council) as an interim cap in June 1995 (Murray-Darling Basin Ministerial Council 1996), confirmed as permanent in 1997, formally adopted as Schedule F to the Murray-Darling Basin Agreement 1992 by the MDB Council in August 2000, and amended and renamed as Schedule E in the 2008 Murray-Darling Basin Agreement.[17] The adoption of the Cap aimed to curtail water resource development below the full level of legal entitlements that were already allocated in 1993/94. There was originally no defined Cap for Queensland and no participation by the Australian Capital Territory, but the 2008 amendment introduced 'baseline conditions' definitions for Queensland and the Australian Capital Territory. The Cap imposes on the participating States[18] the duty to ensure that diversions within each 'designated river valley' do not exceed diversion limits under the Cap definitions. The Murray-Darling Basin Commission (the MDBC)[19] approved the States' analytical models and calculated the annual diversion targets. The MDBC also reported on the implementation of the Cap each year.

In 2000, the MDBC concluded that the Cap had contributed to the MDB Council's aim of achieving the ecological sustainability of the Basin's river systems, but that the then current level of the Cap did not represent a sustainable level of diversions for the Basin (Murray-Darling Basin Ministerial Council 2000, pp. 13–14). While it is likely that the projects for saving and purchasing water for the environment will lead to some modifications in the setting of the Cap (Murray-Darling Basin Ministerial Council 2006, p. 7), there are some fundamental weaknesses in it for the purposes of achieving ecological sustainability for the Basin's water resources. The Cap generally applied only to diversions from storages and rivers for consumptive use. It did not account for the interceptions of water from plantations, from increases in the number and size of farm dams, bushfires, return flows from irrigation and increased use of groundwater (Murray-Darling Basin Ministerial Council 2006, p. 2).

9.3.3.2 The Basin Plan

A significant new factor has been introduced to water planning in the Murray-Darling Basin with the enactment of the Water Act 2007 (Cth). It establishes a Murray-Darling Basin Authority (MDBA) as a Commonwealth body charged with preparing, for the Commonwealth Minister's approval, a 'Basin Plan' that 'will provide for limits on the quantity of water that may be taken from the Basin *water resources* as a whole and from the water resources of each *water resource plan area*' (emphasis added): s. 19. Two key objectives of the Basin Plan are to give effect to relevant international agreements (which include the Ramsar Convention and CAMBA) and to establish and enforce environmentally sustainable limits on the quantities of surface and groundwater that may be taken from the Basin water resources: s. 20. The Act also creates a specific duty on the Commonwealth in making the Basin Plan to give effect to international obligations: s. 21. The statutory expression of those international obligations provides, pertinently, that the Basin Plan 'must' promote the wise use of all the Basin water resources and the conservation of declared Ramsar wetlands, and must also take account of the ecological character descriptions of all declared Ramsar wetlands and other key environmental sites within the MDB: s. 21(3)(a), (b) and (c).

The Act provides the foundation for the integrated management of all the Basin's water resources. It defines 'water resource' comprehensively to mean surface water or groundwater, which terms are themselves defined to include overland flow, water in a watercourse, lake, wetland or aquifer, and all aspects of the water resource that contribute to its environmental values: s. 4. The Act also defines 'Basin water resources' to mean all water resources within, or beneath, the Murray-Darling Basin.[20]

The Basin Plan will set the limits within which the State water resources planning will operate. It will define the 'water resource plan areas' ('management areas') and will stipulate the requirements with which a water resource plan for a management area must comply: s. 22(1), item 11, and s. 22(3). Generally, the Basin States will prepare the water resource plans for the management areas and submit them to the Commonwealth Minister for accreditation: s. 53 ff. If the States' water resource plans are consistent with the Basin Plan, the Minister must accredit them: s. 63. However, if the Minister decides not to accredit a State water resource plan, the Minister may ask the MDBA to prepare a water resource plan for that management area and submit it to the Minister for adoption: ss. 68–9.

The Basin Plan limits on the taking of water from the Basin as a whole and from the management areas will be expressed as 'long-term average sustainable diversion limits' (s. 22(1), item 6) and 'must reflect an environmentally sustainable level of take', a term that is defined: ss. 23 and 4. The State water resource plans must incorporate and apply 'the long-term annual diversion limit' for the water resources of the management areas: s. 55(2). These State limits must, in due course, 'reflect an environmentally sustainable level of take': s. 22(1), item 7 and s. 24.

There are three particular issues in giving effect to that duty and the duty to give effect to the international obligations. First, would the Ramsar Convention Integrated Framework guidelines assist in defining international obligations to provide environmental flows and support the constitutional validity of the Act's provisions and the Basin Plan limits? This will depend on whether the Court accepts the guidelines as being reasonably regarded as appropriate and adapted to giving effect to the Convention obligations.

Secondly, how do these duties interact with the obligation to meet 'critical human needs' for water? Part 2A of the Act, inserted in 2008, directs that the Basin Plan must be prepared, having regard to the agreement of the Commonwealth and the Basin States, that 'critical human water needs are the highest priority water for communities who are dependent on Basin water resources'.[21] 'Critical human needs' are defined (s. 86A(2)) as:

> the needs for a minimum amount of water, that can reasonably be provided from Basin water resources, required to meet:
> (a) core human consumption requirements in urban and rural areas; and
> (b) those non-human consumption requirements that a failure to meet would cause prohibitively high social, economic or national security costs.

The reality is that water cannot be supplied to meet critical human needs unless there is 'conveyance water' in the system to deliver it: s. 86A(1)(b) and (4). Thus, Part 2A mandates that the Basin Plan must provide for a sophisticated three tier set of water sharing arrangements to ensure that critical human needs water can be delivered. The Basin Plan must also specify the arrangements for monitoring matters relevant to securing critical human needs water. Interestingly, the Act provides that the preparation of the Basin Plan having regard for critical human needs water is not to limit the obligations to give effect to the relevant international agreements: s. 86A(1). In times of severe water shortage, it is difficult to see that the two will not conflict.

The third issue is the difficulty for a court of law to enforce the generally worded duties to reflect a sustainable level of take. The Act defines an 'environmentally sustainable level of take' (s. 4(1)):

> … for a water resource means the level at which water can be taken from that water resource which, if exceeded, would compromise:
> (a) key environmental assets of the water resource; or
> (b) key ecosystem functions of the water resource; or
> (c) the productive base of the water resource; or
> (d) key environmental outcomes for the water resource.

Is this concept justiciable? Would a court of law entertain an action for judicial review on the ground that the Commonwealth Minister has approved a diversion limit for the Basin Plan as a whole or for a management area that does not reflect an environmentally sustainable level of take? How would a court identify the key environmental features for the purposes of applying the definition of environmentally sustainable level of take? As a matter of statutory interpretation, the key environmental features to be protected will be identified in the Basin Plan, including the declared Ramsar wetlands: s. 28(2). However, that still leaves the interesting question whether a court of law would review a sustainable diversion limit specified in the Basin Plan on the argument that it is at a level that 'would compromise' those key environmental features. The Government said (2009) that the 'results of the CSIRO Murray-Darling Basin Sustainable Yields Project, together with other information available to the Murray-Darling Basin Authority, are used to develop the sustainable diversion limits for the Murray-Darling Basin'.[22] If a diversion limit approved in the Basin Plan departs considerably from the CSIRO finding, for example, could it be asserted legally that it does not 'reflect an environmentally sustainable level of take'?

Even if one or more lines of argument were upheld on this question, it does not follow that the Court would invalidate the adoption of the Basin Plan: see *Gwydir River Case* (*Nature Conservation Council of New South Wales Inc v The Minister Administering the Water Management Act*) [2005] NSWCA 9 at [90]–[95] where the New South Wales Court of Appeal, applying *Project Blue Sky Inc v Australian Broadcasting Authority* (1998) 194 CLR 355, refused to invalidate a management plan that contained an environmental water allocation that did not meet the statutory requirements. The court may say that the Act's declaration of environmental sustainability is not intended to lead to the consequence of legal invalidity of the Basin Plan, especially if a challenge were brought long after the approval of the Basin Plan – perhaps as a means of challenging the validity of an action done under it or defending an enforcement action for breach of the Basin Plan: Water Act 2007 (Cth), s. 35 and Part 8. Further, what may be an appropriate remedy? An order that the Plan be set aside would leave the Minister subject still to the legal duty to make the Plan, and so it should be made again. It is unlikely that a court would go further and actually direct the Minister as to what would be an environmentally sustainable level of take. Notwithstanding the difficult task that a court would face in undertaking judicial review of a Basin Plan, Parliament's direction should be given some effect because of the fundamental importance of achieving sustainability in the MDB and the clear legislative concern with that goal displayed in the Act's objects and the statement of Basin Plan purposes: ss. 3(d)(i) and 20(b).

9.3.4 Trading Environmental Water

The national water policy proposes that water that is provided to meet environmental and other public benefit outcomes may be defined on a plan rules basis or held as a tradable water access entitlement (Australian Government 2004, para. 35(ii) and (iii)). Any trade of an environmental entitlement may only be on the 'temporary market' when it is not required for the environmental outcomes and provided that such trading does not conflict with those outcomes. The national policy envisages that environmental water held as a tradable access entitlement may form a share of the consumptive pool to be determined under a plan and that the actual volumes of water committed to the environment will be subject to the seasonal determinations of available water. Of its nature, a tradable environmental access entitlement is most easily applied to regulated river systems in which volumes of water can be released into the environment by the operation of a dam, but the instrument is not limited to this context.[23] Only two States, New South Wales and Victoria, have specifically legislated for tradable environmental access entitlements. South Australia provides for water to be allocated to the environment under a water licence by the provisions of a water allocation plan.[24]

Although the Basin Plan will not come into effect until 2011, the Commonwealth has been seeking to increase environmental flows by a program of buying water access entitlements from willing sellers and converting them to environmental flow purposes.[25] Because of Victorian State limits on water trading, there were some political difficulties in 2009 with this program attracting a very large proportion of the sales of water to the Commonwealth from NSW. This led the NSW Government to impose an embargo on further sales of water entitlements to the Commonwealth until Victoria enacted the Water Amendment (Non Water User Limit) Act 2009 to remove the limit on the sale of entitlements to the Commonwealth for environmental purposes.

In addition to the buyback program, the Commonwealth and the States have instituted programs of funding works to improve irrigation efficiency in return for entitlement holders transferring the water savings to the Commonwealth or State Governments.[26]

In the case of the Commonwealth, entitlements from water buybacks and efficiency savings are to be held by the new Commonwealth Environmental Water Holder (CEWH).[27] The functions of the CEWH are to manage Commonwealth environmental water holdings and administer the Environmental Water Holdings Special Account. These functions involve the purchase and sale of water access rights and related rights, making available water from the holdings, and the making of contracts or other arrangements for the taking and use of water from the holdings, as well as maintaining records of the holdings. The CEWH is authorized to perform these functions for the purposes of protecting or restoring the environmental assets within and outside the MDB so as to give effect to relevant international agreements. Although the CEWH must operate within relevant water management plans, and the

Minister may make operating rules for the CEWH, neither the Secretary of the Department nor the Minister may give directions to the CEWH about the performance of its core functions: Water Act 2007 (Cth), s. 107.

While the Commonwealth has the capacity to acquire environmental water, most of the entitlements acquired are not high security and so receive only low annual allocations during drought. Nevertheless, this strategy seems to be proving the most politically palatable method of recouping water for environmental flows. Will it be an adequate strategy to recover sufficient environmental flows to sustain important wetlands in a drying climate?

9.4 CONCLUSION: COPING WITH CLIMATE CHANGE

With the MDB impacted by emergent climate change, there needs to be a change to the water sharing arrangements and a reduction of consumptive use allocations in order to restore essential environmental flows to protect Ramsar wetlands. Have the Australian law reforms provided the framework for meeting the international obligations in the face of climate change? Possibly not. The Chair of the National Water Commission commented in 2009 about the success of the water law reforms (Matthews, 2009):

> … despite a lot of effort in water reform, our water is still in trouble. Australia has been challenged for centuries by a dry and highly variable climate. But climate change has now raised the bar on water reform. The need to take climate change better into account in water management is a key theme in the Commission's report. We have known for years that water reform in Australia was important, pressing and difficult. Now that climate change is with us, important becomes vital, pressing becomes urgent, and difficult becomes downright tough.

There are various immediate responses for coping with the effects of climate change on water resources management: defining water resources more broadly and broadening the scope of water source planning beyond the traditional natural resources; adopting greater flexibility in planning scenarios that use shorter term weather patterns to calculate future water availability; and enhancing demand management (Tan, 2010). A key strategy is to identify and consider climate change impacts in the water planning process (Bates et al., 2010). The uncertainty of climate change impacts are also being considered in more cautious licensing decisions: *Alanvale Pty Ltd v Southern Rural Water* [2010] Victorian Civil and Administrative Tribunal 480.

The MDBA is addressing climate change impacts in the design of the Basin Plan sustainable diversion limits by devising varying water allocation models based on a range of short and long term climate scenarios, acknowledging that it is very difficult to predict future climate change (Australian Government,

Murray-Darling Basin Authority 2009, Attachment A, pp. 46–50). It is presently difficult to assign a legal consequence to the scenarios approach.

The significant issue for climate change is who should bear the risk of the reduced availability of water in a drying climate. The national water policy assigns the risk of seasonal or long term changes in climate to entitlement holders (Australian Government, 2004, paras 46–51). Is it fair to assign the burden of climate change reductions to water availability in this way? Is it even practical? Will governments be prepared to make the necessary reductions to allocations for human consumptive use if the entitlement holders have to bear the reductions without compensation?

There are two models of State response to the national policy formula. NSW implements the national policy formula, providing no compensation for reduction of a water access entitlement on the basis of a review report that such a reduction was the result of restoring water to the environment because of changes resulting from climate change: Water Management Act 2000 (NSW), ss. 46 and 87AA(3). The Victorian model provides for uncompensated changes to entitlements but only after a 15 year assessment, which is not due till 2019: Water Act 1989 (Vic), Part 3, Division 1C. This could be too late and too inflexible to deal with sudden climatic drying, but ultimately provides for no compensation.

In *ICM Agriculture* [2009] HCA 51, the High Court majority found that the reduction in entitlements on conversion from the old to the new statutory regime was not an acquisition of property by the Commonwealth through the NSW legislation. Despite this decision, it will be difficult for Australian Governments to make the political choices to reduce the new proprietary water access entitlements in order to return water to the environment, without compensating the entitlement holders.

Australia should reverse its risk assignment framework for reduction of entitlements caused by climate change. The Australian Government could establish a strict/no-fault liability scheme of compensation by which Australian greenhouse gas emitters contribute to a fund that compensates those who suffer climate change harm, including water access entitlement holders. Such a fund and compensation process could be established by legislation associated with mitigating climate change and be quite specific about the categories of harm that were compensable. It would make it easier to fulfil Australia's international environmental obligations in respect of Ramsar wetlands and migratory birds.

NOTES

1. The States are New South Wales, Queensland, South Australia and Victoria, and the Australian Capital Territory, which surrounds the national capital of Canberra.

2. Australian Government and Department of Environment and Climate Change of the New South Wales Government, 'Draft Macquarie Marshes Adaptive Environmental Management Plan, June 2009', pp. 14–15 and 35, www.wetlandrecovery.nsw.gov.au, November 2009.
3. CAMBA provides the framework for Australia and China to cooperate in the protection of migratory birds (that is, birds identified as migrating between the two countries) and their environment. There are similar bilateral agreements in place between Japan and Australia, and the Republic of Korea and Australia. While these bilateral obligations are more geographically general than the key obligations of the Ramsar Convention, many of the migratory birds to be protected under these treaties are similarly protected by the implementation of the Ramsar obligations.
4. The first two guidelines are, respectively, published as Handbooks 8 and 9 in the Ramsar Handbooks for the Wise Use of Wetlands, 3rd edition (2006), www.ramsar.org and link to 'publications' and 'Ramsar Wise Use Handbooks', November 2009.
5. A fuller discussion of the constitutional framework for water resources management is given in Gardner et al. (2009), ch. 5.
6. *Pape v Commissioner of Taxation of the Commonwealth of Australia* (2009) 238 CLR 1 esp at [229]–[245]: the power to spend appropriated moneys must relate to a purpose that is within a topic of Commonwealth power under the Constitution.
7. *Pape v Commissioner of Taxation of the Commonwealth of Australia* (2009) 238 CLR 1, Hayne and Keifel JJ at [368]–[374] and Heydon J at [475]–[485].
8. It is unclear whether 'resident' in s. 100 includes corporations. It does not in s. 75(iv): *Crouch v Commissioner for Railways (Qld)* (1985) 159 CLR 22 at 24, 27, 34.
9. French CJ, Gummow and Crennan JJ at [46] and, in a separate judgment, Heydon J. Three judges, Hayne, Kiefel and Bell JJ, said that it was not necessary to decide the interaction between s. 51(xxxi) and s. 96: [2009] HCA 51 at [141]. The decision in *ICM* was applied in *Arnold.*
10. Australia currently has 65 Ramsar wetlands: see Australian Government, Department of the Sustainability, Environment, Water, Population and Communities website www.environment.gov.au and follow links to 'water', 'water topics', 'wetlands', 'Australian wetlands database' and 'Australian Ramsar wetlands'.
11. Australian Government, Department of the Sustainability, Environment, Water, Population and Communities, 'Ramsar Management Planning Program', http://www.environment.gov.au/water/policy-programs/wetlands/rampp.html, 14 November 2010. For a description and analysis of the informal Ramsar management planning in the Murray-Darling Basin, see Pittock et al. (2010).
12. *Minister for Environment and Heritage v Queensland Conservation Council* (2004) 139 FCR 24 (the Nathan Dam case) and the subsequent insertion of a definition of 'impact' in s. 527E.
13. EPBC Act referral decision, Lower Lakes Irrigation Pipeline, North to North-West of Lake Alexandrina, South Australia (EPBC 2009/4743) – Notification that proposal is not a controlled action if undertaken in a particular manner; limit on extractions to 30 GL reflecting current ground water extractions and Murray River entitlements; 18 March 2009. See also, Queensland Water Infrastructure Pty Ltd, 'Traveston Crossing Dam, Environmental Impact Statement, Executive Summary, October 2007', pp. 2–25.
14. Statement of Reasons for Grant of Approval under the EPBC Act 1999 (Cth) by the Minister for the Environment to approve the proposal for the Sugarloaf Pipeline (EPBC 2008/3960) 14 October 2008, especially paras 60–82. This decision was taken even though the offsetting measures were to be the subject of a separate future referral; namely, that for the Northern Victoria Irrigation Modernisation Project (the so-called 'Food Bowl Modernisation Project'): Northern Victoria Irrigation Renewal Project; 9 October 2009 referral under the EPBC Act.
15. 'Over-allocation' is defined as situations where the total volume of water able to be extracted at a given time exceeds the 'environmentally sustainable level of extraction' for a particular system. 'Overuse' means where the total volume of water actually extracted in a particular system at a given time exceeds the environmentally sustainable levels of extraction for that system. See Gardner et al. (2009), 16.84.
16. Water Act 1989 (Vic), s. 4A. See also, the second reading speech on the Water (Resource

Management) Act 2005 (Vic), Parliament of Victoria, Hansard, Legislative Assembly, 6 October 2005, p. 1334.

17. The 2008 Murray-Darling Basin Agreement is Schedule 1 to the Water Act 2007 (Cth).
18. The Australian Capital Territory is defined as a participating State: Schedule F cl 2(2).
19. The MDB Commission has now been replaced by the MDB Authority under the Water Act 2007 (Cth).
20. Water Act 2007 (Cth), s. 4, definition of 'Basin water resources'. It does not include the groundwater of the Great Artesian Basin and other water resources may be excluded by regulation.
21. Water Act 2007 (Cth), s. 86A(1).
22. Australian Government, Department of Environment, Water, Heritage and the Arts, 'Sustainable Yields in the Murray-Darling Basin', http://www.environment.gov.au and follow links 'Water', 'Murray-Darling Basin' and 'Sustainable Yields', October 2009.
23. Water Act 1989 (Vic), s. 48B provides that an environmental entitlement may be allocated in respect of groundwater.
24. For example, see Government of South Australia, River Murray Catchment Water Management Board, River Murray Prescribed Watercourse Water Allocation Plan 2009, parts 5.2 and 5.3, http://www.samdbnrm.sa.gov.au/ , follow links to 'Our Plans' and 'water allocation plans' October 2009.
25. Australian Government, Department of the Environment, Water, Heritage and the Arts, "Water entitlement purchasing in the Murray-Darling Basin (water buybacks)", http://www.environment.gov.au/water/policy-programs/entitlement-purchasing/index.html, September 2010. The Commonwealth has committed 3.1 billion dollars to a ten year program of buybacks in the MDB.
26. The initial funding program, agreed in 2002, was called 'The Living Murray Initiative'. The new Commonwealth program, 'Sustainable Rural Water Use and Infrastructure', 2008, committed 3.7 billion dollars to works that will deliver water savings for the environment in the MDB: Australian Government, Department of Sustainability, Environment, Water, Population and Communities, http://www.environment.gov.au/water/programs/srwui/index.html, October 2010.
27. Australian Government, Department of Sustainability, Environment, Water, Population and Communities, 'Commonwealth Environmental Water Holder', http://www.environment.gov.au/water/policy-programs/cewh/index.html, October 2010.

REFERENCES

Australian Government (2004), 'Intergovernmental Agreement on a National Water Initiative 2004 (NWI)', http://www.nwc.gov.au and follow links 'Water reform' and 'National Water Initiative', accessed September 2010.

Australian Government (2006), 'Department of Sustainability, Environment, Water, Population and Communities, EPBC Act Policy Statement 1.1, "Significant Impact Guidelines, Matters of National Environmental Significance"', http://www.environment.gov.au/epbc/publications/nes-guidelines.html, May 2006.

Australian Government (2008), 'National Report on the Implementation of the Ramsar Convention on Wetlands', submitted to the 10th Meeting of the Conference of the Contracting Parties, Republic of Korea, 28 October–4 November 2008.

Australian Government, Murray-Darling Basin Authority (2009), 'Development of Sustainable Diversion Limits for the Murray-Darling Basin, http://www.mdba.gov.au and follow links to 'Basin Plan', 'The Basin Plan: a concept statement', November 2009.

Australian Government, National Water Commission (2007), *National Water Initiative: First Biennial Assessment of Progress in Implementation*, October 2007.

Australian Government and New South Wales Government (2010), Department of Environment and Climate Change, 'Macquarie Marshes Adaptive Environmental Management Plan', June 2010, http://www.wetlandrecovery.nsw.gov.au.

Bates, B., K. Walker, S. Beare and S. Page (2010), 'Incorporating Climate Change in Water Allocation Planning', Australian Government, National Water Commission, Waterlines report series no. 28.

CAMBA (1988), Agreement between the Government of the People's Republic of China and the Government of Australia for the Protection of Migratory Birds and their Environment, signed 1986, entry into force 1988, Australian Treaty Series 1988 no. 22.

Chartres, C. and J. Williams (2006), 'Can Australia Overcome its Water Scarcity Problems?' *Journal of Developments in Sustainable Agriculture*, 1, 17–24.

Commonwealth of Australia, Commonwealth Scientific and Industrial Research Organization (CSIRO) (2008), 'Water Availability in the Murray-Darling Basin: A Report from the CSIRO to the Australian Government', http://www.csiro.au, follow links 'Flagships', 'Water for a Healthy Country Flagship', 'Sustainable Yields Project', 'The Murray-Darling Basin Sustainable Yields Project', and 'MDBSY Whole of Basin Report', and 'Water Availability in the Murray-Darling Basin Report'; see the Executive Summary, September 2010.

Farrier, D. and L. Tucker (2000), 'Wise Use of Wetlands Under the Ramsar Convention: A Challenge for Meaningful Implementation of International law', *Journal of Environmental Law*, 12 (1), 21–42.

Foerster, A. (2007), 'Victoria's New Environmental Water Reserve: What's In a Name?', *The Australasian Journal of Natural Resources Law and Policy*, 11, 145–80.

Gardner, A., R. Bartlett and J. Gray (2009), *Water Resources Law*, Australia: LexisNexis Butterworths.

Government of South Australia (2010), 'Murray Futures: Lower Lakes and Coorong Recovery; Securing the Future, A Long-Term Plan for the Coorong, Lower Lakes and Murray Mouth', June 2010, http://www.murrayfutures.sa.gov.au/lower.php, 17 September 2010.

Matthews, K. (2009), Chair and CEO of the National Water Commission of Australia, 'Australian Water Reform in 2009', presentation delivered to a conference hosted by the Australian Committee for Economic Development, 9 October 2009.

McKay, J. (2006), 'The Quest for Environmentally Sustainable Water Use – Constitutional Issues for Federal, State and Local Governments', *Reform* (89), 2006/2007, 22.

Murray-Darling Basin Ministerial Council (1996), 'Setting the Cap: Report of the Independent Audit Group', November 1996, http://www.mdbc.gov.au, and follow links 'Natural Resources Management' and 'The Cap', and link to the Report, September 2010.

Murray-Darling Basin Ministerial Council (2000), 'Review of the Operation of the Cap, August 2000'.

Murray-Darling Basin Ministerial Council (2006), 'Report of the Independent Audit Group, Review of Cap Implementation 2005/06'.

Paton, D., D. Rogers, K. Aldridge, B. Deegan and J. Brookes (2009), 'A future for the Coorong and Lower Lakes', *Pacific Conservation Biology*, 15, 7–10.

Pittock, J., M. Finlayson, A. Gardner and C. McKay (2010), 'Changing Character: The Ramsar Convention on Wetlands and Climate Change in the Murray-Darling Basin, Australia', *Environmental and Planning Law Journal*, 27(6), 401–25.

Ramsar Convention on Wetlands (1971), Convention on Wetlands of International Importance especially as Waterfowl Habitat, signed at Ramsar in Iran in 1971, Australian Treaty Series no. 48, entered into force on 21 December 1975, and amended in 1982 and 1987.

Ramsar Convention on Wetlands (2005), Conference of the Parties 9, 2005, Resolution IX.1 Annex C, An Integrated Framework for the Ramsar Convention's Water-related Guidance.

Ramsar Convention on Wetlands (2008), Resolution X.1 adopting The Ramsar Strategic Plan 2009–2015, Gland: Ramsar Secretariat.

Tan, Poh-Ling (2010), 'Adaptation Measures for Water Security in a Changing Climate: Policy, Planning and the Law', in T. Bonyhady, A. MacIntosh and J. MacDonald (eds), *Adaptation to Climate Change: Law and Policy*, Sydney: Federation Press, pp. 135–56.

10. Drinking water security in China: a critical justice issue

Ke Jian[1]

10.1 DRINKING WATER SECURITY IS THREATENED BY WATER POLLUTION IN CHINA

After more than two decades of two-digit economic growth, the great challenge facing China now is to break the relationship between fast economic development and the deterioration of environment. Rapid industrialization and urbanization has left much of China's water, air, land and other environmental elements polluted to a dangerous degree.

Because many rivers, lakes and other waters have become polluted with various types of effluent, water security is threatened by the devastation of water sources. This is particularly so with drinking water sources, which have been increasingly threatened by industrial pollution. One of the most crucial issues both for urban residents and rural farmers in China is to get access to clean and safe drinking water.

Because most of China's drinking water supply comes from untreated water sources such as rivers, lakes, pools and underground aquifers, a drinking water crisis is imminent in many parts of China. In 2005, SEPA (the State Environmental Protection Agency) received reports of 76 pollution incidents nationwide, many of which took their toll on the water bodies that provide both rural and urban drinking water (Liu, 2006). China's seven main river basins, including the Yangtze River basin and Yellow River basin, are cross-provincial. They cover a total area of 4.37 million square kilometers, amounting to 44% of the total territory of China and involving 29 provinces, municipalities and autonomous regions. Located in these areas are 88% of the country's population, and 80% of its arable lands. Along the Yangtze River and Yellow River alone more than 13,000 petrochemical factories (out of the national total of 21,000) have been built. Most such factories lack strict environmental protection measures, and the consequences of pollutant spills or other accidents would be devastating.

Over the past few years, China has seen a number of water pollution incidents that have resulted in drinking water supply interruptions on a large scale across the country. The most serious cases include the Songhua River trans-boundary water pollution incident in China's northeast in 2005,[1] and the Yancheng drinking water pollution incident in China's southeast in 2009.[2] In both of these instances, the responsible persons in the polluting companies were eventually investigated, prosecuted and sentenced to jail through the application of the relevant articles in China's Criminal Law and Law on Prevention and Control of Water Pollution (LPCWP). Although criminal punishment has been imposed on the offenders in these cases, the environmental impacts on the health of water users and the economic and other effects on affected societies are certainly harmful and far-reaching.

10.2 DRINKING WATER SECURITY AS A CRITICAL JUSTICE ISSUE

A monthly report on water quality released by the China National Environmental Monitoring Center in 2006 showed that drinking water quality in 16 out of 113 key cities was assessed as below national standards.[3] As a result, the health of a large number of Chinese is threatened on a daily basis by the decline in drinking water quality. Increasing awareness of the harmful effects of drinking water pollution has engendered great health concerns in China nationwide. Reported cases of stomach, liver, and esophagus cancers are much more common in polluted areas than in non-polluted areas. China's two leading infectious diseases are waterborne hepatitis and dysentery.

In the two aforementioned incidents where prosecutions were successful, the biggest concern of governments, media and the public was the safety of the urban drinking water supply. Millions of urban residents are involved. The system is based on intensive purification systems and tap water networks for most urban areas. Whilst contamination and poor water quality does exist in urban areas serviced by such systems, the more threatening situation is for those who directly access waters, rivers, lakes and pools. The problem of water pollution threatens access to clean and safe water for tens of millions of people in China, most of whom live in rural communities. These people must take their drinking water directly from polluted rivers, lakes and pools without the benefit of treatment infrastructures to purify polluted water. Given the serious pollution of water sources, a huge number of rural residents suffer long-term, delayed, complicated and latent health effects through drinking polluted water. In August 2007, reporting to the Standing Committee of the 10th NPC at the 29th session, Zhou Shenxian, Director of SEPA,[4] pointed out that more than 0.3 billion people in rural areas in China are under threat regarding their drinking water security.

For the great number of Chinese people in rural areas, the health impacts and hazards of drinking water pollution are almost inescapable. News reports in China and overseas suggest the existence of hundreds of 'cancer villages' arising from long-term drinking of polluted water in rural villages in China.[5] Given that it is residents in rural areas in China who lack basic sanitary drinking water infrastructures and who must therefore extract drinking water from the polluted water, it is they who bear the environmental costs and health damage to a disproportionate degree. This is compounded by the fact that they can rarely enjoy the fruits of economic development in China directly. The combination of relative poverty and disproportionate exposure to contamination for rural people means that drinking water security is a critical social justice issue in China.

In an attempt to lessen the conflict between economic development and environmental protection and to bridge the gap between different social groups, China's central government has set forth such public policies as 'sustainable development' since the 1992 Rio Conference on Environment and Development, and 'establishing scientific views of development' and 'achieving harmonious societies' in the Governmental Work Reports of the State Council over the past few years. As a political response to the challenges, the central government and the Communist Party have proposed a new political and social conception, 'sharing achievements of the reform and opening policy together', at the National Conference of the Communist Party and the plenary conference of the National People's Congress in 2005 with the objective of balancing the social disparity and bridging the gap. However, faced with the reality of an intrinsic conflict between economic development and environmental protection, some Chinese officials, frankly speaking, see environmental problems as the normal consequences of an early stage of economic growth, which will be naturally resolved through further development.

This author believes such a view is wrong. Since clean and safe drinking water is an essential life-sustaining element, it cannot be denied to anyone. The critical justice issue is: when pollution is a direct threat to the health and lives of the people, why should people have to wait for some indeterminate future time for the problem to be addressed? People might suggest that it is mostly those officials who can afford to drink bottled water, live apart from pollution and eat uncontaminated foods, who see the risk of death as a reasonable price for economic development. It is vulnerable social groups who fail to achieve the full benefits of economic growth who suffer most from water and air pollution (Ma, 2009).

Unfortunately, the wider public in China are far from aware of the social justice aspects of the human suffering and burdens created by environmental pollution and the ecological degradation resulting from the economic boom.

In terms of environmental law development in China, the significant challenge is to turn the high-sounding policy rhetoric I have outlined above into reality, for the majority of people. This involves dealing with the challenge of an environmental externality of industry development which is converted into a fundamental health and social justice problem for those who do not benefit from urban water infrastructures.

10.3 DRINKING WATER SECURITY AS A FUNDAMENTAL LEGAL CONCEPT IN THE 2008 AMENDMENT TO THE LPCWP

The Chinese government has made concerted efforts to legislate for environmental protection, particularly after the Rio Conference on Environment and Development in 1992. In order to combat water pollution, the Law on Prevention and Control of Water Pollution (LPCWP) was adopted in 1984 and amended in 1996 and in 2008 respectively. The law and its amendments provide the main legal grounds for dealing with inland water pollution issues in China. The recent amendment to the LPCWP in 2008, in particular, reflects increased legislative efforts to address drinking water security issues in China.[6]

Triggered by such serious water pollution incidents as transboundary water pollution in Songhua River noted above, the 32nd session of the Standing Committee of the 10th National People's Congress (NPC) in Beijing passed the amendment to LPCWP on February 28, 2008. This came into force on June 1, 2008.[7] The LPCWP amendment reflects increasing concerns in China about the need to achieve better water quality in general and to provide drinking water security in particular. Specifically, the amendment set forth a fundamental legal concept to protect drinking water security by means of amending the legislative purposes of the LPCWP, commencing with establishing a general principle of drinking water security in the law.

10.3.1 Changes of the Legislative Purposes through the 2008 Amendment

In China's statutes, legislative purposes, which are generally provided by the first article of the legislation, play an important role as they provide the core idea which is intended to govern the legislation as a whole.

In the 1984 LPCWP and its 1996 amendment,[8] Article 1 provided that:

> This Law is enacted for the purposes of preventing and controlling water pollution, protecting and improving the environment, safeguarding human health, ensuring effective utilization of water resources and promoting progress of the socialist modernization.

The 2008 Amendment to LPCWP increases the focus on drinking water security. It adds 'maintaining the safety of drinking water' to the purposes of the legislation and removes the expression, 'ensuring the effective use of water resources', suggesting a substantial shift in priorities. Article 1 of the 2008 Amendment states that:

> This Law is enacted for the purpose of preventing and controlling water pollution, protecting and improving the environment, maintaining the safety of drinking water, and promoting sustained economic and social development.

The words of the law, 'protecting and improving the environment' and 'safeguarding human health', attach greater importance to the legal value of social equity, whereas 'ensuring effective utilization of water resources and promoting progress of the socialist modernization' is related to economic efficiency. In 1984 LPCWP and its 1996 Amendment, the two elements of equity and efficiency, were accorded equal importance and expected to strike a balance. It is significant that in the 2008 LPCWP Amendment, the expression, 'ensuring effective utilization of water resources and promoting progress of the socialist modernization', was deleted. By inserting 'maintaining the safety of drinking water, and promoting sustained economic and social development' as a legislative purpose in the law, the safety of drinking water was stressed and the value of equity was given greater importance than utilization and modernization.

10.3.2 'Drinking Water Sources shall Receive Priority Protection' as a General Principle of the 2008 Amendment

Reflecting this change of legislative purposes, the 2008 Amendment to the LPCWP also set forth a general principle to protect drinking water sources as a priority, with the words 'drinking water sources shall receive priority protection'.[9]

In the drafting of legislation in China, the general principle provides a basic legal framework for the legislation and constitutes a legislative junction between the legislative purpose of maintaining drinking water security and specific legal norms, regulations and institutions of protecting drinking water security for the public.

10.4 DRINKING WATER SECURITY IN THE 2008 AMENDMENT

Clean and safe water for such essential human uses as drinking is a common good. Logically, clean and safe drinking water supply should be a governmental social responsibility. To achieve the legislative purpose and the general principle of drinking water security, enforceable legal norms, regulations and institutions have been laid down in the 2008 Amendment of LPCWP.[10] These regulations for the most part provide the specific command-and-control measures for the purposes of maintaining drinking water security.[11]

10.4.1 More Stringent Regulation on Water Pollution

Aimed at improving water quality in general, the 2008 Amendment adopted more stringent regulation measures on water pollution prevention and control. The main regulatory measures included in the 2008 Amendment are as follows:

- Water pollutant discharge activities in excess of the prescribed standards are totally prohibited;[12]
- Such preventive measures as the Environment Impact Assessment (EIA) and 'Three Simultaneousness' requirements are strengthened;[13]
- Total discharges control of permitted water pollutants and requirements for permits for an allowed volume are provided;[14]
- Water pollutant discharge fees are confirmed;[15]
- SEPA's legal competence to monitor water quality and release national water pollution information is granted;[16]
- Administrative fines and penalties for water pollution infringements are increased significantly.[17]

10.4.2 An Independent Chapter about Drinking Water Security

In addition to the general regulation measures discussed above, which are particularly aimed at maintaining drinking water security, an independent chapter, Protection of Drinking Water Sources and Other Special Waters, was added to the 2008 amendment to the LPCWP.[18] The chapter includes the following main measures:

- The state designates and establishes drinking water source reserves. Drinking water source reserves are classified into Grade I and Grade II. Relevant governments are permitted to delimit a certain area at the periphery of a drinking water source reserve as a quasi reserve. No outfall may be set up in drinking water source reserves.[19]
- It is prohibited to build, renovate or enlarge in a Grade I drinking water source reserve any construction projects other than water supply facilities and works for water source protection; for those already in place, the people's government at or above the county level may order their demolition or closure.[20]

- It is prohibited to build, renovate or enlarge in a Grade II drinking water source reserve any construction projects discharging pollutants. For those already constructed, the people's government at or above the county level shall order their demolition or closure.[21]
- It is prohibited to build or enlarge in a quasi drinking water source reserve any construction projects that seriously pollute waters, but rebuilding such projects is allowed provided that it does not contribute to increasing the discharge volume.[22]
- The people's government at or above the county level shall, in light of the actual needs for the protection of drinking water sources, take engineering measures or such ecological protection measures as building wetland or water conservation forests in quasi reserves, to prevent water pollutants from being directly discharged into drinking waters to ensure the safety of drinking water.[23]
- If a drinking water source is polluted and it may threaten drinking water security, the administrative department responsible for environmental protection shall order the relevant enterprises and public institutions to stop or reduce the discharge of water pollutants.[24]
- The State Council and the people's government of any province, autonomous region or municipality directly under the Central Government may, in light of the needs for protecting water environment, prohibit or restrict the use of detergent, fertilizer and pesticide containing phosphor or restrict planting or breeding, etc. within a drinking water source reserve.[25]

10.5 CIVIL RELIEF FOR WATER POLLUTION VICTIMS

The previous analysis of the 2008 Amendment indicates that regulation of drinking water security was mainly focused on the designation and the enhanced protection of drinking water source reserves. Nevertheless, as water pollution is spread through flowing water, drinking water security can hardly be guaranteed without improvement of water quality as a whole in China. Even though the government can strengthen drinking water protection by more stringent 'command-and-control' water quality regulation in accordance with the 2008 Amendment of the LPCWP, the security of drinking water is still in doubt. Given rampant transboundary water pollution nationwide and the weak enforcement of environmental law, civil relief for environmental pollution victims resulting from polluted drinking water is an important complement to government regulation.

While enhancing command-and-control regulation measures, the 2008 Amendment to the LPCWP addresses the reform of civil procedures and remedial actions for the protection of water pollution victims.

The legal grounds for civil claims by pollution victims are built on the foundation of two pieces of legislation introduced in China in the 1980s. These are the General Principles of Civil Law,[26] and the 1989 Amendment to the Environmental Protection Law.[27] The two laws laid down a no-fault liability principle in favor of environmental pollution victims seeking civil compensation for the effects of environmental pollution. The no-fault liability principle tilts the balance in favor of plaintiffs in environmental pollution compensation cases by exempting them from the burden of proof to show the defendants' fault.

On similar policy grounds, a number of follow-up environmental laws on different environmental sectors in China, such as water, air, solid waste and noise, adopted the no-fault liability principle. The 2008 Amendment to the LPCWP, together with the civil liability provisions in the 1984 LPCWP and its 1996 Amendment, stipulate that the party whose rights and interests are claimed to be damaged by water pollution is entitled to ask the party discharging pollutants to eliminate the harm and pay compensation for their losses. Significantly the 2008 Amendment not only inherited the civil provisions of the no-fault liability principle, but also developed further evidence rules and civil procedures that favor the interests of water pollution victims.

- A new evidence rule reverses the burden of proof of a causal link in water pollution compensation cases.[28] With regard to the burden of proof, the basic civil procedural rule in China is 'he who makes the claim must prove it'. This means plaintiffs must demonstrate evidence to prove all of the key elements of their claim to the court when seeking civil remedies. However, in environmental pollution compensation cases, claimants are often unable to do this because they are disadvantaged and because they have difficulties in collecting relevant evidence of a causal link between polluters' acts and victims' damage to health or property, which is always scientifically complicated. No doubt, the new evidence rule will significantly assist drinking water pollution victims to obtain water pollution compensation where they have suffered harm.
- As water pollution is likely to have negative impacts on a number of people, water pollution compensation cases are often class actions. Although class actions are generally provided for in the Civil Procedure Law,[29] there are practical barriers with regard to environmental class actions because of the traditional culture and current judicial context in China. The 2008 Amendment supports class actions in water pollution cases by establishing that if the number of parties whose legitimate rights and interests are damaged by water pollution is relatively large, the parties may select a representative to file a joint action.[30] In terms of drinking water pollution compensation, more detailed and specific

procedural provisions can help victims to file class actions to protect their rights and interests.

- For the first time, legal aid is provided in China's environmental legislation to support civil claimants.[31] The amendment encourages governments, social organizations, legal institutions and lawyers to support water pollution victims in civil water pollution cases. The 2008 Amendment provides that the administrative department of environmental protection and the related social organizations and environmental NGOs may legally support parties whose legitimate rights and interests are claimed to have been damaged by water pollution to file a lawsuit with the people's court. The legislation also affirms that the state encourages law offices and lawyers to provide legal assistance for victims of water pollution by means of lawsuits. With the help of legal aid, drinking water pollution victims will find it easier to get access to justice.
- In terms of drinking water quality, access to relevant information should be a fundamental right of the citizen. To help water pollution victims access relevant information, the 2008 Amendment requires that in any dispute over liability for compensation in water pollution cases, the parties may require the environmental monitoring institution (which is under the control of SEPA or local EPAs in China), to provide the relevant monitoring data. The institution shall accept such an obligation and truthfully provide the required monitoring data.[32]

10.6 CONCLUSION

With regard to drinking water security in China, the legislative foundations have been established by the 2008 Amendment to the LPCWP. This doesn't necessarily mean that the road ahead is smooth and well-lit for drinking water pollution victims who suffer health damage from effluent discharged by polluters, which occurs on a daily basis. Access to clean and safe drinking water is an undeniable right for human beings, no matter where they live and whatever their social status. While being concerned for drinking water security for the public at large and adopting more stringent regulation for this purpose, we should pay greater legal attention to the situation of disadvantaged people, whose health is more likely to be injured through drinking water pollution.

In pursuit of social justice, not only is legislation needed, but also the voice of disadvantaged people should be heard, reliable information about drinking water pollution should be readily available, and the legal channels of justice should be viable for them. No doubt, environmental governance, which should be based on rule of law, brings them new hope.

NOTES

1 The Songhua River runs through many cities in the region before entering Russia. The river is the main drinking water source of many cities and villages it passes through. On November13, 2005, an explosion took place at Jilin Chemical Industrial Co. plant in Jilin. The explosion led to an outpouring of around 100 tons of chemicals, of which benzene was the main constituent, into the Songhua River. The incident caused a serious water crisis in the region along the river. On Thursday November 23, Harbin, a city about 380 kilometers downstream from the plant, had to temporarily shut down its water supply, leaving around 3.5 million people without access to tap water for nearly one week. See Xinhua News Agency (2005), 'Wen Visits Harbin; Russia Offers Apology', *China Daily*, www.chinadaily.com.cn/english/doc/2005-11/27/content_498263.htm (visited January 5, 2010).

2. The tap water supply in the city of Yancheng, Jiangsu province, was closed after the Mangshe River was contaminated with carbolic acid emitted by a local factory, Yancheng Biaoxin Chemicals, on February 20, 2009. Large areas of the city, which is home to 200,000 residents, were left without drinking water. News of the pollution incident occupied the front pages of the national media for the entire week. The local Environmental Protection Bureau, the Ministry of Environmental Protection and the Ministry of Health quickly dispatched emergency response and inspection teams to restore clean water to the city. See Joan Hu (2009), 'Yancheng City's Water Pollution Attracts National Attention and Debate', *Environmental News*, www.greenlaw.org. cn/enblog/?p=713 (visited January 11, 2010).

3. Supra note 1.

4. SEPA was promoted to the Ministry of Environmental Protection under the State Council in 2008.

5. The Institute of Public and Environmental Affairs, a Beijing-based environmental NGO, has created a public interest database of water pollution in China and sets out a map entitled China's Water Pollution Map, which collects hundreds of water pollution cases reported and disclosed by a variety of media in China and overseas. See http://www.ipe.org.cn/ (visited November 6, 2010).

6. The 2008 Amendment to the Law of the People's Republic of China on Prevention and Control of Water Pollution was promulgated on February 28, 2008 and entered into force on June 1, 2008. Its English version is available at: http://www.greenlaw.org.cn/files/laws/water-pollution-prevention-and-control-law.pdf (visited January 9, 2010).

7. To get the public involved in the legislation, the Standing Committee of the National People's Congress (NPC) publicized the draft of the 2008 LPCWP Amendment, which was submitted to the 29th session of the NPC Standing Committee for the first review, inviting the public to convey their opinions through the standing committees of provincial or municipal people's congresses, the Law Committee of the NPC or the NPC website. See Xinhua News Agency (2007), *China Daily*, www.chinadaily.com.cn/ bizchina/2007-09/05/content_6083113.htm (visited January 9, 2010).

8. Law of the People's Republic of China on Prevention and Control of Water Pollution (1996), China Laws and Regulations, see www.86148.com/englishlaw/shownews.asp?id=1617 (visited January 14, 2010).

9. Supra note 6, Art. 3.

10. The initial generation of Chinese environmental laws largely consisted of statements of general principles that were ambiguous and difficult to enforce. China's economic boom roared forward faster than these laws could be implemented and enforced, see Percival (2008), 3. See also Alford and Shen (1997).

11. Such regulations as the Enforcement Regulation of the LPCWP are drafted and authorized by the State Council or its executive body the Ministry of Environmental Protection. The Ministry of Environmental Protection is responsible for the enforcement of the regulations in accordance with the executive powers granted by relevant laws and the regulations.

12. Supra note 6, Art. 9.

13. Supra note 6, Art. 17. 'Three simultaneousness' means that development projects should be designed, constructed and operate with subsidiary environmental protection facilities. It is a unique preventive institution of environmental management in China.
14. Supra note 6, Art. 20.
15. Supra note 6, Art. 24. There is also a call for water pollution taxation reform in China nowadays.
16. Supra note 6, Art. 25.
17. Ibid.
18. In response to the obligations provided in the chapter on protection of drinking water sources, Chapter 7, Legal Liabilities, of the 2008 Amendment provides relevant administrative liabilities for infringements, including warning, fine, suspension of polluters' operation, etc.
19. Supra note 6, Art. 56 and 57.
20. Supra note 6, Art. 58.
21. Supra note 6, Art. 59.
22. Supra note 6, Art. 60.
23. Supra note 6, Art. 61.
24. Supra note 6, Art. 62.
25. Supra note 6, Art. 63.
26. General Principles of Civil Law was adopted on April 12, 1986. Article 124 of the law states that: 'Any person who pollutes the environment and causes damage to others in violation of state provisions for environmental protection and the prevention of pollution shall bear civil liability in accordance with the law.' See www.en.chinacourt.org/public/detail.php?id=2696 (PRC) (visited January 14, 2010).
27. The Environmental Protection Law was first adopted in 1979 and amended in 1989. Article 41 of the 1989 Amendment states that: 'A unit that has caused an environmental pollution hazard shall have the obligation to eliminate it and make compensation to the unit or individual that suffered direct losses.' (Author's translation.)
28. Article 87 of the 2008 Amendment of the LPCWP provides that the party discharging pollutants shall assume the burden of proof for the nonexistence of the relation of cause and effect between its act and the harmful consequences for an action of damage due to water pollution. The evidence rule was first provided as a judicial interpretation in Article 4, Section 3 of the Supreme People's Court Various Regulations Regarding Evidence for Civil Suits, promulgated by the Supreme People's Court on December 6, 2001 and came into force on April 1, 2002. However, the 2008 Amendment of the LPCWP is the first environmental legislation that set forth the evidence rule clearly in water pollution compensation cases. The Tort Liabilities Law, promulgated on December 26, 2009, reaffirmed the evidence rule and extended it to environmental pollution compensation cases generally.
29. The Civil Procedure Law was promulgated on April 9, 1991 and effective on April 9, 1991.
30. Supra note 6, Art. 88.
31. Ibid.
32. Supra note 6, Art. 89.

REFERENCES

Alford, William and Yuanyuan Shen (1997), 'Limits of the Law in Addressing China's Environmental Dilemma', *Standford Environmental Law Journal* 16, 125–48.

Hu, Joan (2009), 'Yancheng City's Water Pollution Attracts National Attention and Debate', *Environmental News*, www.greenlaw.org.cn/enblog/?p=713.

Liu, Yingling (2006), 'China's Drinking Water Situation Grim', www.worldwatch.org/node/4423.

Ma, Jun (2009), 'Defending Water Security', www.chinadialogue.net/article/show/single/en/2847-Defending-water-security.

Percival, Robert V. (2008), 'The Challenge of Chinese Environmental Law', *International Environmental Law Committee Newsletter* 10(4), 2–6.

PART IV

Linking local and international legal innovations

11. The quest for a World Environment Organization: reflections on a failing debate as an input for future improvement

Nils Goeteyn and Frank Maes

11.1 INTRODUCTION

No international organization exists to oversee environmental issues in a comprehensive and coordinated manner. The form and mandate of the United Nations Environment Programme (UNEP) were deliberately designed for such a role, but many observers of the international environmental scene dismiss UNEP as an institutional failure. Given the deteriorating state of the global environment and the lack of a politically authoritative body in the field of environmental policy-making, the idea that a profound institutional overhaul is needed is a compelling one.

One of the advocated alternatives is the so-called World Environment Organization (WEO). For the purposes of this chapter, WEO stands for the concept of a World Environment Organization, without prejudice towards the many different existing proposals, ranging from a Global Environmental Organization that would focus on global issues (Esty 1994); a global bargaining marketplace (Whalley and Zissimos 2001a and 2001b); an upgraded UNEP (among others: Biermann 2000 and 2001); or even a super-sized, powerful and supranational organization (Downie and Levy 2000); the clustering of MEAs (Oberthür 2002; Von Moltke 2005); or a United Nations Environment Organization. It represents the idea of a new or reformed international organization for the environment, in any conceivable form, rather than observing and critiquing one or more individual existing proposals. What this new institution should look like, the mandate it would have and exactly how it could practically be created has long been debated in academic circles. However, so far, tangible political progress towards its creation is lacking. As is the case with all structural changes at United Nations (UN) level, the proposal meets considerable resistance. Developed and developing states alike protest with the to-be-expected arguments (too costly; too tiresome in terms of political and diplomatic efforts), but more surprisingly civil and social stakeholders also do not seem convinced of the need for a WEO.

Examining the debate that has been going on for the last 40 years, it seems that it has failed in its core business: enthralling people for improving the level of environmental protection through an upgraded International Environmental Governance (IEG) system – in which an institutional overhaul of UNEP would be the centerpiece. With the prospect of a RIO+20 conference in 2012, advocates feel that now is the time to press on for fundamental changes on the IEG scene. The 2009 UNEP Governing Council and the subsequent and ongoing ministerial process (the so-called Belgrade Process) make it clear that an institutional shift towards a WEO still is, in the heads of many, a viable solution – even though tangible progress towards its creation remains doubtful.

This chapter investigates why the idea of a WEO is not met with general enthusiasm and acceptance. Why have institutional reform efforts so far proven unsuccessful? We show that many of the critiques of the existing structures, and more particularly UNEP, are imbalanced, overly diverse and as a consequence thereof not convincing. This directly affects the proposed alternatives to the IEG system, which fail to have an effective impact on policymakers. Furthermore, while IEG is arguably much broader than (the reform of) UNEP alone, we argue that the failed WEO debate seriously hampers progress in the deliberations on reforming the environmental institutions and the ongoing IEG debate. Lastly, based on these assessments, we make a number of recommendations for the debate and prognoses for future negotiations.

11.2 THE FAILING OF UNEP

Ever since its conception in 1972, UNEP has been under heavy public and scholarly scrutiny. Adherents of potent environmental governance dismiss it as being too compliant and noncommittal; others consider it to be too intrusive in national policies. Over the years, the current IEG system and UNEP, as its main institutional representative, have been diagnosed with many deficiencies: it has been judged too exclusive (Biermann, 2002; United Nations 2005); too inclusive (Chayes 1972); too Northern-dominated and as a consequence thereof, ill-conceived in the South (Gupta 2005); with too vague and broad a mandate (Elliot 2005); too fragmented - too soft, too hard; too little, too much. Unrelated to the author's vision on the need for a WEO, UNEP has been called both an organization that has 'chronically underperformed' (Charnovitz 2005, p. 93) and one that has been 'immensely successful' (Elliot 2005, p. 32), albeit in varying and limited fields of expertise.

Abstracting the arguments behind these diverse perspectives, the conclusion is unavoidable: the common overall assessment of today's most promment environmental governance structure is that it is not satisfactory. Indeed, if one looks at the state of the world's environmental governance, with its many duplicative or even contradictory efforts in the field of environmental policy-making, the lack of transparency, effectiveness of implementation or a well-functioning coordination mechanism, one is tempted to conclude that the current IEG system, *by itself*, is conceptually inept and a new leaf needs to be turned over. It is '[...]a case of massive institutional failure writ large [...]', and '[i]t is the overall system of [...] incomplete environmental institutions that has failed in its basic design' (Kirton 2005, p. 154).

This line of reasoning is often used to advocate the creation of a World Environment Organization. Various assessments of UNEP start with the premise that the state of the global environment is continuously declining and use this as a point of departure for arguing that today's world still lacks adequate environmental protection and existing structures are failing; that, given this premise, UNEP has underperformed dramatically; and that, therefore, there is an urgent need to create a new organization in the form of a WEO.

We hold this line of thought to be defective, and one of the causes for the failure of the reform debate until today. The two main problems with this argument are that (i) it fails to take into account the changing circumstances UNEP has had to work under; and that (ii) it fails to pose the right questions about what exactly is going wrong within UNEP and the IEG system as a whole, and as a result, the proposed alternatives based on these assessments remain purely academic at best.

11.2.1 UNEP's Original Design

UNEP was created by the UN General Assembly following the 1972 Stockholm Conference on the Human Environment (UNCHE), after proposals made by Kennan (1970) and Chayes (1972). It is not a specialized UN agency, but a subsidiary body of the Economic and Social Council, with the general UN budget covering the Nairobi headquarters' costs. It was not designed to be an organization with sanctioning powers and norm-setting abilities; instead, UNEP was intended to be a promoter of international cooperation in the battle against 'environmental problems of broad international significance', able to set out general policy guidelines and stimulate regional cooperation, and to provide a funnel for scientific assessment and exchange of environmental knowledge, endorse country progress reports, and to serve as an early warning mechanism for newly emerging environmental threats. Furthermore, these tasks would have to be performed 'with due respect to the sovereign rights of States' and with the presupposition that protecting the environment is a task that rests primarily and 'can be exercised more effectively at the national and regional levels'. Lastly, a 'small secretariat' that would 'serve as a focal point for environmental action and co-ordination within the United Nations system' (United Nations 1972, preamble and Part II) was established under the auspices of the Economic and Social Council.

Seeing the broad description and wide range of tasks set forth in the founding resolution, it is understandable for UNEP to have sought a (number of) niche(s) in which it could excel. With its limited staff, its broad array of tasks, its limited funding and relatively slight political weight, there is widespread agreement that at least in the field of agenda-setting and the creation of new legal instruments, UNEP can pride itself on some remarkable achievements (among others: Najam 2005; Andresen 2007).

11.2.2 A Changing Environment and a Changing Perspective

The IEG landscape has altered drastically since 1972 (Shaw 2003; Najam, Papa and Taiyab 2006; Najam, Runnals and Halle 2007). Many contemporary writings on IEG remark that over 500 Multilateral Environmental Agreements (MEAs) exist today – up from 52 major ones in 1972, of which only 23 were global in scope (UNEP 2004). Nowadays, countless international organizations, commissions and programs deal with environmental concerns, both within and outside of the UN structure (for example (non-exhaustively): the World Bank, the International Monetary Fund (IMF), the World Trade Organization (WTO), the Food and Agriculture Organization (FAO), the International Labour Organization (ILO), the Commission for Sustainable Development (CSD) and the United Nations Development Programme (UNDP)). In 1972, however, environmental degradation was a relative newcomer on the international scene. An overwhelming number of stakeholders, both in the political and social sphere, have since entered the field to participate in the deliberations (Kjellén 2008). Environmental issues nowadays are very visible and under international scrutiny. However, this accumulated interest, the great number of organizations involved in environmental governance and the continuously growing number of civil and social stakeholders have not brought a significant improvement to the overall state of the environment – or its institutions (Najam, Papa and Taiyab 2006). Apart from this, the world population has nearly tripled over the last 60 years (United Nations 2000). In the same period, the level of development, both in the developed and the developing nations, has risen substantially and the economy has globalized to unprecedented levels (Park, Conca and Finger 2008). One could rightfully argue that rising pressure on and subsequent degradation of the environment is an evolution to be expected (Kjellén 2008).

The point made here is that, apart from UNEP itself, practically everything around it has changed profoundly from the situation for which UNEP was essentially designed in 1972. It is fair to say that UNEP was designed to be the focal point for environmental action throughout the UN echelons. However, '(...) it had severe obstacles placed in its path (...). It had too little money, too few staff, and too much to do. It had the thankless task of coordinating the work of other UN agencies against a background of interagency jealousy and suspicion, and national governments were unwilling to grant UNEP significant powers' (McCormick 1995, p. 152). This assessment gives cause to believe that UNEP was handicapped from the outset in fulfilling its task. Above this, many states feared that the new Programme would interfere too much with their domestic affairs and were unwilling to let UNEP fully play the role it was designed for (McCormick 1995). It has therefore been argued that UNEP was designed to fail (Von Moltke 1996).

We hold a somewhat different perspective: the creation of the Programme in its original form was the maximum achievable outcome of a political process in the early 1970s. Considering the spirit of the age and the mindset of those creating the institution, and given the low visibility and importance of environmental degradation issues in international forums at that time, the choices in the design of the Programme were defensible and made political sense. Perhaps today it is understood that environmental degradation or institutional coordination at the UN level needs more focus and attention than a minimal *anchor institution* (Ivanova 2005) like UNEP can provide in its current form. That is, however, no just reason to equate environmental degradation with the failing of the institution. The real question that often remains unasked is how *being successful* should be described, given the range of expectations, the available resources and the amount of goodwill the international system as a whole is willing to dedicate to environmental concerns. However much improvement may be needed to the IEG system, the current mechanisms have their present-day form because of their political and economical feasibility at the time of their conception, rather than their sheer efficiency in the struggle against contemporary environmental degradation. It does not serve UNEP, the WEO debate or the IEG system to compare those mechanisms to the present requirements, because it leads to misplaced and distorted conclusions about the problem and the proposed solutions (Newell 2002).

While the pace of change in world affairs and international law has never been greater than during the last century (Bull 2002; Shaw 2003) and attention to environmental concerns is soaring, UNEP has remained unaltered in its core form and substance, apart from some minor (and only partly implemented) alterations after the 2002 World Summit on Sustainable Development (WSSD) through the so-called Cartagena package (United Nations 2002). Because of the growing importance of environmental issues and the pressure on the international system as a whole to alleviate these issues in a consistent manner, the challenge UNEP faces has changed significantly. However, its design, financial resources and founding principles have remained, by and large, unaltered. It is of paramount importance to take into account these changing circumstances and expectations when it comes to UNEP's role in the IEG system and changing public opinion on environmental issues as a whole (Najam 2005; Najam, Papa and Taiyab 2006). In other words, if one is to usefully assess UNEP's overall performance and accomplishments, one must take into account the reasons for which the Programme was created, the budget it was provided with, the source of those resources, and the goals that it was set out to achieve *given the 1972 background.*

11.2.3 Enter the WEO – Or Not?

Kennan and Chayes' aforementioned proposals were followed by an impressive series of failed attempts to improve the level of global environmental protection by overhauling the IEG institutional framework. One could convincingly argue that the debate over a WEO has not ceased since the creation of UNEP in 1972 (Lodefalk and Whalley 2002; Bauer and Biermann 2005; Najam, Papa and Taiyab 2006). The fact that UNEP is perceived as unable to achieve the expected outcomes and carry out its mandate should make the case for its reform even more appealing. However, reality has proven different. After decades of debate and subsequent reform proposals, the only conclusion from the overall lack of progress in the reform process can be that, so far, the debate to fundamentally reform UNEP has failed.

The reasons behind the perceived weakness of UNEP are, as stated above, diverse and plentiful. 'The problems of UNEP stem from its low status within the UN bureaucracy, its disadvantageous and dangerous location in Nairobi, its inadequate and insecure funding, and its detachment from many of the MEAs' (Charnovitz 2005, p. 93). Without wanting to rework the well-known debate we believe this to be an appealing enumeration, because the four distinct elements in it tend to come back in one form or another within most authors' assessment of the contemporary IEG system in general and UNEP in particular. These are also the issues authors try to alleviate in their respective (WEO) proposals.

While these issues are very real indeed and have not made the task UNEP has been faced with any easier, the question that comes to mind is why WEO advocates are so strikingly convinced that a WEO would not face the exact same issues, or why the symbolic act of creating a WEO would achieve success when UNEP has failed to overcome these obstacles. Taking into account the political sensitivity and financial consequences, why do reform proponents keep demanding the relocation of UNEP or its successor from the current UNEP headquarters' hub in Nairobi? Why is it necessary in so many

WEO advocates' to seek to give a WEO a much broader mandate than the environment alone, even if the scholarly and political debate has made it abundantly clear that states are unwilling to accept such a drastic overhaul? Why is it that a WEO would be able to secure a greater budget than UNEP can, knowing that the states that would be funding a WEO are the same ones that have protested vehemently during the last years of diplomatic negotiations against the adoption of the Voluntary Indicative Scale of Contributions, a modest change to UNEP's financial base? And why would a WEO be better equipped than UNEP to overlook and, indeed, govern the existing Multilateral Environmental Agreements (MEAs) or even cluster them, when the present debate makes it perfectly clear that states are unwilling to let anyone meddle with the independence of these agreements?

The point made is that these questions need satisfactory answers before they can be set aside and this is lacking in many reform proposals. While 'form follows function' should be the guiding principle in any international forum, advocates seek to reform institutions without being able to define the mission that this organization would have to, or need to, fulfill. They seem to be 'first positing reorganization and then searching for a mission' (Charnovitz 2005, p. 91). In the rare cases where a concrete agenda for a WEO is formulated, it often goes well beyond the environment. It has authoritatively been argued that poverty reduction has been usurping the environmental agenda (Charnovitz 2005). Strikingly, WEO proposals are often guilty of the exact same defects as has been attributed to the UNEP: building an environmental organization that would have the power to meddle in trade issues, or foreign aid, or any field of policy with ties to the environmental agenda. It should come as no surprise then that neither states nor other existing organizations are eager to have this new and unpredictable WEO tipping the existing balance – however feeble that may be.

It seems therefore more appropriate to alleviate the problems at hand rather than to make a *tabula rasa* of the existing structures, seeing that it is not likely that any UNEP replacement will be allowed more elbow room to do a better job than the present structures and that the proposed alternatives are neither authoritative nor convincing enough to push the reform process forward (Newell 2002; Biermann and Bauer 2005). Furthermore, it is interesting to note that those elements that are being conceived today as the main reasons for the failure of UNEP were considered fundamental assets and strengths of the newly founded Programme in 1972. Indeed, a 'small' secretariat ('no more than 50 professionals' (Chayes 1972, p. 13)) was deemed necessary to maintain the highest possible degree of quality and independence of the personnel, although many WEO advocates feel that the present approximately 450 officials is way too small a number to effectively tackle UNEP's tasks (among others: Biermann 2005, p. 117). The much contested funding from the general budget, which is nowadays considered too little and, because it fluctuates yearly, too uncertain to work with (Charnovitz 2005), was one of the other key elements in Chayes' proposal on the eve of the 1972 Stockholm UNCHE to maintain UNEP's independence. Other than envisioned, however, UNEP was placed under the Economic and Social Council, which Chayes predicted would gravely affect the effectiveness of the Programme.

This is not to say that UNEP, in the present tidal wave of environmental concerns, is sufficiently equipped to be an effective, successful and comprehensive environmental governance organization. We do not argue that diversity in the debate is of no benefit, as it adds to the richness of the discussion; nor do we deny that improvements to the system as it stands today are needed. What we do contest, however, is the idea that the mere existence of today's environmental issues is evidence enough in itself for claiming that UNEP has been 'chronically underperforming'. WEO advocates have failed to properly address the existing issues within the IEG system. It is unclear exactly what it is that a WEO could change in the present situation. There is no convergence in views as to what exactly is going wrong and what might be done to alleviate these issues. Some arguments have not been adequately advocated; others have been proposed in haste and are not ripe to stand the test of a larger debate, if they are not indeed harmful to the cause of an institutional overhaul (like a WEO) in themselves. As a result thereof, the proposed alternatives are too diverse to have any real impact in the field, and the expected improvements they would bring remain highly questionable.

11.3 CURRENT AND FUTURE DEBATE

The 2005 World Summit on Sustainable Development in New York agreed to the exploration of 'the possibility of a more coherent institutional framework (...), including a more integrated structure' (World Summit Outcome Document 2005, § 169) for environmental activities in the United Nations system. In realization of the WSSD outcome document, two co-chairs of the Informal Consultative Process on the Institutional Framework for the UN's environmental activities were appointed. In June 2007 the co-chairs presented their so-called Options Paper in which they gave an overview of the ideas that had been propagated during the past consultations, around seven thematic building blocks. The Options Paper contained a list of over 50 recommendations for an improved IEG system. Strikingly, most of the proposed solutions were not new – they are a reflection of the 1972 resolution founding UNEP, elaborated and – finally – ready to be implemented. Apart from making it clear that the time was not yet ripe to be expecting final results from the reformation process of the IEG system, the co-chairs observed that a political consensus on a comprehensive IEG design may be far off since 'more rapid and more substantive replies to more pressing issues would demand far stronger institutions and financial arrangements, while the exact design of such arrangements would largely depend on new policy approaches which [are] still to be defined' (United Nations 2007, p. 3). Based on these ideas and experiences, the co-chairs saw the IEG reform process develop in two parallel ways. First, there is the reform and strengthening of the existing structures, for which there is a 'wide volume of consensus'. Secondly, there's the debate on a 'broader transformation' of the IEG system (i.e. structural change), an evolutionary process concerned with the 'future needs'. However, the co-chairs concluded that in their experience, 'there is insufficient momentum for a fundamental reform now'.

Consequently the co-chairs came out with the 'Draft Resolution on Strengthening the Environmental Activities in the United Nations System' (United Nations 2008) in May 2008. This consists of two major parts, with the first part reflecting progress on the reform and strengthening the existing structures and the second part concerned with structural changes in the IEG system. There is clear progress on the reform and strengthening of existing structures around the seven building blocks that formed the basis of the Options Paper, with (among other things) the creation of a Global Environmental Financial Tracking System (a database which provides an overview of the financial flows for environmental activities in the United Nations system), appointing a chief scientist at UNEP, expanding and deepening the regional presence of UNEP and extra efforts to fully implement the Bali Strategic Plan. Any real progress on the broader transformation of the IEG framework is lacking. It is only minimally discussed in two rather vague paragraphs, where 'further consultations to explore the possibility of a more coherent institutional framework' are recommended (United Nations 2008, OP 34 and 35). The preamble literally states that: 'The strengthening of IEG is a long-term process, evolutionary in nature, which needs continued discussion in order to reflect emerging challenges and adapt the system to the needs of the international community' (United Nations 2008, § 10).

As far as institutional reform goes, this is indeed a limited and meager outcome. The EU repeated its United Nations Environmental Organization (UNEO) proposal; Brazil reiterated its support for the creation of an umbrella organization for sustainable development. It is striking, however, that both proposals remain vague and no one really seems willing or able to go into the details of exactly how this organization would function and what the implications for the whole of the UN system would be. This gave rise to the belief that both proposals are not much more than repackaged priorities: economic-social affairs for the EU; economic development for Brazil. With the competition between different proposals and the discord on the time frame for the broader transformation, it is probably all that could reasonably be expected. More importantly, it shows that the lack of a common vision on what exactly we expect from UNEP or a WEO, in whichever form, hampers progress on the political level.

The failure of the debate in New York created a window for UNEP to step into the debate, in which it had had only a marginal voice before. The idea that UNEP might indeed be the best placed to revive the reform debate gathered momentum with the publication of the management review of the Joint Inspection Unit in December 2008 (JIU 2008). Apart from a scathing analysis of the current IEG system, the report made several important recommendations about the future technical and organizational features of UNEP, not refraining from praising UNEP for the work it had been doing over the last five years and recommending to the UN Secretary-General use of the UNEP Medium-Term Strategy system-wide. But especially the last part, 'Observations on future institutional arrangements', is interesting from an IEG perspective. The report observes in clear terms that 'Any future institutional overhaul of global environmental governance needs to build on the reform of UNEP (…)' (JIU 2008, § 30–31).

The need to kick-start the reform debate prompted UNEP at the 25th Regular Session of its Governing Council in February 2009 to make IEG one of the two central themes to be discussed in the ministerial conference. The idea was to look at IEG from a country-level perspective and in doing so, to identify the most adverse consequences for national policies of the lack of strength and coherence within the IEG system. In the build-up to the actual negotiations, many delegates in Nairobi had the feeling that the IEG debate had become a nuisance in itself. No progress had been made since the Malmö Declaration, nine years before, and countries were unwilling to abandon their entrenched positions. The perception was that the GC/GMEF was the 'last chance' to save the IEG debate since governments were getting increasingly 'fed up' with it. Therefore, although admittedly the decision is on process rather than content, the importance of the continuation of the process at a high level can hardly be overestimated. It is important to note that the co-chairs of the process in New York have by no means ended their mandate and that the main venue for discussion on IEG is still the UNGA. The ministerial consultations do not create a parallel process, but aim only to help the debate in New York.

The ministerial group met twice in 2009, in Belgrade (27–9 June 2009) and Rome (26–9 October 2009), and presented the results of their deliberations on architectural reform of IEG at the special session of the GC/GMEF in February 2010. The meetings focused, after the principle of *form follows function*, on the functions of the IEG system. The first meeting focused on the classic IEG components, namely the strengthening of the policy guidance of the

GMEF, the strengthening of synergies between MEAs and assistance for capacity building in the developing world. The real institutional debate was explicitly dealt with during the Rome meeting. The result of the two meetings was promising: apart from reaching agreement on a list of *incremental changes*, such as the launch of a bottom-up process to create synergies between the various biodiversity conventions and a closer collaboration between UNEP and UNDP through yearly reports on the MOU between the two institutions, tangible progress was made towards a *broader transformation* of the existing environmental structures. The fact that a number of developing countries were beginning to change their position vis-à-vis the UNEO proposal should be mentioned. Many countries reiterated the view that environmental governance and sustainable development should not be mixed; however, this position was argued from both sides of the debate: the EU considers the environmental structures in the UN to be too weak and wishes to strengthen them, while developing nations seem to be hinting at strengthening sustainable development and eclipsing environmental concerns in one movement.

The 11th Special Session of the GC/GMEF in Bali, Indonesia, confirmed that view. Two decisions were made on IEG (decision SS.XI/1 and part of the Nusa Dua Declaration both deal with IEG). The most important fact is that the Governing Council decided to extend the special ministerial consultations for another year, this time to explicitly focus on the broader transformation of the IEG scene, explore the different options on the table extensively and in depth, and to conclude its workings by the next GC, in February 2011. This will be a necessary step to deepen the understanding around the table about the different institutional proposals. The Governing Council in 2011 is asked to present its findings to the General Assembly and Rio+20 Second Preparatory Committee. That way, the IEG debate could come to a formal conclusion at the upcoming RIO+20 meeting in 2012, provided the ministers can find enough common ground and mutual understanding about the functions and consequent form of a future environmental governance institution.

11.4 CONCLUSION: THE WAY FORWARD

What do we expect from an environmental institution at UN level? Seeing the political debate of the last few years and the outcomes of the recent ministerial consultations on the future of IEG, countries want to have a coordinating agency that serves as an early-warning mechanism for emerging environmental threats, assists developing countries in the execution of their environmental obligations and developmental potential, which would serve as the scientific powerhouse of the UN on environmental issues. It should also encourage synergies between the existing MEAs, without touching the juridical independence and autonomy of these treaties. Strikingly, with the exception of the latter, all of these elements were part of the original proposal that led to the creation of UNEP in the early 1970s. The goals we set today for an environmental institution at UN level are not fundamentally different from those in the early 1970s – so why would the outcome of the debate today be so fundamentally different from what we already have in place?

For over 30 years advocates have tried to convince the international community of the merits of the idea that a more potent environmental organization is needed. So far this has proven to be a fruitless exercise. Indeed, looking back, the landscape of International Environmental Governance is littered with failed attempts to break the political deadlock on the creation of a WEO. It inspired the famous remark that a WEO was the organization of the impossible (Von Moltke 2001). Taking into account the profound changes over the last 40 years and given the unwavering criticism of UNEP, why is it proving so hard to hammer out a World Environmental Organization proposal that is both politically feasible and practically germane?

There is a multitude of reasons for the failure of the reform debate. First, there is no agreement on the different assessments of UNEP. The Programme is benchmarked against contemporary expectations for which it is not equipped. Secondly, WEO advocates have not been able to satisfactorily explain: (i) what exactly is going wrong in the present environmental protection system; (ii) what should be done to alleviate these issues; and (iii) why the proposed WEO would do a better job than what is presently available and being achieved in the IEG system. WEO proposals and alternatives to the present IEG system are based upon very divergent and even incompatible assessments of UNEP and the other presently existing structures. As a result, the argument that there is a real need for a new international structure because the existing ones simply do not meet expectations loses much of its appeal. If there is no agreement on the issues and their underlying reasons, it should come as no surprise that there is no agreement on the best solution to resolve them. Beyond this, proposed alternatives are either insufficiently worked out or fail to take into account the basic elements of the judicial and political requirements that any solution would have to meet. Partly this is explained by the fact that so many different ideas for a WEO exist and that there is no clear unified goal for or rationale behind a WEO in the literature. That is unfortunate, because it is slowing much-needed improvements to the IEG system. Due to the lack of any tangible progress, the permanent negotiations achieve little more than alienating initially interested parties and creating negotiation fatigue among many players.

It is abundantly clear that given the present state of the debate, the prospects for the creation of a powerful WEO, as envisioned by many advocates, are dire indeed. If states are unwilling to go beyond what has been achieved thus far and what is on the table today, proposals for an institutional overhaul of the IEG system will remain fruitless. Cynical and hyperbolic as it may sound, the truth is probably that if nations (or more broadly, the international community) were able and willing to create a powerful WEO, we would have had one by now. Apparently, states are not convinced that a WEO would be beneficial – to them, or to the system as a whole.

At the same time and despite all of these notes of criticism, we believe that there is still room for progress in the negotiations. There is growing convergence in the diplomatic efforts for a step-by-step strengthening of the environmental institutional framework. The main purpose of the ministerial consultations is to put a series of options on the table. It appears that three main options will survive the next GC/GMEF: enhancing UNEP; creation of some form of a WEO (so far meaning no more than that it would be a specialized UN agency); and ECOSOC and CSD reform proposals. A combination of these measures would indeed bring about fundamental institutional change, with far-reaching consequences. The results of the deliberations also mean that the upcoming GC/GMEF will have the means and a fitting time frame to prepare and conduct the actual negotiations on a new institutional framework at the RIO+20 conference, planned for 2012.

A small ministerial group has proved capable of getting results in the past and high-level consultations may be exactly what is needed to give new impetus to the reform process. A fundamental institutional overhaul will only be possible if agreement can be reached on (i) which issues need addressing first, and (ii) a vision for the future structure of IEG. That is an enormous task. If nothing else, WEO advocates have successfully spread the conviction that the present IEG system has got to change and that inaction will come at too high a price.

REFERENCES

Andresen, S. (2007), 'The Effectiveness of UN Environmental Institutions', *International Environmental Agreements*, 7, 317–36.

Bauer, S. and F. Biermann (2005), 'The Debate on a WEO: An Introduction', in F. Biermann and S. Bauer (eds), *A World Environment Organization: Solution or Threat to Effective International Environmental Governance?*, Aldershot: Ashgate.

Biermann, F. (2000), 'The Case for a World Environment Organization', *Environment*, 20(9), 22–31.

Biermann, F. (2001), 'The Emerging Debate on a World Environment Organization: A Commentary', *Global Environmental Politics*, 1(1), 45–56.

Biermann, F. (2002), 'Strengthening Green Global Governance in a Disparate World Society: Would a World Environment Organization Benefit the South?', *International Environmental Agreements: Politics, Law and Economics*, 2, 297–315.

Biermann, F. (2005), 'The Rationale for a World Environmental Organization', in F. Biermann and S. Bauer (eds), *A World Environment Organization: Solution or Threat to Effective International Environmental Governance?*, Aldershot: Ashgate.

Bull, H. (2002), *The Anarchical Society: A Study of Order in World Politics*, New York: Columbia University Press.

Charnovitz, S. (2005), 'Towards a World Environment Organization: Reflections upon a Vital Debate', in F. Biermann and S. Bauer (eds), *A World Environment Organization: Solution or Threat to Effective International Environmental Governance?*, Aldershot: Ashgate.

Chayes, A. (1972), 'International Institutions for the Environment', in J.L. Hargrove (ed.), *Law, Institutions and the Global Environment*, Dobbs Ferry, NY: Oceana.

Downie, L.D. and A.M. Levy (2000), 'The United Nations Environment Programme at a Turning Point', in P.S. Chasek (ed.), *The Global Environment in the Twenty-First Century*, Tokyo: UNU Press.

Elliot, L. (2005), 'The United Nations' Record on Environmental Governance: An Assessment', in F. Biermann and S. Bauer (eds), *A World Environment Organization: Solution or Threat to Effective International Environmental Governance?*, Aldershot: Ashgate.

Esty, C.D. (1994), 'The Case for a Global Environmental Organization', in P.B. Kenen (ed.), *Managing the World Economy: Fifty Years after Bretton Woods*, Washington, DC: Institute for International Economics.

Gupta, J. (2005), 'Global Environmental Governance: Challenges for the South from a Theoretical Perspective', in F. Biermann and S. Bauer (eds), *A World Environment Organization: Solution or Threat to Effective International Environmental Governance?*, Aldershot: Ashgate.

Ivanova, M. (2005), 'Assessing UNEP as Anchor Institution for the Global Environment: Lessons for the UNEO Debate', Working Paper 05/01, Yale Center for Environmental Law & Policy.

Joint Inspection Unit (2008), 'Management Review of Environmental Governance within the United Nations System: Report of the Joint Inspection Unit' (JIU/REP/2008/3).

Kennan, F.G. (1970), 'To Prevent a World Wasteland: a Proposal', *Foreign Affairs*, 48 (3), 401–13.

Kirton, J.J. (2005), 'Generating Effective Global Governance: The North's Need for a World Environment Organization', in F. Biermann and S. Bauer (eds), *A World Environment Organization: Solution or Threat to Effective International Environmental Governance?*, Aldershot: Ashgate.

Kjellén, B. (2008), *A New Diplomacy for Sustainable Development: The Challenge of Global Change*, London: Routledge.

Lodefalk, M. and J. Whalley (2002), 'Reviewing Proposals for a World Environmental Organization', *The World Economy*, 25, 601–17.

McCormick, J. (1995), *The Global Environmental Movement*, London: John Wiley and Sons.

Najam, A. (2005), 'Neither Necessary, Nor Sufficient: Why Organizational Tinkering Will Not Improve Environmental Governance', in F. Biermann and S. Bauer (eds), *A World Environment Organization: Solution or Threat to Effective International Environmental Governance?*, Aldershot: Ashgate.

Najam, A., M. Papa and N. Taiyab (2006), *Global Environmental Governance: A Reform Agenda*, Winnipeg: IISD.

Najam, A., D. Runnalls and M. Halle (2007), *Environment and Globalization: Five Propositions*, Winnipeg: IISD.

Newell, P. (2002), 'A World Environment Organization: The Wrong Solution to the Wrong Problem', *The World Economy*, 25(5), 659–71.

Oberthür, S. (2002), 'Clustering of Multilateral Environmental Agreements: Potentials and Limitations', *International Environmental Agreements: Politics, Law and Economics*, 2(4), 317–40.

Palmer, G. (1992), 'New ways to make International Environmental Law', *American Journal of International Law*, 86, 259–83.

Park, J., K. Conca and M. Finger (eds) (2008), *The Crisis of Global Environmental Governance: Towards a New Political Economy of Sustainability*, London: Routledge.

Shaw, N.M. (2003), *International Law*, Cambridge: Cambridge University Press.

UNEP (2002), Third Global Ministerial Forum (Seventh Special Session of the UNEP Governing Council), Cartagena.

UNEP (2004), *Environmental Law Instruments – Multilateral Environmental Agreements*, Nairobi.

United Nations (1972), Resolution 2997 (XXVII) of the UNGA, 15 December 1972.

United Nations (2000), *Charting the Progress of Populations*, New York.

United Nations (2002), *Report of the World Summit on Sustainable Development*, A/CONF.199/20, 26 August–4 September 2002, New York.

United Nations (2005), *In Larger Freedom: Towards Development, Security and Human Rights for All,* A/59/2005, 21 March 2005, New York.

United Nations (2007), Informal Consultative Process on the Institutional Framework for the United Nations' Environmental Activities, Co-Chairs' Options Paper, 14 June 2007.

United Nations (2008), Revised Draft Resolution on Strengthening the Environmental Activities in the United Nations System, 23 July 2008.

Von Moltke, K. (1996), 'Why UNEP Matters', in *Green Globe Yearbook of International Cooperation on Environment and Development*, Oxford: Oxford University Press.

Von Moltke, K. (2001), 'The Organization of the Impossible', *Global Environmental Politics*, 1(1), 23–8.

Von Moltke, K. (2005), 'Clustering International Environmental Agreements as an Alternative to a World Environment Organization', in F. Biermann and S. Bauer (eds), *A World Environment Organization: Solution or Threat to Effective International Environmental Governance?*, Aldershot: Ashgate.

Whalley, J. and B. Zissimos (2001a), 'An Internalisation-based World Environmental Organization', *The World Economy*, 25(5), 619–42.

Whalley, J. and B. Zissimos (2001b), 'What would a World Environmental Organization Do?', *Global Environmental Politics*, 1(1), 29–34.

World Summit Outcome Document (2005), Resolution A/RES/60/1 of the UNGA, 24 October 2005, New York.

12. Human rights law, refugee and migration law, and environmental law: exploring their contributions in the context of 'environmental migration'

Michèle Morel[1]

12.1 INTRODUCTION

The plight of so-called 'climate refugees' or 'environmental refugees' has become a hot topic for discussion and writings. Geographers, anthropologists, political scientists and lawyers arrange meetings on the issue to debate the existence of such refugees, their number, the causes of flight, and the existing or needed institutional policies and legal frameworks. While people have always used migration as a strategy for responding to environmental changes, it is the increasing worldwide attention to the phenomenon of climate change that has made academics, policy makers and the NGO community turn their attention towards those who are forced to leave their homes due to environmental changes. Importantly, many more people negatively affected by environmental changes lack the necessary funds to move. As a result, despite deserving as much attention and protection, they risk finding themselves neglected and in the shadow of those who are on the move.

The issue of environmental migration raises important questions, some of the legal questions being analysed in this chapter. The existing literature on the topic discusses these questions sometimes within the broad framework of general international law and sometimes within the specific framework of a branch of international law, such as human rights, refugee and migration, or environmental law. In the latter case, which specific framework is used depends on the background and perspective of the author. Human rights lawyers, refugee and migration lawyers and environmental lawyers all take a different approach, so that interaction between the different approaches, especially between the refugee and migration lawyers' approach and the environmental lawyers' approach, is often difficult to find. This raises the question:

what is the contribution of each of these relevant international law branches to the protection of environmental migrants and how do these contributions relate to each other and to what extent are they complementary?

This chapter examines the role of four international law branches in the protection of environmental migrants: international human rights law, international refugee law, international migration law, and international environmental law. A clear overview is provided of which branch of law is relevant in relation to the various aspects of forced migration owing to environmental change. The different aspects identified are the question of the *prevention* of forced migration, the issue of *admission* of migrants onto foreign territory, and the matter of exercisable *rights* in the country or place of arrival. In adopting this approach, it becomes clear that the four different branches of international law have their own specific functions and contributions in the context of environmental migration and, therefore, are fully complementary.

With regard to terminology, this chapter uses the terms 'internal environmental migration/migrants' and 'external environmental migration/migrants'. As will be explained, internal environmental migrants who are forced to move fall under the law of internal displacement and, therefore, belong to the group of 'internally displaced persons' (IDPs). In this chapter the term 'migrant', having no universally adopted definition and consequently no fixed meaning in international law, includes both movements within a country and cross-border movements, as well as both forced and voluntary movements. The term 'refugee' is not used owing to its strict legal meaning and the fact that environmental migrants are not automatically refugees (see below for further discussion on this point). Although both forced and voluntary movements are included in the term 'migrant', this chapter focuses on the former type of movement. Within the category of forced movement, differences exist with regard to the extent of coercion. Some people flee in order to survive (for example, in the situation of a sudden natural disaster), others to escape extreme poverty or health problems related to the environment. For certain purposes it can be justifiable to consider only people who flee to survive. In the context of the admission of migrants onto foreign territory, for example, it makes sense – taking into account the 'great scarcity of entrance places' in the world of today – to give priority to those claimants for entrance with the most valid or strongest claim to international protection (Gibney, 2004, p. 12).

In this context, it is worth referring to the concept of 'survival migrants', developed in 2009 at Oxford University (Betts and Kaytaz, 2009; Morel and Maes, 2010). 'Survival migrants' are characterized, amongst other things, by the *existential threat* they face. Interestingly, the reasons for their flight are not limited to environmental changes, but are mostly a combination of environmental, social and economic factors. As such, the authors emphasize the generally multi-causal character of forced movement. Since the purpose of this chapter is not to find international protection mechanisms only for the 'worst-off', but instead aims to analyse the relevance of different international law branches in the problem of environmental migration, there is no need to prioritize different types of environmental migrants based on the seriousness of the threat they face. Therefore, the term 'survival migration' is not used here. Nevertheless, when using the term 'environmental migration', the above-mentioned complex causal relationships linked to migration decisions should be acknowledged, by bearing in mind that environmental push factors are often accompanied by other (for example, social and economic) elements.

Finally, the word 'environmental' in environmental migration refers to any type of environmental change, whether at the global or local level. This means that not only climate change is considered, but also other changes in the environment, for example due to development projects, industrial accidents, armed conflicts, environmental conservation projects, and deforestation.

12.2 INTERNATIONAL HUMAN RIGHTS LAW

International human rights law is potentially relevant for dealing with the problem of environmental migration in three ways. First, it stipulates the human rights of potential environmental migrants in their country of origin or habitual residence. The most relevant human rights instruments in this regard are: the 1948 Universal Declaration of Human Rights (UDHR),[2] the first global expression of rights to which all human beings are entitled; the 1966 International Covenant on Civil and Political Rights (ICCPR),[3] stipulating in Articles 6, 7 and 1(2) respectively the right to life, the right not to be subjected to cruel, inhuman or degrading treatment, and the right not to be deprived of means of subsistence; and the 1966 International Covenant on Economic, Social and Cultural Rights (ICESCR),[4] protecting amongst other things the right to an adequate standard of living, including food and housing in Article 11. Other relevant instruments, offering human rights protection to specific social groups, are the 1989 Convention on the Rights of the Child (CRC),[5] the 1979 Convention on the Elimination of All Forms of Discrimination against Women (CEDAW),[6] and the 1989 International Labour Organization (ILO) Convention on the Rights of Indigenous People.[7]

If the human rights of people were realized in practice, forced migration would not exist, since displacement in most cases implies human rights violations. Human rights law thus plays a significant role in the *prevention* of environmental migration. However, not all states are party to all international human rights instruments, and where states have agreed to be bound by international obligations, a lack of enforcement often exists due to the unwillingness or incapacity of national governments. Consequently, the practical effectiveness of international human rights law, as a source of rights that people can, in theory, exercise in their country of origin or habitual residence, in tackling the problem of environmental migration, should not be overestimated. The strengthening of human rights law, with an indisputable primary responsibility for national governments, is required to strengthen the prevention of forced migration.

Another way in which human rights law can be useful for environmental migrants is in relation to external environmental migration. International human rights law, since it applies to each person without discrimination, is applicable to foreigners (in this case environmental migrants who have crossed an international border) in the same manner as it applies to citizens. Both legal or regular migrants and illegal or irregular migrants without residence documents – for example, rejected asylum seekers or those who manage to enter and remain in a foreign country undocumented without submitting an asylum application – enjoy the basic human rights stipulated in international human rights law. A special category of persons finding themselves in between the categories of regular and irregular migrants are those persons who do not fall within the international refugee framework but are nevertheless 'non-returnable', meaning that they cannot be legally sent back to their country of origin or habitual residence (that is, the principle of non-refoulement, which is discussed below). The case of a threat of torture can here serve as an example. Non-returnables also fall under international human rights law.

Environmental migrants, having crossed an international border and finding themselves on foreign territory, thus enjoy all basic human rights, irrespective of their (il)legal status in the foreign country. However, in practice, (illegal) migrants are often deprived of healthcare, housing and other social services. Detaining rejected asylum seekers is common practice and more generally they are often treated as criminals (Weissbrodt, 2008, pp. 147–8). The current global climate is one in which migrants are often seen as a threat to the national culture, economy, and security. The enforcement of international human rights law, as a source of rights that people cannot only exercise in their country of origin or habitual residence but also in a foreign country to which they have fled, needs to be strengthened to make this branch of law contribute more substantially in practice to the protection of external environmental migrants. Worth mentioning in this context is the 1985 Declaration on the Human Rights of Individuals Who are not National of the Country in which They Live,[8] adopted by the United Nations General Assembly. This Declaration lists a number of rights that non-nationals shall enjoy in the state in which they are present. While a first group of rights are directed at all non-nationals, whether regular or irregular (including the right to life, the freedom from torture, the right to private life and home, and the freedom of thought), certain additional rights are exclusively reserved for lawfully residing aliens (for example, the right to medical care and the right to safe and healthy working conditions).

Finally, international human rights law may be relevant in the context of the question of the *admission* of persons into a foreign country. The right to be protected against forcible return, known as the principle of non-refoulement, prohibits a state from returning, expelling or extraditing a person in any manner whatsoever to another state where that person risks being subjected to serious human rights violations (Wouters, 2009). The question arises whether this principle protects environmental migrants who have crossed an international border. While this question has been analyzed in detail elsewhere (Morel and Maes, 2010), it suffices here to point out that, based on the interpretation of the relevant provisions of international and regional conventions[9] as well as case law of the European Court of Human Rights,[10] environmental migrants who have crossed an international border are currently not protected by the non-refoulement principle. Indeed, this principle does not protect all types of migrants equally. As a result, any country can legally send them back to their country of origin or habitual residence, provided they are not protected in the context of any other legal framework.

International human rights law is thus not useful in this context at the present time. However, it can not entirely be ruled out that future case law of international or regional human rights bodies may decide that the return of a person to an area where that person faces extremely severe (life-threatening) environmental problems, constitutes a violation of human rights law (based, for example, on the right to life or the freedom from inhumane treatment).

12.3 INTERNATIONAL REFUGEE LAW

International refugee law, in the broad sense of the term,[11] is a set of rules and procedures aimed at protecting persons who seek asylum in a foreign country after having been forced to leave their country of origin for certain reasons specified in the relevant legal instruments. The legal protection granted by international refugee law to the different groups of persons partially overlaps with international human rights law. Indeed, refugee law is closely connected to human rights law. Nevertheless, whereas the human rights regime has a *normative* role,[12] international refugee law deals with the situation whereby the 'human being's one truly autonomous remedy' is 'flight when circumstances become unbearable' (Hathaway, 1995, pp. 293–4), circumstances that amount to a violation of human rights. Refugee law thus has a *palliative* role (IARLJ, 2004).

The international legal framework for forced migrants who have crossed an international border consists of one international instrument, the Convention relating to the Status of Refugees (1951 Refugee Convention),[13] and four regional instruments, namely the Convention governing the Specific Aspects of Refugee Problems in Africa of the African Union (1969 AU Convention),[14] the Cartagena Declaration on Refugees of the Organization of American States (1984 OAS Declaration),[15] the EU Council Directive 2004/83/EC of 29 April 2004 on minimum standards for the qualification and status of third country nationals or stateless persons as refugees or as persons who otherwise need international protection and the content of the protection granted (EU Qualification Directive),[16] and the EU Council Directive 2001/55/EC of 20 July 2001 on minimum standards for giving temporary protection in the event of a mass influx of displaced persons and on measures promoting a balance of efforts between member states in receiving such persons and bearing the consequences thereof (EU Temporary Protection Directive).[17] These refugee instruments deal both with the criteria for admission into a foreign country and, although not in all cases equally specifically, the rights that can be exercised in the host country. The above-discussed non-refoulement principle, by contrast, only deals with the prohibition of return, not with other rights.

The 1951 Refugee Convention defines a 'refugee' and provides legal protection for a person who

> ... owing to well-founded fear of being persecuted for reasons of race, religion, nationality, membership of a particular social group or political opinion, is outside the country of his nationality and is unable or, owing to such fear, is unwilling to avail himself of the protection of that country; or who, not having a nationality and being outside the country of his former habitual residence as a result of such events, is unable or, owing to such fear, is unwilling to return to it. (Article 1(a)(2))

Much research has been done on the applicability of the 1951 Refugee Convention in situations of environmental migration (for example, Cooper, 1998; Falstrom, 2001; Aleinikoff, 2003; McAdam, 2007; Williams, 2008) and there is now widespread agreement that the 1951 Refugee Convention is not applicable: to meet the criteria of the 1951 Refugee Convention, a persecuting 'actor' is required and the persecution must be linked to one of the five convention grounds. Some have argued that environmental migrants constitute a 'particular social group' – one of the five convention grounds – which is composed of persons who lack the political power to protect their own environment (Cooper, 1998). However, this interpretation is controversial and does not seem to be the right approach. Political powerlessness cannot be considered as a permanent characteristic that makes someone a member of a social group and, in the same way, persecution as such cannot define the social group (Falstrom, 2001).

This is not to say that environmental migrants can never be refugees. It is possible that a person fleeing environmental problems also fears persecution on one of the five grounds and thus enjoys the protection of the 1951 Refugee

Convention, for example when a government intentionally refuses to offer relief to a minority group after a cyclone has affected the country. However, this is the exception rather than the rule.

The 1969 AU Convention, dealing with forced migration in Africa, states in Article 1(2), after reasserting the 1951 refugee definition in Article 1(1), that the term 'refugee' shall also apply to

> … every person who, owing to external aggression, occupation, foreign domination or *events seriously disturbing public order* in either part or the whole of his country of origin or nationality, is compelled to leave his place of habitual residence in order to seek refuge in another place outside his country of origin or nationality. [Emphasis added]

Based on a plain reading, environmental problems may be included in this definition, since these can be considered to constitute events that seriously disturb public order (Rwelamira, 1989; Lopez, 2007). However, the AU refugee definition poses serious interpretative difficulties: there are few or no *travaux préparatoires*, case law, or academic literature to rely on (Shacknove, 1985; Okoth-Obbo, 2001; Rankin, 2005). While it is probable that states will offer refuge to foreigners in situations that require temporary protection, this is much less evident where permanent or long-term protection is needed.

In Article 3, the 1984 OAS Cartagena Declaration, dealing with forced migration in Latin America, provides that

> … the definition or concept of a refugee to be recommended for use in the region is one which, in addition to containing the elements of the 1951 Convention and the 1967 Protocol, includes among refugees persons who have fled their country because their lives, safety or freedom have been threatened by generalized violence, foreign aggression, internal conflicts, massive violation of human rights or *other circumstances* which have *seriously disturbed public order*. [Emphasis added]

Like the case of the 1969 AU Convention, it can reasonably be said that environmental migration is implicitly included in this definition given the category of circumstances that seriously disturb public order. However, in a report of the International Conference on Central American Refugees (CIREFCA) interpreting the 1984 OAS Cartagena Declaration, a distinction is made between 'natural disasters' and other events that 'seriously disturb public order' – for example, human-made disasters such as those generated by dams – whereupon it is observed that the victims of the former category of events are not considered as refugees (Lopez, 2007). It should also be noted that the 1984 OAS Cartagena Declaration is not legally binding upon member states of the Organization of American States. Rather, it is a political document (Miranda 1990), that has served as a source of inspiration for national asylum legislation in Latin America.[18]

The EU Qualification Directive provides 'subsidiary protection' in the European Union for persons who 'otherwise need international protection', with 'otherwise' referring to other international protection needs than those dealt with in the 1951 Refugee Convention (that is, persecution on one of the five grounds). According to Article 2(e), a person who is eligible for subsidiary protection is

> … a third-country national or a stateless person who does not qualify as a refugee [in the sense of Article 1(a)(2) of the 1951 Refugee Convention] but in respect of whom substantial grounds have been shown for believing that the person concerned, if returned to his or her country of origin … would face a real risk of suffering serious harm as defined in Article 15, and to whom Article 17(1) and (2) do not apply, and is unable, or, owing to such risk, unwilling to avail himself or herself of the protection of that country.

Article 15 reads:

> Serious harm consists of: (a) death penalty or execution; or (b) torture or inhuman or degrading treatment or punishment of an applicant in the country of origin; or (c) serious and individual threat to a civilian's life or person by reason of indiscriminate violence in situations of international or internal armed conflict.

This list of different types of 'serious harm' is exhaustive and does not explicitly include harm caused by environmental problems. However, the Directive might become relevant for environmental migrants in the future, especially considering the ongoing amendment process of the Directive and the increased concern of the European Commission for the relationship between climate change and migration (EC, 2008a; EC, 2008b). Also, questions can be raised whether and to what extent severe environmental problems amount to torture or inhuman treatment as set out in Article 15(b). We can here refer to the above-mentioned discussion on the non-refoulement principle, which includes the question to what extent returning a person to a place of harsh environmental conditions constitutes a breach of the freedom from torture or other proscribed treatment.

Finally, the EU Temporary Protection Directive, offering temporary protection in the European Union in the event of a mass influx of displaced persons, defines those displaced persons in Article 2(c) as

> … third-country nationals or stateless persons who have had to leave their country or region of origin … and are unable to return in safe and durable conditions because of the situation prevailing in that country, who may fall within the scope of Article 1A of the Geneva Convention or other international or national instruments giving international protection, *in particular*: (i) persons who have fled areas of armed conflict or endemic violence; (ii) persons at serious risk of, or who have been the victims of, systematic or generalised violations of their human rights. [Emphasis added]

The words 'in particular' indicate that victims of other than the specified situations, for example environmental disasters, may qualify for temporary protection. Temporary protection is defined in Article 2(a) as

> … a procedure of exceptional character to provide, in the event of a mass influx or imminent mass influx of displaced persons from third countries … immediate and temporary protection to such persons, in particular if there is also a risk that the asylum system will be unable to process this influx without adverse effects for its efficient operation, in the interests of the persons concerned and other persons requesting protection.

Persons enjoying temporary protection have the right, for a period not exceeding that of temporary protection, to engage in employment activities as well as in educational activities (Article 12). The maximum possible duration of temporary protection is three years (Article 4). As a result, no permanent protection is provided. A weakness of the Directive is the requirement of 'mass influx'. Consequently, the Directive is not applicable where an individual is in need of protection without finding him- or herself in a mass influx situation. Furthermore, the Directive does not contain a definition of this term: the existence of a mass influx should be established by a decision of the Council (Article 5).

Based on the above analysis of international and regional refugee instruments and their applicability to environmental migrants, it can be concluded that some of these instruments are not applicable at all; some are only applicable to certain types of environmental migrants; and that the applicability of some other instruments remains uncertain. Consequently, environmental migrants cannot rely on a clear legal framework. The concrete contribution of international refugee law to the protection of environmental migrants is therefore, although not negligible, not significant. Victims of sudden disasters, requiring mainly temporary protection, find themselves in a slightly better position legally than victims of slow-onset disasters who often need permanent protection. Additionally, the former category of victims can often rely on the (temporary) goodwill of neighbouring and other states.

For national authorities willing to grant protection to environmental migrants, there is, to a certain extent, legal space through instruments whose applicability is uncertain, though not strictly non-applicable. The problem is thus as much related to a lack of political will to protect environmental migrants as it is related to a lack of a legal framework.

In respect of this lack of an effective legal framework, the option of adopting new laws granting environmental migrants the right to enter and stay in a foreign country, as well as other in-country rights, is problematic. First, the political feasibility of such a new law in the (near) future is uncertain. Immigration policy is one of the few remaining strong expressions of national sovereignty: the power to decide on the admission of foreigners onto national territory still lies primarily at the national level.[19] Second, the adoption of new law at the international level is likely to be a long process taking many years, while the problem of environmental migration requires urgent response. Third, there are practical difficulties with regard to the threshold determination: it would be a great challenge to determine who is included in and who is excluded from the definition of an environmental migrant for the purpose of such a new law, and thus who is and who is not eligible for admission into a foreign country. This challenge follows from the difficulty of distinguishing between voluntary *versus* forced migration and between harmful environmental conditions *versus* poor socio-economic circumstances and poverty. Finally, the adoption of an asylum-like international instrument would need to be complemented by the development of international programmes to resettle migrants from the (developing) country of first arrival to a third (developed) country. In the absence of such programmes, it is likely that developing countries would receive the large majority of environmental migrants onto their territories. This is because, on the one hand, environmental migration is likely to occur mainly within regions (poverty prevents many people from crossing continents) and, on the other hand, environmental problems – for example, the effects of climate change – particularly occur in developing countries.

The above examination has dealt with cross-border forced movements of people, or international refugee law. Where the internal movements of people are concerned, there exists the law of internal displacement. The Guiding Principles on Internal Displacement[20] are a set of principles, developed in 1998 by the former United Nations Secretary-General Representative on internally displaced persons, Francis M. Deng, and afterwards adopted by the United Nations, that guide states on the protection of internally displaced persons against, during, and after displacement. The inclusion of the first element – protection *against* displacement – indicates that the Guiding Principles play a role in the *prevention* of environmental migration. The Guiding Principles are mainly based on existing international human rights law and international humanitarian law.

The Guiding Principles apply to all persons forced to move within national borders, irrespective of the cause of the flight (Principle 2) and, thus, also to internal environmental migrants. Since it is probable that the majority of people negatively affected by environmental changes lack the necessary financial and other means to move abroad, and given the reluctance of states to admit foreigners onto their territories, forced movement within countries is in this era of climate change likely to increase on a significant scale. Therefore, the law of internal displacement is highly relevant and important for internal environmental migrants. However, the question arises as to what extent the

Guiding Principles, as a legally non-binding instrument, are enforced by states in practice. Several states have incorporated the Guiding Principles or adapted versions into their national legislation and policy. At this moment, about 20 states spread over different continents have drawn inspiration from the Guiding Principles in the development of their national law or policy on internal displacement.[21] Sub-regionally, the Great Lakes Region in Africa adopted in 2006 the Protocol on the Protection and Assistance to Internally Displaced Persons,[22] in the context of the 2006 Pact on Security, Stability and Development in the Great Lakes Region.[23] At the regional level, the African Union adopted in October 2009 the Convention for the Protection and Assistance of Internally Displaced Persons in Africa (Kampala Convention).[24] These regional and sub-regional instruments draw upon the Guiding Principles on Internal Displacement for their content, including the definition of internally displaced persons.

The law of internal displacement is expanding gradually through national and regional implementation of the Guiding Principles on Internal Displacement. Whether this area of law is concretely useful and effective in the context of the protection of environmental migrants depends on the political will and ability of states to make the rights of internally displaced persons real and observe their responsibilities set out in the above-mentioned instruments on internal displacement.

12.4 INTERNATIONAL MIGRATION LAW

As mentioned in the introduction, the term 'migration' in this chapter includes internal, external, voluntary, and forced movement of people. International refugee law can therefore be considered a branch of international migration law that deals with certain types of forced migration, in particular where the right to life is threatened (for example, persecution- or conflict-induced migration). Migrants not falling within the refugee law framework, although having moved involuntarily due to a threat to life or livelihood, as well as migrants having left their places of habitual residence merely in order to improve their (already decent) quality of life, are other types of migrants falling under international migration law. Amongst them are 'economic migrants' – who wish to improve their standard of living – whereby the extent of coercion in the decision to move can vary significantly.[25] Depending on the particular facts of each case, environmental migrants fit into one of these migrant categories.

A significant component of migration around the world are 'labour migrants'. Labour migrants move from their place of habitual residence to another country or to another place within their own country for the purpose of employment (IOM, 2008, p. 495). Some environmental migrants fit this type of migration pattern. While the power to decide on the admission of migrants into the national labour market currently remains principally at the national level,[26] it is particularly interesting to examine the rights labour migrants can exercise in the country of employment on the basis of international migration law. The most important relevant instrument is the International Convention on the Protection of the Rights of All Migrant Workers and Members of Their Families (Migrant Workers Convention), adopted by the United Nations in 1990.[27] The Migrant Workers Convention defines a migrant worker in Article 2(1) as 'a person who is to be engaged, is engaged or has been engaged in a remunerated activity in a State of which he or she is not a national'. All migrants are included, irrespective of their (il)legal status: regular or documented migrants, undocumented migrants, victims of trafficking who are often exploited and not properly remunerated for their work, and so on. However, to discourage illegal migration, the Migrant Workers Convention grants more rights to documented migrants than to undocumented migrants (Weissbrodt, 2008, pp. 182–3 and 185–6). Based on international human rights instruments, the Migrant Workers Convention merely reaffirms existing human rights norms without developing new norms. Nevertheless, few states have ratified the Migrant Workers Convention so far, and those that have are mainly states that primarily send (not receive) migrants (Weissbrodt, 2008, pp. 186–8). There simply is insufficient political will to protect migrant workers.

The Migrant Workers Convention, along with other international (labour) migration instruments, are in practice only relevant for those environmental migrants who manage to become engaged in a salaried activity in a foreign state.

Returning to the issue of admission of migrants onto foreign territory, the strategy of facilitating permanent or temporary (circular) labour migration through bilateral agreements between governments is a valuable approach to the problem of environmental migration. Instead of considering migration as a last resort to survive, migration can be considered as a positive strategy to adapt to environmental changes. Labour migration programmes, especially those on a circular basis, can contribute substantially to the reconstruction of disaster-hit areas and recovery of disaster-hit communities through the remittances of the labour migrants (IOM, 2009, p. 8). In addition, these labour migration schemes may play a significant role in the environmental adaptation of local developing communities. For developed countries that are confronted with an ageing population and unfilled jobs, foreign (particularly temporary) labour forces are welcome. The win-win-win situation (for the sending country, the receiving country and the labour migrant) makes this adaptation-focused strategy politically more feasible than rights-based approaches such as a new asylum-like convention. The facilitation or accommodation of labour migration can thus make a real contribution to mitigating the plight of environmental migrants. It is about supporting voluntary migration to reduce forced migration (Tacoli, 2009; Newland, 2009; Barnett and Webber, 2009).

12.5 INTERNATIONAL ENVIRONMENTAL LAW

The question can be raised whether and to what extent international environmental law contains principles, rules or provisions that explicitly address (environmental) migration. Most relevant in this context are the United Nations Framework Convention on Climate Change (UNFCCC),[28] the Protocol to the UNFCCC (Kyoto Protocol),[29] the Copenhagen Accord[30] and the United Nations Convention to Combat Desertification in Countries Experiencing Serious Drought and/or Desertification, Particularly in Africa (UNCCD).[31] From these four instruments, only the UNCCD pays modest attention to (environmental) migration:

> *Mindful* that desertification and drought affect sustainable development through their interrelationships with important social problems such as poverty, poor health and nutrition, lack of food security, and those arising from *migration, displacement of persons* and demographic dynamics, ... (Prologue) [Emphasis added]

> National action programmes may include … some or all of the following measures to prepare for and mitigate the effects of drought: (a) establishment and/or strengthening, as appropriate, of early warning systems … and mechanisms for assisting *environmentally displaced persons* .... (Article 10) [Emphasis added]

> The Parties undertake, according to their respective capabilities, to promote technical and scientific cooperation in the fields of combating desertification and mitigating the effects of drought …. To this end, they shall support research activities that ... take into account, where relevant, the relationship between poverty, *migration caused by environmental factors*, and desertification. (Article 17) [Emphasis added]

By contrast, no explicit reference at all can be found to the phenomenon of (environmental) migration in the UNFCCC, the Kyoto Protocol or the Copenhagen Accord.

Although it does not take an explicit approach, environmental law implicitly has a substantial role in dealing with environmental migration. International environmental law is a body of international law that seeks to protect the natural environment, which may be affected by human activities (Sands, 2003, p. 3). Considering the dependence of human beings on the environment, in some regions more than in others and some populations more than others due to their specific lifestyle, the protection of the natural environment often contributes to the protection of the livelihoods of human beings.[32] International environmental law thus has a role in the protection of the livelihoods and more generally the human rights of people, and therefore, this branch of international law is highly relevant with regard to the *prevention* of environmental migration. As an illustration in the context of climate change, we can look to mitigation and adaptation initiatives and activities discussed in the UNFCCC and the Kyoto Protocol. Through mitigation of climate change, one of the causes of environmental migration is tackled. Adaptation to climate change, to the extent that it aims to reduce the current impacts of climate change as well as seeking to increase the resilience of people to future impacts, contributes to the protection of people's livelihood and therefore to the prevention of environmental migration.[33] In the Copenhagen Accord of 2009, which is not legally binding upon the parties to the UNFCCC, 100 billion dollars was promised for poor countries to adapt to climate change. However, a concrete financing plan specifying where this money would come from has not been developed. With regard to climate change mitigation, the Copenhagen Accord contains a commitment to limit the rise in global temperatures to two degrees Celsius. Nevertheless, no concrete goals have been formulated with regard to the reduction of the global emission of greenhouse gases.

12.6 CONCLUSION

This chapter has analysed the role of several branches of international law that are relevant to the protection of environmental migrants. International human rights law, although it requires stronger enforcement, plays an important normative, as well as a preventative role, in the protection of environmental migrants. International refugee law's role is a palliative one, protecting forced migrants whose human rights have been violated. On several regional levels, the legal space exists to include environmental migrants in the existing refugee framework. However, the political will to do so is generally absent at the present time, at least concerning forced migration due to gradual environmental changes necessitating long-term protection. The law of internal displacement is highly relevant for environmental IDPs. Its enforcement, however, must be strengthened. The facilitation of labour migration, by increasing legal labour migration opportunities, can make a significant contribution to the mitigation of the problem of environmental migration. The development of (circular) labour migration programmes, based on bilateral agreements between governments, should therefore be encouraged. International (labour) migration law as it currently exists is particularly relevant with regard to the rights that environmental migrants who have become migrant workers in a foreign country can exercise in the country of employment. However, the relevant law is characterized by low levels of ratification. Finally, international environmental law, while paying only limited attention to environmental migration, implicitly plays a significant role in the prevention of environmental migration by aiming at the protection of the natural environment.

All four international law branches thus have a specific and important role in dealing with environmental migration, with this role being linked to the *ratio legis* of the respective law branches. In practice, however, several shortcomings exist, often linked to enforcement and political will. International efforts should be made to strengthen existing mechanisms and to develop new, effective systems within each branch.

Precisely because of the specific functions of the respective branches of international law, each branch separately is not sufficiently effective on its own to deal appropriately with the problem of forced migration due to environmental change. The contributions of the respective branches are complementary to each other, and, therefore, the four law branches should be united in the form of parallel application to environmental migration. Indeed, a comprehensive solution to the problem of environmental migration covers both (different forms of) prevention and (different forms of) remedy. *Prevention* should be at the heart of the urgently needed global strategy (prevention is better than cure) and the appropriate frameworks for dealing with this are international environmental law on the one hand and international human rights law (including the law of internal displacement) on the other hand. When migration is seen as a form of adaptation to environmental changes, international migration law is another approach that can deal with the prevention of forced migration. For those who have no other choice but to flee across borders due to environmental problems, *international protection* is required. The suitable framework for this remedial part is international refugee law. Finally, strengthening the *human rights* of persons who have left their home in search of a better place is another part of the remedy. Here, the appropriate fora are international human rights law (including the law of internal displacement) and international (labour) migration law.

Human rights law, refugee law, migration law, and environmental law constitute the four pieces of the environmental migration puzzle. Separately they have a specific, limited function, but put together they form a satisfactory whole. Legal researchers, organizations and policy makers should think and work in an intra-disciplinary manner to come up with a comprehensive solution to environmentally forced migration.

NOTES

1. Michèle Morel is a PhD researcher at Ghent University, Belgium, Department of Public International Law. She wishes to thank the Research Foundation Flanders (FWO) for funding her research.
2. 10 December 1948, GA Res. 217(III), UN GAOR, 3d Sess., Supp. No. 13, UN Doc. A/810 (1948) 71.
3. 19 December 1966, 999 UNTS 171.
4. 19 December 1966, 993 UNTS 3.
5. 20 November 1989, 1577 UNTS 3.
6. 18 December 1979, 1249 UNTS 13.
7. 27 June 1989, 1650 UNTS 384.
8. 13 December 1985, A/RES/40/144.
9. The Convention relating to the Status of Refugees, 28 July 1951, 189 UNTS 137, amended by the Protocol relating to the Status of Refugees, 31 January 1967, 606 UNTS 267 (1951 Refugee Convention); the United Nations Convention against Torture and Other Cruel, Inhuman or Degrading Treatment or Punishment (UNCAT), 10 December 1984, 1465 UNTS 85; the European Convention for the Protection of Human Rights and Fundamental Freedoms (ECHR), 213 UNTS 221; and the ICCPR; see note 4.
10. *D v. the United Kingdom* (1997) 24 EHRR 423; *N v. the United Kingdom* (2008) 47 EHRR 885.
11. In the narrow sense of the term, a 'refugee' is a person fulfilling the criteria mentioned in Article 1(a)(2) of the 1951 Refugee Convention.
12. Article 2(1) ICCPR: 'Each State Party (…) undertakes to respect and to ensure to all individuals (…) the rights recognized in the present Covenant (…)'; Article 2(1) ICESCR: 'Each State Party (…) undertakes to take steps, (…) to the maximum of its available resources, with a view to achieving progressively the full realization of the rights recognized in the present Covenant (…)'.
13. See note 10.
14. Organization of African Unity, 10 September 1969, 1001 UNTS 45.
15. Colloquium on the International Protection of Refugees in Central America, Organization of American States, Mexico and Panama, 22 November 1984.
16. Official Journal L 304, 30/09/2004 pp. 12–23.
17. Official Journal L 212, 07/08/2001 pp. 12–23.
18. See http://www.unhcr.org/pages/49e45be46.html (visited 17 August 2010).
19. Note as an example of an exception to the rule the free movement of persons within the European Union.
20. The Guiding Principles on Internal Displacement, E/CN.4/1998/53/Add.2.
21. See the Brookings-Bern Project on Internal Displacement, www.brookings.edu/projects/idp/Laws-and-Policies/idp_policies_index.aspx (visited 17 August 2010).
22. For the text of the Protocol on the Protection and Assistance to Internally Displaced Persons, see www.brookings.edu/~/media/Files/Projects/IDP/Laws%20and%20Policies/Great%20Lakes/GreatLakes_IDPprotocol_2006.pdf (visited 17 August 2010).
23. For the text of the Pact of Security, Stability and Development in the Great Lakes Region, see www.brookings.edu/~/media/Files/Projects/IDP/Laws%20and%20Policies/Great%20Lakes/GreatLakes_Pact2006.pdf (visited 17 August 2010).
24. The text of the Convention can be found on the African Union website, www.africa-union.org (visited 17 August 2010).
25. On migration terminology, see International Organization for Migration (IOM) (2008, pp. 491–501), giving an overview of migration terms and definitions.
26. See note 19.
27. 18 December 1990, 2220 UNTS 93. The Migrant Workers Convention entered into force on 1 July 2003. Other relevant instruments are the several conventions of the International Labour Organization (ILO) on migrant workers. Some of these conventions are widely ratified by states, while others are not (Weissbrodt, 2008, pp. 183–5).

28. 9 May 1992, 1771 UNTS 107, 31 ILM 849.
29. 10 December 1997, 37 ILM 22.
30. The Copenhagen Accord was drafted and agreed by a limited group of states and afterwards formally accepted ('taken note of') by the Conference of the Parties to the UNFCCC (COP15) on 18 December 2009 in Copenhagen. It remains to be seen how many countries will sign up to the Copenhagen Accord. For the text of the Copenhagen Accord, see www.unfccc.int/files/meetings/cop_15/application/pdf/cop15_cph_auv.pdf (visited 17 August 2010).
31. 17 June 1994, 1954 UNTS 3, 33 ILM 1328.
32. The protection of the environment can also have a negative impact upon the livelihoods of people, for example the situation where the conservation of the environment, in the form of designating areas as nature reserves, results in the expulsion of indigenous tribes from these land areas.
33. The Adaptation Fund, financed with a share of proceeds from the Clean Development Mechanism and supervised by the Adaptation Fund Board, finances concrete adaptation projects in developing countries that are parties to the Kyoto Protocol and particularly vulnerable to the negative effects of climate change. See http://www.adaptation-fund.org/ (visited 17 August 2010).

REFERENCES

Aleinikoff, A. (2003), 'Protected characteristics and social perceptions: an analysis of the meaning of "membership of a particular social group" ', in E. Feller, V. Türk and F. Nicholson (eds), *Refugee Protection in International Law*, Cambridge, UK: Cambridge University Press, pp. 263–311.

Barnett, J. and M. Webber (2009), 'Accommodating migration to promote adaptation to climate change', policy brief prepared for the Secretariat of the Swedish Commission on Climate Change and Development and the World Bank World Development Report 2010 team, http://www.ccdcommission.org/Filer/documents/Accommodating%20Migration.pdf (visited 17 August 2010).

Betts, A. and E. Kaytaz (2009), 'National and international responses to the Zimbabwean exodus: implications for the refugee protection regime', *New Issues in Refugee Research*, Research Paper No. 175, Geneva, Switzerland: UNHCR.

Cooper, J. (1998), 'Environmental refugees: meeting the requirements of the refugee definition', *New York University Environmental Law Journal* **6**, 480–529.

European Commission (EC) (2008a), COM/2008/0360 final, Policy Plan on Asylum, 17 June 2008, http://eur-lex.europa.eu/LexUriServ/LexUriServ.do?uri=COM:2008:0360:FIN:EN:HTML (visited 17 August 2010).

European Commission (EC) (2008b), COM/2008/0611 final, Communication on strengthening the global approach to migration: increasing coordination, coherence and synergies, 8 October 2008, http://eur-lex.europa.eu/LexUriServ/LexUriServ.do?uri=COM:2008:0611:FIN:EN:HTML (visited 17 August 2010).

Falstrom, D. (2001), 'Stemming the flow of environmental displacement: creating a convention to protect persons and preserve the environment', *Colorado Journal of International Environmental Law and Policy* **1**(6), 1–32.

Gibney, M. (2004), *The Ethics and Politics of Asylum: Liberal Democracy and the Response to Refugees*, Cambridge, UK: Cambridge University Press.

Hathaway, J. (1995), 'New directions to avoid hard problems: The distortion of the palliative role of refugee protection', *Journal of Refugee Studies* **8**(3), 288–94.

International Association of Refugee Law Judges (IARLJ) (2004), 'The intersection of human rights law and refugee law: on or off the map? The challenge of locating *Appellant S395/2002*Australia/', New Zealand Chapter Meeting, Sydney, 9 June 2004, www.refugee.org.nz/Reference/Sydney04.html (visited 17 August 2010).

International Organization for Migration (IOM) (2008), *World Migration Report 2008: Managing Labour Mobility in an Evolving Global Economy*, Geneva, Switzerland: IOM.

International Organization for Migration (IOM) (2009), *Migration, Climate Change and Environmental Degradation*, Geneva, Switzerland: IOM.

Lopez, A. (2007), 'The protection of environmentally-displaced persons in international law', *Environmental Law Review*, **37**, 365–409.

McAdam, J. (2007), 'Climate change "refugees" and international law', NSW Bar Association, 24 October 2007, www.nswbar.asn.au/circulars/climatechange1.pdf (visited 17 August 2010).

Miranda, C. (1990), 'Toward a broader definition of refugee: 20th century development trends', *California Western International Law Journal*, **20**(2), 315–27.

Morel, M. and F. Maes (2010), 'The curious phenomenon of "environmental migration/displacement" and the role of international law in cross-border protection', in D. French (ed.), *Global Justice and Sustainable Development*, Leiden, The Netherlands: Brill, pp. 273–88.

Newland, K. (2009), 'Circular migration and human development', Human Development Research Paper 2009/42, New York, US: UNDP, http://hdr.undp.org/en/reports/global/hdr2009/papers/HDRP_2009_42.pdf (visited 17 August 2010).

Okoth-Obbo, G. (2001), 'Thirty years on: a legal review of the 1969 OAU Refugee Convention Governing the Specific Aspects of Refugee Problems in Africa', *Refugee Survey Quarterly*, **20**(1), 79–138.

Rankin, M. (2005), 'Extending the limits or narrowing the scope? Deconstructing the OAU refugee definition thirty years on', *New Issues in Refugee Research*, Working Paper No. 113, Geneva, Switzerland: UNHCR.

Rwelamira, M. (1989), 'Two decades of the 1969 OAU Convention Governing the Specific Aspects of Refugee Problems in Africa', *International Journal of Refugee Law*, **1**, 557–61.

Sands, P. (2003), *Principles of International Environmental Law*, Cambridge, UK: Cambridge University Press.

Shacknove, A. (1985), 'Who is a refugee?', *Ethics*, **95**(2), 274–84.

Tacoli, C. (2009), 'Crisis or adaptation? Migration and climate change in a context of high mobility', paper prepared for the Expert Group Meeting on Population Dynamics and Climate Change, UNFPA and IIED, 24–5 June 2009, http://www.unfpa.org/webdav/site/global/users/schensul/public/CCPD/papers/Tacoli%20Paper.pdf (visited 17 August 2010).

Weissbrodt, D. (2008), *The Human Rights of Non-citizens*, Oxford, UK: Oxford University Press.

Williams, A. (2008), 'Turning the tide: recognizing climate change refugees in international law', *Law & Policy* **30**(4), 502–29.

Wouters, K. (2009), *International Legal Standards for the Protection from Refoulement*, Mortsel, Belgium: Intersentia.

13. Climate change: legal impediments to technology transfer

Zhou Chen

13.1 INTRODUCTION

Global warming is an unequivocal threat to humankind happening at a more rapid pace than many expected.[1] To a large extent, the state of the climate today is a result of technology choices we made yesterday; similarly, the situation of climate in the 21st century will be largely determined by the technology we choose now. This technological change is particularly important over the long-term time scales that are characteristic of climate change.[2] The rapid and widespread transfer of the relevant technologies, namely those technologies used to mitigate and adapt to climate change, encompasses an inclusive set of processes in which climate-related equipment, knowledge and experience pass through several basic stages (from supply and interim path to demand among different stakeholders).[3] In addition to the operation of the technology market in the country-based context, there is also a broader performance conducted at the international level. As a positive measure of addressing global climate change, technology transfer has both economic and environmental benefits. It is expected, for example, to improve efficiency in energy use, introduce less carbon-intensive sources of energy, develop renewable energy sources and further achieve a transition to a low-carbon economy.[4] From the legal perspective of global environmental responsibilities, the transfer of technology has been acknowledged to be a fresh avenue for international cooperation in relation to the 'common concerns of humankind',[5] especially where cooperation between developed countries and developing countries is concerned. Indeed, collective cooperation on climate control and technological improvements benefits all nations in comparison with any unilateral strategies.[6]

Recognizing that technology transfer is an integral part of international dialogue on environmental and developmental policies, the intergovernmental community has responded by adopting a number of provisions in multilateral environmental agreements (MEAs) which, directly or indirectly, stipulate that technology transfer should serve as a radical vehicle to assist states in fulfilling their regulatory commitments under the international climate framework, with developed countries taking a leadership role. Not only do these agreements, from Agenda 21[7] and the United Nations Framework Convention on Climate Change (UNFCCC)[8] to the Kyoto Protocol,[9] show consensus on the imperative of a technological solution as an adjunct to the rigid target of emission reduction, but also they internally spawn several technology-oriented incentives to drive technology innovation at an appropriate rate and to facilitate technology transfer worldwide. Typical examples are the Clean Development Mechanism (CDM) introduced by the Kyoto Protocol[10] and the MRV criteria (measurable, reportable and verifiable) under the Bali Action Plan.[11] So far, these provisions have provided a solid basis for implementing technology transfer in practice. More importantly, the key point highlighted by the aforementioned MEAs is that current technology transfer targeted at climate mitigation and adaptation should not be enhanced in the purely market-based traditional economic order, but through favorable, concessional and preferential terms founded on global environmental responsibilities, particularly the common but differentiated environmental responsibilities of states.[12]

Despite the increasing importance of technology transfer which has been illustrated by two facts (the Post-Kyoto agreement negotiations having put it onto the agenda and the Obama administration having claimed that they will 'seek global solutions' to climate change),[13] such transfers are not occurring at a sufficient rate to aid developing nations in mitigating and adapting to the effects of global warming.[14] International practices of technology development and deployment have been proved to contribute little to sustainable development and climate welfare on a global scale.[15] The reasons for this are mainly twofold: first, those technology transfers in existence have not been necessarily in a proper location where they can be best employed to cope with climate change, whether in quantity or in quality;[16] secondly, inadequate effectiveness and potential uncertainties constantly operate as formidable barriers to the transfer process. Apparently, there is an essential inter-linkage between them: the technological potential of environmentally sound technology (EST) which needs further exploitation at a conceptual level appears constrained and undermined largely by various blocks in practice. It is high time to remove these barriers and facilitate technology transfer in accordance with the arrangements of international climate agreements.

Regarding policy, whatever international agreements or national instruments are concerned, they can be designed well or poorly and be stringent or lax, binding or non-binding, or politically attractive or unattractive.[17] In general, barriers present in policy areas are viewed as among the principal obstacles caused by human factors.[18] They arise at any stage and vary widely in concrete detail, which makes identification, evaluation and prioritization of tailored actions for countries extremely difficult. As a result, it proves more appropriate to embark on an in-depth analysis of specific barriers that occur at every stage of transfer (from initial suppliers, intermediate path to end-user recipients).

In this context, the chapter will seek to provide an overview of legal barriers that deter the supply of technologies at the first stage and develop answers to the following research questions: what are these instrumental barriers; where are they emerging from in legislation and practice; how do they manifest themselves in the supply of climate-related technology and to what extent do they impact this process negatively? To approach these questions, an interdisciplinary approach, founded on normative analysis in combination with exploratory inquiry and descriptive research, will be used. First, the author will explore the theoretical basis of legal barriers that occur in the climate-related technology transfer through exploratory inquiry; on this basis, normative resources such as treaties, statutory texts, general principles and customary laws will be further examined; finally, in the light of some descriptive research, the chapter will give an overall introduction to the specific barriers, in a comprehensive and systematic way.

13.2 THEORETICAL BASIS

13.2.1 Market Mechanism

Combating global warming unquestionably calls for worldwide technology sharing and universal participation among states facing different conditions regarding technological sources. It is true that the national needs of mitigating and adapting to climate change are first and foremost conditional on one's domestic technology endowments. Taking a horizontal view, the radical demand for international technology transfer arises from the geographical imbalance of technology distribution.[19] Regional maladjustment in technology supply/demand ultimately contributes to trans-boundary movements. The degree of tension between supply and demand has a direct effect upon the scope and speed of technological internal innovation, and its external diffusion. At this point, technological change primarily takes place in response to market conditions. The demand-pull mechanism has a basic driving role in clean technology transfer and manifests itself in several key factors like market size, partnership pathway, transactional model, capital basis and competition conditions. Among these, the most important impact is to put the private sector, which is the most important player in technology transfer, in an appropriate position.[20]

13.2.2 Market Failure

Apart from its economic function, the unique feature of climate-related technology is that it has public good attributes as well as externalities. Reflecting the legal status of the atmosphere, the 'common concern of mankind',[21] these climate-related technologies spontaneously possess an inherent nature of public welfare and spillover effect which necessitates special treatment.[22] Global climate change is, moreover, a typical negative externality. The implementation of technology transfer utilized for addressing this will create costs and benefits that are not fully internalized by those involved.[23] Specifically, when developing policies to stimulate this process, the following problems occur: (1) failure to internalize the environmental costs of climate change, thereby reducing the private sector incentives to innovate; (2) failure to hold back and otherwise distort private sector investment in technological advances, irrespective of environmental concerns.[24] An optimal policy instrument which balances technology push with demand pull is needed in order to adjust current market mechanisms based on the new circumstances of climate-related technology transfer.[25] This is especially true for technologies applied for adaptation, which is often defined as a development objective. The worldwide transfer of such technologies has occurred not as a result of market forces, but of social intervention.[26]

13.2.3 Government Failure

On one side, government involvement is sought to handle the incapability of the market mechanism. However, when confronting the common property 'atmosphere', there is no corresponding virtual global governance by a supranational government. The arrangements on technology transfer under climate change agreements have to be enforced by state governments individually. At the national level, there are also domestic needs to pursue certain economic and political objectives.[27] Due to the intimate correlation between energy technologies and economic development, most supplying countries are prone to adopt tight controls over them. This would contradict global climate welfare, since the whole world is expected to be the beneficiary.[28] In this two-level game, for national officials and interest groups to act in national and intergovernmental politics is insufficient.[29] A global endeavor to address climate change which goes beyond interest-bargaining is needed and this will, by and large, depend on upcoming optimizations in the international legal order. For instance, the failure of Copenhagen to agree on this issue reflects a generalized truth of climate geopolitics. The focus should not simply be on whether technology transfer needs to be undertaken by developed countries or developing countries, or by public or private sectors, but on what institutional public mechanism is necessary to allow successful implementation of technology through the private sector.[30]

In conclusion, to frame an optimal policy on technology transfer proves difficult owing to market and government failures. This is where the potential paradox emanates from: climate-related technology transfer accommodates public environmental value and private economic interest within one regime simultaneously.

13.3 LEGAL BARRIERS IN SUPPLYING TECHNOLOGY

Climate change is a topic that is as much a political and economic challenge as it is a legal one.[31] Transferring climate-related technology, likewise, reflects problems of global environmental governance and intergenerational equity. So far, there is widespread recognition that North-South technology transfers continue to be important in many industries that can make significant contributions in the field of combating climate change, in particular when it comes to mitigation.[32] In the dynamic process of supplying, technology suppliers, including public or private sectors, make their advanced technologies in international markets easily accessible to recipients in developing countries. Surrounding this process, there are hard and soft environments of implementation involving relevant international agreements, national policies and corporate practices. To give a clear overview about the legal barriers impeding climate sound technology supplying, the chapter outlines them as:

- the lack of an explicit, stringent and applicable legal basis for binding commitments on technology transfer (including substantive and procedural laws);
- the potential constraints in the international legal order (e.g. Intellectual Property Rights (IPRs));
- inappropriate protective laws within national policies (including environmental, technological and economic laws);
- insufficiency of viable, innovative incentives at the level of national instruments (e.g. R&D, Offical Development Assistance (ODA));
- restrictive business practices performed in the private sector;
- the lack of corporate social-environmental responsibilities in the business domain.

13.3.1 Public Sector

The public sector in the technology-supplying countries is a critical player. The public sector's commitment to provide assistance in technology transfer and financial support seems vague, weak and indeterminate in the climate framework.

13.3.1.1 Barriers from international law

When reviewing relevant international law mainly shaped in the UNFCCC proceedings, a progressive path on technology transfer can be identified.[33] The UNFCCC is a legally binding agreement that provides a coherent framework for addressing climate-related technology transfer. 'It assumes universal accession and adherence to a single set of implementing principles and rules.'[34] For instance, the principle of cooperation[35] and the principle of common but differentiated environmental responsibilities[36] aim to maximize the efforts from all nations to apply a technology solution in overcoming climate change. Through them, an equable approach acceptable to the great majority of developed and developing countries has been achieved.[37] With the subsequent implementation of the convention, the international community began to realize that some countries' capabilities and conditions to assume environmental obligations were too limited to achieve a global optimum, in particular developing countries.[38] Technology transfer is therefore introduced as a concrete means of fulfilling mandatory commitments and solidarity under the convention. This initiative provides a portfolio approach to effective cooperation between the North and South, as the wording in the UNFCCC describes:

> The extent to which developing country Parties will effectively implement their commitments under the Convention will depend on the effective implementation by developed country Parties of their commitments under the Convention related to financial resources and transfer of technology and will take fully into account that economic and social development and poverty eradication are the first and overriding priorities of the developing country Parties.[39]

In spite of improvements, the success of the international climate framework in accelerating technology transfer should not be overstated. Attempts to rebalance different interests in combating climate change face many of the political difficulties that have doomed past efforts, even though the UNFCCC or the Kyoto Protocol are the result of considerable political compromise.[40] From the viewpoint of substantive law, there is no an explicit, stringent and applicable legal basis for the binding commitments on technology transfer. Although the expression 'shall'[41] utilized throughout the technology transfer article indicate a relatively strong sense of duty, rather than a mere moral aspiration claimed in the Declaration on the NIEO (New International Economic Order) in the late 1970s,[42] to what extent this duty is considered to be legally binding remains questionable.[43] The MRV criteria used to measure the solidarity assistance obligations of developed countries,[44] on their own, are insufficient to clarify what constitutes the material breadth of these obligations.

Meanwhile, even though the UNFCCC itself is flexible enough to accommodate a wide variety of approaches, there is an inherent difficulty in it (particularly in comparison with the Montreal Protocol): the range of climate-related technologies is vast and their applications span many sectors. 'Only when the technologies to be transferred are very specific and readily identifiable will developed countries be able to make concrete commitments and to effectively monitor compliance with the resulting obligations.'[45]

Implementation is generally regarded as a weak point when it comes to complying with the international climate laws. An elaborate and effective compliance mechanism needs to be designed to ensure that climate-related technologies transfer can be moved from rhetoric to a down-to-earth legal reality.[46] According to compliance with the theory of public policy, the UNFCCC and the 1997 Kyoto Protocol are viewed as only partially fulfilling essential criteria.[47] There are provisions on a 'multiple consultative process' (MCP) under the convention, which by its nature (non-judicial and non-confrontational), is a rather soft measure to avoid and solve disputes surrounding implementation.[48] No penalties or sanctions can be imposed upon non-compliant parties under the MCP, apart from the power to recommend measures to facilitate cooperation and promote understanding of the conventions.[49] At the follow-up COP7 in Marrakesh, a new compliance mechanism was coined to enforce the UNFCCC and the Kyoto Protocol. Two branches: the Enforcement Branch[50] and the Facilitative Branch[51] were created under the Compliance Committee to take charge of determining consequences for non-compliance and providing assistance respectively. Despite its apparent advance, the legal status of this mechanism has not yet been settled. Some countries, especially Japan and Russia, did not want the enforcement mechanism to be legally binding; instead they want to soften the legal status of the mechanism.[52] In the case of technology transfer, eventual disputes will involve not only environmental treaties but also trade treaties. In other words, there is a need to coordinate authority between the multiple environmental agreements (MEAs) and the World Trade Organization (WTO).[53] Whether the MEA, especially the Kyoto Protocol compliance mechanism, is capable of functioning as a counterpart of the WTO on an equal footing seems unclear. In reality, it is the Facilitative Branch that takes into consideration the common but differentiated responsibilities of the Parties and the circumstances pertaining to this such as technology transfer.[54] However, there are no corresponding sanctions in comparison with the Enforcement Branch discussed above.[55]

Besides the limited substantial and procedural stringency, the concrete technology transfer commitment under the UNFCCC agreement is a relative obligation, due to its conditionality qualification 'as appropriate'.[56] It does not indicate any standards of reference. Technology transfer, thus, is assumed to operate within certain legal circumstances, namely the present international law and national law (this will be discussed later), particularly intellectual property protection.[57] Governments' commitments in technology-supplying countries and the costs of clean technologies are two core divergences between North and South.[58] The issue of Intellectual Property Rights (IPRs) is confronted by every government involved at both national and international level. In general, certain regulatory tools on IPRs can both facilitate and hinder the progress of technology transfer; however, the central aspect is whether the target of fostering innovation in IPRs protection can be appropriately reconciled with the public health interest. Climate-related technologies stand for a deeper balance between commercial interests and public objectives. Undue protection of IPRs will, by and large, result in high costs, delayed access and reduced competition.[59] At present, struggles on public interests reveal a compelling need to properly control exclusive rights so that public requirements of adapting and mitigating to climate change through innovation and application of improved technology can be satisfied.[60]

So far, the present regime of intellectual property protection has been mainly shaped by the Agreement on Trade-related Aspects of Intellectual Property (TRIPS Agreement) under the WTO system. Its minimum standards for intellectual property reflect unduly rigorous protection in some ways and have even become a kind of protectionism.[61] Evidence for this can be found in the studies of the European Patent Office (2008), which noted the increasing number and scope of patent claims in wind energy and bio-fuel technologies.[62] Although TRIPS does permit certain flexibilities allowing countries to position IPRs in the context of public policy priorities,[63] there is no evidence to show that their potential contributions are enough to support the rapid and widespread transfer of the technologies that would be needed for climate change mitigation and adaptation. By contrast, the enforcement of these flexibilities has been greatly challenged by restrictive business practices and numerous cases occurring in parallel fields.[64] It is still premature to assume that the benefits of TRIPS are bound to exceed the obstacles it potentially poses to climate- related technology transfer. There has been widespread consensus about the negative consequences of TRIPS. For instance, the European Parliament adopted a resolution which stated that an ambitious post-Kyoto agreement would require 'corresponding adjustments' to be made to other international agreements, including new agreement on IPRs.[65]

13.3.2 Barriers from National Law

There is an essential interaction between the national and international legal system. The absence of a domestic enabling environment, to some extent, corresponds to inactive attitudes embodied by international society on the issue under discussion. Major suppliers in developed countries are reluctant to export their clean technologies unless substantial supervision can be effectively carried out at international level. However, this is not feasible in current practice. With regard to the national legal system, there are two major barriers, rooting themselves respectively in inappropriate litigation and innovative approaches.

Before examining the national instruments that impact technology flows from North to South, it is necessary to recognize that no standardized conclusions can be offered, since related identification, analysis and evaluation of barriers is country-context driven.[66] To make a qualitative-and-quantitative analysis possible, only common practices are specifically referred to.

In general, technology policies, regulatory standards and macroeconomic legislations within a national context are leading obstacles hindering the export of clean technology to developing countries. First, in the name of energy security, climate-related technologies that bear economic potential and environmental effectiveness are placed at the center of strategic competition, and are frequently discouraged from 'spilling over' abroad.[67] Instead of providing technology directly, major suppliers such as Japan and Germany[68] would rather offer finished products in order to sustain their monopoly status in the technology market, which artificially cuts off technologies to recipient countries. Because of the tight grip on the information clean technologies involve tight control exercised by the governments in tech-supplying countries tends to trigger information asymmetry and accountability deficiencies, resulting in additional risks in the process of technology import. Second, some practices amounting to 'regulatory chill'[69] reveal a vague legislative attitude toward regulatory standards when exporting technology. Policy-makers in these countries, for instance Germany, the UK and the USA, usually adopt high product and technology standards in foreign trade. A side-effect of this is to inhibit the outflow of the domestic environmentally sound technologies and to prevent spillovers. They deepfreeze higher standards through the relevant regulations.[70] This has a strong sense of protectionism. Referring to macroeconomic settings, market barriers generally occur. There is often a lack of legal support for an open, transparent trading and financing system in which reluctance to make clean technologies available can be minimized.[71] Very often, improper trade access, technology agreements, currency and investment regulations impose formidable barriers to the smooth diffusion of climate technology.[72] They cause delayed access, cumbersome negotiation, inconsistent funding and most of the time unaffordable costs.

More proactive actions need to be taken at the governmental level in order to create an enabling environment for clean technology transfer.[73] Several innovative approaches aim at this task, ranging from government involvement, joint efforts to achieve voluntary agreement (such as public-private partnership),[74] by which governments could pilot their domestic technology investments into developing countries on more favorable terms. There is great scope for the public sector in tech-supplying countries to adopt substantive and sufficient incentives in technology transfer and financial support.[75] The Official Development Assistance (ODA) as an example. It only accounts for a small part of developmental sources in these countries, but plays an irreplaceable role in certain developing countries that attract fewer private funds, in agriculture, forestry, human health and coastal management. Ongoing projects under the ODA are experiencing an overall decline both in absolute terms and as a percentage, particularly those with a significant impact on technology transfer to developing counties.[76] R&D, which involves direct government funding and investment, is another important channel to transfer technology. The recent facts, however, witness to a substantial decrease in R&D projects in developed countries.[77] The principal reason for the insufficiency of innovative assistance is that it is costly; implementation would virtually increase public expenditure in such countries, at least in the short term. However, the positive outcomes of such assistance are likely to be felt in the long run, such as environmental effectiveness, distributional equity, as well as instrumental feasibility.[78] All of these considerations deserve more weight in the prospective legislation of technology-supplying countries.

13.3.3 Private Sectors

International technology transfer is achieving a gradual increase in the importance for the private sector.[79] Climate-related technologies can be developed in either the public or the private sector, but promising technologies created in the public sector often spin off to the private one, for the latter is regarded as better at exploiting the technologies' market potential.[80] Most of these technologies are centralized in transnational corporations. With the ownership of technology, they engage in foreign trade in the technology market, or directly invest in developing countries through joint ventures. As another crucial participant in supplying technology, transnational corporations play a fundamental role in ensuring the effectiveness of this process. In the remaining part of this chapter, an attempt will be made to explore the potential blocks emerging from the private sector, from a legal point of view.

13.3.3.1 Restrictive business practices

The private sector (particularly transnational corporations), which aims at lower production costs and bigger market shares, is prone to lock in the commercial price for climate-related technologies.[81] Being for-profit entities, the main focus of corporations when providing technologies is on expected benefits, acceptable risks and achievable protection of IPRs. Typically, once the potential benefits exceed production costs, corporations in tech-supplying countries will be willing to sell their technologies. However, owing to the nature of profit maximization and being less aware of social-environmental responsibilities, restrictive business practices (RBPs) have been constantly present and operate under the umbrella of trade liberalism and economic sovereignty.

There has been accumulated evidence on the RBPs in the clean technology transfer. According to an investigation of Korean companies that imported from Japan, among 523 technologies introduced in 1994, 23.3% were accompanied by restrictive conditions. In some cases, even public institutes refused to license technologies benefiting climate, such as the HFC-134a fuel cell.[82] After surveying the evidence, one can see that transnational corporations' RBPs differ marginally at various stages of transfer. For each RBP that occurs, countermeasures also vary legally. At the initial stage of innovation, where there are not yet many other competitors with mature technologies in the international market, it is highly likely for technology-owning corporations to refuse to license technologies or offer any access. In this phase, certain exceptions to IPRs, such as a compulsory license, may be requested at the instrumental level. Once they have entered the market successfully, international corporations begin to adjust their competitive strategies to block the development of similar technologies, or to attach prohibitive, restrictive conditions to transfer agreements instead. By doing so, they try to obtain and sustain competitive advantages, whereby corporations will manipulate the market in any manner that suits their global strategies.[83]

Various RBPs are gradually shaping the supplier market in international technology transfer, exacerbating this imbalance of supply and demand.[84] Compared to the transfer of ordinary technologies, where RBPs can be viewed as an intrinsic monopoly under traditional IPRs protection, in the case of technologies for mitigating and adapting to climate change, RBPs lead to more adverse consequences, breaching both the principles of trade liberalization and sustainable development. In the public policy field, no legal harmonization is in place to ensure that these practices exercised by clean technology suppliers can be avoided. On the contrary, the situation is deteriorating, to a certain extent. For instance, in the area of anti-monopoly law, there have been great changes in the competition rules regulating patent licenses. As a response to mergers between corporations, some practices seen as restrictive business behavior will no longer be questioned.[85] Consequently, although the recipients in developing countries could theoretically get access to climate technologies at a lower price, it is still difficult to obtain benefits like supplementary maintenance and relevant experience, which makes the favorable arrangements in climate change agreements ineffective.[86]

13.3.3.2 Corporate social-environmental responsibility

RBPs and corporations' social-environmental responsibilities are two sides of the same coin, whereas the latter give more weight to external restraints from government, society and publicity. Under the cumulative pressures, corporations begin to take issues into environmental account in their daily managing, to pursue sustainable development. As the EU puts it, 'companies act voluntarily and beyond the law to achieve social and environmental objectives during the course of their daily business activities'.[87]

Climate change has a transformative effect on all types of business, implying a potential change in the configuration of corporations' responsibility.[88] From the internal perspective, their ultimate objective of maximizing profits ought to be achieved in a manner that incorporates environmental needs within commercial profits. Provided that transnational corporations cherish a vision of public good, it is possible for them to create better publicity and gain more competitive advances in the marketplace. To realize this overnight is not an easy task. Not only is strategic insight required,[89] but also a comprehensively supportive legal context should be enabled on a regional, national and international level.

According to key documents, transnational corporations are required to (1) adopt precautionary measures; (2) be proactive in taking action to bear more responsibility; (3) promote innovation and transfer of clean technology.[90] The UNFCCC agreements set out that 'other Parties and organizations in a position to do so may also assist in facilitating the transfer of such technologies'.[91] The statement reflects recognition of the increasingly prominent role that entities other than government are playing in the process of climate technology transfer. However, legislators seemingly did not intend to impose any direct obligations on these entities, given the word 'may'. Instead of an explicit duty associated with social-environmental responsibility, it only requests voluntary cooperation from corporations in transferring climate sound technologies.

Corporate social-environmental responsibilities first and foremost rely on their willingness and, in this respect, it is necessary to have effective guidance as well as viable supervision. On the economic side, industry standards emphasise economic sovereignty and trade liberalism. Hence, their potential contributions to the obligations of transnational corporations in climate-related technology transfer are insufficient.[92] On the environmental side, it is a regret that existing MEAs fail to prescribe firm responsibilities for transnational corporations to transfer their advanced technologies. At the very least, they could make a shift obligatory. It is a government duty to encourage corporations' engagement in technology transfer through the mechanism of institutions.[93] Developed countries' government should either directly transfer publicly held climate-related technologies or finance the licensing of privately held climate-related technologies.[94] The test of success must lie in subsequent developments, particularly the substantive endeavors arising from international climate legislation.

13.4 CONCLUSION

At the latest Copenhagen Summit, technology transfer, which was listed as one of the main 'building blocks' in Bali two years before, aroused great concern once again,[95] with both developed and developing country parties calling for the creation of a technology transfer regime in the near future.[96] The preconditions to achieve such 'meaningful and effective technology transfer regime' are political, legislative and institutional capability.

As far as the current international market is concerned, technology transfer is centralized in the flows between North and South. Relevant technologies originate mostly from Japan, Germany, the USA, France and Great Britain. Therefore, at the initial stage of transfer, good faith, as well as the cooperative performance of technology suppliers, including both the public sector and the private sector, play an essential, even a definitive, role in the success of the entire process. In addition, confronting the irreversible aftermath of global warming and the urgent requirements of sustainable development, an innovative, favorable model of transacting that reconciles intergenerational equity with global climate governance has been introduced by climate change agreements, seeking the removal of legal obstacles and the facilitation of a supplying process. This chapter seeks to provide an overall input to ongoing discussions on technology transfer in the context of the UNFCCC proceedings.

Based on the analysis above, it can be concluded that for climate change, which has great political and economical implications, there are no affirmative commitments under the international climate framework for the technology-supplying countries to transfer their improved climate technology to recipients in developing countries. Due to the inadequacies of external supervision and internal willingness, they are reluctant to adopt domestic incentives to assist technology export. Some protective measures exercised concurrently, to a large extent, decelerate the process of technology penetration. The perspective of stakeholders in technology-supplying corporate RBPs and the absence of a consciousness of their social-environmental responsibilities are two formidable barriers to achieving the environmental potential of climate-related technology.

Climate change is an unprecedented crisis for humanity. But realizing there is a crisis and being determined to change proves to be a turning point.[97] In this, great progress, encouraging the transfer as well as usage of climate-friendly technologies can accomplish the transition from a manufacturing economy to a knowledge economy which targets carbon-free and sustainable development. For all, it is also a valuable opportunity to set out on the path to climate justice, and political and legal civilization.

NOTES

1. See Collins et al. (2007).
2. IPCC Report 2007, WGIII Ch. 2. Framing Issues, p. 119. Decade, or longer time scales are typical of the gaps involved between technological innovation and widespread diffusion and of the capital turnover rates characteristic of long-term energy capital stock and infrastructures.
3. IPCC Report 2001, WGIII Methodological and Technological Issues in Technology Transfer, Section I: Framework for Analysis: Technology Transfer to Address Climate Change, Ch. 1.2: Basic Concepts.
4. ICTSD (2008), pp. 1–8.
5. The totality of the global atmosphere can now properly be regarded as the common concern of humankind. See Birnie et al. (2008), p. 339.
6. See (2004), p. 457.
7. Agenda 21, Ch. 34, Article 4:

> There is a need for favorable access to and transfer of environmentally sound technologies, in particular to developing countries, through supportive measures that promote technology cooperation and that should enable transfer of necessary technological know-how as well as building up of economic, technical, and managerial capabilities for the efficient use and further development of transferred technology. Technology cooperation involves joint efforts by enterprises and Governments, both suppliers of technology and its recipients. Therefore, such cooperation entails an iterative process involving government, the private sector, and research and development facilities to ensure the best possible results from transfer of technology. Successful long-term partnerships in technology cooperation necessarily require continuing systematic training and capacity-building at all levels over an extended period of time.

8. UNFCCC, Article 4.1

> All Parties, taking into account their common but differentiated responsibilities and their specific national and regional development priorities, objectives and circumstances, shall: ...(c). Promote and cooperate in the development, application and diffusion, including transfer, of technologies, practices and processes that control, reduce or prevent anthropogenic emissions of greenhouse gases not controlled by the Montreal Protocol in all relevant sectors, including the energy, transport, industry, agriculture, forestry and waste management sectors;
>
> Article 5: The developed country Parties and other developed Parties included in Annex II shall take all practicable steps to promote, facilitate and finance, as appropriate, the transfer of, or access to, environmentally sound technologies and know-how to other Parties, particularly developing country Parties, to enable them to implement the provisions of the Convention. In this process, the developed country Parties shall support the development and enhancement of endogenous capacities and technologies of developing country Parties. Other Parties and organizations in a position to do so may also assist in facilitating the transfer of such technologies.

9. The Kyoto Protocol, Article 10:

> All Parties, taking into account their common but differentiated responsibilities and their specific national and regional development priorities, objectives and circumstances …shall: (c) Cooperate in the promotion of effective modalities for the development, application and diffusion of, and take all practicable steps to promote, facilitate and finance, as appropriate, the transfer of, or access to, environmentally sound technologies, know-how, practices and processes pertinent to climate change, in particular to developing countries, including the formulation of policies and programs for the effective transfer of environmentally sound technologies that are publicly owned or in the public domain and the creation of an enabling environment for the private sector, to promote and enhance the transfer of, and access to, environmentally sound technologies;
>
> Article 11. 2. (a) Provide new and additional financial resources to meet the agreed full costs incurred by developing country Parties in advancing the implementation of existing commitments under Article 4 paragraph 1 (b). Also provide such financial resources, including for the transfer of technology, needed by the developing country Parties to meet the agreed full incremental costs of advancing the implementation of existing commitments under Article 4, paragraph 1, of the Convention that are covered by Article 10 and that are agreed between a developing country Party and the international entity or entities referred to in Article 11 of the Convention, in accordance with that Article.

10. The Clean Development Mechanism (CDM), which is primarily driven by Certificated Emission Reductions, could also be a vehicle for stimulating technology transfer, but the effects are unclear at this point. It does not have an explicit technology transfer mandate and is not identified as a means of fulfilling the development objective of technology transfer in the Protocol; however, it may contribute to technology transfer by financing emission reduction projects that use technologies currently not available in recipient countries. Particularly, with regard to the key player in climate-related technology transfer – the private sector, the CDM is intended to help channel private investment toward climate- friendly projects. Such government-supported Foreign Direct Investment (FDI) has great potential to trigger abundant ESTs transfer to developing countries.
11. MRV criteria refer to measurable, reportable and verifiable mitigation actions, which could include policies and measures supporting the development and deployment of low carbon technologies, and the provision of finance, technology and capacity-building support by developed countries. In the case of technology transfer, it means: (1) measurable, reportable and verifiable nationally appropriate mitigation commitments or actions by all developed countries; (2) nationally appropriate mitigation actions by developing country Parties, supported and enabled by technology, financing and capacity-building, in a measurable, reportable and verifiable manner.

    FCCC/CP/2007/L.7, distributed early on December 15, 2007, stated: '(ii) Measurable, reportable and verifiable nationally appropriate mitigation actions by developing country Parties in the context of sustainable development, supported by technology and enabled by financing and capacity-building;'
12. Agenda 21, Ch. 34.
13. President B. Obama, Inaugural Speech in Washington, DC, 20 January 2009, at http://www.oregonlive.com/politics/index.ssf/2009/01/obama_inauguration_lifts_troub.html.
14. World Bank (2008).
15. UNDP, UNDESA and the World Energy Council (2000).
16. IPCC Report 2007, WGIII Ch. 11.7: International Spillover Effects and Ch. 13.3: International Climate Change Agreements and Other Arrangements.
17. IPCC Report 2007, WGIII Ch. 13.3: International Climate Change Agreements and Other Arrangements, p. 790.
18. IPCC Report 2007, WGIII Ch. 2.4.3: Definition of Barriers, Opportunities and Potentials, in which barrier is defined as 'any obstacle to reaching a potential that can be overcome by

policies and measures'. From this point onwards, 'policies' will be assumed to include policies, measures, programs and portfolios of policies.

19. See Koschatzky (2005).
20. See Hoekman (2004), pp. 1–3.
21. UN General Assembly Resolution 43/53; see generally Alan Boyle, in Churchill and Freestone (1991).
22. Chapter 28 – Government and Market Failure, at http://welkerswikinomics.wetpaint.com/page/Chapter+28+-+Government+and+Market+Failure.
23. The positive spillover of technology transfer only exists whenever technological information is diffused into the wider economy and the technology suppliers cannot extract the economic value of that transference. A major share of benefits to recipient countries of technology transfer is likely to arise from uncompensated spillovers. Fearing the leakage of this can significantly reduce incentives for technology transfer, while market power created by IPRs will lead to pricing above marginal cost. See Hoekman et al. (2004), pp. 4.
24. See Jaffe et al. (2005), pp. 169–74.
25. See Grubb (2004), p. 9.
26. IPCC Report 2001, WGIII Methodological and Technological Issues in Technology Transfer, Section I: Framework for Analysis: Technology Transfer to Address Climate Change, Ch. 1.8: Technology Transfer Related to Global Climate Change.
27. IPCC Report 2007, WGIII Ch. 13.2.1: National Policy Instruments, their Implementation and Interactions: 'many countries pursue technological advancements as a national policy for a variety of different reasons, For example, to foster the development of innovative technologies, share costs, spread risks, avoid duplication, access facilities, enhance domestic capabilities, harmonize standards, accelerate market learning and create goodwill'.
28. IPCC Report 2007, WGIII Ch. 13.2.2: Linking National Policies.
29. See Stewart et al. (2009).
30. See Chung (1998), pp. 47–8.
31. Birnie et al. (2008), p. 336.
32. See Brewer (2007).
33. See Shepherd (2007), pp. 10544–56.
34. See Heller and Shukla (2003), p. 3.
35. The Rio Declaration, Principle 5, Principle 12, and Principle 13; with regard to international technology transfer, the inclusive principle of cooperation is 'no longer simply aimed at the prevention of damage in neighbor states, but at sustainable (social and economic) development for the entire world community, especially for developing countries'. See Verschuuren (2003), p. 59.
36. The Rio Declaration, Principle 5; Agenda 21, Chapter 34; the UNFCCC (1992), Article 4 and the Kyoto Protocol, Article 10. For this, other authors argue that countries are differentiated by historical responsibility and that such sub-global participation can be effective: Gupta and Grubb (2002), pp. 150–51, argue that under some scenarios one can expect that technology development driven by the international climate regime in Annex I countries could offset some or all emissions leakage in non-Annex I countries.
37. See generally Catherine Redgwell, in Churchill and Freestone (1992), p. 41; Franck (1998), ch. 12.
38. See Mintzer (1992), pp. 7–9.
39. The UNFCCC 1992, Article 4.7.
40. Birnie et al. (2008), p. 337.
41. UNFCCC Article 4.5:

> The developed country Parties and other developed Parties included in Annex II shall take all practicable steps to promote, facilitate and finance, as appropriate, the transfer of, or access to, environmentally sound technologies and know-how to other Parties, particularly developing country Parties … In this process, the developed country Parties shall support the development and enhancement of endogenous capacities and technologies of developing country Parties.

42. See Haug (1992), pp. 219–311.
43. For more details on the differences between the morality of aspiration and the morality of duty in the international environmental law, see Verschuuren (2003).
44. Decision 1/COP.13: Bali Action Plan 1 (d).

> Enhanced action on technology development and transfer to support action on mitigation and adaptation, including, inter alia, consideration of:
>
> (i) Effective mechanisms and enhanced means for the removal of obstacles to, and provision of financial and other incentives for, scaling up of the development and transfer of technology to developing country Parties in order to promote access to affordable environmentally sound technologies;
> (ii) Ways to accelerate deployment, diffusion and transfer of affordable environmentally sound technologies;
> (iii) Cooperation on research and development of current, new and innovative technology, including win-win solutions;
> (iv) The effectiveness of mechanisms and tools for technology cooperation in specific sectors ...

45. See Verhoosel (1999), p. 54.
46. See Littleton (2008), pp. 1–3.
47. IPCC Report 2007, WGIII Ch. 13.3.3: Proposal for Climate Change Agreements: three criteria at least need to be met: (1) consequences of non-compliance have to be more than proportionate; (2) punishment needs to take place when behavior is suboptimal; (3) an effective enforcement system must be able to curb collective as well as individual incentives to cheat.
48. UNFCCC, Article 13; 1997 Kyoto Protocol Article 16.
49. Birnie et al. (2008), p. 369.
50. COP7 Marrakesh Final Report: enforcement Branch decides whether there is non-compliance in a country and hence whether sanctions will be applied. Specifically, it is responsible for determining whether a party included in Annex 1 is not in compliance with its emission targets, the methodological and reporting requirements for greenhouse gas inventories and the eligibility requirements under the mechanism. Once non-compliance is determined, the sanctions including restitution, suspension and action plan will be duly imposed, 2001.
51. The mandate of the facilitative branch is to provide advice and facilitation to Parties in implementing the protocol, and to promote compliance by Parties with their Kyoto commitments. It is responsible for addressing questions of implementation by Annex 1 Parties of response measures aimed at mitigating climate change in a way that minimizes their adverse impacts on developing countries and the use by Annex 1 Parties of the mechanism as 'supplemental' to domestic action.
52. See Hagem et al. (2005), pp. 2112–22.
53. Given that they are independent treaties on an equal footing, neither can automatically be given the right to make a decision in the case of a conflict. See Murase (2002), pp. 301–10.
54. FCCC, an Introduction to the Kyoto Protocol Compliance Mechanism, at http://unfccc.int/kyoto_protocol/compliance/items/3024.php.
55. Besides the potential distinctions that exist in the scope of responsibilities and legal consequences, there are some differences at a procedural level, for instance, no fixed deadlines are provided for the Facilitative Branch, except the three-week deadline given to complete the preliminary examination.
56. The UNFCCC, Article 4.5, the Kyoto Protocol, Article 10 (C).
57. See Pizer (2002), pp. 409–34.
58. In the initial round of talks in 2008, developed countries, including Australia and the US, affirmed that IP was not a barrier, but a catalyst for technology transfer; while Cuba, India, Tanzania, Indonesia, China and others presented the case for there being a strong need to address IP within technology discussions in a systemic and cross-cutting manner. See the first meetings of the Ad Hoc Working Group on Further Commitments for Annex I Parties

under the Kyoto Protocol and the Ad Hoc Working Group on Long-term Cooperative Action under the Convention, Bangkok, April 2008.

59. Littleton (2008), p. 3.
60. See Abbott (2009), pp. 24–6.
61. Sha Zukang, Speech at Beijing High-level Conference on Climate Change: Technology Development and Technology Transfer, Beijing, China, 7–8 November 2008, at http://www.un.org/chinese/esa/desa/ousg/statements/2008/20081107_climate_Beijing.html.
62. ICTSD (2008), p. 4.
63. For instance: exemptions to patentability, exceptions to patent rights and compulsory licenses; see TRIPS. Article 27.1, Article 30 and Article 31.
64. Historically, both South Africa and Brazil suffered from American obstruction in the case of compulsory disclosure AIDS medicines. Herein, the exercise of compulsory licenses in the name of public health turns out to be exceptional under TRIPS, due to the intertwined process which basically includes that the proposed user should make good faith efforts to obtain authorization from the patent holder; the usage must be limited to domestic supply only; the patent owner should be granted 'adequate' remuneration, and a review process needs to be established and so on.
65. European Parliament Resolution (2007/2003(INI)), Trade and Climate Change, 29 November 2007.
66. IPCC Report 2001, WGIII, Methodological and Technological Issues in Technology Transfer, Technical Summary, Ch. 2: Increase the Flow; Improve the Quality.
67. There is an example here: Proposed Rule Revisions and Clarification of Export and Re-export Controls for the People's Republic of China; New Authorization Validated End-User, published by The Bureau of Industry and Security (BIS), The USA, July 6, 2006.
68. See Seres (2008), p. 9.
69. See Neumeyer (2001), pp. 69–78.
70. See Tang Hao (2007).
71. Beijing High-level Conference on Climate Change (2008).
72. IPCC Report 2001, WGIII, Methodological and Technological Issues in Technology Transfer, Technical Summary, Ch. 1.5: Barriers to Transfer Environmental Sound Technologies.
73. The purpose of the enabling environments component of the framework is to improve the effectiveness of the transfer of environmentally sound technologies by identifying and analyzing ways of facilitating the transfer of environmentally sound technologies, including the identification and removal of barriers at each stage of the process. See Enabling Environment at http://unfccc.int/ttclear/jsp/EEnvironment.jsp.
74. See Forsyth (2005), pp. 165–76.
75. IPCC Report 2007, WGIII, Ch. 13.1.1: Types of Policies, Measures, Instruments and Cooperative Arrangements.
76. UN, Finance Issues for Sustainable Development (1997), p. 22. Also see IPCC Report 2001, WGIII, Methodological and Technological Issues in Technology Transfer, Ch. 2.3: ODA.
77. See de Cendra de Larragán (2009).
78. IPCC Report 2007, WGIII, Ch. 13.2.1 Climate Change and Other Related Policies.
79. It is becoming increasingly active in developing renewable energy technologies, after a loss of interest following the sharp decline in oil prices during the 1980s. Several hundred companies are now involved in the manufacture of wind turbines, photovoltaic systems and component devices. IPCC Report 2001, WGIII, Methodological and Technological Issues in Technology Transfer, Section I: Framework for Analysis: Technology Transfer to Address Climate Change, Ch. 1.9: The Changing Roles of Key Stakeholders: Governments, Private Sector, Communities and NGOs.
80. The private sectors hold the largest amount of financing and clean technologies. Given this, some have questioned whether there is a role for the UNFCCC in the regulation, management and direction of private sector investment. See the PEW Environmental Group, 'Technology Transfer: Doing It to Solve Climate Change', at http://www.pewglobalwarming.org.
81. See Fischer (2006), p. 158.

82. IPCC Report 2001, Methodological and Technological Issues in Technology Transfer, WGIII, Ch. 3.5.2: Private Investment and Intellectual Property Rights.
83. See Porter and van der Linde (1995).
84. Seres (2008), pp. 8–9.
85. See Zou Ji and Xu Yan (2005).
86. See Zou Ji (2002).
87. Environmental issues and innovations in employee health management, business education and lifelong learning are equally part of the CSR agenda which is undertaken on a multi-stakeholder basis; see European Commission, Corporate Social Responsibility (CSR), at http://ec.europa.eu/social/main.jsp?catId=331&langId=en.
88. 'Clean Technology: Enabling the Business Responses to Climate Change', at http://www.ey.com/CA/en/Issues/Driving-growth/Sustainability.
89. OECD Guidelines for Multinational Enterprises (MNEs), Part 1. VIII. Science and Technology, 54:

> … When selling or licensing technologies, not only should the terms and conditions negotiated be reasonable, but MNEs may want to consider the long-term developmental, environmental and other impacts of technologies for the home and host country. In their activities, multinational enterprises can establish and improve the innovative capacity of their international subsidiaries and subcontractors. In addition, MNEs can call attention to the importance of local scientific and technological infrastructure, both physical and institutional. In this regard, MNEs can usefully contribute to the formulation by host country governments of policy frameworks conducive to the development of dynamic innovation systems.

90. They are: (1) OECD Guidelines for Multinational Enterprises (2008); (2) Tripartite Declaration of Principles concerning Multinational Enterprises and Social Policy from International Labor Office (2001); (3) ICEM Global Framework Agreements, International Federation of Chemical, Energy, Mine and General Workers' Unions (2000); (4) Norms on the Responsibilities of Transnational Corporations and Other Business Enterprises with Regard to Human Rights drafted by a working group of the United Nations Sub-Commission, E/CN.4/Sub.2/2003/12/Rev.2, Office of the United Nations High Commissioner for Human Rights (2003).
91. UNFCCC, Article 4.5; also see the Kyoto Protocol, Article 10.
92. See Muchie (2000), pp. 201–20.
93. Chung (1998), p. 48.
94. Verhoosel (1999), p. 66.
95. Decision 1/COP.13. These four building blocks are: (1) enhanced national/international action on mitigation of climate change; (2) enhanced action on adaptation; (3) enhanced action on technology development and transfer to support action on mitigation and adaptation; (4) enhanced action on the provision of financial resources and investment to support action on mitigation and adaptation and technology cooperation.
96. FCCC/CP/2009/11/Add.1, Report of the Conference of the Parties on its Fifteenth Session, Decisions adopted by the Conference of the Parties, Copenhagen, 7–19 December 2009.
97. See He Gang (2007).

REFERENCES

Abbott, Frederick M. (2009), 'Innovation and Technology Transfer to Address Climate Change: Lessons from the Global Debate on Intellectual Property and Public Health', ICTSD Program on Intellectual Property Rights, pp. 24–6.

Beijing High-level Conference on Climate Change (2008), 'Climate Change:

Technology Development and Technology Transfer', Technology Development and Technology Transfer Working Paper, Beijing China, 7–8 November.
Birnie, P., A. Boyle and C. Redgwell (2008), 'Climate Change and Atmospheric Pollution', in *International Law and the Environment*, Oxford: Oxford University Press, pp. 336–69.
Brewer, Thomas L. (2007), 'Climate Change Technology Transfer: International Trade and Investment Policy Issues in the G8+5 Countries', Prepared for the G8+5 Climate Change Dialogue.
Chung, R.K. (1998), 'The Role of Government in the Transfer of Environmental Sound Technology', in T. Forsyth (ed.), *Positive Measures for Technology Transfer under the Climate Change Convention*, London: Royal Institute of International Affairs, pp. 46–8.
Churchill, R.R. and D.A.C Freestone (1991), *International Law and Global Climate International Legal Issues and Implications*, Netherlands: Kluwer Law International.
'Clean Technology: Enabling Business Responses to Climate Change', at http://www.ey.com/CA/en/Issues/Driving-growth/Sustainability.
Collins, W., R. Colman, J. Haywood, M. Manning and P. Mote (2007), 'The Physical Science behind Climate Change', *Scientific American*, 65–70.
de Cendra de Larragán, Javier (2009), 'The Position of the EU in the International Climate Change Negotiation', Environmental Law Expert Meeting on the European position towards Copenhagen: A Global Outlook, Maastricht, the Netherlands.
European Patent Office (2008), 'A Special Report on Selected Side Events at the UNFCC SB28', 2–13 June, Bonn, Germany.
Fischer, C. (2006), 'Multinational Taxation and International Emissions', *Trading, Resource and Energy Economics* (28), 155–8.
Forsyth, Tim (2005), 'Enhancing Climate Change Technology Transfer through Greater Public-private Cooperation: Lessons from Thailand and the Philippines', *National Resources Forum*, 29(2), 165–76.
Franck, Thomas M. (1998), *Fairness in International Law and Institutions*, Oxford: Clarendon Press.
Grubb, Michael (2004), 'Technology Innovation and Climate Change Policy: An Overview of Issues and Options', *Keio Journal of Economics*, 9.
Gupta, Joyeeta and Michael Grubb (2002), *Climate Change and European Leadership: A Sustainable Role for Europe?*, Dordrecht: Kluwer Academic Publishers.
Hagem, C., S. Kallbekken, O. Maestad and H. Westskog (2005), 'Enforcing the Kyoto Protocol: Sanctions and Strategic Behaviors', *Energy Policy*, 33, 2112–22.
Haug, David M. (1992), 'The International Transfer of Technology: Lessons that East Europe Can Learn from the Failed Third World Experiences', *Harvard Journal of Law and Technology*, pp. 219–311.
He Gang (2007), 'Climate Change and the Equity Principle', *China Dialogue*, 19 December.
Heller, Thomas C. and P.R. Shukla (2003), 'Development and Climate Engaging Developing Countries', *Beyond Kyoto Series*, 3.
Hoekman, Ernard M., Keith E. Maskus and Kamal Saggi (2004), 'Transfer of Technology to Developing Countries: Unilateral and Multilateral Policy Options', Research Program on Political and Economic Change Working Paper PEC2004-0003, May, pp. 1–3.
International Centre for Trade and Sustainable Development (ICTSD), Trade and Climate Change Seminar (2008), Climate Change, Technology Transfer and Intellectual Property Rights, Switzerland, pp. 4–8.

Jaffe, A.B., R.G. Newell and R.N. Stavins (2005), 'A Tale of Two Market Failures: Technology and Environmental Policy', *Ecological Economics*, 54(2–3), 169–74.
Kemfert, C. (2004), 'Climate Coalitions and International Trade: Assessment of Cooperation Incentives by Issue Linkage', *Energy Policy,* 32(4), 457.
Koschatzky, Knut (2005), 'The Regionalization of Innovation Policy: New Options for Regional Change?' in G. Fuchs and P. Shapira (eds), *Rethinking Regional Innovation and Change: Path Dependency or Regional Breakthrough?*, The Netherlands: Springer, pp. 291–300.
Littleton, Matthew (2008), 'The TRIPS Agreement and Transfer of Climate Change-related Technologies to Developing Countries', DESA Working Paper, No. 71, pp. 1–3.
Mintzer, Irving M. (1992), 'Living in a Warming World', in *Confronting Climate Change: Risks, Implications and Responses*, Cambridge: Cambridge University Press, pp. 1–14.
Muchie, M. (2000), 'Old Wine in New Bottles: A Critical Exploration of the UN's Conceptions and Mechanisms for the Transfer of Environmentally Sound Technologies to Industry', *Technology in Society*, 22, 201–20.
Murase, S. (2002), 'Conflict of International Regimes: Trade and the Environment', Institute of International Public Law and International Relations of Thessaloniki, *Thesaurus Acroasium*, XXXI, pp. 301–10.
Neumeyer, E. (2001), *Greening Trade and Investment: Environmental Protection without Protectionism*, London and Sterling, VA: *Earthscan*, pp. 69–78.
OECD (2008), Guidelines for Multinational Enterprises, ISBN 978-92-64-05597-1.
Pizer, W.A. (2002), 'Combining Price and Quantity Controls to Mitigate Global Climate Change', *Public Economics*, 85(3), 409–34.
Porter, M.E. and C. van der Linde (1995), 'Green and Competitive', *Harvard Business Review*, Issue 9–10.
Qin Tianbao (2001), 'The Study on Basic Principles of International Environmental Law', *Legal Research*, 10, 102 (in Chinese).
Robert R.M. (2000), 'Feathers or Gold? A Civic Economics for Environmental Law', *Harvard Environmental Law Review,* 25, 107–20.
Seres, Stephen (2008), 'Analysis of Technology Transfer in CDM Projects', Prepared for the UNFCCC Registration & Issuance Unit CDM/SDM, Montreal, Canada, 9.
Shepherd, James (2007), 'The Future of Technology Transfer under Multilateral Environmental Agreements', *ELR News & Analysis*, 37, 10544–56, Environmental Law Institute, Washington, DC, available at http://www.eli.org.
Stewart, Richard, B., Benedict Kingsbury and Bryce Rudyk (2009), 'Climate Finance for Limiting Emissions and Promoting Green Development: Mechanisms, Regulation and Governance', Public Law and Legal Theory Research Paper Series Working Paper, No. 09-66.
Tang Hao (2007), 'An Environmental Approach to Technology', *China Dialogue*, 21 November.
UN, Finance Issues for Sustainable Development (1997), 'The Road Ahead', Proceedings of the Fourth Group Meeting on Financial Issues of Agenda 21, Santiago, Chile, p. 22.
UNDP, UNDESA and the World Energy Council (2000), *World Energy Assessment: Energy and the Challenge of Sustainable Development*, New York.
Verchick, Robert R.M. (2000), 'Feathers or Gold? A Civic Economics for Environmental Law', *Harvard Environmental Law Review*, 25, 107–20.
Verhoosel, Gaetan (1999), 'Beyond the Unsustainable Rhetoric of Sustainable

Development: Transferring Environmentally Sound Technologies', *International Environmental Law Review*, 11, 54–66.

Verschuuren, Jonathan (2003), *Principles of Environmental Law*, Baden-Baden: Nomos Verlagsgesellschaft.

World Bank (2008), 'Global Economic Prospects: Technology Diffusions in the Developing World', Development Prospects Group Report 42097, Washington, DC.

Zou Ji (2002), 'Tools and Methodologies in Assessing Technology Needs', Working Paper on the UNFCCC/UNDP Expert Meeting on Methodologies for Technology Need Assessments, Seoul, Republic of Korea.

Zou Ji and Xu Yan (2005), 'Technology Innovation and Transfer to Address Climate Change', Environmental Protection, 1 (in Chinese).

14. Implementing stewardship in Kenyan land use law: the case for a sustainability extension

Robert Kibugi

14.1 INTRODUCTION

Poverty and food insecurity are two serious challenges facing developing countries like Kenya. A large section of the national population, especially in rural areas, earns a livelihood from land-based activities. Credible evidence suggests that engaging in farming or rural agriculture correlates with poverty, which calls into question prior policies focused on agriculture *per se* for generating rural economic growth, and alleviating poverty and food insecurity. Innovative mechanisms have been introduced to supplement agriculture. One is controlled community agroforestry on degraded state forests, known as the *shamba* system. *Shamba* is Swahili for garden or farm. Over time rural agriculture, farm forestry and the *shamba* system have demonstrated declining productivity and failure related to depletion of soils and poor husbandry, which in turn are related to a lack of relevant knowledge and skills.

Passing on relevant knowledge and skills to enhance how farmers use their land to increase productivity and fertility has typically been performed through agricultural and forestry extension.[1] Failures in rural land uses have been linked to inadequacies in the extension function. Where extension has been effective, case studies show a positive outcome. This suggests that extension can enhance sustainable land use, if adapted to support stewardship alongside uses like forestry and agriculture. This chapter is an inquiry into how extension can be adapted as a mechanism available for land use, and environmental law to meet their sustainability goals.

Section 14.1 is the Introduction. Section 14.2 reviews poverty and environmental degradation in view of the sustainability objects of land use (agriculture and forestry) law. Section 14.3 examines agricultural and forestry extension in Kenya, and its potential contribution to behaviour modification for land stewardship. Section 14.4 explores the link between extension and stewardship. Section 14.5 examines the position of African law and policy on sustainable land management. Section 14.6 frames the concept of sustainability extension, and the last section is the conclusion.

14.2 POVERTY, ENVIRONMENTAL DEGRADATION, AND SUSTAINABILITY OBJECTIVES OF LAW

14.2.1 Evaluating Agriculture Land Use

The majority of the Kenyan population inhabits rural areas, and 80% of this population depends on agriculture for their livelihood (Kimenyi, 2002, p. 6). Paradoxically, a national household survey established that poverty is concentrated in rural areas in general and in the agricultural sector in particular. Dependence on or employment in the agricultural sector significantly raises the probability of people being poor (Geda et al., 2001, p. 25). Concurring literature suggests that in developing countries like Kenya, the agriculture-based economy accounts for a substantially higher share of absolute poverty (Ravallion, 2000, p. 1090). However, the literature optimistically suggests that fostering conditions for growth in rural economies is central to effective poverty reduction strategies. In Kenya, poverty is closely linked to food insecurity.[2]

The above literature raises a concern whether land use and environmental law, whose objectives should facilitate land health and productivity, exacerbate this poverty and food insecurity. This is because agriculture, as a dominant land use and economic activity, is a double-edged sword, necessary for basic livelihood but not providing an escape from poverty. Lockwood and Kothari (2006, p. 56) have argued that where poverty and food insecurity are dominant, they provoke short-term behaviour and attitudes towards natural resources in pursuit of basic survival which is inimical to environmental integrity. Mbithi et al. (2005, pp. 195–6) highlight that the interaction of the poor with the environment results in undesirable consequences like poor farming practices or charcoal burning as survival needs conflict with protection of viable agricultural and forestry ecosystems. They cite two densely populated districts in Kenya, Kiambu and Kakamega, which account for a combined 10% of poor households nationally, where this is most marked. Kimalu et al. (2001, p. 14) suggest that poor people depend on natural resources for their livelihoods and are more likely to live in vulnerable areas, putting them at higher risk of suffering from deterioration of the environment. This literature suggests that agriculture, poverty and environmental degradation are linked to an insufficiency of knowledge and skills for land management. This further suggests that the objectives of pertinent land use laws, like agriculture legislation, that are intended to improve environmental conditions in developing countries, have to integrate effective extension to remedy the current situation. Overcoming the shortcomings in land husbandry, degradation, and fertility loss is urgent as rural poverty has reached almost 60% in many areas. About 51% of the Kenyan population is classified as food insecure (Kenya, 2009b, p. 7).

The 1955 Agriculture Act is the main land use law that should uphold land husbandry and land health standards in Kenya, as agriculture is a dominant land use and activity. One of its express objectives, a goal that is fundamental to sustainability, is conservation of soil and its fertility (sections 48–62). However, this law does not place any direct responsibility on land owners such as minimum soil conservation standards they should observe. Instead, it operates on the police power legal concept, empowering the Minister to make mandatory rules regulating land clearance for cultivation, grazing or vegetation clearance. The Minister can also make positive action rules regulating afforestation or reafforestation of land and the protection of slopes and catchment areas, or restrict or prohibit use of any land for agricultural purposes.

This law covers most activities responsible for land degradation, which have continued in spite of statute regulation (Kameri-Mbote, 2002, p. 75). This can be attributed to land shortage and population pressure, making legal prohibition ineffective. Further, the law does not consider any incentives, or public participation in implementation (Kameri-Mbote, ibid.). Public participation is essential for exchange of information amongst local land users, and with government agents like extension workers. Therefore in spite of these legal provisions, a 2009 government of Kenya economic survey revealed that the agricultural sector experienced a 5.1% contraction. The new agriculture policy (Kenya, 2010) highlights declining fertility of land and depletion of soil nutrients, as constraints resulting in declining agricultural yield and environmental degradation.

Although not the only reason, failures in agricultural research and extension services are identified as important causes of this environmental and productivity decline. Extension is the means of transmission of knowledge and skills to farmers to enable them to improve the productivity of their land. Falling productivity is linked to the ineffectiveness of inappropriate extension methods, limited use of science, poor land husbandry practices, and weak research-extension-farmer linkages (Kenya, 2010, supra, p. 24). The need to revamp environmental and land use standards, and in turn reverse poverty trends for the population implies the law must embrace land stewardship as a tool to achieve sustainability. Extension, with its role of providing knowledge and skills to land users, will provide a means for the law to effectively engage with the land-using community, and pursue the sustainability objectives. This chapter will consider extension in relation to food security and poverty, and then evaluate extension as a component in the pursuit of sustainable land use, in line with legal and policy objectives.

14.2.2 Evaluating Forestry Land Use

Statutory provisions on forests in Kenya derive from the Forests Act, 2005 and the Forests Policy (Kenya, 2007). Forests in Kenya, except private and local authority forests, are vested in the state subject to any user rights (Forest Act, section 20). State forests are protected areas using legal restrictions or prohibitions on access and utilization for activities like mining.

Kenya is a low forest cover country (Kenya, 2007, p. iv). The government acknowledges that forestry plays vital roles in livelihood through forest-related goods and services, such as charcoal, timber and trees to regulate water flow. Sustainable forest management is hampered by an increasing population and poverty, which result in rampant illegal logging, illegal charcoal making and encroachment for agriculture and settlement. In contrast to this state of affairs, the express objective of the Forest Act is to govern the establishment, development and sustainable management and utilization of forests for the social and economic development of Kenya (Preamble).

This chapter considers the legal mechanisms applied to ensure sustainable use of state forests managed as protected areas by the Kenya Forests Service, by managing them with local community involvement. This approach is envisaged by section 46 of the Forests Act which allows community participation in state forest management. The chapter argues that the well-intentioned achievement of the poverty, food security and sustainability goals of this law is not likely to occur unless complementary investments in extension also take place.

Community involvement in state forests was historically implemented without explicit legal provisions. It was termed the *shamba* system; *shamba* being a Swahili word meaning farm or garden. The system was pursued in plantation establishment since 1910, with the intention of producing wood for industry and domestic uses away from natural forests. Lax controls and oversight led to an influx of people, higher demand for more forest land to set up *shambas,* poorly tended *shambas* and low survival rates of planted trees. The system was suspended by a Presidential decree in 1987 (Oduol, 1986, p. 366) with no arrangements for alternative forest plantations. This resulted in the stagnation of reforestation. A resulting lack of fast-growing non-indigenous timber for industry, firewood and the like led to indigenous forests being targeted instead. All forest workers and other people living in forest villages were evicted in 1988, leading to a loss of social amenities, sources of food and employment (Oduol, ibid.).

The system was reintroduced in 1994 as Non-Resident Cultivation (NRC) (Kagombe and Gitonga, 2005), with the non-residential component being an attempt to reduce the risk of cultivators claiming squatter rights.[3] Political manipulation and disregard of environmental or sustainability considerations resulted in indigenous forest areas being cleared for farming without replanting. The *shamba* system was again terminated by Presidential decree in 2003.

The 2005 forest law with a clear objective of sustainable management embeds community participation in state forests. The *shamba* system is now reorganized as the 'Plantation Establishment and Livelihood Improvement Scheme'[4] but *shamba* remains the popular term of reference. The programme is intended to implement cost-effective tree growing, while making a significant contribution to food security and the socio-economic well-being of rural communities.

The government proposed to open up 8,000 hectares of fallow forest area for immediate cultivation and reforestation in phase one.[5] Farmers in zoned areas must belong to registered and active Community Forest Associations (CFAs), the legal entity with which the forest service can conclude *shamba* agreements (Forest Act, section 46). Success or failure of this iteration of the *shamba* system depends on effective planning and implementation.

The literature on the suitability of this system of forest management is divided in its assessment. Some literature cites the *shamba* system as one of the worst forms of forest management, citing it as a stimulus for encroachment into indigenous forests (WWF, 2006). Wangari Maathai (Maathai, 2009, p. 241) also argues that *shamba* plantations are monocultures with little biodiversity value, and are an excuse for encroachment into indigenous forests. While this criticism is well deserved considering the history of the *shamba* system, other assessments make credible positive claims. Plantation forests contribute to the maintenance of ecological processes, offsetting pressure on primary/old-growth forests. They provide local employment and development with the involvement of local communities (United Nations, 1992). Kagombe and Gitonga (2005, p. 40), who analysed the *shamba* system in 2004 prior to its reintroduction, note that exotic forest plantations, while being monocultures, have a role in conservation. They reduce pressure on natural forests. They found that in areas benefiting from the *shamba* system, food production declined significantly after its cessation, with peasant farmers with few alternative resources facing severe food insecurity.

Other research (Hodas, 2007, p. 58) argues that land use reconfiguration, such as this, must somehow promote ecosystem and biodiversity protection. We argue that a structured extension system for ensuring knowledge and skills for ecosystem and biodiversity protection by land users is an important mechanism to ensure sustainable land use and forest management. Perhaps with hindsight into the poor state of forests and history of ineffective extension, the Forest Act requires the forest service to provide extension services by assisting forest owners, farmers and associations in the sustainable management of forests (Section14. 5). This provision evidently anchors extension as a primary component in meeting sustainability objectives of forest law, for the benefit of forest health, private forest owners, farm forestry, and local communities involved in the *shamba* system. This legal recognition reinforces our argument that extension is crucial to realization of the sustainability goals of the forest and other land use laws, a discussion pursued later in the chapter.

14.3 THEORY OF EXTENSION

Rural extension is the function of providing need- and demand-based knowledge and skills to rural populations in a non-formal, participatory manner with the objective of improving their quality of life (Qamar, 2005, p. 1). Considering that land use activities like agriculture are inherently influenced by broad social-cultural, economic and political forces, the role of the extension function is to inculcate behaviour change and managing these multiple forces is an imperative for sustainable land use (Vanclay and Lawrence, 1994, p. 1; Qamar, 2005, p. 1).

The term 'extension' has various applications, such as agricultural extension, or forestry extension. It has a dual focus. The first is communications, which involves transferring information about new practices and technology from research to potential users and obtaining feedback for the researchers (World Bank, 1985, p. 71). This transfer of knowledge aims to generate behavioural change by land users, seeking major modifications in production systems (World Bank, ibid.). This communication focus of extension is synergistic with the education focus. The education function of extension involves land owners and users working with researchers and other experts. This mainly involves the exchange of ideas, to guide people in adapting their production systems.

Extension includes two crucial components: function and organization. Function relates to the role or the relevance of extension services (Gautam, 2000, p. viii). The traditional extension function targets the dissemination of information and advice with the intention of promoting desirable knowledge, attitudes, skills and aspirations (Rivera and Qamar, 2003, p. 7). Organization relates to how the agency or department responsible for extension organizes itself to execute the extension function (Qamar, 2005) or designs a particular extension project (Gautam, 2000, supra).

14.3.1 Agricultural Extension in Kenya

Agricultural extension is intended to help rural families make the best use of productive resources at their disposal (Muyanga and Jayne, 2006, p. 1). Agricultural extension provides farmers with important information such as patterns in crop prices, new seeds varieties, management practices in crop cultivation and marketing, and training in new technologies (Muyanga and Jayne, ibid.). Kenyan farmers have traditionally benefited from two major types of extension organization: publicly funded government extension; and specialized commodity extension (Muyanga and Jayne, ibid., p. 3). Early public extension had limited success in most instances for many reasons, but was highly successful in the dissemination of hybrid maize technology (Gautam, 2000, p. 7). The focus of extension programmes run by the Ministry of Agriculture has been food crops and livestock (Muyanga and Jayne, 2006, p. 3). Essentially, this is production extension, as it is concerned with how to increase production and yield of food crops, or livestock products.

While agriculture law implicitly embraces a sustainability objective through its soil conservation and fertility goals, it is silent on role of extension. This is probably the reason the Kenyan government has historically pursued a project-based approach to extension organization. Prior to the 1982 National Extension Programme (NEP), there were uncoordinated donor-supported efforts (World Bank, 1999b, p. 15). These extension arrangements were found to *lack a consistent national strategy*, were *expensive*, *inefficient*, and largely *ineffective.* At the close of NEP, the World Bank commissioned an evaluation which found the agriculture extension function and organization up to the end of the project 'lacked a strategic vision, had no appreciable improvement in its effectiveness and suffered from weak management' (Gautam, 2000, p. 10).

This approach failed to deliver the kinds of relevant information desired by farmers, instead disseminating simple agronomic and maize-related messages. This failure vitiated the cost-effectiveness of the main 'face-to-face' oriented training and visit (T&V) system (Gautam, 2000, p. 52). Most farmers surveyed several years into the T&V system indicated that the availability and quality of information and services declined within a few years (Gautam, ibid., p. xv). World Bank evaluators were quick to highlight that the failure of a *particular* extension project (organization) does not extinguish the rationale or utility of extension function *per se* (Gautam, ibid., p. 7).

Reflecting this background the government undertook a review, resulting in the agricultural extension policy of 2001 (Kenya, 2001b). The policy acknowledges the need to address persistent poor agricultural performance; and to reassess the role of government in extension services (Kenya, ibid., p. 1). The policy acknowledges that extension is concerned with effecting change through adoption of innovations and changed practices and attitudes (Kenya, ibid., p. 9). The policy extensively focuses on increasing productivity. It also addresses environmental issues, albeit briefly, indicating that farmers should receive training on soil and water conservation especially as it relates to agricultural and livestock production (Kenya, ibid., p. 23).

Implementation of the extension policy is undertaken through the National

Agriculture and Livestock Extension Programme (NALEP).[6] NALEP frames the principal goals of extension function as being to enhance the contribution of agriculture and livestock to social and economic development and poverty alleviation in the country. Implementation of these goals also focuses on transfer of knowledge and skills to increase land productivity, and marketing strategies. This suggests that land stewardship may be a subsidiary outcome during extension, through high productivity farming initiatives, but the sustainability link is indirect and unclear. NALEP, however, embraces farmer participation, a useful component of land stewardship, in its implementation, therefore marking a departure from the prescriptive provisions of current agriculture land use law.

NALEP implementation revolves around the participation of farmers and other stakeholders in the broader agricultural field, including private sector players. It is decentralized to the district level; the highest district organ being the District Stakeholders Forum. This forum comprises farmers, agribusiness representatives, and sectoral ministries such as Agriculture, Livestock, Fisheries, Forestry, Co-operatives, Water and Provincial Administration.[7] In a series of interviews with agricultural extension workers, this author established that NALEP is administratively implemented on the basis of focal areas, selected by the District or Divisional Stakeholder forum. In practice, due to budgetary constraints, every district will have one focal area in operation at any time. Based on the interviews, the following paragraph summarizes the organization of the NALEP project in one district, and is representative of the national arrangement.

The district stakeholder's forum selects a focal area, ideally a new area or a repeat if the district was previously covered. Where a district comprises several administrative divisions, the district forum selects one division. A divisional stakeholder forum is selected, reflecting the composition of the district forum. The divisional forum identifies a focal area with a relatively high population density, poor agricultural output, or similar characteristics. A survey is undertaken on poverty and farming options. This forms the basis of an action plan for the focal area. An initial meeting for the focal area is usually held in the form of a *baraza* – a meeting convened by the local chief. At this meeting farmers elect suitable groupings, or Common Interest Groups (CIG). The CIGs elect leaders from among their members. At this meeting, and similar ones, a Common Action Plan is determined for the year-long duration of the project.

Some farmers interviewed for a mid-term assessment of NALEP indicated that they have managed to improve their production and food security considerably (Cuellar et al., 2006, p. 6). However, the programme faces several challenges. NALEP services are restricted to one focal area within an administrative division at any one time. Second, NALEP is structured as 'demand-driven'. Outside an active focal area, training and visits by extension officers to other farms are predicated on a request for service. This may be suboptimal in public policy terms, as those whose actions would most benefit from extension support may not be those who request it. The poor agriculture performance, attributed to loss of soil fertility, suggests that the extension policy direction to train farmers on soil and water conservation has been ineffective, especially since extension has been implemented on such a limited scale nationally.

Some officers attached to the extension units and specializing in agriculture, social and home economics provided positive reviews of the programmes to this author.[8] They pointed out that the NALEP programme had offered opportunities for men, women and youth in agriculture, and had generated some attitude change, with farming being viewed as a business rather than as subsistence, especially supporting on-farm value addition to products. This positive effect of agricultural extension, especially supporting increased agricultural productivity and quality of land stewardship, was visible to this author during field trips to private farms.[9] However, because extension advice is offered actively in few focal areas at any time, or only on demand, this significantly limits the overall impact on a nationwide scale.

The literature, and empirical information suggest agriculture extension, even though focused on production has some positive impact on public participation. It also achieves some attitude change, evident from farmers' willing uptake of farming, value-addition and marketing advice. This potential can be tapped as a means to communicate and educate on the urgent need for sustainable land use, thus providing an implementation tool for the law. Successful implementation of these sustainability objectives of both agricultural and environmental law is crucial due to the importance of agriculture as a productive economic sector in Kenya.

14.3.2 Extension Function in Forestry

Forestry extension follows the same approach as agricultural extension. Forestry extension involves facilitating the flow of knowledge, skills and technology to farmers or other people involved in forestry. Forestry extension also aims to widen the knowledge of people beyond the range of their food crops and animals, to understand more fully how forests fit the pattern of their lives and whether they are being managed as wisely as they should be (Sim and Hilmi, 1987, pp. 1–2).

With the 2005 Forest Law making provision for forestry extension, the administrative structure of the Kenya Forest Service includes a Forest Extension Services Division, and a drylands and farm forestry branch within this division (Kenya Forest Service, 2009, p. 19). All forest officers are expected to play an extension role, including rendering extension service to communities involved in the *shamba* system and to private land owners. There are about 250 extension offices countrywide.[10] However, interviews with forestry respondents suggest that forestry extension staff lack mobility due to underfunding and lack of vehicles.[11]

Kagombe and Gitonga (2005, p. 25) found that where the *shamba* system has been successful, this was due to a large component of extension education, whereby the local forester had actively engaged the local community on forestry management. The failure of past models of the *shamba* system suggests that overall forestry extension was ineffective.

There is experience of success in forestry extension in Kenya, analysis of which will provide useful insights on the potential role of extension in meeting sustainability objectives of forest law. A Kenyan pilot scale extension project, intended to enhance on-farm forestry was the 'Intensified Social Forestry Project' (ISFP). A five-year donor-funded pilot project from 2004, and concluded in March 2009 (Kenya Forest Service et al., 2004a, 2004b),[12] it focused on forestry development in the expansive arid and semi-arid lands (ASAL). Its objectives included providing social forestry extension to farmers in focus districts, and ensuring that farmers and other stakeholders obtain sufficient practical knowledge. The project was carried out in three focus ASAL districts of Kitui, Mbeere and Tharaka, all in Kenya's eastern province.

A baseline study undertaken in 2004, before the ISFP project, found that tree planting was prevalent in all three project districts, but with very low survival rate because of limited knowledge on tree growth and management (Kenya Forest Service et al., 2004b, pp. 80, 81). A mid-term survey of the ISFP project in 2007 corroborated earlier findings by Kagombe and Gitonga that extension services bring about positive outcomes. The ISFP project had enhanced extension training, building the capacity of forestry officers, and training farmers, including as peer trainers to other farmers at village level (FAO, JICA, 2007, pp. 11–12). There was remarkable evidence of increased farm fertility, productivity, tree planting and survival. There was an average 14% expansion of lands for food crops for farmers who received training (FAO, JICA , ibid.).

The analysis of such information suggests strongly that forestry extension is functionally important in meeting the objectives of sustainable forest management, meeting the needs of local communities and addressing unsustainable land use. This suggests that extension is an important practical consideration in the pursuit of sustainability objectives, which are of course intrinsic to environmental law. This makes extension a component in any legal strategy for sustainability.

14.4 LINKING UTILITY OF EXTENSION FUNCTION TO LAND STEWARDSHIP

Developing countries like Kenya, whose populations face a crisis of livelihood due to poverty and the absence of food security, face complex tasks. A large section of the population depends on land for income and food, but land productivity is declining, sending more people into destitution. The decline in agricultural productivity is linked to falling soil fertility, poor land husbandry and a failure in extension services, and it puts pressure on land users to over-exploit the land and prejudice sustainability. Action must be taken to alleviate poverty and food insecurity, by reversing the decline in agricultural productivity, and enhancing policy attempts to integrate forests and farming, such as the *shamba* system. Achieving this may be a Herculean task when the immediate objective for people is the next meal. Undoing poverty and hunger is a priority, but so is ensuring that land regenerates to sustain life and increase productivity.

14.4.1 The Basis for Stewardship

The sustainability objects and tools of land use and environmental law come into focus when evaluating means for reversing environmental degradation, poverty and food insecurity, such as land stewardship. Principal land use legislation, on agriculture or forestry, incorporates some sustainability objectives captured as 'conservation of soil and its fertility', or 'sustainable forest management'. Agriculture law, however, continues to embed command and control approaches, prescribing orders to farmers on land use measures. From the information reviewed in this chapter, the current state of land use, soil fertility loss, and poor agriculture productivity does not support any suggestion that mandatory orders are effective in modifying attitudes of farmers toward land stewardship.

The Kenyan Forest Law, enacted in 2005, is more recent and states its sustainability objectives more succinctly, and even embeds a role for extension. However, this law has to contend with massively degraded forests, and an adversarial relationship with communities resulting from decades of exclusion from forests, and poor implementation of the *shamba* system. Recognition of extension as a key tool to achieve sustainable forestry management, and integration of local communities through the *shamba* system, is perhaps a first step towards shifting the attitudes of these communities to appreciating the need to maintain a healthy forest ecosystem.

The ability of current agriculture and forestry extension models, highlighted in Section 14.3, to realize some measure of attitude change and better land husbandry is indicative of the direction law and policy should follow, in search of sustainable land use. It is arguable that a statutory duty of care that sets out minimum land use standards for land users, and mandates attitude change, is preferable. However, examining the nature of such a duty will involve in-depth analysis of property rights in land, and is beyond the scope of the current chapter.[13] Instead, I focus on how law and policy can integrate measures which aim to bring about changes in attitude and behaviour such that people appreciate that land health is irrevocably linked to land productivity, which they need for basic livelihood. The magnitude of this change in attitude and knowledge to achieve the goals of sustainability law and policy is substantial. This section considers the extent of this challenge, and suggests that, without effective extension, it may not be possible to create effective sustainability law in rural communities in developing countries.

14.4.1.1 Stewardship from a land ethic

A way needs to be found to guide farmers to understand that, unless the health and fertility of the land are upheld, productivity will decline, and poverty will increase. Extension is critical to reversing land use damage. New methods are needed to change the attitude of land users, through education and building their capacity. This implies that embedding a land ethic, based on a human duty to care for the earth, is a conceptual basis for changing human attitude towards sustainable land use.

This land ethic reflects an individual responsibility to the land. A key proponent is American forester Aldo Leopold (Leopold, 1981) who explains *land health* as the capacity of the land for self-renewal. Leopold argues that human beings need an ecological conscience which involves love, respect and admiration for the land beyond a focus on its economic utility. Leopold suggests that human beings must recognize a *pyramid* in which land is a biotic mechanism comprising soil and a fountain of energy flowing through a circuit of soils, plants, and animals.

It is argued that if human beings understand this they will care for the land and the associated ecosystem (e.g. river catchment, wetlands) which may not possess discernible commercial value but are crucial for healthy ecosystem function. This does not prevent the use of land, which Leopold urges is a resource. Rather human beings will use land resources but accept their individual responsibility to ensure the ability of the land for self-renewal (Leopold, ibid., p. 216; Jamieson, 2008, p. 149). This outlook is not to be restricted within the boundaries created by property rights, for it talks of responsibility for a complete natural system. It implies the need to depart from the *business as usual* attitude towards integrating responsible caring for the land.

What is apparent is that pursuit of sustainability potentially involves significant changes to the attitudes, knowledge and land use practices of a large number of disadvantaged land users. Land stewardship, which is often an implicit objective of environmental law, implies adoption of significant innovations in behaviour change, resulting in land use practices that are in sync with upholding land health. Extension, with its dual focus on communication and education, is a ready means of passing on knowledge about the land ethic and stewardship to land users, as well as cultivating behaviour change. This in turn indicates the importance of extension in achieving the objectives of environmental law.

14.4.1.2 Demonstrating utility of extension to land stewardship

Agriculture, the main economic activity for significant rural populations in Kenya, is closely linked to poverty. Most small-scale farmers are farming degraded soils and rainwater is scarce due to degraded forests (Maathai, 2009, p. 241). A loose causal link suggests that if no corrective action is taken, even the current version of the *shamba* system will fail, pushing participating farmers deeper into poverty and resulting in significant forest degradation. Learning from history, the failure to integrate local communities' land use activities with the protection of forests has frustrated the realization of sustainable forest management throughout Kenya.

Extension offers a tool to nudge land use towards sustainability and an ethos of stewardship, avoiding a situation such as illustrated above. Extension can play a major role in influencing the behaviour and attitudes of farmers, mostly to enhance the economic benefits from agriculture and related activities. Leopold suggests that a major obstacle to a land ethic culture is the attitude of the farmer for whom the land is still an adversary (Leopold, 1981, p. 223). Small-scale farmers and other users of land thus need to be nudged in the direction of stewardship by all possible means if the objectives of law and policy are to be achieved. This suggests that the legal tools and institutions responsible for sustainable land use/forestry need to embrace extension as a legal mechanism necessary to meet their sustainability objectives. This will shift extension and extension institutions from focusing on production and encourage a focus on achieving sustainable land use and higher productivity at the same time.

14.5 INTEGRATING THE EXTENSION FUNCTION FOR SUSTAINABLE LAND USE: AFRICAN UNION (AU) TREATY AND SOFT LAW POSITION

In 2003, during an African Union summit in Maputo, Mozambique, African leaders adopted the Revised African Convention on the Conservation of

Nature and Natural Resources (African Union, 2003a). While this treaty is yet to come into force,[14] it introduced a firm environmental right for African people, and a corresponding legal duty on African states, like Kenya, to ensure realization of the right to development that is favourable to the environment (African Union, ibid., article 3). The treaty also addresses the health of the land and the soil. Article 6 binds African states to take effective measures to prevent land degradation, and develop strategies for the conservation and sustainable management of land resources, including soil, vegetation and related hydrological processes. These strategies should include, among others, steps to improve soil conservation and introduce sustainable farming and forestry practices, which in turn will ensure the long-term productivity of the land.

The convention implicitly embeds the concept of extension and highlights its importance for the goal of sustainable land use. Thus article 20 requires African states to promote environmental education, training and awareness creation at all levels in order to enhance people's appreciation of their close dependence on natural resources and their understanding of the reasons and rules for the sustainable use of these resources.

During the same 2003 Summit, the assembled African leaders adopted the 'Maputo Declaration on Agriculture and Food Security in Africa' (African Union, 2003b). Implicitly, the Maputo Declaration stands out as the accompanying policy statement to the continental treaty law on the environment. It focused on the important linkage between land health, biodiversity, food security and human survival. The declaration discloses an Africa-wide agenda on agriculture and food security. It expresses a concern that 30% of the African population is chronically and severely undernourished, and that the continent has become a net importer of food and the largest recipient of food aid in the world. The African leaders were convinced of the need for Africa to utilize its potential to increase food and agricultural production.

Two resolutions from the Maputo Declaration are directly relevant to this chapter. The first resolution involves revitalizing the agricultural sector through policies and strategies targeted at small-scale and traditional farmers. The strategies developed emphasize human capacity development, and removal of constraints on agricultural production and marketing, including poor soil fertility and water management. The second resolution involves the active participation of small-scale and traditional farmers, women and youth associations in all aspects of agriculture and food production. The resolutions resonate with the treaty, and reiterate connectivity between the quality of land health and husbandry, the needs of local communities, and the role of extension in building human capacity and modifying attitudes in favour of land stewardship. This connectivity is highlighted as imperative for realizing the sustainability objectives envisaged by law and policy.

14.5.1 African Model to Implement Sustainable Land Use Policy Agenda

Through the Maputo Declaration, the African Union committed itself to implementing, as a matter of urgency, the Comprehensive Africa Agriculture Development Programme (CAADP), and to develop African policy action plans at national, regional and continental levels .

The CAADP was designed by the New Partnership for African Development (NEPAD) Agency of the African Union in 2002 and the UN Food and Agriculture Organization (FAO). It was endorsed by African Ministers for Agriculture in June 2002. A summit of Heads of States and Governments of the AU, meeting in Abuja, Nigeria in December 2002, committed itself to pursuing vigorous action for the implementation of the main pillars of action of the CAADP (African Union, 2006) The Assembly in Maputo resolved to implement the CAADP as a matter of urgency.

The CAADP is organized into four pillars, each targeting a core aspect necessary for successful implementation (African Union, NEPAD, n.d., p. 5–12):

- Pillar 1 – to extend the area under sustainable land management and reliable water control systems;
- Pillar 2 – to improve rural infrastructure and trade-related capacities for market access;
- Pillar 3 – increase food supply, reduce hunger, and improve responses to food emergency crises; and
- Pillar 4 – to improve agricultural research, technology dissemination and adoption.

The first and fourth pillars are especially relevant to this chapter. They embody the potential of extension to bring about change in the direction of sustainable land use across the African continent.

The objective of Pillar 1 is to reverse resource degradation and ensure widespread and rapid adoption of sustainable land and forestry management practices by the smallholder and commercial sectors. The activities include supporting national research and extension systems for conservation-friendly forestry and farming technologies. This entails community-based reforestation and conservation, including interventions in soil health, restoring soil fertility with mineral fertilizers, agroforestry, etc. National governments are expected to implement these activities, including mainstreaming land management and conservation programmes into national research and extension systems.

The objective of Pillar 4 is a flow of technologies to resolve the challenges facing African agriculture. This would be done through national agricultural technology systems such as national research and extension functions. According to the CAADP agenda, the most effective way to reduce poverty and food insecurity sustainably is to raise the productivity of resources upon which poor people depend for their livelihood. These resources include agriculture and forestry resources that provide a subsistence livelihood but face significant sustainability challenges.

The CAADP reflects the African agenda to infuse sustainability into agriculture land use, to increase productivity and food security for the long and short term. The forestry agenda includes sustainable forest management, strengthening community and other participatory approaches, and enhancing research, education, training and extension (African Union, NEPAD, 2006, pp. 20–22). The role of the extension function in achieving sustainable land use and constructive engagement between government and land users stands out prominently.

14.5.2 Implementing the AU Sustainable Land Use Policy Principles at Country Level

The CAADP is an African sustainable land management policy drawing inspiration from the environmental principles of the 2003 revised African convention, and the Maputo Declaration. To achieve an impact on the realization of sustainability objectives, these policies have to be adapted to national situations and aligned with sustainability objectives of national law. The AU has also carved out a role for the Regional Economic Communities (RECs) within the African continent. It is the role of the individual member state that is pertinent. The RECs assist member states to develop CAADP Country Compacts to guide and mirror national level implementation.[15]

The country compacts represent a commitment by each country to implement the CAADP agenda, within national priorities. Developing a compact involves identifying major areas of agriculture that require significant investments. Importantly, it involves integrating the CAADP agenda into national policy areas that touch on agriculture such as forestry, land, as well as related research, training and extension functions (NEPAD, 2010). Twenty-two countries, including Kenya have signed compacts with the AU/NEPAD. In addition, Kenya has recently adopted an agriculture policy that acknowledges the CAADP agenda (Kenya, 2010, p. 7). Through such mechanisms a responsibility for supporting sustainable and productive land use is incorporated into national policy and it is assumed that this will be reflected in the legal and administrative arrangements governing land and forest management.

14.6 TOWARDS A SUSTAINABILITY EXTENSION FUNCTION

Stewardship is closely linked to the idea of sustainability and the individual human responsibility to ensure that land and its life support systems are sustained. It suggests the human being is ceasing to be the conqueror of the environment and becoming a citizen of the biotic community. Sustainability is conceptualized as a higher norm amongst the norms of human interaction with the natural environment. It requires human concern for land that goes beyond considering the economic utility of land, to ensure survival of all components of land, including those lacking economic value. To change the attitude of farmers, or inculcate a change of behaviour or transfer skills and relevant knowledge, extension is ready to play a useful role.

14.6.1 Framing the Concept

Traditional extension has been concerned with the transfer of knowledge, technology and skills to land users from extension agents. The new knowledge is aimed at improving productivity for the farmer. Whether the extension function is rendered by a public agency, or a private sector player, adapting the technology is generally voluntary. Unless there is a distinct benefit to the farmer, they may readily ignore any advice. This perspective heightens concern that while extension primarily serves a positive function, the focus on short-term private benefits may inadvertently enhance anthropocentric focused land use practices.

Frank Vanclay provides a justification for seeking to include a dominant imperative of sustainable land use in the objectives of extension (Vanclay and Lawrence, 1994, pp. 4–5). He suggests that, in traditional extension, the decision to adopt new technologies was always an individual decision, with consequences restricted to the farmer. When it comes to land use like agriculture or forestry, the effects of unsustainable practices affect people beyond the land users, including future generations. Since land is non-replenishable, the resource declines through degradation. The community has a vested public interest in ensuring that legal, policy and administrative measures guarantee sustainable land use. As opposed to entirely private benefits conferred by the traditional extension function, sustainability extension confers both private and public benefits on the land owner/user and the public. This would mark conversion from production extension to sustainability (plus productivity) extension.

This reorientation of extension toward sustainable land use is crucial for developing countries such as Kenya. They are faced with a land use crisis, whereby the majority of the population depend on agriculture or forestry-based activities, yet levels of degradation are high, and the prevalence of poverty and hunger is extremely high. Sustainability extension will be positioned as a key mechanism, aiding the law to meet those sustainable land use/forestry objectives necessary to reverse environmental degradation, and address socio-economic requirements needed to mitigate poverty.

14.6.2 Framing the Principles

The negative effects of unsustainable land use affect the public and ecosystems. The execution of unharmonized sectoral land use objectives exacerbates the land use situation, with consequential effects on livelihoods. Integration of production extension with sustainability extension offers a useful opportunity. The following concerns are critical:

(a) In their use of land, human beings should allow room for regeneration to sustain land health and vitality, which will in turn support human life and economic advancement;
(b) Developing countries such as Kenya are faced with a land use crisis. The majority of their populations depend on agriculture or forestry-based activities, yet levels of degradation are high, and the prevalence of poverty and hunger is extremely high. The desire to fight poverty and hunger must not divert from the pursuit of sustainability in land use.

Land use, and environmental laws that set sustainability objectives, should be guided by these concerns. They should also embed extension, such as the 2005 Forestry Law, as a legal mechanism that is integral to realization of these sustainability objectives. When extension is clearly identified as a means to achieve the sustainability objectives of land use law, it is conceptually transformed from production extension to sustainability extension. The education and communication role of extension then focuses on skills and knowledge pertinent to stewardship, including information on the close proximity of stewardship to any meaningful and sustained productivity of land.

While embedding sustainability extension as a mechanism for different land use laws like agriculture reinforces its purpose, land use is fragmented, with distinct sectoral implementation. This suggests it is essential to develop unified and common extension principles that can incorporate the sustainability agenda, and guide sectoral implementation by legal institutions.

14.6.2.1 A unified national sustainability extension policy

A unified policy will enable a holistic approach to extension, refocusing from simple technology transfer for enhanced land productivity, to building human capacity for, and providing guidelines and targets for, land stewardship. The priorities should be set based on national land use challenges and opportunities. Declining land fertility, poor husbandry, falling food crop production, and forest degradation are some of the identified challenges. Opportunities include implementing a policy of land stewardship, and engaging the local communities to achieve this goal. The policy should also address legal and institutional arrangements on common sustainability objectives, and institutional coordination amongst concerned agencies.

14.6.2.2 Common goals and objectives

A baseline objective should be a quantifiable target for the outputs of the sustainability extension. This mainly entails having a common agreement between the sectoral authorities on the general land use responsibilities of land owners/users for sustainable land use. This should include the content of sustainability education or knowledge. It also includes strategies for land user/owner participation in the extension, including approaches such as training of farmers to be trainers of their peers, and local monitoring. Implementation to achieve these targets is then the role of sectoral agencies.

14.6.2.3 Utility of knowledge

A major challenge facing extension involves the utility of extension advice about sustainable land use to land users. This requires shifting from basic knowledge on how to increase productivity to broader knowledge on how to sustain land health and high productivity at the same time. This does not necessarily suggest a top-down approach where the extension agents are presumed to know. In order to enhance the contribution of extension to sustainable goals of land use laws, extension policy must create mechanisms of participation, information sharing and feedback between farmers and extension agents or researchers. When implemented properly, this could combine the breadth and quality of information from local knowledge with scientific research into knowledge useful to sustain a healthy and productive land base.

Traditionally, participation in a typical extension programme is voluntary for private land owners, and uptake of technical advice depends on the tangible benefits it brings to the farmer. Land stewardship revolves around changing the ethics and attitude of people so they uphold the health of the land as they utilize it, which is crucial to sustainable land use. Sustainability extension is the proposed mechanism for infusing values of stewardship into the practices of land owners/users. If extension is anchored in land use law as one primary mechanism to meet sustainability objectives, it will become one of the basic, default legal tools accessible to public agencies implementing land use laws on a national scale.

14.6.2.4 A broad legislative and policy mandate

The mandate of the sustainability extension function could be extended beyond merely being repositories and transmitters of skills and knowledge. Farmers and other users of land should be tapped for information, since once the importance of stewardship is highlighted, they may have on-the-ground knowledge on how best to practise it. The same channels of education and communication applied to extension can be used to address multiple law/policy objectives that affect sustainable land use. These include civic education and action in areas like gender rights, HIV/AIDs and other diseases, illiteracy, etc.

This should also address institutional arrangements, vesting policy-making roles and oversight for implementing sustainability extension in a broad-based supervisory body not directly involved in the delivery of extension. Its other role would be to coordinate staff training to harmonize information and methods. It would also design policy and strategy to coordinate extension implementation by sectoral ministries, including providing a legally mandated linkage between front-line extension agents, and research institutions. Such a body should be created as part of the proposed national extension policy.

There is a need for public sector investment in a nationwide programme. It may be argued that such a broad undertaking will result in large costs to the public sector. However, the failure to take such measures will result in further unsustainable land use, and undermine the activities on which the livelihoods of millions of Kenyans today and in the future will depend. The values of sustainability and extension were firmed up by the 2010 constitution of Kenya. Article 69 binds the state to ensure sustainable management of the the environment and natural resources. It also binds the state to encourage public participation in the management of the environment and natural resources. Extension manifests public participation as well as public education, both of which are essential to attitude change. The constitution was recently approved by 67% of the voting population,[16] and therefore is not only basic law, but also captures the aspirations of the Kenyan people. State policies and statute law should peg their design and implementation on the constitution. Making a case for sustainability extension as a mechanism to implement the sustainability objectives of law begins this process.

14.7 CONCLUSION

Interaction between people and natural resources such as land is evident through land use activities. Land use and environmental laws ideally should determine the legal norms by which these land use activities should adhere. Sustainability, deriving from the concept of sustainable development, emerges as a dominant legal norm. Therefore land use legislation, such as agriculture and forestry, should contain sustainability objectives, and mechanisms to meet these objectives.

Agriculture law in Kenya specifies some objectives to ensure conservation of soil and its fertility, which are instrumental to sustainability. However, this law pursues a strict regulatory regime with no room for incentives or public participation. The regulations are based on prescribed orders, and offer no guidance on the actual responsibilities of land owners/users in realizing sustainable land use. There is massive land degradation, poor land productivity and lost fertility, which suggests the need for a different approach to enable the law to meet its sustainable land use objective. In spite of the law, the available literature and information suggest that people do not exercise responsibility over the health of land. A structured system is therefore essential to transfer knowledge on land stewardship, given the relationship between stewardship and higher productivity.

Forestry law too specifies its objective, ensuring sustainable forest management and utilization. Kenya experiences high forest degradation, an adversarial relationship between local communities and forests, and previously failed attempts to integrate local communities and protected forests. The 2005 Forest Law anchors community co-management in state forests, and also embeds extension as a core mechanism. The *shamba* system requires a tremendous investment in extension to ensure that it does not fail, in which case forest degradation and poverty levels will rise. Extension is required to adjust local communities' attitudes so that they look upon forests as valuable resources they need to exercise stewardship over for present and future generations.

Collectively, the challenges facing forestry and agriculture concern mechanisms to implement the sustainable land use objectives of the sectoral laws. Land stewardship as a value or ethic system brings to the fore human responsibility to ensure the health of the land, even as people use land as a resource.

Agricultural and forestry extension functions provide a tool for law and policy that can be tailored to assist those engaged in land use. Typically extension has been focused on transmission of skills and knowledge to increase productivity. I have argued for and proposed a shift to a sustainability extension which will prioritize land stewardship. Land stewardship is the crucial bridge towards sustainability in agricultural and forestry land use. It can help ensure healthy ecosystems to support the economic utility of agricultural and forestry land. Achieving this goal will involve transforming erstwhile production extension into sustainability extension. The principal aim of a sustainability extension will be communicating that human attitudes on land use need to change and land owners/users must take responsibility for sustaining land health. This reoriented extension function should be guided by a unified policy, responsible for setting common baseline objectives on standards of human responsibility for land, and quality of knowledge.

The overriding concern of this chapter has been to make a case for a sustainability extension that is a key component in sustainable land use. The urgency of this task is amplified by the high levels of land and forest degradation, poverty and food insecurity, cyclically attributed to land productivity. Addressing these challenges requires strategic action that is in consonance with the local people, and which facilitates implementing the sustainability objectives of the land use laws and policy. A system of extension that is designed to promote land stewardship provides a useful mechanism to restart this quest for sustainability in land use. This sustainability extension should be anchored in land use laws, and identified as a primary mechanism available to implement sustainability objectives.

NOTES

1. Agricultural and forestry extension functions are discussed in greater detail throughout the chapter, especially in Sections 14.33–14.66.
2. Quesada, Charo (2001) 'Amartya Sen and the Thousand Faces of Poverty', para. 5, http://www.globalpolicy.org/socecon/develop/2001/1205sen.htm, 27 February 2009.
3. Obare, Lynette and J.B. Wangwe, 'Underlying Cause of Deforestation and Forest Degradation in Kenya', para. 1.3, online: www.wrm.org.uy/deforestation/Africa/Kenya.html, 30 September 2010.
4. Mwiraria, David (2007), speech during the launching of the 2007 Eastern Rainfall Regime Tree Planting Season at Lower Imenti Forest, Meru Central District [Minister of Environment and Natural Resources]. Online: http://www.kfs.go.ke/pub/meru%20speech%20minister%20 sundayt.pdf, 22 March 2009.
5. David Mbugua (speech), 'Kenya Forest Service to Roll out New Organized Shamba System', http://www.kfs.go.ke/html/news%20events.html, 4 April 2009.
6. The first phase (NALEP I) ended in 2005 after five years, and NALEP II commenced in 2006.
7. Interviews undertaken by the author, June–August 2009, Kenya.
8. Interviews undertaken by the author, June–August 2009, Kenya.
9. ibid.
10. Website: http://www.kenyaforestservice.org/index.php?option=com_content&view=article&id=93:about-kenya-forest-service&catid=70:about-kenya-forest-service, 30 September 2010.
11. Interviews undertaken by the author, June–August 2009, Kenya.
12. See website for the Intensified Social Forestry Project in Semi-Arid Areas: http://www.isfp-fd.org.
13. See, for instance, Shepheard, Mark and Paul Martin (2009), 'The Multiple Meanings and Practical Problems with Making a Duty of Care Work for Stewardship in Agriculture' *Macquarie Journal of International and Comparative Law,* 6, 191–215.
14. The treaty has only been ratified by eight states, and requires 15 ratifications to come into force. http://www.africa-union.org/root/au/Documents/Treaties/List/Revised%20Convention%20on%20Nature%20and%20Natural%20Resources.pdf, 2 November 2010.
15. See CAADP, 'The Role of Regional Economic Communities', http://www.nepad-caadp.net/role-regional-economic-communities.php, 22 September 2010.
16. The constitution was approved at a referendum on 5 August 2010, and promulgated into law on 27 August 2010.

REFERENCES

African Union (2003a), Revised African Convention on the Conservation of Nature and Natural Resources, http://www.africa-union.org/root/au/Documents/Treaties/Text/nature%20and%20natural%20recesource.pdf, 2 November 2010.

African Union (2003b), *Declaration on Agriculture and Food Security in Africa,* Maputo, Mozambique: Assembly of the African Union, Second Ordinary Session, Assembly/AU/Decl.7(II).

African Union (2006), *Resolution of the Abuja Food Security Summit,* Abuja, Nigeria: Summit on Food Security in Africa, FS/Res(I).

African Union, NEPAD (undated), *Implementing the Comprehensive Africa Agriculture Development Programme and Restoring Food Security in Africa 'The Roadmap',* Midrand, South Africa, New Partnership for African Development (NEPAD) Secretariat, ftp://ftp.fao.org/TC/TCA/CAADP%20TT/Background%20%20documents/Main%20document/Roadmap%20of%20implementing%20CAADP.pdf, 30 September 2010.

African Union, NEPAD (2006), *Companion Document: Comprehensive Africa Agriculture Development Programme – Integrating Livestock, Forestry and Fisheries Subsectors into the CAADP,* Rome, Italy: Food and Agriculture Organization.

Cuellar, Melinda, Hans Hedlund, Jeremy Mbai and Jane Mwangi (2006), *The National Agriculture and Livestock Extension Programme (NALEP) Phase I Impact Assessment*, Nairobi, Kenya: Swedish International Development Agency (SIDA), Department for Africa.

FAO, JICA (2007), 'Kenya: Intensified Social Forestry Project in Arid Areas Impact Assessment Report', Rome, Italy: Food and Agriculture Organization and Japan International Cooperation Agency.

Gautam, Madhur (2000) *Agricultural Extension, The Kenyan Experience: An Impact Evaluation*, Washington, DC, US: The World Bank.

Geda, Alemayehu, Niek de Jong, Germano Mwabu and Mwangi Kimenyi (2001), 'Determinants of Poverty in Kenya: Household-Level Analysis', Nairobi, Kenya: Discussion Paper No. 9, Kenya Institute for Public Policy Research and Analysis (KIPPRA).

Hodas, David (2007), 'Climate Change and Land Use in Africa', in Nathalie Chalifour, Patricia Kameri-Mbote, Lin Heng Lye, et al. (eds), *Land Use Law for Sustainable Development,* Cambridge, UK: Cambridge University Press.

Jamieson, Dale (2008), *Ethics and the Environment: An Introduction,* New York, US: Cambridge University Press.

Kagombe, Joram and James Gitonga (2005), *Plantation Establishment in Kenya: A Case Study on Shamba System,* Nairobi, Kenya: Forestry Research Institute & Forest Department.

Kameri-Mbote, Patricia (2002), *Property Rights and Biodiversity Management in Kenya,* Nairobi, Kenya: Acts Press.

Kenya (2001a), *Poverty Reduction Strategy Paper for the Period 2001–2004: Prepared by the Government and People of Kenya,* Nairobi, Kenya: Government Printer.

Kenya (2001b), *National Agricultural Extension Policy,* Nairobi, Kenya: Government Printer.

Kenya (2007), *Forest Policy in Sessional Paper No. 1 of 2007*, Nairobi, Kenya: Government Printer.

Kenya (2009a), *Economic Review of Agriculture,* Nairobi, Kenya: Ministry of Agriculture.

Kenya (2009b), *Food Security Situation 2009*, Nairobi, Kenya: Ministry of Agriculture.

Kenya (2009c), *Report of the Government's Task Force on the Conservation of the Mau Forests Complex*, Nairobi, Kenya: Office of the Prime Minister.

Kenya (2010), *Agricultural Sector Development Strategy 2010–2020*, Nairobi, Kenya: Ministry of Agriculture.

Kenya Forest Service (KFS), Kenya Forests Research Institute (KEFRI) and Japan International Cooperation Agency (JICA) (2004a), *Intensified Social Forestry Project in Semi-Arid Areas in Kenya: Baseline Survey*, Nairobi, Kenya: Development Consultants.

Kenya Forest Service (KFS), Kenya Forests Research Institute (KEFRI) and Japan International Cooperation Agency (JICA) (2004b), *Pilot Study for Intensified Social Forestry Project in Semi-Arid Areas in Kenya*, Nairobi, Kenya: Development Consultants.

Kenya Forest Service (2009), *Strategic Plan: 2009/10–2013/14,* Nairobi, Kenya: Kenya Forest Service.

Kimalu, Paul, Nancy Nafula, Damiano K. Manda, Germano Mwabu and Mwangi Kimenyi (2001), 'A Situational Analysis of Poverty in Kenya', Nairobi, Kenya: Working Paper No. 6, Kenya Institute for Public Policy Research and Analysis (KIPPRA).

Kimenyi, Mwangi (2002), 'Agriculture, Economic Growth and Poverty Reduction', Nairobi, Kenya: Occasional Paper No. 3, Kenya Institute for Public Policy Research and Analysis (KIPPRA).

Leopold, Aldo (1981), *A Sand County Almanac with Other Essays on Conservation from Round River*, New York, US: Oxford University Press. Reprinted in Donald VanDeveer and Christine Pierce (eds) (2003), *The Environmental Ethics and Policy Book,* California, US: Thomson/Wadsworth.

Lockwood, Michael and Ashish Kothari (2006), 'Social Context', in Michael Lockwood, Graeme Worboys and Ashish Kothari (eds), *Managing Protected Areas: A Global Guide*, London, UK: Earthscan.

Maathai, Wangari (2009), *The Challenge for Africa: A New Vision,* London, UK: William Heinemann.

Mbithi, D., M. Phiri, H. Gibbon and E.N. Mugo (2005), 'Forest and Woodland Management in East and Central Africa: Emerging Models for Improvement in Livelihoods and Natural Resource Management in Kenya and Zambia', *International Forestry Review*, 7(3), 193–207.

Muyanga, Milu and T.S. Jayne (2006), 'Agricultural Extension in Kenya: Practice and Policy Lessons', Nakuru, Kenya: Tegemeo Institute Working Paper 26/2006, Egerton University.

NEPAD (2010), *Comprehensive Africa Agriculture Development Programme: Post Compact Review Guidelines*, http://www.nepad-caadp.net/pdf/POST%20 COMPACT%20GUIDELINE%20-%20English.pdf, 30 September 2010.

Oduol, Peter Allan (1986), 'The Shamba System: An Indigenous System of Food Production from Forest Areas in Kenya', *Agroforestry Systems*, 4 (1986), 365–73.

Qamar, Kalim (2005), *Modernizing National Agricultural Extension Systems: A Practical Guide for Policy-Makers of Developing Countries*, Rome, Italy: FAO.

Ravallion, Martin (2000), 'What Is Needed for a More Pro-Poor Growth Process in India?', *Economic and Political Weekly,* 35(13), 1089–93.

Rivera, William McLeod and Kalim Qamar (2003), *Agricultural Extension, Rural Development and the Food Security Challenge,* Rome, Italy: FAO.

Sim, D. and H.A. Hilmi (1987) *Forestry Extension Methods*, Rome, Italy: FAO Forestry Paper 80.

United Nations (1992), *Non-legally Binding Authoritative Statements of Principles for a Global Consensus on the Management, Conservation and Sustainable Development of all types of Forests*, UNGA, A/Conf.151/26(Vol. III), 14 August, available at http://www,un.org/documents/ga/conf151/aconf15126-3annex3.htm, accessed 25 September 2011.

Vanclay, Frank and Geoffrey Lawrence (1994), 'Agriculture Extension in the Context of Environmental Degradation: Agricultural Extension as Social Welfare', *Rural Society*, 5(1), 1–13.

World Bank (1985), *Agricultural Research and Extension: An Evaluation of the World Bank's Experience*, Washington, DC, US: The World Bank.

World Bank (1999), 'Agriculture: The Kenyan Experience', *Précis*, 198, Winter.

World Bank (1999b), *Agricultural Extension Projects in Kenya: An Impact Evaluation*, Washington, DC, US: Report No. 19523, The World Bank 1999, http://www-wds.worldbank.org/external/default/WDSContentServer/WDSP/IB/1999/11/04/000094946_99092004315349/Rendered/PDF/multi_page.pdf, 30 September 2010.

WWW (2006), *Poverty and the Environment Initiative – Kenya*, Nairobi, Kenya: World Wildlife Fund, UNEP, UNDP.

Index